BLUE
MELODY

TIM BUCKLEY REMEMBERED

LEE UNDERWOOD

Backbeat Books

San Francisco

Published by Backbeat Books
600 Harrison Street, San Francisco, CA 94107
www.backbeatbooks.com
email: books@musicplayer.com
An imprint of the Music Player Group
Publishers of *Guitar Player*, *Bass Player*, *Keyboard*, and other magazines
United Entertainment Media, Inc.
A CMP Information company

CMP
United Business Media

Distributed to the book trade in the US and Canada by
Publishers Group West, 1700 Fourth Street, Berkeley, CA 94710

Distributed to the music trade in the US and Canada by
Hal Leonard Publishing, P.O. Box 13819, Milwaukee, WI 53213

Text Design and Composition by Michael Cutter
Cover Design by David Hamamoto
Front Cover Photo: Michael Ochs Archives.com
Back Cover Photo: Don Paulsen

Library of Congress Cataloging-in-Publication Data

Underwood, Lee.
    Blue Melody : Tim Buckley remembered / Lee Underwood
        p. cm.
    Includes discography (p.) and index.
    ISBN 0-87930-718-8
    1. Buckley, Tim. 2. Singers—United States—Biography. I. Title

ML420.B86 U53 2002
782.42166'092—dc21
[B]   2002066674

Printed in the United States of America
02 03 04 05 06   5 4 3 2 1

PART II

Timewinds

CONTENTS

PART I

Blue Melody

THE LIFE

TIM BUCKLEY: 1966–1967

GOODBYE AND HELLO: 1967–1968

HAPPY SAD: 1968–1969

IN REMEMBRANCE

Timothy Charles Buckley Jr.,
The Father

Timothy Charles Buckley III,
The Son

Jeffrey Scott Buckley,
The Grandson

ACKNOWLEDGMENTS

*OUR
LIFESONGS SANG
IN THE SUN
LIKE WIND CHIMES*

HEARTFELT THANKS TO—
Tim Buckley, his music, his life, his laughter, his memory.

And to Jennifer Stace, Jainie Goldstein, Larry Beckett, Manda (Bradlyn) Beckett, Dan Gordon, Carter C.C. Collins, Daniella Sapriel, John Balkin, Maury Baker, John King, Bob Campbell, Michael Cavanaugh, Barry Schulze, Charlie Jones, Crazy Terry, Philip, Night Owl Mary, Jacqueline Klein, Natasha Reatig, Hope Ruff, Meneli, Carol Zeitz, Bobby (Jesse) James, Artie Leichter, Toledo Red, Atlanta Darlin', and those many other wonderful people who cared about us and so generously shared their lives with us along the way.

Together we were gypsy children, dancing in the sunshine of our astonished and astonishing youth. The songs we sang with laughter, kisses, tears, and joy shall be remembered forever in our hearts. Listen closely . . . Those were the days, my friend. . . . They remain with us forever, eternal music singing inside memory's windsongs. . . .

WITH SPECIAL THANKS TO—
Sonia Crespi for sharing her life, her heartfelt care, and her illuminating insight with me, and creating a healthy, vibrant, energizing context in which love and music and writing have flourished for nearly three decades.

Stu Goldberg for starting me off on guitar, which led to my life with Tim, which led to this celebration of Tim and his work.

Dr. Richard J. Rosenthal for helping me learn how to live life affirmatively.

Anne Marie Micklo, Bill Henderson, Sam Bradley, Michael Davis, Frankie Nemko, Bob Garcia, Paul Eberle, Chrissie Hynde, Susan Ahrens, Steve Lake, Steve Turner, Martin Aston, Bob Niemi, and Jack Brolly for knowing how to ask good questions, and how to listen, and how to write well. I am indebted to each and every one of these journalists. Their interviews with Tim and some of his associates have been most helpful in illuminating Tim's viewpoints and serving his life and work with dignity, understanding and appreciation. On Tim's behalf as well as my own, I thank one and all.

Judy Buckley, Cool Richard, Joe Falsia, Carter C.C. Collins, Elaine Buckley, Katy

Buckley, Jeff Eyrich, Bob Campbell, and John Balkin for taking the time to share their experiences and perspectives with me in exclusive interviews.

Musician Scott Sechman for connecting me with Jay Kahn at Backbeat Books, thus making it possible to get *Blue Melody* published.

All of the good people at Backbeat Books who recognized this work, supported it 100 percent, and gave it wings in the marketplace, including Publisher Matt Kelsey and Sales Manager Jay Kahn. Thanks to Production Editor Michael Baughan, who was most helpful both professionally and personally during some of the tougher times that arose while getting this book launched. Thanks to Bob Doerschuk, who worked directly with me editing the manuscript the first time around. His knowledge, skill, insight, and gracious tact helped bring *Blue Melody* alive. Extra-special thanks to Executive Editor Richard Johnston. Without him and his wisdom, tact, consideration, skill and good judgment, *Blue Melody* would not have made it through that last and most difficult mile.

Karen Stevenson for her extensive research on the web on Tim's behalf, her kindness and generosity of spirit, her gentle friendship.

Alex Crespi, who calmly and professionally soothed my frantic brains while expertly solving my computer problems.

All the beautiful people on the Starsailor website (http://groups.yahoo.com/group/Starsailor) and the TimBuckley.com website.

Louie Dula and Howard Wilson for enthusiastically sending me dozens of articles.

Producers Veit Stauffer and Urs Rageth and their band for their love, dedication, and comprehensive selection of Buckley songs in their 1987 Swiss cover-album, *Comebuckley* (Boy-001—"Because of You").

PRELUDE

I
A STARSAILOR'S LIFE

When Tim Buckley and I met in Greenwich Village in the spring of 1966, we were a study in contrasts. He was a Loara High School graduate from Bell Gardens and Anaheim, California, who had attended nearby Fullerton Junior College (now Community College) for two months and dropped out. I had graduated from San Francisco State College and done some graduate work at UC Berkeley. Tim had worked at a Taco Bell. I had worn a suit and tie and taught English for one year at The Peddie School in Hightstown, New Jersey, a posh private high school for boys near Princeton.

Tim hailed from Orange County's blue-collar neighborhoods, and had abandoned his wife, Mary, to come to New York, where, according to him, he was later informed she was pregnant. He had written a handful of songs that constituted a synthesis of the lives he and his friend and talented co-lyricist Larry Beckett had experienced in high school. He had just signed a recording contract with Elektra Records. I owned three acoustic guitars, had abandoned my wife, had one year's experience singing and playing my own songs, but had no contract with anybody, and no work in sight. I didn't care. I was taking my shot. So was Tim. The Big Apple. We liked each other and teamed up, with me as his lead guitarist.

For some seven years we worked and played together—clubs, concerts, records, TV shows, wine, women, song. The last time I performed with him was on a *Greetings From L.A.* tour in early 1973. In April 1975, I saw him perform at the Golden Bear in Huntington Beach, where I met his ex-wife Mary and their eight-year-old son, Jeff, who was later to become a first-class singer and songwriter in his own right. The last time I saw Tim on stage was May 9–11, 1975, at a three-night whirlwind get-down roadhouse funk-rock gig at the Starwood club in Hollywood. I attended every performance, and had never seen him in better shape.

The last time I saw him at all he was dead. An overdose of alcohol and heroin killed him on June 29, 1975, age twenty-eight.

II
MULTIPLE PERSPECTIVES

Part I, Blue Melody: The Life is a celebration of Tim Buckley and his multifaceted personality, a musical appraisal, a partial biography, a heartfelt memoir. I focus on

Tim not only as a young man coming of age, but as a dedicated artist whose evolutionary creative journey was nothing short of extraordinary.

Part I draws from direct personal experiences, showcasing my recollections of playing lead guitar with Tim during the sixties and early seventies, including behind-the-scenes anecdotes with explicit details about the wild, wonderful, strange, whimsical, and sometimes dangerously crazy things we were involved with. It also draws from exclusive interviews, conversations, and letters, as well as solid research into interviews and articles written by others while Tim was alive. It spotlights his story, my story, and the music we played, celebrating the people we knew and the tumultuous times we lived in.

Part II, Timewinds, touches upon a few of the many complex circumstances surrounding Tim's rather sordid death, the funeral, the aftermath.

I am happy to include exclusive interviews of my own with some of Tim's key family members, friends, loved ones, and bandmates, and to bring to light certain biographical information and quotes from writings by various outside journalists. However, it is not my intention to include everybody's viewpoint, or to reduce all viewpoints to equal value, or to cover each and every external detail of Tim's life. I leave that to biographers.

For the most part, I discuss events and conversations in which I participated. I often quote from Tim's interviews with other writers, giving appreciation and due credit to them in the Sources section, so we might have his exact words regarding matters he spoke directly with me about, or regarding matters that need to be included for their insight and informational value, whether I was personally present or not. Also, in the interest of readablity I have used quotations to reflect certain conversations between various people, although I may not have been present at the time the conversations took place. While the words in these quotations likely were not the exact ones used, they reflect the substance of those conversations as they were told me.

Tim was intelligent and insightful right from the beginning, but it is fascinating to watch the ways in which his language evolved as he himself evolved psychologically and artistically. Linguistically, he moved from the blue-collar profanities and light-hearted street-rat vulgarities of his youthful background in Bell Gardens and Anaheim, to the obscenity-free, highly articulate, and even graceful elegance of his later interviews with Frankie Nemko, Sam Bradley, and Michael Davis.

My loyalty is to the truth of Tim and the music and to my own experiences of the context in which we lived—the music, the times, the people we knew. That does not mean I am blinded by friendship. To the contrary—I am no idolater, and know all too well he had his faults and weaknesses. But I also know that I see clearly the totality of his contributions as an individual and as an artist. I have come to see the whole of the man and his life and work—the goods and bads, the ups and downs, the strengths and limitations, the joy and heartbreak—and that is what I am presenting in this book. I am equally forthright about my own strengths, contributions, weaknesses, mistakes, and shortcomings during those years.

What an extraordinary adventure Tim's musical voyage has been! And the music lives on, happy to say, vindicating those who from the beginning knew it would endure. This is very satisfying, of course. Very satisfying, indeed.

III

THE CREATIVE ODYSSEY

"When it's true, man, it's true for a long time."

Tim Buckley

I toured and recorded and played lead guitar with Tim on seven of the nine albums released while he was alive and on numerous posthumous CDs that continue growing in number. From the time we met until the time he died, we remained the closest of friends.

He was a boy when I met him. He became a man through his music and his work and play—in studios, on the road, in bar rooms, bedrooms, executive offices, concert halls. Every step of the way he displayed exceptional creative abilities, although, to be sure, he did not always make wise or even pragmatic decisions.

Not only did he possess an astonishing voice—approximately 3 ½ octaves (he enjoyed boasting of 5)—but he also taught himself how to use it. On the one hand, his voice was an aurally pleasing vehicle that carried words, concepts, and verbal imagery in conventional popular music fashion. However, he also came to utilize it as a nonverbal instrument that was as multifaceted and expressive as any I have ever heard. Transcending words, moving into pure vocal sound, he could coo and whisper, he could charm and seduce, he could rage, bark, shriek, and rant. Intimacy, sorrow, pain, love, humor—Buckley felt it all, and could sing it all both verbally and nonverbally with unparalleled intensity. Eventually with Buckley, music was no longer an exclusive matter of repeatable hummable melodies and communally shared verbal images. He became quintessentially contemporary when music also became a much broader palette for him—not just the 12 tones of a piano octave, or Harry Partch's forty-plus tones, but also the control of sound in its full range of colors and permutations.

While a majority of musicians seek and then commercially exploit a single successful style until it runs dry, Buckley joined the ranks of those few artists who dare to evolve, like Picasso in painting or Miles Davis in jazz. In fact, Buckley's creativity led him through no fewer than five conceptual/aesthetic periods— through the early folk orientation of Tim Buckley. Through the hippie-flavored folk-rock influences of *Goodbye and Hello*. Through the mellow jazz impressions of *Happy Sad* and *Blue Afternoon*. Through the surrealistic, darkly hued, contemporary exploratory innovations of *Lorca*, which phased into *Starsailor*—the ferocious, gentle, intellectually complex avant-garde album that he told me he regarded as his masterpiece. Finally, his journey took him into the impassioned rhythm and blues sensuality of his last three albums, *Greetings from L.A.*, *Sefronia*, and *Look at the Fool*. Nine years, nine albums, a vast spectrum of songs, styles, emotional levels, and intellectual dimensions.

Throughout his amazing creative journey, he enjoyed those times when his concepts and songs happened to match and mirror the public's ways of thinking and feeling, as they did with *Goodbye and Hello* and *Happy Sad*. But he did not sell out or abandon his creativity when new directions beckoned, even when they carried him far away from the securities of conceptual repetition and commercially successful pop forms, as did *Lorca* and *Starsailor*.

Like a Starsailor, indeed, Tim Buckley maintained his integrity, refused to buckle under in the face of commercial disaster, followed inspired new musical dreams with courage, fire and, to my way of thinking, stupendous strength. He was a rebel *with* a cause, a fighter and hero with a musical purpose, an uncompromising vision-ary with a dream, unafraid to go against the grain of crippling commercial pressures and popular rejection. There were times when he was forced to walk in the rain. But rain or shine, damned or adored, he walked his own path and did so with convic-tion, even when he staggered in pain along the way. He was not a showbiz enter-tainer. He was a dedicated artist who reaped creative rewards even as he paid a severe price for innovation.

With his struggles, aspirations, triumphs, and failures, he became the kind of man his World War II warrior father might have been proud of, although Tim never received that satisfaction. Tim's father, and the relationship Tim had with him, is very much a part of this story. The reactions Tim had to his father's influence great-ly contributed to Tim's fiery artistic ascension—and to his personal downfall.

Tim had impressive physical grace and beauty, dazzling intelligence, sparkling and often scathing wit, an inventiveness in music, humor, and life that nobody else in my life has matched. For all of his talent, charisma, and productivity, he was also a lad whose soul had been fractured—by his father's confusion and rage; by the demands of a ruthless commercial system that avariciously insists that art be sub-servient to the idols of greed and profit; and to some extent by a spoiled, fickle and occasionally vicious public. Whether as artist or listener, it takes courage and imag-ination to sail beyond comfortable familiarity into the unknown, to explore the new and, in so doing, to challenge and expand the core of one's deepest self. Tim had the courage, but he paid an exorbitant toll for it.

Even as Tim aspired to great artistic heights, he sometimes fell into the darkest psychological valleys, in which frustration, anger and disappointment turned into self-destruction. Inwardly divided, and riddled with doubts, he sometimes desper-ately needed to assuage his demons with the comforts of oblivion, or savagely lash out at others with caustic sarcasm. He was not always a nice guy. I know the pain he felt. I understand what he needed and why. I wish he had made it through to the other side. He almost did.

But almost is not quite.

Obviously, we all die. The question is not death. The question has to do with quality—with how we live and die. Tim lived well, as a cerulean blue melody that served music with every breath and created some of the most moving albums of his day. He also lived sloppily, damaging his talent while attempting to mollify emo-tional pain. He died sadly, poignantly, wastefully—tripped up on the comeback trail, even as bright new success beckoned.

When all is said and done, we can witness how Tim Buckley ascended the moun-tain. In spite of certain demeaning judgments by some of his critics, he did not compromise his integrity, his musical visions, or his life—including the final peri-od in which he played white-funk rock 'n' roll. Everything he sang and wrote came from the heart. Near the end, it also came from pragmatic desperation fueled with heartfelt aspiration. He wrote and sang his own music with integrity, even when those who did not care for it deemed him either an obnoxious elitist avant-garde purist or a rock 'n' roll sell-out.

For nine short years, he performed live on stages across America, Canada, and

Europe, vocally improvising at a level of brilliant creativity, technical sophistication, and raw emotional intensity that normally only instrumentalists attain. As I said in my 1977 *Down Beat* article about him, he did for the voice what Miles did for the trumpet, Coltrane did for the sax, Cecil Taylor did for the piano, and Hendrix did for the guitar.

On his journey to the heights, he recorded but a small portion of what he envisioned and performed. We have only a handful of albums to listen to—but there's magic and mystery in those works. In every musical period—from folk, across the rainbow spectrum to funk-rock—we can hear the pain, beauty, passion, intensity, integrity, and enormous love that fueled his life and brought vitality into the lives of his listeners.

He signed with Elektra in 1966, over three decades ago. While others appeared and disappeared, Tim Buckley remains.

> Your blue melodies sing on, Starsailor.
> God bless, old friend.
> I am with you always.

IV
A BRIEF EXPLANATION

Shortly before press time, the publisher that handles the songs that Judy Buckley controls refused to grant permission to use Tim's song lyrics in this book. I went through the text, eliminated all lyrics controlled by her, and worked my way through the obstacle course as deftly as I could. I ask you to join me in sailing up and beyond these obstructions into the open skies above, where Tim's blue melodies enliven one's ears, touch the heart, clear the eyes, cleanse the soul, and make everything all right again. I am sure that is the way he would want it.

Lee Underwood
Oakhurst, CA

Seminal concepts, 1977
Initial Effort, 1997
Second Effort, 1999
First Manuscript, 1999
Placement, 2001
Publication, 2002

PART I

Blue Melody

THE LIFE

TIM BUCKLEY: 1966–1967

CHAPTER 1

FROM NEW YORK TO L.A.

MEETING IN THE VILLAGE

The first time I saw Tim was really the second time. It was in Sean O'brien's Greenwich Village apartment building, late May of 1966. A friend of mine, Natasha Reatig, knew Sean managed Jesse Colin Young, whose Youngbloods were about to break into the Top Ten with a rousing version of Dino Valenti's "Let's Get Together." She recommended I look up O'brien, razzle-dazzle him with my original folk tunes and fancy pickin', and see if he could line me up with gigs in the Village—maybe the Café Au Go Go, the Bitter End, the Café Wha.

Tim had only recently arrived from L.A. with his girlfriend, Jainie Goldstein. His manager, Herb Cohen, had set him up with O'brien, who got Tim the apartment next to his.

I trudged up the stairs to the second floor, carrying all three of my guitars strung together with a rope and slung around my neck, huffing and puffing, making a racket. With instrument cases swinging in every direction, banging on walls and steps, I tried to make it to the second floor without falling. Reaching the landing, I looked through an open door to the right. A skinny short guy with high cheekbones and a huge mass of brown curly hair walked across the room with no shirt on. As he picked a guitar up off the couch, he looked out the door—and we recognized each other.

Two months before, I had driven down to L.A. to play in one of the Monday night hoots at the Troubadour in hopes that owner Doug Weston would hire me. I had already played numerous coffeehouses in San Francisco, made something of a reputation, and felt ready for the next step. At the Troubadour I played and sang my songs (but got no gig). Tim came on later. He was good, of course, but a little on the gentle side, not as fierce or as blues-oriented as I was, so I wasn't overly impressed.

Backstage, after he performed, somebody rushed over to him and exclaimed, "I talked to Herbie today—Elektra signed us!" It was Larry Beckett announcing the good news. "I know," said Tim. "Ain't that great?"

I couldn't help but gasp with a mixture of admiration and envy. Since beginning my own folk journey a year or so before that, it had been one of my fantasies to record with Elektra—the same label as Judy Collins, Josh White, Theodore Bikel, Tom Rush, and my all-time favorite blues hollering seven-string guitar picker,

Spider John Koerner. Buckley had struck the mother lode I still hoped to find. All the best to him. Plenty of room for everybody.

Tim and I said Hi on the stairs and introduced ourselves, remembering each other from the Troubadour. Sean invited us in. "My place is small," he said. "Let's go over to the studio." At Sean's studio I sat in the center of the room on a folding chair, played my six-string Martin D-28, my 12-string Guild, and an old metal 1930s Dobro, singing, picking, and strumming as passionately as I could.

"I can get you a gig in a folk house down in Baltimore," Sean said.

I shook my head. "Thanks, man, but I didn't come all the way to New York so I could play Baltimore. I'm looking for work here."

Tim said, "I've got a contract with Elektra. We'll be going into the studio soon. I've also got a gig here in the Village for six weeks at a club called the Night Owl. You wanna play lead guitar for me on the gig?"

"I don't remember your stuff very well," I said. "Let me hear what you're doing."

At his apartment, sitting in the kitchen, he strummed his guitar and sang "Song for Jainie," "Aren't You the Girl," "She Is," and one or two others. In this context, sitting close to him, listening intently to the music, I could hear the magic in his voice, appreciate the harmonic originality of his songs, and at least glimpse what Jac Holzman and Elektra producer Paul Rothchild saw in him.

To be sure, I was touched by the beauty in his voice and music, but wasn't awed—that came later, as he grew and developed into the astonishing singer, songwriter, and conceptualizer he started becoming a year or more down the line. Perhaps I wasn't able to fully appreciate what he was already doing, simply because I was a blues guy—get-down, hard-edged, sexy, and literary all at once, and his style didn't mirror my own. His gentle approach to music, even with its passion and undeniable sincerity, seemed a bit airy for me, a little too sweet, too young.

Again, maybe I was missing. I was older than he—Tim had been born on Valentine's Day, February 14, 1947, in Washington, D.C. He was barely nineteen when I met him in New York, while I was twenty-seven, eight years his senior. Plus, he had a gig in the Village, a recording contract, and respect from people such as Herb Cohen, Jac Holzman, and Paul Rothchild. I suspect my age, my predilection for blues-oriented material, and a tinge of envy prevented me from fully appreciating what Buckley was doing. He was a Bambi-eyed choirboy with a hip pocket full of teenage love songs—not entirely wrong, but not entirely fair, either.

In addition to his singing, which moved me, he did something that day that impressed me. As we talked about music, I said, "Here, let me show you something." I trotted out a bluesy riff that Stu Goldberg, the guy who started me on guitar, had shown me in college a few years ago. I had not pursued guitar then, but later used the riff in one of my tunes when I left my wife in New Jersey to become a foot-stomping folk and blues picker in San Francisco. "You know this already?"

"No. Show me again."

I showed him. He learned it immediately, and later incorporated part of it as one of the foundations for "Gypsy Woman."

He asked about a second pattern I had played in Sean's studio. I showed it to him, but it required the placing of his left index finger across the board of his six-string electric Gibson and pressing down all of the steel strings simultaneously, known as a barre chord.

"I can't do that," he said, smiling. He waved his crooked index and middle fin-

Lee in San Francisco, 1965, with his 1930s steel-body National Dobro, one of three guitars he played when performing in coffeehouses and nightclubs.

gers. "Broke 'em my freshman year in high school, quarterbacking football. Can't barre a chord."

(He often appeared to barre a chord when playing, and on nylon-string guitars he could. But on his steel-string electric Gibson, and later, on his acoustic 12-string Guild guitars, the barre was partial, pressing down only a few strings. He did not develop systems of open tunings, as stated by certain other writers, but did create imaginative new voicings within standard tunings.)

"Tell me something. Is Tim Buckley your real name?"

"Yeah."

"Well, Tim Buckley, I like your songs."

"You wanna play the Night Owl?"

"If I can play on the recording too."

"Sure."

"When do we rehearse?"

"How about tomorrow morning, 10 A.M.?"

Tim had shown me that he was a good singer and songwriter, and that he was quick to learn and eager for more. It spoke well for him and made me feel good.

I also realized that here was a "real" singer, a guy with a great voice and a unique and appealing sense of melody. Although I didn't dwell on it, I knew I didn't have a voice anywhere near as good as his. Nobody else did either, of course, so I pushed that doubt down into the cellar of my mind and temporarily ignored it. I would gig with him at the Night Owl, record on the album, see what happened.

The next morning, carrying my six-string Martin, I knocked on his door at ten o'clock. No answer. Knocked again. No answer. Knocked a third time. Tim opened the door, in his underwear, wearing no shirt, rubbing his eyes.

"Aren't you ready? It's time for rehearsal."

"Sorry."

Jainie Goldstein shuffled into the kitchen. "It's so early," she complained, turning on a yellow plastic AM radio. Cheesy rock 'n' roll blared thinly out of the speakers, grating my ears and offending my sensibilities, especially since I was already miffed at Tim for being late.

"You still listen to *that* stuff?" I inquired.

"What's wrong with that?" Jainie defensively shot back.

Tim looked at me closely.

"I've just moved on to other things, I guess."

Jainie yawned, put on some coffee. She was about nineteen years old, short, dark-haired, hazel eyes, barefooted, wearing a knee-length cotton nightdress.

"Like what?"

"Oh, Miles Davis, Bill Evans. You know, jazz people."

"Cocktail music," Jainie sneered.

"Ha! I can tell how much you've listened."

Tim smiled. "Have some coffee. I'll be ready in a minute."

That quick, quiet smile indicated a lot. Tim was a close observer—and he liked what he saw. At that moment, of course, I had only an inkling of what I later discovered—how intelligent he was, his desire to learn, how receptive and bright he could be in handling new ideas, information and concepts.

Years later he laughed at himself and quipped, "Basically, ol' buddy, I'm just an ignorant genius." Indeed, he was ignorant—but he knew how to learn quickly, and over the years learned a lot. It turned out that perhaps my greatest value to him lay in my knowledge of books and music, beyond whatever contributions I made to his music.

I grew to love him, and spoke to him of music, musicians, literature, poetry—he absorbed all of it instantly and, without copying or imitating, transformed it into conversation or songs that often spun in bold new conceptual directions.

He led the way on our journey, forever the Odyssean Starsailor, and I gave in devotion whatever knowledge or insight I had that might help him fulfill his dreams. Much of the content and direction of the music he created emerged from specific conversations we had, notably *Happy Sad*, and to no small extent, *Lorca* and *Starsailor*. That is, when he found himself wondering which way to go, I offered knowledge and ideas, which he either rejected, or utilized and developed in unique ways. Far from feeling used, I felt honored to serve his talent, for he was, in Thomas Mann's sense of the word, a true artist, "one upon whom nothing is lost."

I also felt a certain degree of pride, because I lasted. Others came into the circle, gave whatever they had, were absorbed quickly, and suddenly found themselves back out on the street. Tim inhaled everything in a whoosh—knowledge, ideas, musical styles, people, whatever was relevant to his interests. His appetite for insight and information was sometimes scary, sometimes thrilling, always exciting. In this respect, he was not a predictably compassionate person, if only because he burned with a sense of purpose and direction that transcended personal considerations—his own as well as others'. He took from people whatever knowledge he needed to fuel the creative fires that, in turn, used him as a vessel to serve music. He gave far more than he took. He was one of the most interesting, complex and stimulating persons I ever met. As he himself might have said, "Bucking frilliant!"

TALL TALES AND MANAGER HERB COHEN

As time passed, I discovered Tim was quite a storyteller, not exactly a liar, but a whimsically creative inventor. Tim's sister, Katy, said their father shared this trait. In fact, the whole family did.

"With us, it wasn't like lying," she said. "I mean we lied, but they weren't really lies. We would never slander anybody or anything like that. We were just having fun, making life brighter. We were actors and actresses, theatrical people, that's all. . . . It was the creation of characters and stories that lightened things up, you know?"

"I took up guitar, and played in a bunch of country bands," Tim said for a Warners biography. "The only one that toured was Princess Ramona and the Cherokee Riders. I got to dress up in a yellow hummingbird shirt and a turquoise hat and play lead guitar. I was about fifteen. I'd get $60 a week plus gas money and a room. I'd usually stay at a motel next to the bar. You know how those clubs in the Midwest and South are, with a motel right next to the bar, and I could play in the bars in that part of the country because they didn't care.

"It was Princess Ramona who told me: 'Folk music is going to be it.' So I started playing folk music. There were three kinds of clubs in L.A.: folk clubs, black clubs, and country music clubs. It was easier to get laid in folk clubs."

"I was a kid, still in school, and the folk thing really got to booming," he told writer Michael Davis.[1] "The kids in the suburbs needed guitars, because it was very important to be just like the Kingston Trio or the Limelighters.

"So I was buying up Martin guitars in downtown L.A. pawnshops. The guys in the pawnshops didn't know what they had. A lot of those great old Martins dated back to the '30s, collectors' items. Now, of course, they've got them in vaults, you know?

"So I was buying Martins from the pawnshops and running them out to the suburbs, meeting these strange people who were rich and buying their kids guitars. The

---

1. Writers' names appear in the text. Their articles from which quotes have been extrapolated appear in the Sources at the end of the book, along with publication information.

kids have since gone on to become lawyers or wiretappers, whatever comes out of that breed. That's how I got into Orange County."

"I started off with only five or six notes to my voice, when I was about 12 years old," Tim told writer Frankie Nemko. "Then all of a sudden, on one of the big band recordings my mother and father had, I heard a trumpet player playing things way up there, and I tried to get the note. I heard Little Richard—sometimes he got that note, like a falsetto scream.

"I figured, 'There's gotta be a way of getting to that.'

"So I'd ride my bike next to busses, and scream right at them, and try to get that note.

"Then one day, I heard the opposite end, a baritone sax, Gerry Mulligan. 'There's gotta be a way to get down there.' Well, I can get down there, a couple of notes, after a few nights singing.

"So I practiced, screamed, practiced some more, and ended up with a five- to five-and-a-half octave range. Yma Sumac. I don't know if she's from Brooklyn, or actually an Aztec princess. It's hard to tell."

Sometimes Tim's tales were tall indeed, as with the Princess Ramona fabrication, or running Martin guitars—or driving a taxi in L.A., or disguising himself and becoming Sly Stone's chauffeur. These and other tales were his way of impressing interviewers and having fun. He used to wink and laugh and say, "Feed the legend."

But some of the tales were as true as they were colorful.

"In Orange County, I found a few clubs there that served sassafras tea and coffee, actual coffee houses, with no liquor, which meant a brat of my age could play there," he said in a label bio, talking about professional beginnings. "I put together a group with bassist Jim Fielder, poet/drummer Larry Beckett and guitarist Brian Hartzler, an amazing guy. He started off on a Stratocaster, and now he's writing operas. We worked the folk clubs and coffee houses.

"But we needed a real gig to establish ourselves, so we went up to Hollywood to a club called It's Boss. We auditioned for the guy—and never got to finish a single tune! We played about twenty-five tunes, and halfway through each one he'd say, 'Okay—lemme hear the next one!'

"We had an amazing repertoire. We did everything. We didn't know about the Top 40 thing at the time. We figured, 'God, they're gonna love us—we wrote all our own songs!' Not so. He wanted Top 40 covers, things like 'Knock on Wood.'

"But we hadn't wasted our time. We met Jim Black at It's Boss. He was one of the drummers for Frank Zappa's band, the Mothers of Invention, and Zappa was managed by Herb Cohen. Jim liked us and set up an appointment for us with Herb at a club on Sunset Strip, a place called the Trip. I told him we had our own songs. He liked that. Then he heard us, made a six-song demo with just me and Fielder, sent it to Jac Holzman of Elektra Records, and Jac signed us. After that, we went to New York and played the Night Owl."

"Jim said Herb had managed Lenny Bruce, and that impressed me," Tim told me one day in the Village. "When I first met Herb I was 18. He looked like a dope smuggler or somebody out of *Che!* He's short, stocky, strong. Black curly hair, a Van Dyke beard. He wears only one kind of shirt, those white Guyabera shirts with four pockets and pleats down the front. In hot countries like Spain, Cuba and Mexico, they're

Herb Cohen, Tim's manager.
Smart, tough, a great ear for music.

considered formal wear, and Herb likes them. We didn't talk a lot. But he was straight and direct with me. I liked that. He's the first person I've talked to in the business who is honest and who believes in me.

"When I met him, neither one of us had much. He carried all his money in a shoebox! Not really, but he didn't have a lot of bread at the time, you know? When he found out I didn't have anything and wasn't even eating, he took me in and let me live with him for six months."

Tim said Herb was not only tough and smart in business, but had had considerable martial experience when he was younger. "Yeah, man, he used to run guns down to Cuba. I think he was a mercenary, helping Che Guevara in the revolution."

Tim told me hostile people quite often put down his spectacular mass of hair. In those days, only shortly after the Beatles had made long hair fashionable, any man who wore long hair was readily targeted by rednecks.

Back in L.A., Tim recalled, he and Herb had just finished eating in a diner. They were waiting to pay, when some guy made a sassy remark about Tim's hair and cherubic looks. "What are you, a girl?" he sneered.

Herb was holding car keys in his hand. He stepped right up to the guy, poked one of the keys into his chest hard, backing him up. As he poked, he said to the guy with a hiss, slowly and forcefully enunciating each word, "Watch . . . who. . . you're . . . fucking . . . with."

According to Tim, the guy was considerably bigger than Herb, but Herb's intensity was so heavy, and the menacing gesture with the keys so pointedly violent, that the guy wisely dropped the matter and backed off.

Tim's point was simple enough: Herb was a fighter, not only in the world of business, but physically as well. Not one to be tampered with. Tim was impressed with Herb, and wanted me to be impressed with himself because Herb was his manager.

I didn't necessarily believe Tim about the gunrunning, but I certainly believed him about Herb's physical courage, his willingness to challenge and intimidate the guy with his keys.

I once heard Herb say, "Ninety per cent of the business is hype." And yet, he had an incredible ear for music that often showed not only commercial potential, but was high-quality music as well—Fred Neil ("Dolphins," "Everybody's Talkin'"), Frank Zappa, Tom Waits, Linda Ronstadt, and others. Some of the best singers and musicians in the business got their start because of Herb Cohen's good judgment—including Tim Buckley.

Tim and I were hanging out at a party in Boston, toking pot, drinking beer. The apartment was thick with smoke. Lots of hippies and gorgeous gals. People talking, drinking, necking in the corner.

Herb opened the door, came in, looked around the room, headed my way.

"Where's Tim?"

"Over there." I offered him a lit joint. "Toke?"

He looked at it disdainfully. "I never touch the stuff. Rots your brain." He walked away.

He was the first person I had met in the business who to my knowledge didn't indulge in drugs of any kind.

Years later, Bill Henderson interviewed Tim in England. . . .

I gather your manager, Herb Cohen, is OK?

Yeah, he is. I mean, it's all a necessary evil. He knows it. I mean, I don't like reality, y'know?—he faces it every day. It's hard for me to be around him; it's hard for him to be around me. . . . I mean, I couldn't answer the phone that many times a day, but he's good at it.

Well, it seems to have been a successful working relationship—it's lasted.

I don't know how successful it is—but it's lasted! Well, he believes in me to a certain extent, in my earning power.

It's degrading—to be thought of in terms of dollars. I feel like a racehorse. But once you get over that, and realize everything has its place, then you accept it, and remember that the main thing is the people that you play for. . . .

It's the compromise of wanting to get through to as many people as you can, but to do that, you've got to go through the record companies.

Sure. It takes a lot of hate and a lot of love to keep doing it. I know guys who are incredibly talented, but they get sucked in by the business and therefore ruined, 'cause all they're thinking about is the money. . . . They're not thinking at all about their heart and soul, and what they want to say. . . .

In Tim's interview with John Lawless, Herb said, "Tim doesn't regard material things at all. The one and only thing in his life is music. . . . Some people might think that would give me, a businessman, a headache, but it doesn't. The average life of a teenybopper pop group is twenty-one or twenty-two months. That's their entire career, and they make good money in that time.

"But Tim is going to be around for a long time, because what he is doing is valid.

Tim in New York, age 19 or 20. Among his many gifts, he photographed as well as he sang.

He does not depend on record sales, and he'll still be here as long as there are people who can hear.

"I'm not saying that I would object to a big seller, although I would think he might, because of what it might bring. He is making more through concerts than the majority of Top Twenty artists. Theirs is a false market. Tim's is a market that lasts."

FROM THE NIGHT OWL TO L.A.

It felt great being in New York. Exhilarating. Exciting. Traffic roared in the streets, people yelled at each other in cars and on the sidewalks, taxi cabs rattled and banged by at forty miles an hour, bums panhandled tourists and washed car windows at stop signs for a dollar, cop cars and fire engines wailed their sirens, hot-shot characters on bicycles whipped in and out of traffic, nobody obeyed the stop lights, cars ran them, people walked through them, shop keepers shouted about their wares, massive trucks double-parked and clogged traffic, men in tank-tops and women in floppy blouses sat in apartment windows, bored, smoking cigarettes, watching the high-energy street scene parade below them like a Fellini movie. New York in the springtime, New York all the time, New York any time, every time, a colorful, cacophonous insane asylum.

We carried our guitars and walked over to Sean's studio three blocks away to rehearse. Tim didn't wear conventional jeans, a tucked-in shirt, orthodox shoes. He wore a sky-blue faded work shirt, tails dangling outside his brown corduroy pants like rags, a brown suede jacket, and beige-colored, high-topped Indian moccasin boots with leather laces.

He walked with his head forward and down, shoulders slumped, often sliding or dragging his feet rather than stepping. Peering out from underneath that enormous mass of curly brown hair, he had the largest and most expressive dark brown eyes I had ever seen. They gave him a delicate, vulnerable look, awakening an urge in me to treat him gently and protect him. His fragile beauty and incredible shyness made me feel strong in his presence, as well as loving, protective, and nurturing. On the other hand, there was something so passive about him that it made me feel a little boorish and impatient, yet inhibited—the eggshell syndrome—as if I had to be careful not to ruffle or hurt him by being harsh or crude or too direct.

At the studio we went over the songs that would eventually become the first album, *Tim Buckley*. The more we worked, the more impressed I became.

Some of Tim's harmonic changes were fresh, offbeat, original, perhaps especially in "She Is." His melodies had an instant appeal and flowed well, delighting the ear with their originality. "Strange Street Affair Under Blue" featured an enchanting choir-boy interlude in the middle (it was my idea to gradually accelerate the piece, like a Greek dance), while "Understand Your Man," a blues-based tune, not quite finished yet, offered an aggressive energy many of the other pieces lacked. It also gave a hint of the vocal range that began to find fuller expression on the second album, *Goodbye and Hello*. "Wings" had a charm and simplicity that instantly reached all who heard it, and "Valentine Melody," a birthday song for Tim as well as a Beckett love song, was one of the prettiest, most sensitive tunes I had ever heard.

"Song Slowly Song" and "Song of the Magician" were two spacious, whisper-quiet compositions that had a mysterious, atmospheric presence above and beyond the lyrics. When the album came out, writer Brian Van der Horst agreed. He regarded

"Song Slowly Song" as "a thoroughly haunting piece." He called "Song of the Magician" one of the best tracks on the album, saying it "seemed to be casting a spell of white magic and love." Both performances also included interludes for improvised melodic lines on the guitar, which featured my "bell-toned" harmonics that for a while became something of a trademark for me. The intimacy of these twin gems was as intense as it was subtle, as sensual as it was mind-caressing. I played well on them, and they won my heart forever.

In this dimension of Tim's music I left foot-stomping behind and discovered my better side—a flowing, gentle, lyrical sense of melody, not at all brash or aggressive. Here, in the realm of whispered intimacy, more than anywhere else in the scope of Tim's work, I felt most at home.

During this period, Tim's concept of composition, rehearsal, and performance perfectly fit the norm. He sang the songs the same way each time. I conceived melodic lines and rhythmic phrases for guitar, and wrote out chord charts. We devised specific parts and concrete arrangements, which I memorized and performed onstage and on the recording, except for the improvisations in "Song Slowly Song" and "Song of the Magician."

At this time, Tim's pieces were "objects," rather like sound sculptures—a conventional, well-rehearsed approach to composing that fit business interests, AM radio, and both of our sensibilities at the time, but which later became dramatically irrelevant.

Once I felt comfortable with the tunes, Tim and I rounded up a local drummer and electric bass player whose names I don't recall, and opened at the Night Owl at Third and Macdougal. The place was packed.

Tim wore a black turtleneck sweater, leaned into the mike, strummed his six-string guitar and started singing. Joe Marra, the owner, stood at the cash register, chewing gum, listening intently. He nodded his head in approval. An acquaintance of mine heard him say, "At least he ain't wunna deez fuckin' lames."

Playing my six-string Martin into a microphone, knowing I couldn't be heard very well, giving it everything I had, I watched people's reactions.

Many listeners immediately fell in love with Tim's voice, his songs, his presence, and virtually everybody enjoyed us, clapping heartily. As might be expected, some of the radio-conditioned teenage listeners didn't quite know how to relate to the music initially, because it wasn't rooted in blues clichés, nor was it based on lust, rage, misery, or screaming. As Tim's ethereal voice sailed out into the smoky spotlights, people softened, opened their hearts, and the music won them over. Before long, everybody in the house was attuned. Magic in New York City.

During intermissions, people in the club listened to the Lovin' Spoonful wailing "Hot Town, Summer in the City," the Mamas & the Papas sentimentally chortling "California Dreamin'," The Who singing "My G-g-g-generation," the Beatles crooning "Michelle," and dozens of other fresh, new rock groups breaking into the charts.

Numerous people took photographs at the Night Owl, including Bill Harvey, who snapped the performance shot that appeared on the back cover of *Tim Buckley*. The bass player can barely be seen on the left edge of the cover, while the drummer and I are completely omitted.

My acoustic D-28 was not loud enough at the Night Owl, so Tim suggested I purchase an electric guitar. Together we visited a hock shop and found an old second-hand hollow-body jazz-toned Epiphone. We liked it, but I worried about the money. I had come to New York with only $700, had spent much of it already, and the Epiphone cost $300. Tim smiled, looked me in the eye, and said, "Don't worry. Everything will be all right." I took a deep breath and bought the Epiphone.

Before rehearsals, we ate breakfast at a diner called the Hip Bagel. Tim ordered scrambled eggs and bacon (burnt black) every time. The Bagel had a great jukebox: Thelonious Monk playing "'Round Midnight," Bud Powell playing "April in Paris," trumpeter Donald Byrd playing Duke Pearson's melancholy "Christo Redentor."

Outside, in holes in the sidewalk, scraggly trees, optimistically yearning for the sky, sprouted yellow-green leaves. Springtime in New York. Peaceful moments in the big city.

Throughout the years, Tim had no difficulty relating to good music of any generic style, an unusual trait and another indication of his musical intelligence. During this early period, he was connecting primarily with folk music, but he was not alien to other forms, including jazz.

"There were two people who really made me want to be a musician," he told writer Frankie Nemko years later. "The first was seeing the Duke Ellington band on TV, between 1956 and 1959. They were all dressed in white, and they themselves were all black. It might have been on *The Nat King Cole Show*—and of course when I saw Nat King Cole sing, it was love and beauty. But when I saw Duke play I realized, 'Jesus, music can be like that.' They sounded like a quintet. They always played that well.

"And the other person who kept me going, because obviously I couldn't play that way—I was only around nine or ten—was Pete Seeger. He had that same kind of communication with people. That's when I picked up the banjo."

At this early time in his life, 1966, Tim was developing the Pete Seeger dimension of himself. Later, beginning with *Happy Sad*, when he started composing with his own musicians in mind, Tim developed the Duke Ellington dimension, which included strong influences from Nat King Cole and Johnny Mathis. He never imitated anyone in figurative or literal ways. As do virtually all serious artists, he learned selected underlying principles that helped him springboard into creative originality. With each new step, he learned new concepts from new artists in new genres. As he absorbed one level and evolved upward into the next, so his music changed and evolved, as did his musical reference points. The exceptional evolutionary journey he took in music constituted our shared Odyssean Starsailor adventures in life as well.

Shortly before we opened at the Night Owl, a disturbing event took place that stuck with me. Tim and Jainie told me about it over breakfast at the Hip Bagel.

They had to move to a new apartment, because Tim had gotten into an argument with the landlord over a matter of $10. Tim lashed out in anger and hit the landlord in the face. The landlord of course threw them out.

That shocked me. Tim was not a big fellow, perhaps 5'5", maybe 130 pounds. He was not a pug, did not seem to be violent, had not been crude or coarse around me—and of course sang like the sweetest cherubic angel this side of a Walt Disney cartoon.

"My God, Tim, how could you do that?"

Lee playing guitar onstage for the first time, in a shopping-mall coffeehouse hootenanny in Princeton, New Jersey. He was so shy Jennifer had to push him onto the stage. The audience loved his flashy finger-pickin' and clapped for more.

"He pissed me off, that's how."

"He was big, too," Jainie said.

"My dad taught me you don't back down from anybody, not even a Mack truck. Besides," Tim smiled gleefully, "I played quarterback on the football team, remember? Ran down the sidelines for touchdowns, kissing cheerleaders all the way."

That incident unsettled me. This little guy facing up to an enraged landlord—and hitting him? Oh, well. Tougher than he looks.

When I left my wife in New Jersey a year before coming to New York, I ran away, first to Mexico, then to San Francisco, with a beautiful, warm-hearted, fun-loving dancer named Jennifer Stace. We met and fell in love in Princeton, where her father, Professor Walter T. Stace, was a world-famous philosopher and author (*Teachings of the Mystics*). Bored with Princeton's respectable straight life, Jennifer and I left her ten-year-old son Michael Cavanaugh with Jennifer's parents and took off to see what adventures the world might hold for us.

In San Francisco, we brought Michael out to live with us. Jennifer danced in a go-go bar. I taught guitar at my friend Stu Goldberg's Marina Guitar store by day, and played and sang my own songs in coffeehouses by night. After a year of performing, capped by opening for the then-famous John Handy jazz group at the Berkeley Theater, I left Jennifer and Michael in San Francisco and traveled to New York.

Two or three times a week, I wrote them from my rented room in the Village, letting them know what had been happening since my departure. Jennifer was thrilled I was working, "But what about your own music?" she asked. "I don't know," I said. "Right now, I'm gigging with Tim. I'll have some money after the recording, and will then see if I can get booked on my own. Meanwhile, I can't wait for you to hear this guy sing. He's good. I see why Elektra signed him."

Although I had initially been hesitant about serving as a sideman for someone else, that feeling gradually vanished. Tim and his music had an irresistible charm, and I soon found myself thoroughly involved, if not yet totally committed. At this point I was simply feeling my way into the situation, enjoying myself and Tim and the music more and more as we moved along.

At Tim's new apartment, we broke out red wine and had a party. Larry Beckett had arrived from Anaheim, a gentle soul with introspective eyes, blond wispy hair, thick glasses, a good sense of humor, and a quiet, intelligent way of speaking.

"I'm into Dryden, Donovan, Donne, and Dylan," he said, a twinkle in his eyes.

"Sounds like a law firm," I said.

"Well, it's Bob Dylan," he said, "and Dylan Thomas. I love the magic language can create. Shakespeare, Keats, Bobbie Burns—maybe someday Larry Beckett, too!" he laughed, took a drink, smiling, a little tipsy. I expected him to say, "I'm a poet, and know it, and my feet are long fellows," but he didn't.

He pushed his plastic-rimmed glasses up the bridge of his nose with his middle finger. I liked him. Behind his glasses and underneath his thin blond hair, he was clearly a bright, well-read fellow, and a perceptive observer with a good sense of humor.

He and Tim had been the closest of friends throughout their years together at Loara public high school in Anaheim, where their intellectual brilliance, their unorthodox artistic values, their relative maturity and sense of purpose gained them a reputation as a kind of "fearsome twosome."

As Mary Guibert, Tim's ex-wife, years later told writer Bob Niemi, "It was great fun being with them, lots of laughs. . . . Tim was totally himself all the time, a breath of fresh air in my otherwise 'do it right' life. He told jokes, did impressions, made comments full of irony and wit. He always made me laugh.

"He and Beckett were inseparable in high school. They'd recite ancient English poetry in the quad during lunch and blow all those tidy people away. Everyone thought they were either crazy or brilliant—I belonged to the latter."

In high school, and off-and-on throughout Buckley's career, Beckett and Buckley collaborated on songs. Very often, Larry wrote poems, then Tim put music to them. On other occasions, Tim wrote both the lyrics and the music. In high school, they hung out and listened to recordings by Pete Seeger, the Kingston Trio, Odetta, the Weavers, the Limelighters, Judy Henske, and Bob Dylan. They attended the various open-mike hoot nights at folk clubs like Leadbelly's, the Trip, and the Troubadour, where Tim sang the songs he and Larry had penned. I liked Larry and looked forward to knowing him better.

Jainie came over while I poured myself more wine. "Are you drunk?" Her typically blunt way of asking carried with it an air of innocent sincerity.

"Smashed out of my mind," I replied.

"You don't look it or sound like it."

"Many years of practice in the finest schools of Europe," I said. "Here's to you, Jainie, and to the Night Owl gig." We smiled at each other, raised our glasses.

I liked Jainie, too. At first she seemed a bit crude, a little awkward. But as I got to know her better, she began to shine in her own sweet way. True, she lacked polish or sophistication, but at the same time, she had a shy, insecure little girl quality about her that was charming. She lacked education and artifice, but her warmth and spontaneity were instantly endearing. When she smiled, her cheeks glowed and her hazel-blue-green eyes lit up the room.

"Your eyes have little brown specks in them," I said. "Really pretty."

"Thank you," she smiled. "Some people say those specks mean I'm a prophet."

"Are you?"

"I dunno," she laughed. "I just inherited them from my father."

"Where'd you meet Tim?"

"At one of the hoots at the Troubadour in L.A.. When he came offstage after singing, I told him I thought he was really good." Jainie blushed, recalling the moment. "It wasn't like I was the only one in the place who knew he was good, but he seemed to like me saying it, and liked me too. We've been together ever since."

"I noticed that your name on Tim's lyric sheet for your song is spelled J-a-i-n-i-e. Is that his spelling?

"No," she blushed. "It's mine. I just wanted to fancy up my plain-Jane name, give it a little bi-zazz."

Jainie loved Tim, sensed his artistry and his vulnerability, and did everything she could to help and protect him. She paid the bills, balanced the checkbook, shopped for groceries, did the cooking, and served as a buffer between Tim and the harsh vulgarities of mundane reality. She was the perfect Jewish mama, tough on the outside, heart of gold inside, and a rock of strength and stability. At this point in Tim's life she was perfect for him.

Tim once chuckled and said that Night Owl owner "Joe Marra didn't quite understand what we were doing musically—so he kept us on an extra month." Word spread throughout the Village, and before long Tim packed the place with people who came specifically to hear him.

Tim was with Jainie, but I was alone until Mary, one of the Night Owl waitresses, took me under her wing. She had long black hair, New York-chapped lips, and a kind of punchy urban gruffness that I liked. She knew how to drink too much without losing her cool and she had a good sense of humor, both of which helped me relax. She was fun and she was a comfort, a refuge in the midst of New York's brutal madness.

I didn't always feel good on the road, because everybody related to Tim, paid attention to him, fell all over him adoringly, while I was comparatively ignored. Mary's companionship helped ease the loneliness of too many isolated days and nights in that atmospherically violent town. She understood and appreciated me, and to this day I thank her.

"Herb says we gotta go back to L.A." Tim said, his eyes bright with excitement.

"What for?"

"To record the album."

"I thought we were doing it here."

"We were. But everything's changed. Showbiz, y'know?"

"How will we get there?"

"I don't know."

"Let me call Jennifer in San Francisco. She can drive here, then we can toodle out to L.A. together in her car."

"You, me, Larry, Jainie, and Jennifer? That's five," Tim said.

"If there's not enough room, Larry can fly back. And you're gonna love Jennifer. She's got long dark hair, golden skin, a fantastic smile with big horse-teeth, a great sense of humor, a laugh that makes everybody else laugh too, fabulous gazoombas, and she's a terrific dancer. Believe me, you're gonna love her."

"Give her a call!"

Jennifer arrived a week later, and we piled into her car. Guitars and suitcases jammed the trunk, and there was hardly room for all of us. Larry insisted on riding with us to L.A. instead of flying.

"But Larry, there's no room to sit," I said. "And you've got all those LPs—there's no room in the trunk, either."

"I'll sit in the corner of the back seat and stack the records on the floor in front of me."

"That's crazy, Larry. You won't have any leg room. Someplace in Missouri you'll be hurting."

"No, I won't, and even if I do, I won't say a word. Promise."

Larry rode all the way to Los Angeles, scrunched up in the back seat, his feet to the side of the LPs or propped on top. For over 3,000 miles he rode that way, night and day, without a single complaint.

Late at night, somewhere out in the Kansas plains under a clear black nightsky gleaming with blue stars, Tim drove the car and talked about his life. I rode in the front seat while the others dozed in back. It was on this particular night that Tim spoke to me about several things from his past that proved to be significant in his life, including Mary Guibert, the Loara High School sweetheart he had met in French class, then married at the St. Michael's Episcopal Church in Anaheim on October 23, 1965, with Larry as best man.

"Yeah, she's cute," he said. "Cute, but real straight. We both thought of her as Miss Goody Two-shoes. She's from Anaheim, which is kind of a clean, white, middle-class, upscale type of place—real proper, you know? She's a musician too, a good one, piano and cello, but she's lazy. All she wants to do is stay home close to her mother and not do anything with her music. Classical music. That was kind of a problem. She's into Beethoven and those people. I'm into Pete Seeger, Odetta, Fred Neil."

"Did she like your music?"

"She liked it, especially at first. But as we went along I didn't get the feeling that she *really* liked it. It isn't 'great' music in her eyes. It isn't like Mozart or Vivaldi or those other dead white classical guys from Europe."

"Did you love her?"

"Yeah, but it was high school love, you know? I don't think I would have married her if she hadn't said she was pregnant."

"Was she?"

"She said she was, and we got married, but it turned out she wasn't."

"She lied to you?"

"I don't know. Maybe she did, just to get me to marry her. But maybe not. Probably one of those imaginary pregnancies women get sometimes—all the signs, but no bread in the oven."

"Why did you leave her?"

"Well, Herbie got me a deal with Elektra. And music is my life. It's everything I ever wanted, and it's what I'm *supposed* to do. It's my destiny, you know? So when Herbie said I should come to New York, what else could I do? And then in New York, about the time I met you, I got word that she really had gotten pregnant, just before I left. 'Sposed to have the kid in November."

"You didn't know about the pregnancy when you came to New York?"

"No."

"Really?"

"Definitely not. And it was real ironic, too. I had written to my mother, asking her to find out about California divorce laws. Just as Mom was writing back to me, there came a knock at her door. It was Mary, who smiled and patted her belly and said, 'Well, you're gonna be a grandmother.' There was my mom, writing to me about how to get a divorce, and Mary waltzes through the front door pregnant—ha!"

"What are you going to do?"

"I don't know. If I go back to her, I'll have to get my old high school job at the Taco Bell, and put up with Mary's condescending attitudes about my music. What would you do?"

"Anybody can be a father. Not many are gifted with music."

"I'll have to think about that."

"Lot of guilt involved if you leave her."

"Yeah, that would be the price."

"Not easy to carry that kind of guilt."

"Maybe I can make it up to the kid later."

"What about money?"

"I don't have anything now. If the music happens, I'll send her money."

Tim and Mary divorced. Mary gave birth to Jeffrey Scott Buckley on November 17, 1966. Tim pursued his music, making sure his accountant sent a child support check for $80 every month. Jeff grew up to become a singer and songwriter too, one of the best and most-loved talents of his generation.

Years later a reliable source told me that Tim knew very well Mary was pregnant when he left for New York, and called her regularly while he was there.

When we arrived in Hollywood, Tim, Jainie, Larry, Jennifer, and I lived together in a cheap motel on Santa Monica Boulevard, across the street from the (now defunct) Tropicana Motel, where rich and famous rock stars stayed. On hot plates, we cooked potatoes and hamburgers, or bacon and scrambled eggs, and life was fun. We brimmed over with excitement and optimism about the upcoming recording.

At Sunset Sound in L.A., we recorded all the songs we had played at the Night Owl. This was our first time in the studio. We felt nervous and excited, of course, but producer Paul Rothchild, calm, competent, professional and famous for his work with the Doors, helped us relax and take care of business. Everything went smoothly—no snafus or dramas or personality clashes with the technicians. Amazingly, we completed the job in only two days. Musician Van Dyke Parks came into the studio alone a few days later and overdubbed keyboard tracks. Arranger Jack Nitzsche added string parts, which in many people's opinion, including my own, did not enhance the musical quality. Although *Tim Buckley* is not often hailed as one of Tim's greatest works, it is nevertheless a gem of an album—innocent, pure, in some ways ethereal and extremely imaginative, especially in "Song Slowly Song" and "Song of the Magician." It is an emotionally and stylistically varied album, an auspicious debut and pleasure to listen to.

After the sessions, the five of us moved into a house on Eleanor Street in Hollywood, along with Tim's old high school buddy, bassist Jim Fielder, who soon thereafter joined Buffalo Springfield (which promptly folded) then the just-beginning Blood, Sweat & Tears (which became a hit).

Feeling rich, Tim purchased two rusty old 1938 Chevrolet cars for $75 apiece, with running boards and big square box-like trunks on the back. He had the engine from one put into the frame of the other, and drove that funky, clunky car until it gave out. It kept gathering parking tickets until the city hauled it away.

One day I was strumming my 12-string and writing a new song, "There Ain't No Such Thing as Hard Times," singing it over and over again, trying new lines, working it out. After an hour or so of this, an irritated next door neighbor shouted from his second-story window, "Hey, Hard Times! Knock it off—I'm tryna sleep!"

Tim rushed out of the house into the front yard and shouted up at the guy, "Shut the fuck up, you son-of-a-bitch, or I'll bash your face in!"

The guy didn't say another word. I put my guitar away. My heart was pumping fast. I appreciated Tim's loyalty to me, but found the ferocity of his words upsetting.

During this period, on a binge with Jennifer that wheeled and reeled us down to the bullfights in Tijuana, I dealt with a major question. I knew I could never be an accomplished singer, and my songs were good but not great. Boo-hoo. However, from the time I was a kid idolizing Gene Autry and Roy Rogers, I had always wanted to be a guitar player. And Tim was giving me that opportunity.

Without saying anything to Jennifer either during or after the Tijuana trip, I gave up the dream of a solo career as a singer/songwriter that she and I had shared. In my heart I made a full commitment to Tim, embarking on a ship into the unknown, having not the slightest idea how things might work out. That decision reverberates down to this day, in these very words. Never once have I regretted that choice.

Back in Hollywood, I kept my Guild 12-string, but sold my D-28 and Dobro. I bought a Fender Telecaster electric guitar with a maple neck, and added two Humbucking pickups with a "mellow" switch. Along the way, I purchased a Fender Super Reverb amp and customized it with two 12" Electro-Voice speakers.

Jennifer and I felt like innocent hicks from the sticks those first years in the city of stars and lost angels. One night early on we met Theodore Bikel in the Ash Grove—the first of many recording artists and movie actors we encountered in Hollywood. And one night Tim and Jennifer and I invited my folk-blues hero Spider John Koerner over to the house on Eleanor Street after his gig at the Ash Grove. Tim and Larry and Spider and I got drunk, had a wonderful time.

The evening ended around 3 A.M. when Spider John climbed up on the front porch cement banister and tried to leap over the bushes into the front yard. He couldn't clear the bushes, tripped up, and sprawled on the lawn, unhurt. We stood on the porch, cheering for him as he laughed, lurched to his feet, staggered to his car and drove off into the night, singing my favorite tune of his, "Hal C. Blake, he was a real good friend of mine. . . ."

The hazy sky overhead reflected Hollywood's bright lights, glowing pink and gold above us like an all-night sunrise.

CHAPTER 2

THE FATHER SONG

Tim's father, Timothy Charles Buckley Jr.—known as Buck—had an enormous influence on Tim. He tried to love, but found it difficult to do so; as a result, he was not so much a loving parent as he was a powerful force, a presence who lived mentally and emotionally isolated in a violent, unhappy interior world of his own. His volatile nature left permanent imprints on Tim's psyche that generated both constructive and destructive behavior later on.

Because Tim's father was physically present, but not very often in nurturing ways, Tim, in effect, did not have the father he needed. He rarely got the love, recognition, and supportive approval a capable father would have given. There was a hole in Tim's soul. Ironically, and in a very different way, Tim passed the father-suffering on to his own son, Jeff.

While Tim's father was a volatile *presence* who left a huge emotional emptiness in Tim's life, so Tim was an enormous *absence* who left a gaping void in Jeff that could never be filled. Tim and Jeff both grew up desperately yearning for love and respect and emotional nourishment from fathers who simply were not able to fulfill those primal needs.

The love they felt for their fathers inevitably turned to resentment and anger. In both of their psyches a battle raged between love and hate. In part, it was that battle that drove them toward public performance, where, onstage, they might be able to attain the stature and acquire the love from the public that they could not get from their fathers.

When Tim drove us over the Kansas plains in Jennifer's car that summer night on our way from New York to L.A., he told me several disturbing stories about his father, later confirmed by his mother, Elaine, and his sister, Katy.

Many questions about Tim's creative talent, his emotional outlook, his deep-seated doubts about his self-worth, his inner conflicts and, to a degree, his self-destructive fears of success, can to some extent be traced to both parents, perhaps especially his father.

TIM

"Dad was brilliant," Tim said, "and he could have been a great writer. But World War II got him, and then later on he had an accident in the plant where he worked [more on this later], so he was never able to really express himself as a writer, except in letters. He had an incredible mind, witty, funny, very bright. He was a good man too, in his way a moral man, a man of integrity, but he lost his purpose and direction. Probably too good for the world, you know? He had high principles and high ideals—maybe that's why he never fit anywhere, except in the military."

"Was he in the fighting?" I asked.

"Yeah. A lot. He was in World War II right from the beginning, drafted in '42. He was in the African/Sicily campaign, and a bunch of others, and then volunteered for the 101st Airborne division so he could parachute behind enemy lines.

"Those 101st guys were legendary. It was a volunteer outfit, called the Screaming Eagles, so tough that only one in three applicants qualified, and he was one of them. For their first combat mission, they had to drop behind German lines at Normandy at night and clear out the Nazis from Utah beach so we could bring in infantry troops by boat. He said it was June 6, 1944. They called it D-Day.

"It was crazy, because the American pilots flying our guys into battle panicked under German artillery fire and broke rank. When Dad jumped, it was in the dead of night, with artillery fire exploding all around lighting up the sky. The plane was too low and too far behind the lines. He lost his rifle and had to fight guerrilla-style back to the beach. He said that was okay, because every paratrooper had been trained as a one-man army. He said it took a month before they could win at Normandy.

"He did five tours over there and was in all those famous battles. . . . One of them was called Operation Market Garden, in Holland. They jumped in daylight, cleared out the Germans. The townspeople welcomed them and cheered for them and treated them like kings. Then the Germans counter-attacked, and he and the guys had to fight for sixteen miles of road that became known as 'Hell's Highway.'

"He loved it. Some people don't, but some do, and he did. He used to talk about the battle of Bastogne in the Ardennes forest in Belgium. They called it 'the Battle of the Bulge,' and it was horrendous. I guess about 65,000 men got wiped out there. Dad said it was December 1944, and the 101st was trapped and surrounded by Germans in sub-zero weather without food or medical supplies. Everybody lived and slept in foxholes. Some didn't have blankets. A lot of guys froze to death.

"The Germans pounded them with artillery fire and bombs day and night, attacked with tanks. Dad said they were like sitting ducks, but they didn't break. They held off repeated assaults by six German divisions. Even when the Nazis demanded surrender, the 101st leader said, 'Nuts!' The guys held their ground until General Patton broke through enemy lines with tanks and saved them. Eisenhower awarded the entire 101st Airborne division the Distinguished Service medal.

"Dad was in all those battles and stayed in the 101st until they disbanded in 1945. The Eagles saw action only that one year 1944–1945, but even today military guys respect the 101st as the ultimate attack division of World War II.

"After that, Dad was in the 105th Infantry. He was a demolition expert who blew up bridges and trains and roads, clearing the way for Army guys or preventing Germans from breaking through. He really liked being a warrior, and that's what he was, a good one. He came back in December 1945.

"Like his own Irish father, Dad hated the English, called them lousy Limeys, said a lot of them didn't take the war seriously enough to suit him, like it was some kind of tennis match. Dad was crazy about George Patton, loved 'Ol' Blood and Guts.' Hated Eisenhower, couldn't stand him, but said Bradley was a great man, that Bradley was the one running the show anyway. After the war, he never stopped talking about the adventures he had, the enemies he killed, the towns he marched into, the people he met.

"But things weren't right with him. I don't think he made it higher than sergeant, but he'd go around saying he was General Buckley, you know? He'd wear his business suit and put on his paratrooper combat boots and tuck his pants down inside, get his green beret, take out all his war medals—he was wounded a lot—had a lot of scars, even had a metal plate in his head from a land mine. Anyway, he would take out his Purple Hearts and his Bronze Star and Distinguished Service badge and a lot of other medals and put them on his chest. He'd pin his Screaming Eagles Paratrooper silver wings on his green beret, and walk outside the house onto the street and parade around like that, slapping his thigh with his riding crop, waving it in the air. He'd even go to church dressed like that!

"After the war, he never fit any place, and he suffered a lot because of that—an outsider, a kind of wandering outcast. I was born in Washington, D.C., where my mother lived, but we soon moved back to Amsterdam, New York. It's just a funky blue-collar town with a lot of factories. Dad was born there in 1916. He worked a factory job at General Electric in Schenectady, then sold all our household furniture and moved us to Bell Gardens in Orange County, California, partly for the sunshine, mostly for new work opportunities.

"But even when he was selling the furniture, he did a number. It was really nice furniture, but nobody wanted to buy it and we couldn't get rid of it. So Dad started going on and on to people about how many Germans he killed—it was a big thing in those days to have killed Germans. The Jews in town came to see the furniture, and Dad would say, 'I killed 300 Nazis.' Well, maybe he did and maybe he didn't, but he did his General Buckley routine so well that he sold all the furniture in the house!

"Bell Gardens is another blue-collar town, full of *Grapes of Wrath* Oakies and Southern rednecks from Arkansas, Texas, Louisiana, right out of *Tobacco Road*. People used to buy these flimsy prefabricated tract houses for $100 down and $25 a month, and raise cows and hogs and goats and chickens in their front yard. They even called the area we lived in 'Billygoat Acres.'

"Everybody loved country music, honky-tonk stuff, Hank Williams, Johnny Cash, George Jones, all those guys. So did I. I used to sneak out of the house by myself at night sometimes and drive down to Eastern Avenue. I'd park the car and walk on the sidewalk just so I could see the neon signs up close and hear music pouring out of those bars. It was great.

"In Bell Gardens Dad got a job as a laborer in the Recold Corporation, a refrigeration and air conditioning plant. Pretty soon he worked his way up to foreman, then superintendent. That's when everything went wrong.

"There was a leak in a refrigeration unit, way up on the ceiling. He climbed a ladder and fixed the leak. They had had a heavy rain the night before and the floor was wet. When he climbed back down, he slipped on the wet floor and fell. He hurt his back and couldn't move his legs. He hit his neck and the back of his head too. They put him in traction and then in physical therapy, because he couldn't walk for a long time.

"From that point on, he was never the same. Mom and I both noticed heavy changes in his personality. He just wasn't mentally right. He started getting crazy—and mean. Mom wanted him to see a psychiatrist, but he wouldn't. He said he wasn't the one who was crazy—she was.

"Pretty soon he lost his job at the factory. It was hard on him, because he was over 45, and he couldn't get another factory job because of the insurance companies. In this country, insurance companies rule everything. So he was out of work a long time. The only other job he could get was a security guard. That snapped him. He was an incredible writer, a reader, a great warrior—and now here he was, physically broken, and degraded to a security guard.

"In one place he worked, he said he got radiation on the job and it had affected the metal plate in his head. I don't know if that's true. Maybe the earlier fall just knocked the plate out of place. But he insisted it was radiation in his brain, and kept getting crazier and crazier.

"He couldn't sleep. He was a high-strung man anyway, but now he was hyperactive. So he'd stay up and turn the stereo on full-blast all night long while everyone was trying to sleep. Sometimes he'd take the car and leave for two or three days at a time. Or he'd take me out of school and insist that I had to come back home and clean house. Or he'd drag my sister Katy out of school and take her to Disneyland. We had a swimming pool in the back yard. He'd drain it dry just to irritate my mother.

"Then two very heavy things happened that finally made me leave home."

"What were they?"

"Last summer he called his mother in Amsterdam, New York, and said we were driving out to see her. He grabbed me and Katy and we took off—heading completely the wrong way, towards Mexico. Every place we stopped, he got into arguments with people. He was wearing his paratrooper uniform and his green beret. He had his medals on, and the riding crop in his hand. 'I'm General Buckley,' he'd proclaim. 'I killed a thousand Nazis and I'll kill a thousand more if I ever get the chance.' He'd go on and on like that. People didn't know how to handle him.

"Then he made me drive. We headed east. I'd pull off the road and pretend we had a flat tire, hoping the cops would stop and take him away, but they never did. Then the car broke down. Somebody towed us to New Mexico.

"We got stuck in a hotel in Albuquerque. Dad and I got into a huge argument about continuing the trip. I insisted we stop this craziness and go back home. Dad refused, shouting at me, 'We can't! We have to go to Amsterdam. My mother is expecting us!' We shouted back and forth, then we'd both ask poor Katy, 'What do you want to do?' She'd break down and cry and say she wanted to go back home, and then she'd get an asthma attack and start wheezing and gasping. It was awful.

"Dad grabbed me by the throat and heaved me up against the wall and we started yelling and hitting each other. Katy was terrified, afraid we were going to kill each other. It was a heavy trip. There was a gun in the room too.

"Then Dad left us in the hotel. He got the car fixed, drove around town on one of his expeditions, and pretty much totaled the car along the way. Katy and I were going to split and just leave him there, but he finally came back—with a bunch of Indians. I don't know if he was drunk or not. I think he was. Finally, we called Mom, and she came and got us."

"Had to have been painful."

"It was, but he was having a mental breakdown. He was hurting inside and didn't know how to express it. He was a beautiful guy. It made me feel sad to see him this way. I hung in as long as I could, didn't leave home until the last incident."

"What happened then?"

"He was drinking and hauled me out to the garage. He grabbed me by the throat, yelling at me, calling me a faggot, saying he was going to kill me.

"'Fuck you!' I yelled back at him.

"'That's right,' he said. "Get mean! Don't put up with my crap, or anybody else's either. Don't *ever* back down—you hear me? Spit on me!'

"'No!'

"'Then hit me. Come on—hit me!'

"'I love you—and I won't hit you.'

"'Whatsa matter with you? Chicken?'

"'I'll never hit you! I love you too much!'

"'You gutless little pansy. Hit me! You're not a man if you don't hit me! Take this gun—take it! I've been a total asshole to you. If you're any kind of man at all, you'll shoot me—go ahead, do it, shoot me!'

"'No! I love you!—And what kind of a man are *you*? You think you're an artist, but you never write. You can't finish anything you start. You're no artist—you're nothing!'

"'You little prick. What did I ever do to deserve you? Why do you shame me like this? I curse the day you were born!'

"I just smiled at him, a giant, exaggerated smile. He threw a crystal glass punch bowl at me, but I ducked. It smashed against the wall, broke into a thousand pieces.

"'I'm not the coward,' I said. 'You are! You just dream of being an artist—and you could be; in your heart, you really are—but you don't do the work. Well, I do. I'm ready to go out there and put my ass on the line!'

"'What's the point of finishing anything?' he said. 'What's the point of even trying? What's the use? Look at this hideous world—hard, cold, greedy, insensitive, selfish, vain, barbaric—there's no place for an artist anywhere!'

"'Bullshit! And even if you're right, I've still gotta try. I'm gonna give it my best shot, and I don't give a damn what you think!'

"'It's not worth it. The business cannibals will eat you up and spit you out and never look back. You simple-minded dummy, you'll never be able to do it. You're not even man enough to hit me when I call you a faggot. You will *never* succeed. They won't let you, don't you understand that?'

"'Yes, I will succeed! I'll show you—I'll prove it! You're the one who's scared, not me. Even if you tried, you couldn't cut it. So you don't try, you only sit around and put everybody down who does! More than that—you're scared that if you *do* succeed you won't be able to bear the pressure. You're the weak one, Dad, not me. You can't handle the spotlight and the criticism. That's really why you hate me. You're scared—and I'm not!'

"'Get outta here!'

"'I love you, Dad, but you're a real bastard.'

"'Get outta here!'

"'Out with the bile! I can laugh again!'

"And I left. After that fight I moved out and lived at Larry Beckett's house until we came to New York. At the end of July, just a few weeks ago, Mom moved out of the house too. She and Katy drove back to D.C. They're living with mom's father now."

"Jesus, man. . . ." I was shaking, appalled by the violence of language and deed Tim had just described. "Well, at least by *not* doing what he wanted, you did what he wanted anyway."

"What do you mean?"

"You refused to hit him or shoot him, right? You didn't break down under pressure. He wanted you to be a man. He wanted you to stand up to him. Well, you did that. You stood up to him—and you did it *your* way, not his. He may not see the paradox, but you can. He put you to the test—and in terms of your *own* values, you passed it. He should feel *proud* of you, man. And you can definitely feel proud of yourself, don't you agree?"

Tim looked at me, gave me a smile.

"Here comes the sun, Tim. Let's pull into that diner up there, get a cup of coffee."

"Okay."

ELAINE

Tim and his mother, Elaine, were extremely close. They spent hours sitting around the kitchen table while Tim talked about his high school problems and dreams, his adventures, challenges, triumphs, and failures. After he left for New York, Tim wrote to her and telephoned. During the ensuing years until his death, he maintained close contact by telephone and with occasional visits.

When I interviewed Elaine in 1977,[1] she said that from Tim's earliest years she sensed the presence of the artist in Tim, the sensitivity, the beauty. "I have to say this, that very early, when he was a baby, not even a year old, I always had the feeling that he was never going to live long. Poets and people like that always die young, don't they? It just came out of the blue one day, like a poignant melody—I had the feeling he wouldn't last long. Maybe that's why I needed to give him so much attention. He used to say he would never hit thirty. You probably heard him say that kiddingly, right? Basically, he was too good for this world. I knew he was a poet and a dreamer, an artist, and I was right. He was born in the wrong period of time. His music shows that, too. Maybe in twenty or thirty years his music will be appreciated. This is the wrong period of time."

Elaine remembered Tim's happy childhood. "He was always a happy-go-lucky kid, but he was also a worrier, and so we talked a lot. We used to joke around together and have a good time. He was always a good kid. He would listen closely, absorbing what you were saying. He read a lot, too.

"We went on trips when he was small. He especially liked Laguna Beach, with the ocean and the art galleries and the sidewalk restaurants.

"We always had music in the house. He became involved early on. I liked all the music that came out of the forties, Frank Sinatra, Nat King Cole, and a lot of jazz albums, Miles Davis, Ella Fitzgerald, Stan Kenton, June Christy. Tim didn't particularly care for Sinatra, but he liked Nat King Cole, and he loved Johnny Mathis, his voice. We had good country music too, including Johnny Cash. Tim used to love singing Johnny Cash's 'Big River.'"

Tim fell in love with the Kingston Trio, the Limelighters, Pete Seeger, and other folk musicians at age twelve. Elaine and Tim's father bought him a banjo for his thirteenth birthday.

"I remember my dad and I went to get a new car," Tim recalled in a Warner Bros. bio. "We went to Cal Worthington Dodge. Cal had a country music TV show that was broadcast from the lot, Cal's Corral. My dad saw all those musicians up there on the flatbed truck, and all the lights and cameras, and said, 'Son, there's money there. You should get a guitar and learn how to sing.' I loved that moment. I'll never forget it."

---

1. Data regarding exclusive interviews with various relatives and friends of Tim's is contained in the Sources at the end of the book.

His folks bought him a six-string guitar the very next Christmas.

"Mr. Beaman at the music store gave him guitar lessons for about a month and a half," Elaine said, "then told us he couldn't teach him anymore. In fact, he said, the kid could teach him a few tricks!"

In Bell Gardens, Tim met Danny Gordon, who became one of Tim's long-lasting friends. Danny and Tim put together a trio with Lauralie Reader, and played dances and assemblies at school. Tim's family lived in Bell Gardens for seven years, then moved to Anaheim. At Loara High School in Anaheim, Tim met bass player Jim Fielder and poet Larry Beckett, who became lifelong friends of his.

With Tim on guitar and vocals, Fielder on bass and Beckett on drums, they formed two bands, a quasi-rock group called the Bohemians, and an acoustic folk group called Harlequins 3.

"They used to have hootenannies in high school," Elaine said, "and Tim started singing in those. I knew he had started singing, but I had never heard him, because they practiced at school. Well, he wanted to surprise his father and me, so he invited us to one of those hootenannies.

"That was the first time I heard him sing—I was shocked! He sang one of the Limelighters' songs, 'Whistling Gypsy.' He wanted to surprise us, and he did! It was beautiful, really beautiful.

"From then on, I went to see him sing and play in the coffeehouses. Every place he performed, I used to go. I knew he was going to be great. He did everything well. He was just one of those kids—he had it."

"In his boyhood, Tim had a lot of good times with his father," said Elaine. "His dad used to go fishin' all the time. He used to work third shift, and I was working during the day, so during the day he'd take Tim up to the lakes. We had a little boat with a motor there, and they'd go out fishin'.

"We had a hunting dog, a beagle hound named Mickey. His dad showed Tim how to shoot the rifle and to hunt rabbits and things like that—of course, Tim couldn't kill them little rabbits, you know. Still, he liked going out with his father. They used to have a lot of good times together. That was before things went bad.

"Tim's father was wounded quite a bit, three or four times during the course of the war, mostly the second time he went overseas, and he had a lot of plastic surgery done on his face. He had scars up here on his forehead. He got shot in the mouth. His nose was broken quite a bit, which is not unusual for a paratrooper. He also got shrapnel in his prostate gland, had to go to the doctor to get antibiotics. High fevers, things like that. And he had a metal plate in his head.

"Tim's dad was a very intelligent Irish Catholic. His father, Timothy Charles Buckley Sr., came over straight from the southern part of Ireland, and of course hated the English. He lived in New York, then Amsterdam, a mill town in central New York, and worked as an ice cream maker and an auto mechanic.

"Tim's dad, Timothy Charles Jr., went to Catholic schools in New York City all the way through Manhattan College. I don't know what he studied, but he was an intellectual. There wasn't a subject you could touch on that he didn't know something about. He liked writing and was a very good writer. He probably could have been a great writer, but he didn't pursue it. He used to write me beautiful letters when he was overseas.

"He was in the war from the beginning. He came back on a furlough in 1944.

That's when I met him. I knew him only two weeks, then he went over to Normandy, and he was still overseas when the war ended. I didn't know him before the war, so I don't know how the war changed him, but it changed him. I know it did.

"After the war, he wasn't right anymore. And after he took that fall in the factory and hurt himself, things got progressively worse. He started getting obnoxious towards me and Tim. He wasn't obnoxious to Tim's little sister, Katy. She was still young. I took him to the company psychiatrist, but he wouldn't go in. He got right up to the front door, but refused to open it. He turned on me, saying, 'I'm not the one who's crazy—you are!' . . .

"Then he had that huge ugly fight with Tim in the garage. Not too long after that, I couldn't stand his craziness any more. I almost killed him.

"He was a security guard then, and he had a gun. He threatened me with the gun and said, 'I'm gonna kill you!' I said, 'Go ahead—kill me!' I mean, at that point, who the hell cares, right?

"He laid the gun down and said something, and then hit me. I picked up the gun and pointed it at him—and I was going to kill him. Then I thought, 'Jesus, why should I go to jail?'

"So I took Katy and got in the car and drove down to the Anaheim police station and told them what happened, and told them to check the gun in, which they did. That's when I moved out of there.

"It was so hard, you know? Tim always had a great deal of respect and love for his father, especially respect for his brilliant mind, so clever, witty, a good man. I loved him, too. But the war, the fall . . . So hard to see someone like that just be broken apart . . . destroyed . . ."

KATY

"My dad was a complicated man," said Katy, eleven years Tim's junior. "I saw him as a sad person, always a melancholy person. I think he lost touch for a lot of reasons. For one thing, he was an artist, a writer. But he couldn't bring himself to complete anything. He was a writer who couldn't write. Well, he could write letters, but couldn't write anything professionally. That used to bother Tim.

"Tim really wanted to be close to Dad, but he couldn't, partly because he was stuck in this heavy mother-son relationship, and partly because he was disappointed that his dad wasn't a strong masculine influence, even with the combat boots. . . .

"There were just a lot of things wrong, and a lot of those things affected Tim— too many spacey things and too many arguments over lack of love and lack of responsibility. Tim felt his dad was a weak artist and therefore a weak man. Dad would blame it on the world, on the system, on how shitty things always are. Tim wouldn't buy into it, so they fought a lot.

"Dad hated the system. He was always fighting against it. I remember one time in school, when I was in first grade, I got sent home from school around Christmas because I didn't want to put glitter on a pine cone. I wanted to leave it just the way it was, and spray snow on it. So the teacher freaked out and sent me to the principal's office, and they sent me home.

"My father took me out into the back yard garden. He pulled a pussywillow and picked a weed.

"'Kathleen,' he said. 'Sit down. What is the difference between a pussywillow and a weed?'

"'A pussywillow is symmetrical, and a weed grows wild.'

"'Well, you're a weed, because you're wild,' he said. 'And you're never gonna fit into this society, because you're artistic, and that's worse than having leprosy.'

"He told me this when I was six years old.

"Tim resisted that kind of thinking, you know? There was a lot of hope in the sixties, and Tim tried to be strong. He'd say, 'No, things are gonna change.' After the sixties, a lot of people had burned themselves out. That's when I think Tim started understanding what his father was trying to say.

"But at that earlier time, there was a fighter in Tim, and he wanted to prove it to his dad. He did prove it too—he made his recordings, he made it to Carnegie Hall. That's pretty damn good. But by that time Dad was too crazy and too burnt out, stuck off in a V.A. mental hospital in Chattanooga, Tennessee. I don't think he ever had any idea of the great things Tim did, and Tim never got that satisfaction of knowing his father's love and pride for what he had accomplished."

I said to Katy, "Maybe Tim's father would have hated him for becoming successful, resented him for proving him wrong and Tim right."

"I don't think so. I think he would have been proud."

"Yes, that, too. Surely, he would have felt proud too. But he might have resented him, as well. And from Tim's side, it's also possible that Tim might have felt ashamed for achieving a victory in the war between them."

"How could he feel shame for being successful?"

"Because *he* could do it, but his dad couldn't. It's complicated. A double-edged sword."

"Dad wasn't always irrational or violent," Katy said. "He was a very bright man, always checking things out, exploring stuff, looking into things. Like, he was into East Indian religion before anybody else was. He had a guru friend, a swami from India who didn't speak much English. I remember one time, I came home and Dad had sold all the furniture. Now there were hanging beads, and wicker elephants, floor pillows, and incense burning. He got rid of all the meat in the house, and had all these vegetables and vitamins and curries.

"My father spoke several languages enough to converse, or at least bits and pieces—French, German, Swahili. He was constantly blowing people's minds, because he was an actor. He was never just one whole person. He was all these different people. He would begin lots of things, but never finish anything. He never had a complete personality. He was scattered.

"He had a heart of gold too. He was always trying to help people out, people who were worse off than he was. They were really strange types—like, a man without any fingers, or some down-and-out artist, or a person who was completely weak and had no money, or an illiterate person he would try to educate."

"Dad loved us, and he loved natural things. He would defend people or things that needed help. Part of his nature was incredibly loving, even though he was kinda crazy.

"Like in Bell Gardens, we had a huge maple tree in the front yard that had grown up into the telephone wires and was leaning over on to the street lamp. The tree itself was all overgrown and half dead. It was covered with bushes, and dimming the streetlight. The neighbors wanted to chop it down. Dad was willing to chop down the dead side of it, but not the living side—but it was the living side that was up in the wires and all over the street lamp.

"Dad went and got the buzz saw and cut down the dead side, but the neighbors said, 'No, cut off the other side, too.'

"That's when Dad got mad and ran into the house and came back out waving his gun. 'Don't you sons-of-bitches come near this tree! You touch it, and I'll blow your balls off! This tree is God's creature. It's alive, and I'm here to see that it *stays* alive! I'm a paratrooper, I've done five tours of Europe, I fought at Normandy—and I'll fight every one of you to the death right here!'

"Well, the neighbors got all upset and called the police. When the police came, Dad had on his green beret with the medals on it and his paratrooper boots and was waving his gun. The cops made him put the gun away and asked what was happening.

"Dad said, 'I'm General Timothy Charles Buckley the Second. I'm a war hero—see these medals?—and I'm defending this tree against those bastards over there who want to kill it.' He sounded just like Patton, and he went on and on about the Nazis and World War II, being a paratrooper and a hero and a general—and finally the cops said, 'Okay, you win. The tree stays.'

"He used to get away with things like that all the time."

TIMOTHY CHARLES "BUCK" BUCKLEY JR.

> *I saw the best minds of my generation*
> *Destroyed by madness.*
>
> Allen Ginsberg

On September 18, 1978, Katy called me on the telephone and asked if she could share the following letter. "It's undated," she said, "and I don't know what happened to the envelope, but I would like to read it to you and have it be part of our interview. Is that okay? It's from my dad. It's not one of his greatest letters—I think he was a little drunk when he wrote it—but it says a lot about how he felt about things and about how much he loved us."

POSTCARDS FROM THE INNER BRAIN
OR
DR. MYTHALAMUS AND HYPOTHALAMUS ARE BISEXUAL—
WHAT CAN YOU DO?

As I lovingly climb back into my tree, and I really need my tree, I leave these words of Nothing to a screwed up world or to nobody. No letters, no messages, rather a farewell speech to my brain which I leave in trust to Vincent Price rather than the others, because—

No, I refuse to explain. No Hellos, no Dears, Dearests or Darlings. They're literary bullshit. Just words, tiny letters stretched out to form tiny words. And maybe, just maybe, all stuck together they will spell out TRUTH.

But then again, maybe it's just my hypothalamus having a good time exploding in one grand, final orgasm, giving all the rage and fear one final exit through the murky passages of my inner brain. . .

So read on, or not. . .

No commas no periods no adjectives verbs or nouns no clarity no wisdom no nothing. Like a heavy laxative, I'm exorcising my brain so I can be free again. I'm being screwed over. I'm being turned sideways, and, white man, I don't need it.

My wife sits doing jigsaw puzzles. Two of my daughters rush off to school [*Robin and Desiree, from his marriage to Joanne, prior to Elaine*]. My lovely daughter Kathleen is in purgatory—or L.A., if you wish. And I'm standing on twenty million tons of TNT and laughing at the whole insane scene as the electronic flashing red tube neon EXIT sign beckons. I stand screaming out words, big explaining words, and I feel like Katy must feel—"To hell with it, man, nobody's listening."

When you exorcise, you drive out, you cleanse. So what better way? In the end, the world is nothing, my brain is nothing, but so what? If I want a clean nothing-brain, so be it. God, how fast we get trapped, squeezed, conveyed. What am I? What am I? I'm nobody, I'm no place. What am I? Dead? Free? I like it, as I need nothing or nobody. Insane—hallelujah! But so is Nixon, Milhaus, Richard, and all the other ruling bodies of the world. What do they rule? Nothing, not even their own inane destinies. Man, I feel the need for a good funeral.

But back to what I am. I got a guy Joe I work for, who offers me the world. What does he want? The money I make and bring him? The precious time I put in? He gives me large chunks of perverted money, and offers me more if I move to the south of France. What the hell is the south of France? He thinks I like him and his money. I don't like anyone. And I hate money. So that ain't what I am.

I got a wife. Eight years worth. Sex, companionship, love, protectiveness, talents unused, children, understanding, easy to live with, inner beauty, kind, considerate—Jesus, it sounds like a Boy Scout. I'm there. It's all right. But it still comes out—LONER.

The EXIT sign keeps blinking.

She keeps talking softly, but the drums of oppression beat loudly in my ears, and my fragile brain disintegrates into spinning, whirling meteorites of nothingness. Get a home in the country. Get a horse. Move out, move in, do this, do that—the All-American Dream, prepackaged crap, tied with multi-colored ribbons. Plastic. "It's just around the corner." "It's logical." "Happiness lies just ahead." "It's somewhere tomorrow."

To hell with logic. I can only hack it today. To hell with tomorrow. It never comes.

Katy, Kathleen. Beautiful, sensitive child-lady, fifteen years late. Magic, warmth, daughter, love, cry, hurt, pain, lonely, happiness, sorrow, memories, Mickey Mouse, gone away, sadness, real, sunshine, Los Angeles, wrong, tilt, obligations, puzzles, confusion, black magic, intelligence, trap, get out, August, September, the days dwindle down—Goodbye everyone. I'm leaving wife, children, five college coeds, see the whole messed up countryside, sit and watch the sunset-sunrise, smell a garbage pit, climb a mountain, sit on a rock, walk barefoot, sandy beaches, look at trees, smell the rain, look at a flower. . .

Twenty years, man. Twenty years of being me. Loner deluxe. Screw the system. Nobody, no one close. Only the family. Now it's—Get a home, move to the south of France, make money. I was happy just living and observing. Now, wham, all this shit comes down. It's heavy. Dear John, it's nice, but I'm falling out the EXIT. Stop this merry-go-round, I want off.

I remember my daughter Desiree, a little love she gave, a little security I gave. Okay, she still loves, she's mine, but she'll go. I'll let her. Rule Number One of the universe: At Point B, like a mother bear, you turn them loose on society, where they can get beat up and trashed. You're free, Desiree. I turn you loose. . . .

Robin, you're ahead of the game. You need no one. You'll make it. Just take a little pity on those who get in your way.

Daughter Kathleen, gone, never knew . . . Oh, well. The sands of time run faster. I walk with you hand in hand down the windy sandy beaches of my mind, soft hands, warm hands, sensitive, expressive hands. Where are you? I need . . . but then again, I need no one. Goodbye, Kathleen. I know you, but I never really knew you. What is Katy? Who is Katy? Who knows? Happy, calm, peaceful. Soft child-lips, woman-lady, apart, wasted time.

Today's the day—nevermore.

Exit son, blazing, red, "I love you, dad, but you're a bastard!" Scary, screaming, "Out with the bile! I can laugh again!"

Goodbye, family—Elaine, Katy, Joanne, Desiree, Robin. Tim? Who's Tim? I'm all alone, Tim, but here when you need me. I'm in my tree. I need no one, but I want you all. I love you all. You are my link to sanity—or insanity—whatever the case may be.

I'll sit in my tree and watch the barbaric madmen of the world take over, and laugh. Happy, now—laugh! Never cry. Funny world. Nothing so screwed up could be so sad. So laugh, laugh, laugh! Who cares?

Nobody, because there is really no one, and that's life, baby. You're born, you die, and there's nothing in between, except for late-late commercials—"Pornographic passages by Donald Bahn, alias Nobody." "Cinnamon, by Westinghouse—Progress is our most important Nothing." "Wardrobes by Polyester." "Los Angeles appears through the courtesy of Fate and the Foul Fiend."

Time is but emotion, leaving fifteen sands of distant misty memories to visit the mysterious crevices of my mind. Each day without each other, your bittersweet thoughts will live our short moments together while I use up the run-down clock of time.

I do love you—Dad.

I

L
O
V
E

Y
O
U

CHAPTER 3

ON THE ROAD:
ALBERT HOTEL & THE BALLOON FARM

December of 1966 rolled around, Elektra released *Tim Buckley*, and we couldn't wait to get on the road.

A picture of the album appeared on the cover of *Billboard*, and it was selected as "Pick of the Week" by *Cashbox*.

Sitting on a living room couch in our Eleanor Street house, Tim held a copy of the LP up to the light, looked at the cover photo—high cheekbones, pouty unsmiling lips, big brown eyes. Hand-in-pocket, knee bent, leaning with his left shoulder up against the stucco wall of Herb Cohen's apartment building, wearing the black turtleneck sweater he had worn at the Night Owl, a black-and-white checkered houndstooth sport jacket casually draped over his right shoulder.

He looked at it and laughed. "How do you like my pretty little dike shot?"

The liner notes on the back described him as "an incredibly thin wire," the "quintessence of *nouvelle*."

"What the hell does that mean?" he asked, wiggling his eyebrows like Groucho Marx.

He read the rest of the notes—"sensitivity," "a study in fragile contrasts," "the magic of Japanese watercolors."

"Blah-blah-blah," he chuckled. "All hype. I had nothing to do with it." He threw the album over his shoulder behind the couch and never looked back.

Between the recording of *Tim Buckley* and its release, we needed money. More importantly, we needed to get out of the house and play.

Jennifer was working as a waitress at the Galaxy, a dance club on Sunset Boulevard in Hollywood, just up the street from the Whiskey Au Go Go. She introduced us to the woman who owned the club.

"Okay," the owner said, "I'll give you one Monday night." We were thrilled, but Herb wasn't. He refused to allow Tim's name to be placed on the marquee. "I don't want everybody in this town to know you're playing an off-the-circuit dump like that." With Jim Fielder on bass and Johnny Sider on drums, we played the gig—the Monday night room was virtually empty, but we didn't care. We had a wonderful time just being onstage.

We landed another job, at Bido Lido in Hollywood, a small, one-room, back alley club off Ivar Street, on Cosmo, with a modest platform for a stage and one microphone. The place was later remodeled and named the Ivar Theater, then the Opium Den. We had a three-night weekend gig, as I recall, again with Fielder on bass and Sider on drums. There was no advertising for it, and very few people showed up—but those who did were devoted, enthusiastic listeners who loved the music. I think we earned $15 apiece, but the job gave us a chance to fulfill our nature—giving wings to music, expressing ourselves, connecting with an audience.

The Galaxy and the Lido were our first two gigs in L.A. They are but distantly remembered dreams now, cherished moments of innocence on time's long path, little gems that forever sparkle with quiet light.

Tim and I piled our guitars into the rear of a Volkswagen panel truck Herb had rented for us, and drove coast-to-coast to New York with Johnny Sider. Johnny was a first-class drummer. He was also an intelligent, happy-go-lucky guy with an extraordinary memory and marvelous sense of humor.

We stayed at the Albert Hotel, in Room 1268, as I recall, but Johnny insisted years later that it was Room 1216. I have a good memory, but because of Johnny's *exceptional* memory, I'll go with him—1216. The Albert was a famous—or infamous— home away from home for some of the most popular and influential rock musicians of the era—Frank Zappa and his band, the Mamas & the Papas, the Lovin' Spoonful, the Butterfield Blues Band, Spanky and Our Gang, the Byrds, the Doors, and dozens of others. The graffiti on the seventh floor corridor wall said, "Jim Morrison is sex, but Ray Manzarek is love."

As Lillian Roxon wrote, paraphrasing Charles Dickens, "The Albert Hotel is the best of hotels, it is the worst of hotels; its prices are ridiculously high, its prices are astonishingly low; its corridors are filled to the brim with life, its corridors are perpetual reminders of death; staying there is the wildest, most exhilarating, dizzying, around-the-clock trip of all time; staying there is the most wretched, lonely terrifying, around-the-clock bummer of all eternity."

Louie Dula, drummer and leader of an all-woman rock band called the Bittersweet, remembered meeting Tim.

"I didn't know who Tim Buckley was when I got to the Albert," she wrote to me, "although I had seen his picture on the wall and thought, 'Cute guy.' One day I was waiting for the elevator to come down. When I pushed the button my purse strap got tangled up in my beaded necklace. The necklace broke and the beads scattered all over the floor. I was down on my hands and knees like a fool, trying to catch them. The elevator door opened, and I looked up—to see this beautiful face looking down at me and smiling. From the angle I saw him at, being down on the floor looking up, the elevator light seemed to form a halo around his curly hair. I remember thinking to myself, 'My God, it's an angel!' He bent down and started helping me gather up all my beads, saying funny things about how cute I looked crawling around on the floor.

"The next day at the front desk there was an envelope for me. Inside was a really pretty necklace with a note from Tim that said,

> 'To replace what was broken,
> I thought you'd like this small token.'

"I couldn't believe he would do something that nice for a stranger. He won my heart for life. . . .

"Sometimes he would take me to Central Park and we'd hang out and go to the zoo and watch people. Did you ever hear him imitate a seal? That used to crack me up.

Lee and Tim at the Balloon Farm in the Village, opening for Frank Zappa's
Mothers of Invention. At this point, Tim was strumming a six-string Gibson electric.

"There was a horse that used to stand by the street as you went into the park by
the Plaza, and we'd see it all the time. I felt sorry for it, so I would always take it
apples or carrots. The guy who drove the carriage got to know me and Tim from
feeding his horse all the time. One day he said he'd give us a free ride around the
park. Tim made the guy get into the back of the carriage. He put the guy's big crazy
hat on and sat up front and took the reins and drove us around the park himself!
He looked so funny, and had so much fun.

"I remember going up on the hotel roof, over to where an air shaft was. Tim
would make all these weird-sounding noises with his voice. He'd yell them down
into the air shaft, and we'd wait and see how long it took for people to come to their
windows and look up to see what in the heck that noise was. Tim was always making me laugh. He could really be funny when he wanted to.

"I'm of Hungarian descent, and Tim would always tell me how he liked my 'gypsy eyes.' Every time he'd do something that would bug me I'd tell him I was going to put a gypsy curse on him. He'd laugh and wiggle his eyebrows up and down in that funny way he had. I could never stay mad at him."

At the Balloon Farm, which later became the Electric Circus, we opened for Frank Zappa and the Mothers of Invention. Zappa came on like a long-haired Svengali leading a pack of eight or ten chuckling, stringy-haired madmen, each a superb musician, including Don Preston, one of the first synthesizer players in pop music; Buzz Gardner on trumpet and his brother Bunk on saxophones (later on, members of one of Tim's Starsailor bands); and Ian Underwood (no relation) on sax and keyboards. Zappa's compositions were new and fresh at the time, loud, complex, dissonant and amazingly sophisticated both as pop music and as contemporary quasi-classical music—Schoenberg and Varesè meet "Louie, Louie."

At the same time, his lyrics reeked of irony, his instrumental compositions of mockery. For all of its technical flash and aural bombast, it seemed to Tim and me that Zappa's music had no heart. He laughed at everything. If he wasn't mocking something ironically, he was putting it down directly. In his eyes nothing remained sacred, innocent, tender, or beautiful—precisely his appeal for those who paid to see him.

As far as Tim and I were concerned, Zappa remained an emotional coward, a crude, empty, predominately mean-spirited cynic. His compositions were impressively complex, no question about it. But they also seemed emotionally sterile at the core, great for pseudo-intellectuals, New York sophisticates, and arrogant neurotics dead from the neck down, but boring and irritating for musicians who sang from the heart and played from the soul. In our eyes, Zappa's strident cynicism and very real technical achievements did not compensate for his lack of humanity or warmth. Irony was not in any way a satisfying substitute for compassion.

Compared to Zappa's musical tornado, Tim and I and Johnny Sider and a bass player whose name I don't recall sounded like wisps of mist. Next to Zappa's, our music was simple, quiet, and instrumentally threadbare. Tim looked shy, intimidated, lost, out of place. He stood with his shoulders hunched, which gave him a weak, vulnerable look, and he almost never said anything to the raucous stoned-out crowd. He seemed afraid. In fact, he was. It took him a year or so to be able to disclose himself onstage with confidence.

Writer Michael Thomas said of Tim's appearance somewhat later than this, "When he walks onstage, he looks like a raggedy kid, dressed in skinny corduroys and old suede boots, his shirt hanging out, like he's just hitchhiked all the way from California cuddling his massive 12-string guitar, and hasn't had the time to get the crows-nests out of his hair. . . . He's frail and restless, his face is bony and delicate, and all the time he barely opens his quick black eyes. He looks a little forlorn."

The Balloon Farm was an upstairs room, about the size of a basketball court, high ceilinged, cavernous, atmospherically cold, acoustically boomy. We stood on a stage at one end of the hall and spilled our tunes into the ears of an audience that remained mostly indifferent, largely because of Tim's innocent music and introverted persona, and partly because of their own desensitized urban-psyches.

We ran through the tunes on the album, plus a few by other people, including two of my favorites, "Big River," by Johnny Cash, and "I'm Just a Country Boy (Got Sand All in My Shoes)," based on a line by Fred Neil, as I recall. Two of Tim's tunes were visceral and strong—"Grief in My Soul" and "Understand Your Man"—but

Tim with his new Guild 12-string.

the majority were paeans to boy-girl teenage love, written by two sweet high school kids from Anaheim's smog-shrouded wastelands. I loved that early music and the first album. But this material seemed far too intimate for the size of the Balloon Farm and far too gentle and ingenuous for Zappa's jaded New York audience.

At one point, I said to Herb Cohen on the stairs during a break, "Tim won't talk to the people. We're not reaching them. Can't you ask him to tell a few stories between songs, liven things up?"

"He's only nineteen, f'Chrise sake. He'll learn. Let him do it his way."

I found Herb's blunt words soothing, his harsh tone consoling.

I got my first taste of on-the-road pleasure, necking with a lovely college girl on the floor behind the dusty stage curtains, with Zappa's band blaring only a few feet away. Another taste with a different girl, necking on the floor of an empty room off to the side—until she jumped up and cried, "Oh, my gosh, I gotta get home and study for tomorrow's chemistry exam!"

Back at the Albert a few days later, Johnny, Tim, and I were a little stoned when Johnny, wearing a tall, black stovepipe hat, said, "I think it's real important to know the lyrics to a song. Yeah—I'm just a drummer. But I think I play a hell of a lot better when I know the lyrics, what a guy's saying, you know? So I learn the words too. How 'bout you?"

He and Tim looked at me, waiting. I didn't quite know what to say, so I spoke the truth. "I don't know. I can't follow the lyrics when I'm playing. Words are words and music is music. I feel what's happening through the music."

"Don't you think you should find out what the words are all about too?"

To my everlasting regret, I said, "No, I don't."

Tim looked away. Johnny was right. I was wrong. Even though I knew I was wrong, I didn't have fortitude enough to admit it. Ego. We never spoke of it again, and I did what I could to pay attention to the words after that, but I knew I had missed the boat in that discussion. Ah, well. Bless you, Johnny. You helped me grow.

Tim said, "Somebody's coming up in a few minutes."

"Oh? Who?"

"I don't know, somebody from the *Village Voice*."

"What for?"

"To interview me."

"To interview *you*?"

"Yeah," he smiled. "First time."

My perspective of Tim subtly shifted. He wasn't merely the scraggly poetic kid I saw in front of me wearing a t-shirt in a funky Albert Hotel room. He was going to be *interviewed*.

At that moment, I flashed back on our first major concert, at the Santa Monica Civic Auditorium shortly before we drove to New York, opening for Joan Baez. Right there, I felt strange. Baez was a big star. We were on the same bill with her. Two thousand people in the audience. Something was going on, something was happening.

Onstage, I usually stood on Tim's right (so I could see his left hand on his guitar fretboard), but at one point I walked behind him. The spotlight was on him, creating a brilliant blue-white aura in his hair. Silhouetted in front of me, his hair a dazzling halo of light, he sang the songs that had now become familiar and close to me. At that moment, however, listening to the music, feeling the rush of energy from him and the crowd, looking at that blue-white light in his hair and surrounding his body, nothing felt familiar. Everything seemed strange, huge, immensely expanded, absolutely new. Something was happening—in that blinding moment, I became aware of it for the first time.

In New York at the Albert, when he was about to participate in that first interview, I flashed on that Santa Monica Civic concert and experienced a similar feeling. I may have been older than Tim, more knowledgeable, a little wiser at that point, but things were taking place that I had not foreseen. I had vaguely thought we might play a few gigs here and there. But this was more than that. Bigger things were happening.

A few days after the interview, Tim received a fan letter from an ecstatic high school girl. She gushed about how beautiful he was and how much she loved his music, "and please, please, please, Tim—don't ever change."

Frowning fiercely, Tim crushed her letter in his hands, wadded it up in disgust, contemptuously threw it into the wastebasket. "Of *course* I'm gonna change."

GOODBYE AND HELLO: 1967–1968

CHAPTER 4

GOODBYE AND HELLO

It was in September of 1967, just after sundown in Venice, when Tim said, "Come on, I want to show you something."

He and Jainie, Larry, Jennifer, and I hopped into Jennifer's car and drove up to Hollywood, listening to the radio. On the way, just as we came to Sunset Boulevard with all of its blazing neon lights, hotels, bars, restaurants, and towering office buildings, Tim's song "Pleasant Street" boomed out of the speakers.

We cheered, "Yeeeaaaa!" I felt goose bumps up the back of my neck—first time we had heard Tim on the radio.

At Sunset Boulevard we turned west. Tim pointed straight ahead, "There."

On the left, high up in the air, a gigantic billboard with Tim's picture on it looked down on us—the cover of *Goodbye and Hello*. There was Tim's smiling face, his curly hair and white teeth, the Pepsi bottle cap whimsically stuck under his right eyebrow like a monocle. His blue work shirt contrasted vividly with the bright yellow background. That incredibly warm smile of his beamed down on the boulevard like sunshine.

We gasped, awestruck, then cheered again. What a rush!

Months earlier, after we had played *Tim Buckley* music at the Balloon Farm in Greenwich Village for a couple of weeks in January, Tim sent me and Johnny Sider back home, while he went out as a solo performer. Tim was free to explore city life to the hilt. And that's what he did.

He played several gigs in New York, including Andy Warhol's club, the Dom, on the same bill with Nico, and Izzy Young's famous Folklore Center. During this period, shortly after the Balloon Farm gig, he bought his first Guild 12-string guitar. He traveled upstate and played Swarthmore College (where, according to writer Jay Hoster and others, he stole the show from the Jefferson Airplane).

He met conga player Carter Crawford Christopher Collins on the road. They teamed up as a duo, a musical and personal friendship that lasted for many years. It was my understanding that they met at Bard College, when Tim, a solo performer at that time, was auditioning students to accompany him on the gig that night (including Chevy Chase on drums and future Steely Dan leader Donald Fagen on piano, neither of whom got the job).

Carter auditioned too, and fit in well with Tim's music. Plus, he was not the least bit in awe of Tim's Bambi trip or all those little groupies sitting around swooning while Tim crooned. When Carter said something outlandish and funny to Tim—he was good at quick, startling remarks—Tim loved him for it and hired him.

In April of 1967 they played the Mainpoint just outside of Philadelphia, where Jay Hoster interviewed Tim downstairs in the dressing room after the first set.

"Buckley was sitting on the floor doing something to his guitar," Hoster wrote. "He made his answers brief. He became more verbal when he was interviewed on WHAT-FM later that night, but even then he spoke no more than two or three sentences in reply to any one question. . . . [At the end of the radio show] Buckley said, 'I've always felt very awkward about talking to people.' I think I understand: Whatever Tim Buckley has to say to the world he does it through his songs."

Tim and Carter zipped up to New York City, where they played a breakthrough gig at the Cafe Au Go Go. George Harrison of the Beatles liked Tim's music. He brought his manager, Brian Epstein, to the Go Go opening. Judy Collins showed up; so did Paul Simon, Linda Ronstadt, and Odetta. Even Tim's mother showed up from Washington, D.C. Word spread fast from the downtown club—a breath of fresh air swept through the city.

"I remember walking into the Tin Angel across the street from the Go Go," said bearded Bob Campbell, one of several people who became close friends with us. "Odetta was there. She had just come from the Go Go and was very emotional, crying tears. When I sat down she said, 'You'll have to excuse me, Bob. I'm overwhelmed right now.' I couldn't tell if she meant good or bad. I said, 'What is it?' As if pronouncing the name of a saint, she said, 'Tim Buckley.' She was too overcome to talk about it."

CBS taped Tim performing "No Man Can Find the War" at the Go Go and featured two brief segments of it in a TV documentary called *Inside Pop—The Rock Revolution*, hosted by Leonard Bernstein. Although *Goodbye and Hello* had not even been recorded, Tim was already scaling the mountain.

When he wasn't gigging, he was writing new *Goodbye and Hello* songs in his room at the Albert Hotel, occasionally exploring his own mind through psychedelics and other fashionable substances. Tim was an explorer in a multitude of ways, and drugs was one of them. Sure, sometimes he needed pot or alcohol for comfort. But he didn't take psychedelics merely to get high or have a party. As far as he was concerned, psychedelics were energizing awakeners. As psychotropic tools, they helped him tap into mind-zones he felt he could never reach on his own—or that would take him years to discover by orthodox means. "I don't have long," he said more than once, perhaps following his mother's deeply implanted ideas about poets dying young. "Gotta do it while I can."

As an artist, an authentic creator, he drew the content of his music from his own experience, subjectivity, and universal humanity. Love, sex, relationships, drugs, life itself—all were valid and viable sources of material. He wasn't concocting commercially formulated decorations to flatter audience preconceptions. He was giving us the core of his life, the soul of his being, a cry of love from the heart. Tim Buckley burned with a very special flame. The light he gave us was his own. He was the real thing, and his music was the real thing too. Along the way, a variety of substances played a role in his process of creation and discovery, with different substances answering different needs at different times in his life.

Carter C.C. Collins at the congas—an immaculate, fiery,
intelligent musician with a great sense of humor.

"I don't have anything really against drugs," he told writer Paul Eberle. "It's just that when a musician uses a drug, it's more a religious thing than when somebody uses it just to go walking down the Strip. . . . It's very religious, man. You get down to yourself and what you mean and what you're gonna do about it."

It was not enough to just get stoned and waste the energy. It was important to utilize the energy as fuel for creativity. "You can't take drugs and not do anything," he told writer Sam Bradley. "You have to go into something you work at. I'm not condoning them. It just has to go into something you're doing, whether it's painting a house or writing music or anything else. You have to work off the energy, or else it just burns out. You're just burning out the currents."

It's too bad—an outrage, in fact—that some people define Tim only in terms of substances, and only in terms of substance *abuse*, at that. Before making such judgments, observers might distinguish between the qualities and effects of different drugs. Pot, LSD, methamphetamine, alcohol, cocaine and heroin, for example, are vastly different. Observers might then distinguish between the various periods of his life when Tim used different drugs for different effects, and take into consideration his motivational needs. They might also consider that even as he was not alone in his generation, so he was also far more than merely one of a herd. He wrote enough music to fill nine albums, plus a half-dozen or more posthumous CDs. He is remembered and loved more than a quarter century after his death—and his memory is likely to endure. Many people got stoned. Very few created anything worth remembering—but he did.

The defining element in Buckley's life was not his wants and needs, and certainly not the substances he used along the way for whatever reasons, but his evolving personal and artistic lifestyle, the choices he made, the fire of his creativity, his courageous commitment to his art, and the final results he gave us—the extraordinary music we hold in our hands and hearts today.

"There are things you can learn from different people in the past," he told Bradley. "When I mention their names, it's basically their biographies that interest me, what period of time they worked in, what kind of energy was necessary in their life, and what obstacles they had to confront. It's the lifestyle that's the art."

Along the way during these years, Tim grew dissatisfied with his Guild F-512 guitar. It was a stress-back 12-string, rounded on the back with no braces inside for support, and constructed of light wood. He asked Guild to build him a new customized Jumbo guitar—Brazilian rosewood, flat on the back with braces inside, mother-of-pearl inlay between frets, double rods inside the neck, and the bottom section of the body unusually large and resonant. He used heavy-gauge strings. (I don't recall which brand.)

Over the course of the years, he lowered the tuning from bass E, to $E\flat$, D, $D\flat$, and finally to C, using a piano string for the low C string (an octave below middle C, as I recall). He kept relative pitch intervals standard between strings, *e.g.* C-F-$B\flat$-$E\flat$-G-C. Therefore, although he might be playing a first-position E chord (in the C mode), the pitch of that chord would be C. As stated earlier, he did not use open tunings, such as dropped-D or G tunings.

His new customized F-512 was amazing in tone, resonating power and looks, a beauty to the ear, a beauty to the eye as well.

While Tim was on the road, Jennifer and I moved out of the Eleanor Street place and rented a one-bedroom guest house on Monroe Street in Hollywood. We slept together on a narrow single bed until Jennifer absolutely insisted we purchase a double. We enjoyed a wide green lawn, a lemon tree, red and yellow flowers, a quiet neighborhood.

On a few prior occasions, we had smoked pot but never gotten high. Here on Monroe Street, we tried again while watching bald-headed, fast-talking Ralph Williams peddle used cars on TV. The pot kicked in, and suddenly Jennifer and I were laughing at Ralph until tears came to our eyes, rolling on the floor, holding our bellies, gasping, hollering—hilarious!

She worked as a waitress at the Galaxy on Sunset Strip, a couple of doors up from the Whiskey Au Go Go . She came home breathless one night, exclaiming, "You've got to come see the new group they just brought in—an incredible singer and dancer named Tina Turner!" I joined the Bill Beau quartet—vocalist, Hammond organ, guitar, drums—playing jazz standards and Jimmy Smith–type blues.

In early May of 1967, Tim and Larry showed up, Tim with his guitar. "We've got some new songs," Larry beamed. "Wanna hear 'em?" Sitting on the front steps, Tim played "Pleasant Street," "Once I Was," "Carnival Song," and "Morning Glory."

I was impressed and quite moved, but it wasn't until I walked into the Western recording studios a couple of weeks later that the music really hit me—Tim, Carter, bassist Jim Fielder, and drummer Eddie Hoh were playing "I Never Asked To Be Your Mountain."

Tim's guitar thundered. The rhythms were fierce, urgent, far more intense than anything I had heard Tim play before. His voice soared into the air with a new strength, grace and power. Everything about this music was assertive and free, full of pathos, drive, transcendent emotion. There was no other word for it: *grand*. As I stood in the booth, looking through the glass while they played, adrenaline winged through my veins. Who *is* this guy?

Later that week, Tim called me in for two tracks. In one of the sessions, we played "Phantasmagoria in Two" (a.k.a. "The Fiddler"), which we often performed onstage. This song appeared in two posthumous albums as well—one with Tim's vocal, on *Dream Letter: Live in London 1968*; the other without Tim's vocal, on *Works in Progress* (the original instrumental track recorded in these *Goodbye and Hello* sessions).

For the second session, in the morning, he had me bring my 12-string acoustic Guild. We worked on each separate stanza of Larry Beckett's massive "Goodbye and Hello" poem. I improvised melodic lines to Tim's 12-string guitar accompaniment until I got the feel of it. Then we recorded the stanza together.

Throughout his career Tim did not write notes on paper. He played and sang the music. Other musicians listened, learned, then added their contributions either in rehearsals or live, on-the-spot.

After we recorded the sections to "Goodbye and Hello," Tim later spliced the various stanzas together into a unified composition and recorded his vocal tracks over it. It is my understanding that Joshua Rifkin wrote the fourteen-piece orchestral arrangements afterward (uncredited), occasionally utilizing my melodic lines as springboards. (Others credit Jerry Yester.)

To this day I stand amazed at the fact that Tim could compose music for Larry's lengthy, complex poem. He had no formal musical education, no extensive knowledge of chords, and no knowledge of composition. But he did it. And he did it well.

Years later, in an interview with Ben Edmonds, Larry Beckett was quite complimentary about my contributions to "Goodbye and Hello," saying, "Lee played like I never heard him play before or since. He played magnificent, inspired lines to all of these pieces that were stylistically diverse. The sound of his guitar was also magnificent; instead of playing his electric, he was playing a rich acoustic 12-string. His motivic ideas were *so* brilliant that when Jerry Yester took the tape home to write the orchestrations, he found himself drawn to Lee's countermelodies. In fact, he based many of his charts on them, and as a result some of the arrangements lie right over some of Lee's best guitar parts. So you can almost consider Lee Underwood the secret composer of 'Goodbye and Hello.'"

I thank Larry for these appreciative comments, and extend the same respect to him for his noteworthy skills as a song lyricist and for his outstanding evolutionary development as a poet. He has always been an intelligent, sensitive individual who has weathered life's difficulties well while sustaining full commitment to his own creative capabilities.

Goodbye and Hello was an impressive and deeply moving album. Among other things, it perfectly reflected the youth culture of the day. As a result, it became something of a hit—nothing huge, but it did reach 171 on *Billboard*'s charts and put Tim on the map in the international marketplace. More importantly, it touched young people everywhere.

There was an irresistible poignancy in Tim's singing, a delicacy and fragile intimacy in his presentation that cannot be communicated simply by discussing it. It must be heard and experienced to be known. The words touched people, the music touched people, *he* touched people. Listeners told their friends, who told other friends. As a result, *Goodbye and Hello* became a steady seller over the years. For many listeners, it became the single work by which Tim was, and still is, identified.

Larry's song lyrics, and the acrostic poem he wrote for the jacket (with I LOVE TRACY spelled out in the descending first letters of each line), constituted a high water mark in 1967's popular music scene. Larry dug into his social values on this album, dramatically protesting the Vietnam debacle in the very first track, "No Man Can Find the War," wherein he pointed out how the guns and flames and other external horrors of war are extensions of the war inside our own minds.

In the title track, he said goodbye to the older generation and its established modes of greed, fear, corruption, pragmatism, exploitation, and violent conflict. He said hello to the new generation that understood peace, love, courage, joy, nature, creativity, and higher consciousness. Beckett's political and social protests matched the sociological currents of the day. He fulfilled his exceptional literary talent, his temperament, and his intelligence on this album, and had every right to feel proud of himself.

Beckett and Buckley weren't the Beatles, but this was their *Sgt. Pepper*. They weren't Bob Dylan, but this was their *Blonde on Blonde*.

Buckley wrote the music for all ten songs on *Goodbye and Hello*. Although he penned lyrics for five, he was already beginning to pull away from working with Beckett as a team. The first album, *Tim Buckley*, had been an assemblage of separately written songs. For *Goodbye and Hello*, the songs were written with the whole album in mind. If Beckett tended to be socio-political in poetic ways, Buckley tended to be emotional, human, and personal. In contrast to Beckett's literary protests, Buckley wrote impassioned heartsongs of love, death, and yearning. Together, Tim and Larry covered all the bases—and the album clicked.

There was a tenderness in Buckley's "Carnival Song," a vulnerable childhood wistfulness that made this piece a favorite among many listeners. Dave Guard (formerly of the Kingston Trio; a.k.a. Ghar) played kalimba, known as an African thumb piano. It is a hollow, rectangular wooden box, easily carried in hand, with a soundhole in the center. Several thin metal bars extend over the hole, like little piano keys. For at least a year, Buckley himself carried this instrument with him everywhere he went, holding it in his hands, plunking keys with both thumbs, playing kalimba music on Venice Beach, in bars, restaurants, at home, wherever.

It was an endearing quality, very much like the way he tapped water glasses with spoons or butter knives at the dinner table, listening to their bell tones, or rattled wind chimes, or tapped his fork on tables, salt and pepper shakers, candlesticks, listening, always listening, whimsically creating music wherever he went.

"Music is my business," he said. "Every sound can be musical. You just have to know how to do it."

Buckley's "Once I Was" (harmonica played by Henry Diltz, uncredited; songwriter's credit given only to Tim on the original album, although Larry participated in writing the lyrics) spoke of the sad passing of man–woman love, the fading away of love's dreams, of his own inevitable demise, poignantly asking us if we would ever remember him after his departure. This song, one of Tim and Larry's

goodbye and

TIM BUCKLEY

The cover shot for *Goodbye and Hello* appeared on a gigantic Sunset Strip billboard. (That's a Pepsi-Cola bottle cap whimsically stuck in his eye.)

best and most enduring, was later used in three films, Hal Bartlett's *Changes*, the Oscar-winning *Coming Home*, and the Emmy-winning *Dear America: Letters Home from Vietnam.*

The scorching rhythms of the love song, "I Never Asked To Be Your Mountain," underlie a powerful explanation to his abandoned Pisces ex-wife Mary. She didn't understand his love; she didn't know why he tried to be the fullest person he could; he never asked for the responsibility of her love in the first place—all sung with a musical brilliance and emotional intensity unparalleled in popular music at that time and, in my view, still unmatched today (although Jeff did an incredibly impassioned rendition of this song in his debut New York performance at the Tim Buckley Tribute in St. Ann's Church, in which he included additional lyrics of his own).

"Pleasant Street" proved to be one of Buckley's very best songs and one of his personal musical favorites, which he performed onstage right to the end. Its descending chord progression immediately gives the song potency with listeners, partly because of the familiarity of the pattern. Buckley's lyrics are as emotionally captivating as they are aesthetically beautiful.

He speaks of the hard, loveless ways the people of today are living, and the way they dress in somber, tradition-oriented, moralistic black suits rather than celebratory, spiritually liberated rainbow attire. He can't wait to escape the ugliness of mainstream straight life and get back to Pleasant Street's comforts of oblivion, in whatever form. It is a drug song, yes, but also a deeply moving, highly poetic musical work, whether or not one knows anything about drugs or any other kind of sweet release and relief.

(At an early gig of ours in Boulder, Colorado, where I was born, I had pointed out to him the house I had lived in as a child—on Pleasant Street. I don't know if this was the source of the song title later on, but it may have been.)

There have been numerous interpretations of "Pleasant Street." In an interview with Jack Brolly, *Goodbye and Hello*'s producer Jerry Yester said he *knows* it is about heroin, because "they" told him so, although he does not say who "they" were. Tim told me personally that he was writing about speed's mellow, sensual dimension, and, as far as I know, he had no significant involvement with heroin during these early years (although there were numerous unfounded rumors, including certain completely unsubstantiated speculations spread by Elektra's Jac Holzman). Beckett told Jack Brolly "Pleasant Street" was a song about "any surrender to any seduction, even if degrading," certainly a viable interpretation.

Others interpret the song as an anti-drug, anti-freeloader, anti-hippie song; a make-out song; a song about experiences while briefly living on Pleasant Street in Cambridge; a castigation of the clergy in their morbid black clothes; a castigation of hard, cold businesspeople in uniform suits; a castigation of straight society's moralizing against joyful pagan hippies; a socio-political statement about how capitalism doesn't work and destroys both nature and the soul. I myself prefer to let the intricacies of the imagery remain as mysteriously beautiful as they were when the song was conceived.

I would guess that Beckett provided the whimsical, quasi-literary title for "Phantasmagoria in Two." In any case, Tim penned the lyrics as well as the music and justifiably felt proud of them. It was his first non-rhyming song, a step forward in skill and confidence. It was also a poignant piece, asking for comfort and security in the midst of rain and fear, expressing empathy for his companion's pain and need for her sheltering love.

"Morning Glory" (a.k.a. "The Hobo") was another sterling Beckett/Buckley collaboration, later covered by Linda Ronstadt, Blood, Sweat & Tears, Ian Matthews, Chrissie Hynde, This Mortal Coil, and on an unauthorized recording by Fairport Convention. It tells the tale of a narrator lighting a candle of purity and innocence close to his window, catching the eye of a passing hobo and asking him to tell him stories. The hobo refuses and walks away. The enchanting melodies to this song are captivating, and the poignant emotional climate of the piece proved irresistible to thousands of listeners. The choir voices in four-part harmony were done by Tim and producer Jerry Yester, singing each part in unison. "The Hobo" became one of Tim and Larry's most popular songs (although in one of our concerts, Buckley turned to me after performing it and said, smiling, chuckling, "I've never had the slightest idea what that song means, do you?")

To my ears, one of the best pieces on the album is "Hallucinations," a spacious, intimate Beckett/Buckley love song, atmospherically reminiscent of "Song Slowly Song" and "Song of the Magician." In this piece, Tim revealed his growing interest in sonic textures above and beyond conventional words and melodies, showcasing shakers, rattles, his African kalimba, and washes of percussive/melodic, surrealistic, dreamlike psycho-sonic instrumental "weirdness" between stanzas. On certain verses he consciously departed from a fixed 4/4 rhythm for the first time, something he later explored in depth with *Lorca* and *Starsailor*.

Elektra's Jac Holzman loved this album and threw the weight of his budget behind it. He made a foldout LP cover, with Larry's poem and the lyrics to all songs printed inside. He printed large color photographs on three of the four surfaces. He placed ads in magazines and newspapers. He rented the Sunset Strip billboard in September—that's when we all drove up from Venice to see it. He gave *Goodbye and Hello* his full attention and support. This was great music, and he was a happy guy.

Until Tim made a smart-ass *faux pas.*

In his first interview with writer Bob Garcia, Tim had complained that the record company executives at Elektra were thinking too much about business and not giving him enough respect for his music. During their second interview, just after *Goodbye and Hello* had been released, Bob asked Tim why his relations with Elektra had improved so much.

"Well, you see," said Tim, "before this album, a record exec I know hadn't taken

Tim weaving his magical spell, circa '67–'68.

acid. In fact, [when he first heard *Goodbye and Hello*] there was one track on the album that he even wanted to cut down—'I Never Asked To Be Your Mountain'— until he listened to it smashed. Then everything was groovy. That was the beginning of his knowing where I was at. . . . That's when it all started—when he truly listened."

When he told me this story, Tim laughed and said, "Yeah, he was real pissed about it—'Whatta you mean, letting everybody know I took acid?!' But it couldn't be all that bad. I mean, what the hell, they hand the article out in press kits, don't they? Let 'em eat hype."

Shortly after the recording sessions in May 1967, Jennifer and I and her son Michael Cavanaugh moved from Monroe Street down to Venice. Tim completed the mixing of *Goodbye and Hello* and asked me to come back on board for the road trip. He brought Carter C.C. Collins to my house for a rehearsal. We set up in the living room and worked on material new for me, beginning with "Once I Was."

Carter never wore jeans or rumpled shirts, but always dressed immaculately. He wore well-pressed slacks and tank-top shirts, choosing colors such as russet or yellow or red that beautifully complemented his dark black skin. His tank-top shirts left his muscular neck, shoulders, and arms exposed, which looked terrific when he played congas. He polished his shoes and boots until they gleamed. He wore a modest beard, shaved his head bald—unusual in those days—and wore small rimless granny glasses (often with dark-green lenses to shield his eyes from the sun, as he was gradually going blind from glaucoma).

In addition to his charismatic physical presence, Carter had a penetrating intellect and a sharp sense of humor. I rarely heard him speak of personal matters, but he often sent fans backstage into peels of laughter, especially when he affected a garrulous, punchy, street-rat voice and said outrageous things like, "I don't mean to scare you, honey, but I got nine inches soft!" He'd gleefully peek over his glasses at the shocked expressions, wait for the laughter, then conclude with a coarse, guttural growl, "Haaaaaaugh?" that ascended from the low range to high. "Saya-fuckin'-ara, bitch!" Squeals of laughter.

Unlike the vast majority of musicians we met, and certainly unlike many fans we encountered, I don't recall Carter's ever once smoking pot or drinking alcohol. I never knew him to have a girlfriend or to have any sexual involvement with anyone. Carter was flamboyant in his language, but otherwise a very private person. To me, although not necessarily to Tim, his intimate thoughts and personal life remained a mystery.

I can't speak for Carter, of course, but on my part I felt a twinge of insecurity. The three of us enjoyed each others' company and loved playing on stage together. But Carter and Tim also shared a strong separate bond that did not include me. I had been used to sharing that kind of bond with Tim on an exclusive basis. Now, rather like an older brother, I had to deal with a new sibling in the family. It was a subtle thing, and never became blown out of proportion or destructive. Musicians give of themselves and often come to love each other in deep friendship. The fact that I felt a little possessive of Tim and resentful of Carter simply reflected my own uncertainties.

Meanwhile, the three of us worked well together for the next few years. Tim had enormous respect for Carter and worked with him extensively during the *Goodbye and Hello* and *Happy Sad* periods. He continued to periodically bring Carter into recording sessions through *Greetings From L.A.*

As a human being and as an American and a black man, Carter Collins cared deeply about racial issues. For some time, blacks and sympathetic whites had been marching in protest against the ugly racist views that seem to forever grip this country. Muhammad Ali was raising not only his fists, but also his voice, embracing Elijah Muhammad's black separatist Nation of Islam. In addition to the Vietnam conflict, the whole of America was in the throes of an escalating black-white conflict that promised to become only more violent.

One day as Carter and I walked on the Venice boardwalk talking music, he said he and other blacks no longer respected the blues. I said, "Why? It's just a 12-bar song form, great to improvise on, and it's the basis for at least fifty percent of pop music. Except for the fact that it's overdone these days and boring, what's wrong with the blues?"

"It's not merely a musical form," he replied. "It has to do with words and feelings too. It's a holdover from the days when blacks were slaves, from times when we couldn't do anything except suffer and complain. It's more than just a 12-bar structure."

"I guess that's why Tim says nobody except Jews from Brooklyn and white boys from England plays the blues anymore, right? And blacks won't have anything to do with blues. But tell me this, Carter," I asked innocently. "As long as we're talking about these things, why is there so much discussion about what black people are called these days? I mean, what's wrong with Negro?"

Carter looked askance at me. "I know you mean well and think you're not prejudiced, but it's impossible to be white in this society without growing up prejudiced. 'Negro,' for example, is the white man's label for a black man. So is 'spade,' 'spook,' 'coon,' and all those other epithets. Blacks don't want to be identified with those labels any more. That's why Muhammad Ali rejected the Cassius Clay name. Cassius Clay was a slave name. He wanted a Muslim name and a name that he elected to take for himself. There's a new identity emerging. That's why we would rather be called blacks and African-Americans."

"Are you saying I'm prejudiced? Jesus, man, I've been a jazz lover all my life, have played music with you and dozens of other black people, have hung out . . ."

"I'm just saying there's a new vision growing, and you need to be aware of it. There's a new spirit of independence and racial pride among blacks. We want a freedom we've never had, a dignity we've never had, and we're willing to fight for it. That's what's happening today. Just look around. You see it everywhere, don't you?"

"You're right, Carter. I hadn't thought about it. Thanks, man."

CHAPTER 5

VENICE BY THE SEA

When Jennifer and I moved to Venice we rented a pink house at 59 Navy Street, near the corner of Ocean Avenue, two blocks from the ocean. We named it "Big Pink," after the Band's album of the same name. Larry lived across the street, upstairs at 42 Navy Street. Tim and Jainie lived in Topanga Canyon, but soon moved to an apartment at 613½ Ocean Park Boulevard in neighboring Santa Monica to be near the rest of us. They and numerous friends, including Manda Bradlyn, an aspiring painter, and Danny Gordon, Tim's old friend from Bell Gardens Junior High and Anaheim High School days, hung out at our place.

Venice was an innocent, enchanted seaside jewel back then. Wooden houses surrounded by palm trees and red and yellow flowers lined both sides of freshwater canals in South Venice, where white ducks floated among the reeds and people paddled row boats as if they were gondolas. In North Venice, where we lived, houses and buildings still had the dilapidated look of early twentieth-century architecture—stucco apartment buildings, wooden homes, funky old individualistic structures painted pink or lime green, yellow or washed-out orange—and wide vacant lots still existed.

The summer skies were infinitely blue, the rolling ocean clear and unpolluted, the glittering yellow-tan beaches wide and clean, nights full of stars, days awash with sunlight. Not too many people, plenty of parking spaces—and the world was ours.

On weekends, sun splashed down on hundreds of locals and visitors who leisurely wandered back and forth on the Venice boardwalk—an outdoor circus in the sun.

People wore all kinds of attire—red bandanas, great hats with feathers, baggy Renaissance pants, tie-dyed T-shirts. Golden suntanned girls wearing bikinis swished by on roller skates. Other people wore bell-bottom pants, cutoff blue jeans, tennis shoes, sandals, beards, long hair, beads, eagle feathers, circus clown makeup, tank tops, no shirts at all. Bathing suits, black skin, white skin, brown skin, everywhere naked skin gleaming in the sun. Clean sweat, patchouli oil, perfume, cologne.

Street bands played: singers, guitars, fiddles, harmonicas, guitar cases spread out open on the sidewalk catching change and dollar bills from passers-by. Jugglers juggled, mimes mimed, magicians pulled cards and quarters out of peoples' ears.

Every weekend a crowd surrounded a group of black drummers gathered in the shade of a sidewalk gazebo: five or six conga players and cowbell players, shakers, rattles, washboards, bald heads, rastas, beards. Hands flashing, pounding. Fast grooves, Afro-chants. Sweat on foreheads, necks, shoulders. At least 50 people listening, blacks, whites, Chicanos standing in a circle, dancing, swaying, drinking beer, smoking grass, eyes closed, shiny faces tilted to the sun, drums urgent, intoxicating, rhythms pulsing.

Further down the boardwalk, individual folksingers, country singers, and rock singers stood with their guitars and sang heartfelt life-songs. Groups of steel drummers spun out silvery cascades of Caribbean melodies and reggae rhythms. People sauntered along, listened, smiled, threw dimes, quarters, dollar bills into instrument cases, passed on.

Vendors displayed wares in booths or on rugs spread out on sidewalks—spunglass sculptures, plastic toys, old books, magazines, hot dogs, ice cones, secondhand clothes, earrings, gold chains, pendants, T-shirts, dolls, tattoo artists, massage tables.

People carried radios on their shoulders up close to their ears, or set them on blankets spread out on the sidewalk. Live music and radio music overlapped with the sounds of voices talking and laughing, mingled with soft summer winds blowing across ageless sands. Little kids drank Cokes and Dr. Peppers. Hippies and bikers smoked pot. Old-school Venice bums who had lived in the alleys for years sat on lawns drinking wine. Men and women painted bright red, yellow, blue, and green murals on building walls—whales, dolphins, roller skaters, weightlifters, swimmers, sunbathers. Psychedelic posters advertising rock bands decorated store windows and wooden fences. And out across the ocean sailboats swayed in warm summer winds. . . .

Almost every day we put on swimming suits, grabbed towels, and toodled down to the beach. While Jennifer and Jainie lay on the sand basking in the sun, Tim and I plunged into the sea, frolicking like seals, laughing, playing, teaching ourselves how to body-surf waves. Young and strong, we slid down the slopes of the big ones,

"Big Pink" in Venice was the center of the universe. It was only two blocks from the beach; no liquor store had been built yet; across the vacant lot to the west we could see the ocean. Tim, Jainie, Larry, Manda, and Dan visited Lee and Jennifer regularly. It was a family, it was a party, it was summer sunlight forever.

The Venice boardwalk—a circus under the summer sky.

tumbled under in roaring water and foam and sand, leaped to our feet near the shoreline, swam back out to catch another big one. Our bodies glistened, our friendship warmed, our hearts pumped with confident optimism.

Back at Big Pink, Jennifer and Jainie prepared big salads or turkey sandwiches or soups or stews while Tim and I sat in the living room, guitars in hand, smoking pot, drinking beer, playing music. Jennifer and Jainie became great friends, laughing, gossiping, sharing the stories of their lives, comforting each other in times of stress. Larry dropped over. Manda visited. Sometimes in the late afternoon Dan Gordon showed up, and we would all step out on the back porch to watch the sun set in glorious red-orange tapestries beyond the blue ocean's rim.

We put on music—Aretha Franklin singing "Respect" and "Unchain My Heart," or Dr. John the Night Tripper—"Gris-Gris," "Mama Roux," "Jump Sturdy," "I Walk on Gilded Splinters."

At Big Pink we talked and laughed, generating amazing freeflight conversations about art, life, business, and music. Philosophical insights flew high, pierced deep.

Although Beckett originally aspired to be a mathematical physicist, he loved to talk about literature, particularly Shakespeare, Keats, Robert Burns, Poe, and other classic giants, as well as more recent writers, perhaps especially Dylan Thomas and Bob Dylan. He had a keen, inquiring, well-educated mind and a well-honed literary propensity, especially in poetry. He didn't smoke pot, but he sipped a little wine, got a little loose, not drunk, and thoroughly enjoyed fencing playfully in the realm of ideas.

I found conversations with him to be stimulating, because he raised challenging questions and offered thought-provoking insights that were as subtle and complex as they were well-articulated. I don't think it mattered to either of us whether we agreed or disagreed. It was a matter of adventurously exploring interesting viewpoints, ideas and values. I found him to be a marvelous conversational comrade.

Manda Bradlyn eventually got together with Beckett, lived with him, and married him. She was a lovely blue-eyed girl, perhaps nineteen at the time, a budding modern painter and a good one. She observed things carefully, but rarely said anything, a quiet person, gentle, introspective, shy. She usually walked barefooted and wore an off-white, one-piece sleeveless cotton dress that hung down below her knees. Whenever she walked on the beach with us, she often strolled by herself, gently turning round and round, slow dancing with the seabirds and the wind.

Of all of the people who knew Tim, Manda was one of the few who knew him well, it seems to me, looking back. She loved him, deeply appreciated him, and had intelligence enough to understand his every word. She did not betray him while he was alive, and did not betray his name after his death. Tim could not have asked for a better friend than Manda.

Larry loquaciously and eloquently celebrated concepts of peace, love, universal justice, and human dignity, and it was a pleasure to hear him discuss these matters. He detested the war in Vietnam and swore he would never go. He believed that violence was not inherent in human nature, that love was the key to our salvation. Insight, meditation, education, and the power and grace of positive intelligence would change the face of the human race. Politics united with love and understanding could enlighten humanity. He would never go in the Army, never support that ghastly conflict, never allow himself to be enslaved by the Industrial War Machine. In its multitude of forms, art could save the world.

When he eventually got drafted, however, his pacifism and antiwar principles seemed to evaporate. I began to question Beckett's sincerity and courage. Maybe he was indeed an artist of insight, integrity, and commitment, courageous enough to

Jennifer and Jainie in bikinis on sunsplashed Venice beach.

Larry Beckett in a group shot taken in front of
Big Pink, circa 1968. Front row, left to right: Blanche
Stace (Jennifer's mother), Michael Cavanaugh
(Jennifer's son, age 13), Larry Beckett. Back row:
Jennifer Stace, Lee Underwood.

put his life on the line for poetry. Time would tell. He talked the talk, and talked it well, but could he live the life? Meanwhile, in the Army or out, he remained a beautiful human being with a first-class mind and a loving heart.

A few years before this, I had evaded the draft by claiming to be an asthmatic (which I had been in childhood) and by obtaining a new prescription for asthma pills. Had they called me, I would have been rejected. Asthmatics wheezing in foxholes make undependable killers and poor poster images.

Buckley had managed to escape the draft before I met him. He proudly boasted that he got staggeringly drunk the night before, claimed he was gay at the interviews, and behaved like a madman. He also said they detected a slight heart fibrillation—and let him go—although I got the impression he concocted that detail out of thin air, on the spot, as part of a very colorful story.

(Elaine, his mother, said, "I don't know how he got out. I think he played crazy and just outsmarted them, which isn't hard to do when you're dealing with the military." When I asked her directly whether or not Tim had a bad heart or a heart murmur of any kind, she stated "No," categorically.)

At this point in his life, Tim was opposed to the war in Vietnam and in support of the various peace movements gaining momentum across the country. He seemed to sit on the fence a bit on the questions of politics versus art, social action versus creative independence, loyalty to society versus loyalty to music. As we traveled along, singin' a song through the years, his views transmuted in very interesting ways.

Dan Gordon didn't smoke pot, but he liked his red wine and enjoyed the conversations that went on in Big Pink. When Dan insisted that high principles only got one into trouble, and financial success was far more important than struggling against the system in an effort to realize lofty artistic ideals, I thought he must be kidding. If he feels that way, why is he here?

He would laugh and contemptuously point out that people don't want depth or reality, they want flash, sass, entertainment, escape. They want sex not love, laughter not poetry, speed not tranquility, sitcoms not art, mirrors not insight. They don't want to transcend the mud. They want to wallow in it.

Hmmmm.

To his credit, Gordon was absolutely out-front about his cynical materialistic values. To hell with beliefs, edification, and art. Principles and visionary ideals were for losers. Give 'em what they want. Write third-rate TV and film scripts. Tell 'em fantasies they want to hear. Take the money and run. He was clear about it—I just didn't get it. If Dan really believed that, I reasoned, he wouldn't be Tim and Larry's friend, and he wouldn't be hanging around Big Pink. Besides, he said it with such wit and charm that I was sure he wasn't serious. He had a fantastic sense of humor and a quick mind. Surely he was simply provoking me into higher flights of idealistic rhetoric. But he wasn't. He meant it. He wound up in Hollywood, "giving 'em what they want" and filling his coffers well.

During those days, of course, none of this mattered. We were having great fun, and all of us loved each other. Our youthful, vibrant present moments sparkled like dewdrops on roses in the early morning sun. The future was ours, full of hope and possibilities, wide open for the taking, and life was good.

One of the reasons life was good was because Tim and Dan were brilliantly funny. Some of the greatest times we ever had at Big Pink were when Tim and Dan got on a roll, improvising wisecracks and one-liners, building stories and images lickety-split-quick with impeccable timing, playing off each other, reveling in each others' comebacks, fencing like French duelists, improvising words and laugh-lines like musicians improvising music. They'd have Jainie, Larry, Manda, Jennifer, Michael, me, and various other friends rocking back and forth in our chairs, tummies about to split, holding our sides, sometimes laughing until the tears came.

On the road one time, Tim and I played a trio gig with Carter on Long Island at a small club called My Father's Moustache. Martin Mull was on the same bill. In those early days, before his TV acting success, Martin was a first-class guitarist and stand-up comedian. Backstage between sets, he and Tim would get to riffing back and forth the way Tim and Dan did back home, with Martin improvising right along with Tim, fleet, witty, quick, keen, deft, bright-eyed, the both of them keeping us howling with laughter.

The same kind of spontaneously improvised comedic fireworks took place one evening in Hollywood a few years later when Tim and Dan and I found ourselves standing in line at a movie theater with former Rat Pack member and TV comic Joey Bishop. Tim and Dan couldn't resist challenging Joey with wisecracks, and Joey did not back off. He didn't mind in the least. In fact, he responded to the challenge line-for-line, thoroughly enjoying himself, and pretty soon the three of them had me and everybody else within earshot laughing our buns off. It was a highlight comedy show right there on a Hollywood sidewalk, "free for nothing."

Undoubtedly, one of the major reasons Dan and Tim were such good friends was because of Dan's quick-witted, intelligent sense of humor. Dan and Tim stimulated each other, bringing laughter into the room wherever they went. When Dan spoke

Jennifer's painting of Pacific Ocean Park, circa '67–'68, with the ocean in the background. This was the view from Big Pink's back porch.

of his intention to write screenplays, I thought surely he would write comedies. He didn't, but that in no way detracted from his gifts as a natural humorist.

Jennifer worked nearby as a waitress in the Oar House. With money from her parents, we sent young Michael to Happy Valley, a private school in Ojai. During the summers Michael stayed with us. When he was thirteen, he decided he wanted to play piano, so we rented one. I showed him a few chords and riffs, and we paid for lessons. Eventually, Michael became a professional musician, gigged regularly around town, and appeared as a studio sideman on several albums.

Jennifer started teaching herself how to paint, and, to my astonishment, showed amazing talent almost immediately. She painted a large-scale green-and-blue picture of Michael playing piano; a large picture of me sitting at the kitchen table, hair aflame, talking with three young women; a large canvas of a huge obese nude woman; another large picture of several down-and-out drunks who stayed next door for a while.

Jennifer was a jewel and even nicknamed herself Jennifer Jewel. She was tough and tender, danced like a sex diva, and loved to sing and laugh. She sentimentally related to underdogs and downtrodden losers, one of her most endearing qualities. She did not enjoy confrontations, but did not back down from them. Like her gentle father, she preferred compassion and understanding over anger and conflict. But when she had to be defiant, persistent, or determined, she did so with gusto and flare, very much like her mother. She was already a feminist, before the movement had gained momentum. Yes, she loved men, but was also wary of them. And yes, she dearly loved women, but was not a lesbian. She never felt quite like a mother to Michael, so the two of them became the best of friends. She was rebellious in her thinking, he more conventional. Together, they were devoted and loyal to each other, a mutually supportive, loving team, each helping the other through difficult times.

With Jennifer painting, me playing guitar, Michael playing piano, and Tim, Larry, Danny, Jainie, and Manda as our best friends, those days were a joy for all of us, the sunshine summers of our lives. Surely they would last forever.

Big Pink stood alone on an empty lot. We could look west and see Pacific Ocean Park (POP), built on a pier extended out over the ocean, with its roller coaster, its merry-go-round, its Ferris wheel and food stalls and game booths. If we listened, we could hear the roller coaster clattering on its rails, its passengers squealing with delight. Throughout the day and into the night, merry-go-round music tinkled distantly inside ocean breezes. Jennifer painted a picture of this POP scene.

Later, when we moved to 136 Park Place in Venice, she painted a portrait of herself smiling out from within a veil of green vines and rose-colored flowers. She also painted a portrait of Tim with his guitar, my photo of which later appeared on the cover of *Works in Progress*, a 1999 posthumous CD. These pictures hang in my studio today.

Next to POP was the Cheetah, a rock 'n' roll concert and dance hall. One night I snuck in alone and listened to Janis Joplin, who astonished me with her visceral power. At a later date, Tim and Carter and I played there ourselves.

Everywhere in those halcyon days, a positive vibration filled the air. Optimism in youthful eyes, smiles on faces, a sense of purpose, destiny, value. A new generation graced the aged houses and apartment buildings of Venice. A sense of creativity, hope, and strength pervaded the air. Vibrant colors shone in the clothes, in the ideas, in the music, in peoples' faces, in the sunbright atmosphere itself.

We walked down to the beach at night, the wide sands empty, quiet, only soft breezes blowing among shadowy palm trees and through the giant pilings supporting the Cheetah and POP pier. Once in a while, a red tide rolled in, glowing phosphorescent blue-green-white inside the waves. We'd go swimming, laughing and splashing water refulgent with blue-white light. When the mist blew off the ocean and thinned overhead, we saw glittering blue stars in the black sky high above. The air smelled heavily of sea salt, especially at night, and especially when waves glowed in the red tide.

In the winter, after the crowds departed, on those overcast days when fog clouds rolled in slowly from the ocean, in November and December when the air grew hushed by the shoreline, we could barely make out the forms of surfer boys in black wetsuits sliding down slopes of giant waves that broke out beyond the pier and tumbled in, whispering all the way to shore. Seabirds flew out of mist-clouds like quiet thoughts on silent wings, disappeared back into fog.

For two years, yes, in every season, yes, our hearts swayed with the music and the tides and the rhythms and the moods of Venice by the sea.

ON THE ROAD: EXTENDED FAMILIES

Our primary family lived on the West Coast, but we had friends and extended families in a number of East Coast cities, especially New York, a poppin' town, compressed, vertical, a vastly different world than sprawled-out, laid-back L.A.

Everywhere we looked in New York, marquees blazed with big names of the day.

To this day, Jennifer's portrait of Tim hangs in Lee's studio above her POP painting.

Folk artists such as Richie Havens, Phil Ochs, Odetta. Rock acts like the Doors, the Byrds, Canned Heat, the Fugs, Blue Cheer, Jefferson Airplane, Velvet Underground, Iron Butterfly, Pink Floyd, Van Morrison, Moby Grape, Steppenwolf, Country Joe and the Fish. Jazz artists such as Nina Simone, Thelonious Monk, John Coltrane, Charles Lloyd, Chick Corea, Gary Burton, Larry Coryell.

Theater was booming as well: *Hair* was playing at the New York Shakespeare Festival Public Theater, *Mac Bird* at Circle in the Square, *Fortune and Men's Eyes* at the Actor's Playhouse, *The Beggar's Opera* at the McAlpin Rooftop Theater.

Then, as now, New York crackled, aflame in neon glory. And many of our closest friends lived there.

John King, whom we met in 1967, proved to be one of our best buddies in New

York. He lived in a tall apartment building at 88 Bleecker Street for a while, where he looked out his fourth floor window and threw nickels and dimes down to the bums on the sidewalk. He then moved to 15 King Street, a funky one-bedroom basement apartment in a Village building where Edgar Allen Poe once lived. Tim and I often stayed there, and often got just as loaded as ol' Edgar did.

The first time I met John, at his Bleecker Street apartment, he hauled a jumbo tin can out of his bedroom, pulled the lid off, and dumped 2,000 swizzle sticks on the floor. Red, yellow, green, blue—hundreds of them. "When I run for president," he quipped to Tim and me and a mutual friend, Charlie Jones, "I'll pass these out as souvenirs." At Louie's bar next to the Tin Angel, he'd line up five or six gin and tonics, drink them down—and pocket the swizzle sticks. I never saw him stagger, never heard him slur a word. He was a first-class serious boozer.

John hailed from a wealthy old-school American aristocratic family in northern New York. He cut his red hair short, wore green blazer jackets and pin-striped button-down shirts, had a low-keyed sardonic wit, especially about politics, and joked about spraying long-haired flea-infested hippies with Raid.

He owned a house and several acres of land in upstate New York, near Craryville, not far from Woodstock, which eventually became our haven from the city. It was a large house, several bedrooms, surrounded by trees and fields, with a stream running nearby. The nature-connection at John King's "farm" (as he called it) became essential for us, perhaps especially for me.

Meanwhile, down in the city, John hung out with us whenever we came to town. He'd pick us up at the airport in his Excalibur automobile, a breath-taking luxury convertible with an eight-foot elongated hood, high arched fenders, sparkling beige paint, three six-inch chrome exhaust tubes extending out of both sides of the hood, gleaming wire hubcaps, an imposing box-trunk in back with a locked spare tire container on the outside. We sat in plush leather seats and rode with the top down, waving at people who stared and pointed as we drove through New York's raucous streets.

John wore a woolen golf cap and a red scarf that fluttered behind him in the wind while he drove. He was the decadent aristocrat. We were his madcap hippie friends, merrily on the rise to stardom. It was a golden time, straight out of the 1920s—but this was the sixties, a time all our own.

Bob Campbell and Barry Schulze roomed together in Greenwich Village, hung out with musicians, and took photographs.

Bob was in his early thirties, bearded, very bright, well-read, a musically literate fellow who did not graduate from college. When I asked him why, he said, "Because I majored in Student Union. I like books and read a lot, but I don't study. When reading becomes work, a task, then that's it. My seventh- and eighth-grade guidance counselor accused me of learning by osmosis. My mother got burned up at my motto in the yearbook: 'I'm not lazy. I'm just tired.'"

Bob met Tim in the Tin Angel. "A couple of days before I met him," Bob said, "Barry had been saying, 'Man, you gotta hear Tim Buckley at the Go Go.' Then Odetta told me about him. I was getting to know Tim before I ever heard him play. Musically, he was an unknown quantity to me.

"When we were introduced, he was sitting at a table with four other people. He had that mass of hair, and I thought, 'Oh, Christ, another one.' That's all the Village needed, was more hair.

Bob Campbell's self-portrait, circa '67–'68. Bob was an exceptionally good photographer, with a bright mind and a marvelous sense of humor. He had enormous respect for Tim.

"Then he said a couple of things, and I thought, 'Oh, a smart-ass—but a very *smart* smart-ass.' He and I wound up just talking—and talking and talking. I liked the way he handled himself with me and other people who came in and out. We talked jazz and classical music until the Angel closed. He paid close attention, and invited me to a rehearsal the next night.

"When I got home, I told Barry I had met Tim Buckley. Barry and I both went to the rehearsal, at one of the first twelve-track studios in New York. You got into a freight elevator that had an elevator shaft with black light and day-glow patterns painted on the walls. Introductions were made, then somebody's amp blew up and Barry fixed it—we were off and running.

"Several days later, Tim came over to our place for the first time, and I played all of my MJQ records: *Concorde*, *Collaborations* (with Laurindo Almeida), and the first ten-inch album, when Kenny Clarke was the drummer—*The Modern Jazz Quartet*. He said you had talked to him a lot about jazz. He was very receptive to me too. And he learned fast.

"I think that's what drew me to Tim the most. He was smart. That was basically it. There was a lot going on in the Village then, a lot of interesting people, but not many people you could sit down and talk to. I mean, I was living with gigantic Barry

Schulze in a tiny room this size! That's like living side-by-side with Mauna Loa inside a cowboy hat. So I'd go out and talk—or try to talk with people. When Tim came along, we could do that.

"I remember calling him one day and saying, 'Are you receiving company?' He was standoffish at first. Then I said, 'I just feel like talking to somebody who understands what I'm saying.' He said, 'Oh, yeah, I got you. Come on up.' He changed from that remote thing into 'Oh! Sure!'

"He was uneducated, but he was bright and sophisticated. He hadn't gotten knowledge through the educational system. He knew he had to get it some other way, so he wasn't the least bit afraid of having people around him who knew more, such as [vibraphonist] David Friedman or [bassist] Johnny Bongo [Miller] or you. He sought such people out, because he knew that's where he was going to get his knowledge. That was one of his sterling characteristics.

"Our friend Charlie Jones was going to get us in to see Taj Mahal at the Electric Circus one night. When you guys played there it was called the Balloon Farm. We got roundly stoned on pot at John King's house, then went to the Circus and were standing around in the vestibule. We were there for about a half-hour, just standing around in that blue room staring at each other. Finally, Buckley turned to me and

Rare photo of Barry Schulze, Tim's road manager and "pet giant," nicknamed "Bear." Now deceased, Ol' Bear was one of Tim's most devoted friends.

said, 'Beethoven quartets?' I said, 'Beethoven quartets. Come on over to my house.'
And we listened to Beethoven quartets."

Barry Schulze stood some 6-foot 7-inches tall, perhaps more, and weighed at
least 270 pounds, a gorilla-sized man. He wore a droopy handlebar moustache, and
his eyes were always half-lidded, sleepy looking. His hair was thin on top, long and
stringy on the sides. He walked and sat with his shoulders stooped, and always had
to duck going through doorways. He wore rumpled dirty shirts, his pants sagged in
back, he shuffled when he walked, he had worn the heels and soles of his shoes
paper-thin. He could hardly roll a joint because his hands were so big and his fingers so thick. Tim called Barry his "pet giant" and nicknamed him "Bear."

Bear was good at fixing things—amplifiers, sound equipment, cars, whatever.
He had a kind of primitive practical intelligence, although when he spoke he
sounded like a slow-minded dullard. Timmy kidded him by addressing him as
"Heeey, dummmie."

There are those who say Herb hired Barry as a kind of watchdog over Tim. That
may be true, but I don't think so. I don't think Herb knew Bear before Tim did, and
not once did I get the impression that Barry's loyalties were to management and not
to Tim. Bear never came on as any kind of cop. We did what we wanted whenever
we wanted, and Bear got us to the gigs on time. From the night Tim met him at the
rehearsal in the Village and hired him, Barry became a devoted friend who worked
as Tim's roadie and sound man for several years. Bear loved Tim as much as anybody Tim ever knew.

Laying up on beds in motel rooms smoking pot and watching TV, Timmy would
say, "Heeey, dummmie, move your webs so I can see the screen." "Okaaaay," Bear
would reply, shifting his enormous feet.

They were quite a pair—Tim short, quick, smart; Bear towering above him, tall,
huge, sluggish of mind—but a comfort to have on the road. He carried our luggage
and equipment, dealt with gas stations, hotel clerks, airplane personnel, and ran
sound systems at the various clubs and halls we played. I figured he would be
immensely effective in any sort of physical conflict—big, strong, intimidating. I was
glad he was with us, just in case.

Dianne Quinn ("Aysha") met Tim in 1967 at Max's Kansas City, where she was a
waitress. At Elektra publicist Danny Fields' apartment she and Tim hung out and
talked about Tim's marriage to Mary, the pregnancy, the anguish. From the moment
she met Tim she loved him, although they had sex only once and went their separate
ways as platonic friends. Tim was still with Jainie, and later with Judy. Over the years,
Dianne became a fashion model, an actress, and eventually an acting teacher. In New
York and L.A. she saw Tim on occasion, remaining a friend until the end.

"I remember sitting with Tim at the Tin Angel, and Al Kooper came in," she told
me. "He was the organist and leader of Blood, Sweat & Tears. Al saw Tim and got
all excited.

"'Hey, Tim!' he beamed. 'We're just about to record your song, 'Morning Glory'!

"'Oh?' said Tim. 'Well, listen, Al—just try not to fuck it up too bad.'"

Back in those days, Tim had a way of doing a passive little-boy poet thing that
thrilled the girls. They yearned to cuddle him, hold him, protect him. He loved it.

The wispy, frail image worked for him, but he also had a mind as quick as a cobra. Sometimes he could be lethal—or he could transform savagery into hilarity at a moment's notice. Most of the girls who adored him also bored him.

But when Hope Ruff, a lovely dark-haired Jewish woman, swept into our lives, smiling grandly, her flamboyant floppy hats tilted to one side, furs or boa feathers draped around her shoulders, slit skirts, high heels, long cigarette holders, she spotted Tim, Tim spotted her—and they clicked instantly, first as friends, eventually as lovers.

As I recall, she was four or five years older than he, a quick-witted, fast-talking pianist who knew how to laugh well. To earn her way, she transcribed music from demos (including some of Tim's songs). Waving her long cigarette holder, smiling like the flashing sun, she won Tim's heart with her perky beauty, her assertiveness, and her ebullient extroversion. She was smart, tough, funny, and knew how to handle Tim's exploitive or dictatorial moods. Sassy and scintillating, she made him laugh. He made her laugh too. In many ways, they were a perfect match.

At one point after Tim broke up with Jainie, he said to me, "I think I love Hope." I chuckled, knowing how Tim's "loves" usually faded quickly. "No," he insisted. "I really do, and I'm thinking about marrying her."

I felt a little uneasy when he said that. They were good together as friends and lovers, but marriage? Hope didn't seem quite right for him. She was extremely independent, already a liberated woman—and Tim still lived in the pre-liberated Neanderthal era. Me man, you woman. Me artist, you slave. A wife to him was somebody who washed his laundry, cooked his meals, sucked his pecker, and knew only two phrases, "Yes" and "Thank you."

Hope was not about to be Jane to Tim's Tarzan. She had her own views and was very much her own person. She was willing to please, yes, but she also had strong notions about equality without having to resort to manipulation. It turned out they did not marry, but she was a major love in his life. It was always a joy to see Hope in New York.

Crazy Terry showed up at John King's downstairs Poe-house apartment on King Street to sell us hash. He was an outlaw with a sense of humor. Bob Campbell said Terry knew how to steal cars, for example, and was good at it. Terry could boost a British Motor Corporation product in five minutes with a stick of gum, put it in the fuse box just right, and get a short that would start the car. A couple of times during the days we knew him, he pulled up in a Triumph or MG and hollered, "Wanna go for a ride?" Terry had style.

That first time Terry walked in, he shocked us. "Mind if I take off my leg?"

He dropped his jeans and took the whole thing off. He had no left leg. It had been cut off about eight inches below his hip. He carried the hash stashed in his wooden leg. Well, hello!

At one time, Terry was a soldier of fortune and a Green Beret, but that's not how he lost his leg. It hadn't been shot off. He was working in a factory on the front lines of one of those Israeli conflicts and fell into a machine. After amputating the leg and cleaning Terry up, the doctor gave him the tourniquet and said, "Here's the schedule—when to tighten, when to let go. It's up to you."

Terry held his life in his own hands. "I wasn't too quick to make a decision about this, you know? There I sat, with incredible pain—and the means to shut it off. All

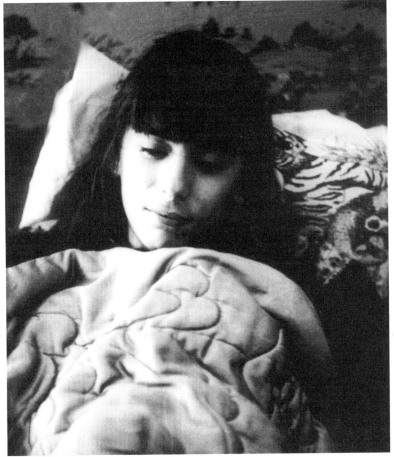

Hope Ruff was already a liberated woman: self-reliant, flamboyant, intelligent, musically talented, a delight in every way. Tim was smitten with her, understandably so. Portrait by Bob Campbell, one of his best.

I had to do was let go, and I was tempted to do just that. Obviously—I didn't! Wanna get high?"

Scattered among so many faceless strangers who passed without sound, there were dozens of acquaintances and friends who touched our lives. I treasure them all. Some made us laugh. Some brought intensity and sexuality into our lives. Some flashed and quickly faded. Others pierced our hearts and changed our lives, perhaps a little, perhaps a lot. Still others awakened love for a night, a week, two weeks. Some remain vivid in my mind to this day, poignant in the heart, a tear, a quiet smile, unforgettable.

Voices, hotel and motel rooms, smoke rings, old songs, lost streets, vanished lives . . . echoes of our shimmering youth . . . autumn leaves, timewinds . . . Tilted memories blurring in and out with the tides. . . .

CHAPTER 6

WEST COAST/EAST COAST, ALL AROUND THE TOWN

CALIFORNIA DREAMIN'

In a rented car that Zappa and his band had used the week before, Tim and I drove up to San Francisco in mid-June 1967 to play at the Magic Mountain Music Festival in Marin Country.

While Tim drove, I dipped into the plastic bag of new pot we had just bought and rolled a joint. We smoked and wheeled along the freeway, enjoying the sunny day. As we approached Ventura, Tim was talking about California cops.

"They'll bust you for no reason at all, you know. Yeah, I've been pulled over just because my hair is long. They hate us."

"Come on, Tim. I can't believe they'd stop you just for long hair."

"Yeah, they will. It's happened to me more than once. If you talk back to them, they'll beat you up too."

"I've never heard of such a thing. Sounds kinda paranoid."

"Cops can get real vicious in California," he said.

Just then, swirling red lights flashed in the mirror. A siren went off. A police car with a whirling party hat crowded up behind us, pulled us over.

"My god, Tim, whatta we do? Where do we hide the dope?"

"Stick it under your belt."

"Get out," the state trooper ordered. "Put your hands on the hood and roof, spread your feet."

"What's wrong?"

"You were weaving on the road. We're checking you for drugs."

The cops started searching us. With my hands on the roof of the car, I looked over the rooftop, across the highway as he cop patted me down. Under my arms . . . cars whooshing by, blue sky . . . down my sides . . . telephone wires, meadow, green grass, summer trees . . . over my stomach *and belt*—heart pounding—on down my legs. He missed it!

The other cop looked inside the car, reached down to the floor, raised his hand. "What's this?" He held a single marijuana seed between his thumb and index finger. "Okay, bust 'em."

"This is a rented car," Tim said.

"Yeah?"

"Frank Zappa and his band use it all the time. That's not our seed. We're clean. Look again. We're clean."

"All right," said the cop who had searched me. "We're state troopers. We'll let you go. But pay attention to your driving. Don't let local Ventura cops stop you. They'll throw you in jail real quick—understand?"

"Yessir!"

We drove off, singing "Rock Island Line"—"We fooo you! We fooo you! We got aaall good grass! We got aaall good grass!"

In July, Tim, Carter and I opened for Jimi Hendrix at the Earl Warren Show Grounds in Santa Barbara. I still had not caught up with the new generation, and had not even heard of Hendrix.

Back in the dressing room after we played our set, I wondered who this guy Hendrix was, dressed in white tights and American Indian beads, fringes on his shirt, hair in a giant Afro, wild eyes. And when he went onstage, plugged in, cranked four Marshall amps up to 10 and started whanking out blues clichés on the guitar without even singing particularly well, I decided to go outside and watch the rodeo.

I motioned to Tim, Jainie, and Jennifer. Tim didn't say anything about staying, so we left and watched a bunch of redneck cowboys riding horses, swinging ropes, wrestling innocent, terrified calves into the dirt.

Missing Jimi Hendrix was a learning experience. I missed because I could see in him only what I already knew and understood. Blinded by partial familiarity and closed to the new, I had not been able to fathom the blazing originality he was bringing to popular music, particularly through the guitar. Once I eventually realized this profound limitation in myself, I kept my mind open, my heart receptive. How could I learn or feel anything new if I were unwilling and therefore unable to venture beyond the boundaries of my own experience? It wasn't long before I came to love Jimi's music.

TONIGHT SHOW

We flew to New York in July 1967, and appeared on Johnny Carson's *Tonight Show*, but Johnny wasn't there. Alan King was. Back in the Green Room, Herb Cohen told Tim to play "Wings," a simple, not particularly interesting tune from the first album, and not at all what we were into now. It seemed to me a strange choice. But Elektra had released it as a single several months before and it had gone over big *in Spain*, so we played it.

Afterwards, Tim sat in the hot seat and Alan King kidded him about his hair, something to the effect of, "What are you, a hippie? Ha-ha-ha." Tim shifted uncomfortably in his chair, crossed one leg, folded his arms, stared at his knee, didn't say anything. Alan asked him, "Where does anybody get a crazy 'do like that?" Tim muttered something about how "It just grows." Alan cut to a commercial, brought on the next guest. That was it. Over.

Tim was furious with himself. Even as Hendrix was a learning experience for me, Alan King was a learning experience for Tim. From that time on, he watched talk shows and paid attention to how quick-witted guests managed to come up with flash-and-slash one-liners without being intimidated by circumstances or abrasive talk show hosts. In time, he taught himself how to improvise conversation as brilliantly as he improvised music. "After Alan King," he said to me, "I knew I had to learn how to talk."

That show stayed on his mind, irritating him. Even as late as 1969 he discussed it with interviewer Anne Marie Micklo. In his humorous way, he embellished the facts, of course:

"I was on with Alan King, the suburban fascist. He was barking at me: 'Find you have much trouble with your hair? Ha-ha.' I said, 'Uh, no, it just grows, man.' 'Where do you have it done? Har-har-har.' So I told him, I said, 'You know, it's really surprising—I always thought you were a piece of cardboard.' That cooled him out and he didn't talk to me any more."

The "cardboard" comment had not taken place, but it sounded good in interviews. The important thing was Tim's new desire to learn how to speak well under the gun and in the glare of the spotlight.

THE CITY OF BROTHERLY LOVE

The very next day Tim, Jainie, Carter, and I flew down to Philadelphia, the "City of Brotherly Love." We arrived mid-afternoon in a blinding rainstorm, took a cab to the Robert Morris Hotel, unloaded our gear in the rain, and dragged our equipment and soaked selves into the lobby. Tim told the clerks we had reservations. The chief clerk, an older man with gray hair, looked at Tim as if he were an insect. He checked the reservation list—yes, we had reservations—leaned over and said something in his younger assistant's ear and turned back to Tim.

"I'm sorry," he said. "But we are full. You can't stay here."

"But we have reservations."

"We have the right to refuse service to anyone."

Carter deliberately affected his low-life street-rat accent—"Haaaaaagggh? Whatta we got here—muthafuckin' honkies?"

Rainwater dripping from his hair, Tim argued with the clerks. Carter paced back and forth in front of the desk, working himself up—"We got muthafuckin' hypocrite redneck bigots here? Haaaaaahhh?"

"We don't allow hippies in our hotel," the manager insisted, growing nervous.

"We aren't hippies," Tim said. "We paid you money. We've got our reservations. It's raining like hell outside. Give us the keys to our goddam rooms!"

Carter was striding up and down behind Tim. "Muthafuckas dead from the neck up? Hangovers from the glory days of cotton fields and lost plantations? Haaaagghh?"

I felt mortified and riddled with anxiety. "Cool it, Carter," I said.

Carter didn't pay the least bit of attention. "Ain't nobody mess wid me, see? I got a bucket full of balls and enough hair on my ass to fill a mattress! I oughtta slash yo' muthfuckin' white asses thinner'n bacon, haaaaaahh?"

Carter was on a roll. Tim argued louder. The clerks were clearly frightened by now, sweating, eyes fluttering. God forbid, here was an enraged black maniac creating havoc and his two rabble-rousing commie hippie friends with wet girl's hair, all of them teaming up to destroy Everything Our Great Country Stands For—yikes!

The clerks huddled and conferred. In fear and trembling they gave us the keys. We had prevailed.

Upstairs, Tim and Jainie stayed in one room, Carter and I in another. We unpacked, undressed, climbed into bed to rest up before the gig that night. As we were dozing off, suddenly there was a loud knock at the door.

"Open up! This is the management!"

I opened the door a crack, and they barreled their way in. They flashed badges. "I thought you said you are the management."

"We're the police."

"You have a warrant?"

"Yes. Step aside. We're searching your room."

It was illegal of them to have lied about who they were at the door, and that made it an illegal entry. Nevertheless, they checked suitcases, the bathroom, opened a top bureau drawer, took out my shaving kit, looked inside, pulled out an amber bottle, opened it and sniffed. "What's this?"

"I don't know."

"It's marijuana. You're both under arrest."

They hauled all four of us downtown, threw us into the drunk tank, and booked us. The cop who was fingerprinting Tim said, "Didn't I see you on TV last night?"

"Yup."

"You were great, man."

"Thanks."

"Roll your finger like this. Gets the ink on good."

One of the cops, a short, white, mean-looking aggressive guy, appeared to hate "hippies" and threatened to cut Tim's hair. Carter intervened immediately. He boldly stepped between Tim and the cop and leaned down into the cop's face and hissed, "Ain't no way you're gonna cut his hair. You mess with him, you deal with me."

The cop's eyes flashed lightning. His white face flushed crimson. In 1967, in white society, and in racist Philadelphia, it was unheard of for a black man to argue with a white cop. It simply was not done. Carter was risking a major beating, and he knew it, but he cared more about Tim than he did for his own safety, and he didn't back off. The cop snarled like a pit bull and reached for his gun. A black police sergeant standing nearby saw rage and racist fire in the short cop's bloodshot eyes and stepped between them.

"Cool it, man," the sergeant said.

"How dare that son-of-a-bitch! Did you see what he did? I'll bust his fuckin' ass!"

"No, you won't! Gimme your gun."

"He can't talk to me like that!"

"I gave you an order!"

The short cop turned over his gun. The sergeant walked him into the next room, where an argument ensued, growing progressively louder. Finally the sergeant yelled, "Get outta here! Go on! Go home! Get gone!" The short cop left.

Carter was lucky. For that matter, we all were. To Carter's credit, not only in this instance but in others, he remained loyal to Tim throughout Tim's life, something I learned to value and respect. He was one of the few friends in Tim's life who actually walked the talk.

Two hours later, a local disc jockey showed up. Somebody had heard about our bust and called him, and he put the word out on the radio. Earlier, Herb had phoned a Philadelphia lawyer, who bailed us out, then the disc jockey arrived and drove us to the gig at the Trauma Club.

"Sorry for the delay, folks. We had a run-in with Philadelphia's Brotherly Love patrol."

"We arrived way late," Carter said, recalling that evening. "It was about 11 P.M., but the place was packed. Some people had been amazingly patient, waiting for us since eight o'clock; others had heard on the radio about the bust and our release, and came down to catch a set. There were candles on the tables, every seat was taken, and there was a full line waiting outside. We got a standing ovation just for walking in!

Lee, Tim, and Carter at the Troubadour in L.A., late 1967.

"Tim improvised a new song full of anger and humor telling everybody what had happened, and the people loved it. We played well, really getting into it, and Tim was brilliant, fiery, inspired. It was an incredible blend of tension from the bust and jail, and the release of it in performance, a night I will remember forever, one of our very best performances."

After the gig, the disc jockey drove us out to his home. Sitting in his living room under a spread-out red-and-white paneled parachute he had rigged up on the ceiling we smoked good pot, ate good food, and enjoyed good conversation. We slept well upstairs and made it back to the airport the next morning without a hitch.

Several months later, we returned to Philadelphia for the trial. The district attorney made his case: The police had searched the rooms legally, found two baggies of marijuana in Tim's room and two small whiskey bottles containing marijuana in Underwood and Collins's room, and arrested us. Here are the whiskey bottle containers, Exhibit A, marijuana still in them.

Our Philadelphia lawyer's turn. He spoke on Tim's behalf, all of which was a blur to me in my nervousness, and the case against Tim was thrown out.

He then leaned over to me. "Would you like to take the stand?"

"No."

I had seen too many movies.

Our lawyer stood up, addressed the judge. "Your Honor, although Exhibit A was found inside a shaving kit in the hotel room's bureau drawer, the district attorney has failed to establish ownership of that shaving kit. It could easily have been left by a previous guest, not by our clients. Because the district attorney failed to establish who owned the shaving kit and therefore who owned the marijuana, I ask you to dismiss this case."

"Case dismissed."

Wow!

Carter later said a club that was hostile to the Trauma had set up the bust to punish the Trauma's owners. That might have been so, especially in light of the fact that the cops said they had search warrants and were pounding at our doors only 20 or 30 minutes or so after we had retired—and it usually takes hours to obtain a warrant. However, the clerks behind the desk looked genuinely frightened of us, truly and honestly upset. In no way did they appear to be acting, playing a role in a preconceived drug bust. Nevertheless, according to Carter, the younger clerk testified that he had been bribed by the police and the Trauma's rival club—and that is why the judge threw out the case against Tim.

A couple of weeks after the arrest, I complained to Herb on the phone, "This would never have happened if you hadn't booked us into that hotel. It was a Methodist hotel, completely suppressive."

"It wouldn't have happened if you guys hadn't been carrying dope, schmuck."

"Bullshit. Grass is a part of our lives. It's part of who we are."

"I don't give a fuck. You shouldn't take it on the road."

"You should book us into hotels that won't hassle us."

"Wake up, dummy—it's not the hotels. It's the dope. Don't take it on the road, period."

Herb was right, of course. Nevertheless, needless to say—

We don't care
What poppa don't allow
We'll take it on the road
Anyhow!

THE BIG APPLE

About this time, the fall of 1967, events started swirling faster, like a kaleidoscope spinning out of control.

Herb lined us up for a one-nighter at Carnegie Hall on September 22. We were impressed with the name and the fame of the place, but the gig itself was not exclusively ours. I told my folks not to drive down from Connecticut, because this was just a hootenanny hosted by Pete Seeger, featuring several folk artists—Tim, Janis Ian, Len Chandler, and others. The folks came anyway. Status gig, Carnegie Hall, had to be there.

Pete Seeger, of course, was one of Tim's idols from high school days. Tim approached Pete backstage with love and respect in his eyes, held out his hand, said, "I've always admired you, Mr. Seeger." Pete hardly noticed, shook his hand, muttered thanks, passed on by. Almost a rebuff. Tim shook it off.

Other singers performed. By the time Tim and Carter and I took the stage, the crowd was restless, waiting for Pete to play. "Seeger, Seeger," they started chanting. Tim looked down at his guitar strings, tuned one, looked up and said, "I'm just a baby boomer tryna make it." The crowd chuckled, settled down, and listened well.

It is infinitely easier to play for strangers than it is for hometown friends, so when in October we took the stage in L.A. at the Troubadour for the first time, the adrenaline pumped. We felt the breathlessness that comes with excitement, anxiety, joyful anticipation, all-out dread. Our loved ones and greatest supporters, Jennifer and Jainie and Larry, were out there, along with dozens of friends and acquaintances from Venice, Hollywood, Anaheim, and elsewhere. Doug Weston watched from the balcony. Herb showed up with Elektra executives. Newcomer comedian Robert Klein opened the show with his silly jokes.

Then we played our asses off—and everybody loved us.

Herb booked us for one night at the Garrick Theater in Greenwich Village on November 13. It was a 300-seat auditorium and a fabulous setting for a small group such as ourselves. He insisted that Tim memorize "Goodbye and Hello," and that I take my 12-string—for just that one song. We performed the song in each of two sets—and never played it again. In addition to Tim, Carter, and myself, we brought in Ian Underwood (of the Mothers) on electric piano, organ, and clarinet; Bunk Gardner on saxes; and Billy Mundi on drums for the one night. (I seem to recall Jim Fielder's playing bass on that gig, but am not sure.)

Robert Shelton of *The New York Times* commented on Tim's voice, calling it "a high and sweet instrument that is not quite a counter-tenor, but certainly a tenor to counter with." He praised the group's improvisations as "quite remarkable in their passion and drive."

Speaking of "Goodbye and Hello," Shelton said, "It would take some study to discuss [Beckett's] lyrics, which alternate between found poetry and labored, pretentious reaches beyond his literary grasp." He went on to say, "But the feeling at this concert was that had Mr. Buckley been singing the New York Telephone Book, he still would have impressed his audience."

We played the Go Go again, this time on the bill with Canned Heat, a raucous blues band, lotta clichés and noise, little substance. During our breaks we split across the street to the Tin Angel.

On one of those nights, Tim left me in the Angel, said he'd send Carter over to get me when it was time to go back on. I sipped a beer, talked with people. After a while, it seemed like Canned Heat was playing an awfully long set, so I walked back over to the Go Go.

Tim and Carter were just finishing up. They had played without me! Back in the dressing room alone with Tim, I swore at him, "What the fuck are you doing?"

"I sent Carter over to get you. He said you weren't there."

"Not there? Of course I was there! How could you go on without me? What is this? You send a blind man over to look for me? And then play the set without me? You think I play this gig for the piddling piss-ant wages you're paying?"

Tim's eyes sparkled gleefully. He laughed, enjoying the turbulence.

"Well, I'm not, see? I play because of the music, asshole, not the money. Don't ever do that again, man. God *damn*, Timmy!"

Indeed, he never did it again, and I never missed a set on my own.

The three of us knew we sounded good together. And years later, quite unexpectedly, it was something of a heart-warmer when a woman named Sassy Suzy wrote about us on the Web. She was not a critic or record company exec, just a regular person, somebody who had heard us 30 years ago.

"Lee and Tim were a wonderful match musically," she said. "When Tim, Lee, and Carter CC Collins were a trio, it was amazing to me how complex and intense the music was. It always made me high. . . . There was something very special about the three of them together. I wish everyone could have heard them live. Tim did a 'high wire act' with them."

BACK IN L.A.

Jet planes roared, and before we knew it we were back in L.A. playing the Troubadour again, November 31–December 3. The girls loved us; the sensitive young men adored us. Tim crooned and sighed, bringing tears to their eyes.

Some journalists, regularly subjected to macho rantings from rock 'n' roll masters of rot-gut boogie, found Tim's stage presence refreshing. They raved about his "fragile vulnerability," his "delicate face that looks like it might cry any minute now in delirious love or fever." As did Phil Arkow, they often swooned over his "cries and shivers" and celebrated him as "this dangerously tender, hauntingly lonely, tensed-up and explosive sound dynamo."

Needless to say, not everybody raved. Larry Beckett, for example, put Tim down for his "weepy-eyed crucifixion complex." He said Tim didn't have to be a martyr to misery. Life could be a joy too. Larry appeared to feel extremely uncomfortable in the presence of emotional pain, perhaps because that kind of pain reduces the human intellect to impotence. Larry seemed to fear whatever his very bright mind could not understand or control. In later years, perhaps especially after Tim's demise, this created perceptual and interpretive problems. It seemed to me that Larry understood Tim well in high school and throughout the first two albums, but not very well after *Goodbye and Hello*. As things moved along and Tim journeyed through several changes, the gap seemed to widen.

Writer Malcolm Terence thoroughly appreciated the Troubadour performance and commented on how Tim's "perilous transitions into falsetto voice with breathtaking control, growled, screamed, placated."

However, Terence also agreed with Beckett, saying, "There's more to the world than unrequited love and alienation, although you wouldn't learn it from the bulk of Buckley's lyrics.

"They dote on the difficulty of love, the prettiness of rain, the dark spaces between people's minds and other stuff that seems a little irrelevant in an age when it's all right for music to be optimistic.

"At the end of the set we felt inescapably that Buckley had never been unhappy for two unbroken weeks in his whole life, and his music has become a kind of sad-eyed documentary, as a consequence. If he could shake this burden, in his songs and his psyche alike, his music overall would be as delightful as his remarkable pipes."

Without saying anything to me about it, Tim performed a solo version of "Song to the Siren" on a Monkees TV show.[1] Wearing his usual funky blue work shirt and brown cords, he sat on the fender of a wrecked blue car and crooned the song that eventually became the piece for which he is best known. Although "Song for the Siren" went out into the air on TV, it did not come out on record until *Starsailor*.

He later told British writer Tony Wilson, "I used to know Mike Nesmith before he became a Monkee, back when he used to write all his own music. He asked me

---

1. The final Monkees show, "Mijacogeo," Program Number 26 of the second series, aired in March 1968.

Amping up the intensity.

to sing on the show. Mike turned up in his mohair suit. I turned up in my work shirt and corduroy trousers.

"Mike said, 'Hey, I see you're still wearing the same old clothes.' I replied, 'Yes, and I'm still singing my own songs.'"

In mid-March, Tim, Carter, and I played the Riverboat, a folk club in Toronto, after which Tim and Carter went back to New York while I stayed and played a week-long gig with folk singer Tom Rush, a musical hero to me during my own early folk days.

While Tom's renditions of Jackson Browne's "These Days" and his own classic "No Regrets" were as captivating as I remembered them, I quickly realized that Tom was singing every song exactly as he had sung them years before, note for note. Absolutely nothing had changed, and although he was never a prolific writer, he had failed to come up with even one new song. With Tim, every moment was a thrilling moment-to-moment adventure in living music, nearly all of it improvised. Even if we performed the same songs, they were never sung or played the same way twice. To my dismay, Tom was only a smooth-talking cardboard frontman putting on a charming act that was as superficial and retrogressive as it was dead at the center.

However, Duke Bardwell, Tom's friend and bass player, was a reasonably intelligent guy with an easy-going sense of humor, so he and I hung out together.

On one of our afternoons off, Tom, Duke, and I attended a Gordon Lightfoot concert. Once again I was confronted with a performer who had stopped living and growing. Gordon sang all of his great songs in that wonderfully warm voice of his— but without out an iota of living vibrancy. If I had wanted to hear only reruns of the albums, I could have stayed home and played the records. With both Tom and Gordon, there was nobody home. I found that enormously upsetting. Why had these talented guys locked themselves in like that? What had happened? Running on empty? Business? Whatever it was, they had turned their backs on life itself. All we listeners were getting was product that had no more vital presence in it than a tombstone with faded names.

I abruptly got up to leave. Duke said, "What's happenin', man?" I said, "We're listening to a zombie. I'm splitting back to the Riverboat to play guitar." Duke said, "Me, too."

In the empty club (which didn't open until 7 p.m.), we dropped MDA (a marvelous stimulant similar in effect to Ecstasy), played Buffalo Springfield's recording of "Rock and Roll Woman" through the sound system over and over again, picked up our instruments, and wailed all afternoon.

Playing free like that and stretching out and soaring into the rock 'n' roll skies woke us up, cleansed our systems, set our hearts and minds free. It was an incredible release and relief from the oppressive, stultifying pseudo-musical context Tom Rush and Gordon Lightfoot offered. I had once loved those guys, but now it was time to move on.

I finished out the week at the Riverboat and returned to California and my beloved Jennifer.

PHILADELPHIA II—FRIENDS IN NEED AND DEED

When we returned to Philadelphia for the drug trial, we again played the Mainpoint coffeehouse in nearby Bryn Mawr, this time with vibraphonist David Friedman. Barry Schulze was with us, running the sound system. We had to play three sets.

After the second set, we decided to walk across the street for a beer. Outside, the line of customers waiting to get in for the third set extended to the end of the block. As Tim, Friedman, Bear and I crossed the street, we suddenly found ourselves surrounded by a pack of short-haired straight dudes. Hippie bashers out for a Saturday night kick-ass festival.

"Look at that son-of-a-bitch faggot," one of them sneered, pointing at Tim. We kept walking across the street. "I oughtta smash his face in."

The guy swung at Tim and hit him on the left cheekbone. I yelled and ran at the guy, kicking in blind fury. He danced away from the pack, leading me toward the pumps of a closed gas station. I didn't want to get separated too far from the group, so I ran back, kicking at a second guy moving in to hit Tim. We scooted as fast as we could toward the bar. Tim did not yell or swing his fists, or in any way try to defend himself.

None of the customers standing in line rushed to help. I looked for Bear. Where was our great defender, our personal gladiator, our much-needed body guard? To my astonishment, Tim's "pet giant" was shuffling as fast as he could for the tavern door without even looking back. So was Friedman. Fear shot through me.

Snarling and yelling, lashing out with fists and feet, I kept the bashers from grabbing Tim. He made it into the tavern. I covered his back. Before I ran inside, one of the guys broke a bottle and threw the jagged neck at me. It gleamed red in neon light. I averted my head a fraction of an inch. Glass gashed the side of my face, just above the right eye. Blood streamed down into my beard.

We played the third set anyway.

LOUIE'S BAR

The reviews of *Goodbye and Hello* were fabulous across the board. Crowds flocked to the gigs. Stages, bar rooms, the night and neon lights swirled.

Between performances, during the day, we remained in John King's basement apartment on King Street, played music, smoked pot, avoided the outdoors, and the public and their weird straight trips. When people live lives based on fear, greed, and ruthless ambition, their faces don't look right, especially if you don't live the same way and you're whacked on good grass.

At night, we hung out in the Village at Louie's bar downstairs next to the Tin Angel, an authentic old-school New York joint with sawdust on the floor and a good jukebox.

One night Tim and Linda Eastman (McCartney), Bob Campbell, Bear, John King, my friend Mary from the Night Owl, and I were drinking at Louie's. John lined up his gin and tonics. We lined up our beers. Music and laughter filled the air.

At one point, a Beatles' tune was playing—"Yellow Submarine," maybe "Eleanor Rigby." I commented on how the Beatles sounded stiff, like a marching band on Veterans Day. Tim laughed and remembered it.

The night spun on. Slouched in his chair, Tim casually leaned over to one side, puked into the sawdust, wiped his mouth on his sleeve, kept talking. Mary and I staggered out, tried to make it to her apartment. To my astonishment, I found myself falling to the sidewalk, couldn't stop. Mary had to help me up. That was the first time anything like that had happened to me.

Months later, Tim told me Linda Eastman had been trying to "get him" ever since she photographed him at the zoo not far from the Albert Hotel. He boasted that Linda gave him the clap that night after Louie's. Linda, however, said otherwise. She said she had bundled him into a cab and taken him to her place. He told her, "Get out. I'll pay." As soon as she got out, he ordered the driver to move on, leaving her standing in the street.

EUROPE '68

Suddenly it was April 1968, and Tim, Carter, and I were in London, opening for the Incredible String Band at the Royal Festival Hall, trying to reach a huge crowd of emotionally repressed English teenagers who didn't quite know what to do with us— applaud, pray, cry, or laugh. They sort of sat there, stunned. When the Incredible String Band brought them back up to the surface of their psyches, they relaxed.

Although critics praised our performance in the papers the next day, we didn't feel fulfilled by it, so we accepted an invitation the same night right after the concert to play at Jim Haynes' personal art studio, a small private hall on Drury Lane (called the Speakeasy, if I recall correctly). Word spread fast. The place was packed with eighty or so devoted fans who knew how to drop their mannered veneer, how to listen and appreciate and applaud with enthusiasm. Tim, Carter, and I felt freed from the comparatively reserved inspection we had received at Festival Hall. For no money, simply for the sheer music of it, we played one of our best sets.

At the Middle Earth, a cavernous downstairs London rock club with brick walls and eerie Day-Glo light, we went on after a couple of blaring blues bands. The crowd was stoned-out on ludes and smack. Nobody was interested in Tim's fragile, forlorn personage or his sweet melodic vocal trip or his increasingly impassioned hollerings. In total frustration, Tim stopped playing in the middle of a song and walked off. We packed up and left.

Back at the hotel, Tim launched into a towering drunken rage. "Those mutha-fuckin' emasculated Limey bastards," he ranted. "Are they alive or dead? Can't feel a fuckin' thing. No heart, no feelings, no brains, no music inside their rotten hearts. Limey zombies, hard as stone. Love me! Hate me! Something! Anything! At least react!"

He snatched a lamp off the bed stand, smashed it through the window. It fell down the well-shaft 12 floors, crashed on cement. People gawked out of their windows. "Hey, shut up! We're tryna sleep!" Somebody knocked on the door. I handed the security guard $20, told him everything was under control, only a mishap.

One day, I said to Tim, "Come on, let's get out of the room, maybe go visit the Tate."
"What's that?"

"A world-famous art gallery—Monet, Cézanne, William Blake, William Turner, Dali, Van Gogh—beautiful stuff, man. It'll lift our spirits."

"No," he said. "I'll stay here." He rolled one of his gigantic king-sized joints, lit it, took a toke.

"Come on," I said. "This is a great opportunity. Let's get out of this hole and put something in our skulls that'll give us a little strength."

"Don't mock the afflicted," he smiled, offering me a toke.

"Fuck it, man. Marijuana leads to harder stuff—like ice cream and chocolate cookies. I'll go myself."

I hopped on the top level of one of those incredible double-tiered London busses and rode in the front seat to the Tate Gallery, where I spent the afternoon surrounded by magic, color, beauty, genius.

A couple of days later, we played a few tunes on John Peel's *Top Gear* radio show (released on *Morning Glory,* a posthumous CD, later re-titled *Once I Was*), and got modestly tiddily in the BBC canteen with a garrulous drunken screen actor, Richard Harris, who was buying drinks for everybody, pompously boasting about how brilliant he was. I bought my own beer.

On the other side of the Channel, in Amsterdam, we ate lunch at a very fancy, very white, very proper, *vedddy* respectable upper class establishment called Le Grande Hotel. Outside—sprawling green lawns, circular driveway, valet parking, red and yellow flowers, a wide red roof, white wrought-iron latticework on the balconies, poodle dogs, diamond collars. Inside—high ceilings, crystal chandeliers, white tablecloths, sparkling glasses, silver utensils, long-stem roses, crystal vases. In the center of the room, a great fountain, green ferns, white lilies, a gorgeous waterfall tumbling into a porcelain tiled pool.

As we ate lunch, Carter felt uneasy. He looked out the side of his eyes. European patrons stared at him, unsettled by his presence. Stodgy gentlemen in white suits raised eyebrows. Old ladies wearing diamond necklaces and gold-plated eyeglasses with neck chains frowned, sniffed indignantly, looked away.

Abruptly, Carter picked up his soup bowl, raised it to his lips, slurped the soup loudly. He slurped again, even louder. Elderly grand dame ladies in pink chiffon dresses and wide-brimmed hats stared aghast in open disapproval.

Carter stood up, knocking his chair over backwards, fiercely grabbed his bowl and plate, strode over to the cascading fountain—and started brazenly washing his dishes in the pool! Everybody in the room gawked at him, shocked.

"Figure a black sum-bitch like me, straight off the plantation, should be out in the kitchen moppin' floors and washin' dishes, haaaaaaghh? Upset that a colored lackey like me is in here sippin' soup with you aristo-fuckin'-cratic fat cats, haaagggh?" He scrubbed his dishes hard and fast, loudly addressing everybody in the room. "Wanna hear me say, 'Yaw-zuh, massa? Lemme shine yo' shoes an' peel yo' potatoes, massa?' Haaaaagggh?"

"Jesus, Timmy, tell him to stop," I muttered, embarrassed.

"Why should I?" Tim said. He motioned his hand contemptuously at the upper-class crowd—"I don't need *their* good opinions."

Carter raised his plate and soup bowl high—and let them drop into the fountain's pool. "Too bad there ain't no slave ships bound for America these days, haaaaagh?" He strode back over to our table, threw down a $20 bill, sneered at the whole crowd, "Sy-ya-fuckin'-ara, whitey! Outta here!"

In the car, slapping high-fives, Tim and Carter laughed uproariously. "Am I low-class?" Carter beamed. "Am I one muthafuckin' low-class sum-bitch? No class! No class at all!" They howled with laughter.

I had mixed feelings about it. Couldn't join them. Later, however, I realized Carter was absolutely right in what he did, and Tim was absolutely right in his response to it. It took me a while to understand, but finally I got it, and felt liberated from another middle-class blind spot.

In Amsterdam and Copenhagen we played clubs, radio, a TV show—at which time everything blurred out for me. Somewhere in there, I got lost in my own mind.[2] When we returned to the States, Buckley sent me home, not in anger, but with compassion and understanding. He knew I needed to return to Venice and Jennifer and the merciful ocean. I needed a break.

STRANGER IN A STRANGE LAND

Success was profoundly difficult for me, and for Tim, too, although during these early days he handled it better than I. In New York and other places, I felt completely out of my element. More accurately, I never had an element to begin with. No inner source of strength and equilibrium. A deep sense of inadequacy, sometimes of outright fear when confronted with anything new. And on the road, everything and everybody was new every single day.

It seemed that the people we met belonged wherever we were. It was their territory, their home, their context. I felt like an outsider, a stranger. I could not and did not feel connected. When attention focused on me, I cringed. When it focused on Tim but excluded me, I felt invisible, isolated, starved. I desperately needed understanding and loving human contact, but didn't know how to get it, receive it, or deal with it. He got it just by being there. Charisma.

---

2. In addition to the gigs in London already mentioned, we taped a BBC-TV show, called "Late Night Line Up." In Copenhagen, we played either a nightclub or a concert or both, while in Amsterdam we performed a televised show at the Fantasio Club.

When I talked with Bob Campbell about this, he said, "It isn't only you who's out of his element. Everybody is. That's what the whole scene is about. The Village and all these other places are nonconformist clubs. You're out of your element, but so are they. That's the key thing to remember. Everybody feels the same way. A friend of mine once said, 'You know all those people in the Village we think are crazy? We're right: They are.'"

Tim tried to help too. "Nothing is ever like you imagine it will be," he once said. "Stay open to whatever happens. Don't criticize it for not fitting your preconceptions. Accept, enjoy." On another occasion, "You gotta develop style, Lee." I didn't know if he meant clothes or thoughts or conduct. What the hell does "style" mean?

Nothing helped. Smoking and drinking only made things worse, of course. I needed out.

As I always did when returning from road trips, I dropped my suitcase and guitar on the living room floor without unpacking, and immediately jogged down to the ocean and plunged in. Profound relief.

God bless Venice, God bless these ancient sands, these healing waters. Cleanse me, ocean mine, O cleanse my heart, cleanse my soul, wash my body, renew my mind. Please, O please—give me birth and new life once again.

HAPPY SAD: 1968-1969

CHAPTER 7

TIMES THEY ARE A-CHANGIN':
THE SOUNDS OF JAZZ

SOCIAL UPHEAVAL: PICK YOUR OWN RIOT

By 1968 and 1969, and on virtually every front, the Western world in general and America in particular writhed in the throes of upheaval.

John Birch Society–type right-wing fascists in the Nixon administration and in society at large stridently insisted that the war in Vietnam was just like World War II: A "they," whom nobody knew, were "bad guys"; we were "good guys," and America's fighting youth should volunteer to kill or be killed.

Those who resisted and protested the war were draft-dodging, Commie, faggot, pinko, hippie sons-of-bitches who oughtta be jailed, hung, electrocuted—or shot dead on college campuses (like Kent State). Coast to coast, young men burned their draft cards and refused to serve. Muhammad Ali said he didn't have anything against the Viet Cong and refused to be drafted. Needless to say, All-American white middle-class John Wayne Nixonites stripped Ali of his title and banned him from fighting for three years at the height of his boxing prime.

Increasing numbers of intelligent, insightful, avant-garde men and women marched in protest of the war, shouting what former Defense Secretary Robert S. McNamara later confessed: The war was stupid, unjust and unwinnable, a political hoax and big-business rip-off scam that never should have been waged in the first place. Ironically, the protesters who were damned by right-wing killerboys in the sixties and early seventies were vindicated by the right wing's own spokesman—but not until 1995, much too late to save thousands of people who were maimed or killed.

Under leadership by Martin Luther King Jr. and Malcolm X, American blacks marched in city streets across the nation, protesting Whitey's slave-master plantation mentality, refusing to ride in the back of anybody's bus or cater to any man, white, black, yellow, or otherwise. King, Malcolm, and Bob Kennedy were murdered along the way, of course, which added fuel to the conflagration and helped accelerate the process.

Women everywhere rose up against further enslavement by male chauvinist pigs, burned their bras in symbolic protest, attended group meetings, struggled to identify their complaints and needs, began emerging from the darkness of unconsciousness into the light of freedom, self-respect, and gender equality—in bed, in business, and in the courtroom.

Freedom's energies were thrusting off psychological and socio-political chains that had imprisoned millions of people for centuries. Racial equality, gender equality, homosexual equality, religious freedom, sexual freedom—on every level, "freedom" was the watchword.

These and related social issues affected Tim and the people who listened to him. As society was moving forward, so was Tim. By the time he entered the *Happy Sad* period, 1968–69, he was personally pulling away from prior ways of perceiving, thinking, and feeling, and forging new, independent, self-reliant creative paths that would eventually lead him well beyond the mainstream.

ON THE OTHER SIDE OF THE REVOLUTION

Disenfranchised from the "antique" Roosevelt/Eisenhower politics their parents embraced, and liberated from the simple-minded mythological dogma of orthodox authoritarian religions, sixties youth for a while found itself with an open window. It was a great opportunity for psychological and social transformation on a large scale, perhaps permanently. They had freed themselves from the shackles of the old, but had no new direction to follow, which was good. If they could remain in the transitional state, open and receptive, they had a chance to create a new human psyche and a new world. Unfortunately, freedom is enormously difficult to bear, almost impossible. The Sixties generation had energy, but no focus or direction. As a result, many young people wanted and needed leadership.

They tended to set musicians up as pop saviors and "easy gods," which always bugged Buckley. Be our gurus and leaders, they seemed to cry, venerating Bob Dylan, Phil Ochs, Joan Baez, Arlo Guthrie, Judy Collins, the Jefferson Airplane, Country Joe and the Fish, and dozens of others. And some of those artists tended to fall into that role all too easily.

Fueled by ancient time-honored multi-cultural religious practices of Tantric ecstasy, hallucinogens, and trance music—Sex, Drugs, and Rock 'n' Roll—modern youth boogied its way to spiritual connection with the All, seizing on rock and folk musicians to give them insight, guidance, and focused momentum. As far as Buckley was concerned, growing spiritual awareness was great, but the choice of "leaders" left much to be desired. He neither wanted to lead, nor to follow. He was his own man, and did not want to use or be used by anybody else. He felt it was important to keep the "freedom window" open. So did I.

After listening to *Goodbye and Hello*, writer Mike Jahn enthusiastically proclaimed, "Tim Buckley is the chief propagandist for the New Children. . . . His words stir hope for a world of love without exploitation, beauty without plasticity, passion without destruction."

But Buckley wanted no part of political propaganda, especially by the time *Happy Sad* was in the works. He told writer Paul Eberle, for example, "As far as business and politics goes, the whole procedure is very obsolete and nobody knows what direction they should take it in. The first direction, I guess, is to take America away from being a business and put it in the hands of the people.

"All those left-wing people and all those Birchers are in a business, and I think that's what's got to end, because the society can't go down without having a styled art. In music and everything else, the only creative form we ever had is chaos. The cats who

Naked honesty, a cry from the heart. Central Park, 1969.

are really involved in music don't give two diddly fucks about what people think, or whether they're changing anything. . . . It's worthless the way it is now, and I'm waiting for it to change. But if it doesn't change, I'll still always be the way I am. . . ."

Originally, Buckley had been anti-war and pro-flowerpower. By this time, he was pulling away from both, asserting his personal independence and artistic autonomy. When writer Nadine Drake asked, "What about the Love Generation?" Buckley replied, "I'm not a hippie and the word 'love' when used in connection with the 'love generation' annoys me. There are two types of killing going on today. One is killing with weapons and the other is with love.

". . . I am not a revolutionary like Phil Ochs and others in the field. I am not a leader. I don't want to be anybody's leader. I don't want the responsibility of being some pop godhead. In a way, I don't want to make it big. Sometimes when you get to the top you become complacent, content and lazy. I don't need that. I just want to be *there* onstage, and do my thing."

Politics isn't even the real problem, he said to writer Anne Marie Micklo in New York: "When people start doing politics in music, like Baez or anybody—rock 'n' roll especially does that a lot—I can't make it. I can't listen to it, 'cause it's such bullshit hype. . . . It's not even talking about the real problem, which is between man and woman. That's what I think is the real problem. Anybody who ever wrote anything great was relating to that first."

Tim treasured his independence above all. "I really wish people would try to live their own lives and stop trying to make musicians do it for them," he told writer Michael Williams. "There's a lot more to music than sex. I play heart music."

ROCK AS BUSINESS MUSIC

Right from the beginning with Buckley, the music industry's business categories never fit. Buckley was unique. He played "Buckley music," but because he strummed a 12-string acoustic guitar, he had to put up with the label "folk artist," a misnomer that never left him. "I was never a folkie," he told journalist Michael Davis. "I always dug African rhythms."

Then writers added the equally inadequate misnomers "folk-rock" and "rock musician." By the time *Happy Sad* rolled around, Buckley was leaving rock well behind, moving into jazz-oriented concepts, surging forward into new lyrical and musical zones both as a listener and as a creator, and nobody knew what to call it.

Then (as now), recording industry labels created effective marketing categories, which in turn created musical barriers. There was folk, rock, jazz, country, R&B, pop, classical. Each excluded the others. Buckley was one of the forerunners of a new sense of musical universality. He refused to be caged within categorical walls. He began fusing influences together and developing new concepts. Old labels did not fit anymore. This was an important element of his creative evolution.

"People don't hear anything," he told Williams. "That's why rock 'n' roll was invented, to pound it in. My new *Happy Sad* songs aren't *dazzling*. It's not two minutes and fifty seconds of rock 'em, sock 'em, say lots of words, get lots of images. I guess it's pretty demanding. . . ."

"I had Carter Collins on conga drums and Lee Underwood on guitar," he told Davis, "and we played rock concerts for years, until it got ridiculous to go on after people who plugged into Grand Cooley Dam. Go out behind Pink Floyd or Blue Cheer and you sound like a fart after a hailstorm.

"Blue Cheer, they were the ones—they hold the record for dropping more beats than anybody else, and no one could tell, because it was so loud—just pure noise, pure energy. They were great [chuckles]."

"I like Hendrix," Tim once told me. "He's taking guitar music to new levels. At the same time, he starts out at full volume and tries to go somewhere from there. Where can he go? No place. So he burns his guitar at the end, and everybody says it's logical, it's the only thing left. I don't think so. As far as I'm concerned, destroying his guitar is a kind of sin. If he stopped depending on volume so much and started working on subtlety, he wouldn't have to do that, and we'd all be better off for it."

"Most rock musicians are businessmen," he told Williams. "The focus is more on clothes than music—you change your clothes every day, ride around in limos and airplanes, and never see the ground. . . . And [the recording industry] wants to control you. They don't want you to be yourself because then they can't say, 'Look, now he's gonna do this. Watch him do that.' Dangle, dangle."

"These white middle-class assholes talk about vibrations," he told Micklo, "but they don't really feel anything. All they see is velvet pants and long blond hair—a perfect person with spangles and flowered shirts. And that's vibrations to them.

"But what the rock guy's playing, they don't know. Well, I can tell, man, I can tell. That's three weeks of learning Clapton licks. That's all it is."

"I believe more in Buckminster Fuller than I do in rock," he told interviewer Sam Bradley.

And it seems eerie in hindsight to read Tim's concluding words to Williams, as if he had a premonition about *Lorca* and *Starsailor*, which came later, and public reactions to them: "I can see where I'm really headed, and it will probably get farther and farther from what people expect of me.

"My old lady [Jainie] was telling me what she was studying in school: Plato, Sophocles, Socrates, and all those people. And the cat, Socrates, starts spewing truth like anybody would, because you gotta be honest. And the people kill him. Ha! I don't know if I'm being pretentious, but I can see what happens. It happened to Bob Dylan. . . . I don't know what to do about that."

During this period, one of the few to get it right regarding Tim was writer Jane Ferguson, who said, "I've decided to stop trying to classify and just listen."

"I'M NOT A POET"

In addition to politics and various forms of pop music, Buckley was also pulling away from the notion of poetry in music—a major change in the overall scope of his evolving creative perspective. It was during this period that Buckley and Larry Beckett separated as a songwriting team.

Tim had enormous respect for his old friend, and included him on all but three albums—*Happy Sad*, *Lorca*, and *Blue Afternoon*. "When I was writing with Beckett," he told Micklo, "I had a lot of good ideas, but I couldn't get the words out. So he would finish them, 'cause he's Mr. Word, you know." "I'm not the giant of the lyric that Beckett is," he told Davis. "I think he's extraordinary."

But to writer Tony Wilson, he said, "Poetry is poetry and songs are songs. I know poets who write things I could never write." And in the oft-quoted remark to writer Michael Williams, Buckley said, "A song is a song, not a poem. I write songs. If people want poems, they should read Dylan Thomas."

Along with formal considerations, content and compatibility were important matters too. Larry Beckett was locked into formal poetry and interested in social protest, while Tim had moved away from both. The days of *Goodbye and Hello* were gone—"I really like listening to the music [of the song 'Goodbye and Hello']," Tim told Micklo, "but I hate the lyrics—I just hate the motherfucker. It's like, 'Okay, you motherfuckers, you want a protest song'—the record company was bugging the hell out of me, so I figured, just this once, man, but I'll never have to do it again."

"By the time of *Happy Sad*, we were writing differently," Buckley told Davis. "When you can't write together, you're usually good enough to know when you can't. What I was doing on *Happy Sad* was a lot more musical. . . .

"At that time, I believed, and I still believe, that things cannot be changed in the world by hammering into peoples' minds that some things are good and some things are bad. . . . You can't pound in a point of view or a lifestyle. You can't do it that way. . . . It doesn't affect anybody. You can't do it directly. It has to be done by example.

"So I do songs on one-to-one relationships, and how you deal with your lifestyle, or how I deal with mine. That's the thing that is truly a movable force, because you're talkin' about rudimentary things, the things we all live on.

"I don't regret doing the political trip with Beckett. I just regret that the American people haven't been told anything. Not that it would help me and my career at all, but that was part of the purpose at the time, to tell people about things. That's what we were writing about."

BYE-BYE BECKETT

Even years afterward, Beckett apparently did not understand why Buckley dropped him:

"He decided to write everything on his own," Beckett told writer Scott Isler in 1991. "My feeling was—and this is just my stupid opinion—that he was afraid that the success of *Goodbye and Hello* was due to my lyrics. See where he's coming from? He respects me and tends to believe the worst about himself."

Unquestionably, the lyrics to the album's title track, "Goodbye and Hello," constituted some of the better poetry of that generation. And as literary, essayistic words, they were intellectually engaging, even brilliant at times. But as materials for a song, Buckley felt they were cumbersome and pretentious, rooted in English Lit 101 and emotionally a far cry from the intimate, heart-felt music-words that Buckley could write. Beckett's cerebrally titillating efforts had all the elegance of an equation in mathematical physics, and they undoubtedly impressed thoughtful adolescent whiz kids, but remained forever lost in the dustbins of so-called "art songs" made fashionable by Judy Collins and others of her day. Nat Hentoff, one of America's sterling music journalists, put the matter succinctly: "In many places, the lyrics [to 'Goodbye and Hello'] confuse rhetoric with feeling."

Beckett himself wrote to me in June 1977, denouncing his own writing. "As for 'Goodbye and Hello,' like all but one of my old lyrics, it isn't worth a first reading." He didn't stop there. He went on to say, "If I could, I'd burn them, all but one, as I have my poetry of those years. I'm embarrassed to have my name attached to them."

Contrary to Beckett's covert assessment in the Isler quote about Tim, it is entirely possible that it was Beckett's writing, not Tim's, that held *Goodbye and Hello* back from *greater* success on the charts. It could also be argued that whatever success that album did enjoy was due, not to Beckett's lyrics, but to Tim's—in such magnificent songs as "I Never Asked to Be Your Mountain," "Once I Was," "Pleasant Street," and "Phantasmagoria in Two."

Buckley explained the break to writer Bill Henderson: "Well, you know as well as I do that, first of all, [Larry] is a poet, and he's doing that first and foremost, and a lot of the things we had written together weren't even close to being acceptable by the public . . . too complicated, too involved, too much story. . . . [I wanted] to keep it as artistic as possible, but more geared to getting across to people. So for a long time, old Larry and I couldn't . . . we saw eye to eye, but together we couldn't write the things that were right to be written then."

"You see, I'm more of a musician than anything else," he told writer Ted Scourtis. "I'm much more musically oriented than lyrically. . . . I started writing songs, not because I thought that they were important, but because there was something I thought was being left unsaid, or that wasn't being said right, or said the way I wanted to hear it."

In a letter to me dated May 4, 1977, Larry put his finger on some of the ways in which he, the cerebrally detached physicist, and Tim, the musician, had complemented each other so well. "I divided myself into mind and heart, I believed in my mind, and while I was scared of my heart, I was fascinated by it. . . . We worked together for a few years, the singer and I, symbols to each other of passion and reason: In the face of each other, we couldn't be complacent, be ourselves. We instinctively knew what Goethe taught, 'Take into yourself that which is opposed to you'. . . . We grew towards each other, our polarities kept us apart—but across the distance we stretched a song."

During the emergent *Happy Sad* period, those complementary unities became exclusive opposites for Tim. Buckley wanted the head to serve the heart, not vice versa, and therefore he needed to fly with his own wings.

There was another very important element involved in this crucial shift of perspective in Tim's life: Memorizing somebody else's words was not the same as singing lyrics that bubbled up organically from within.

"It's like, you live with a song," Tim told Micklo. "I can't explain what goes down. . . . You can't move without the whole feeling inside of you, or else you're just writing things you don't mean."

THE WORST—OR THE BEST?

Early on, as an innocent eighteen-year-old college dropout, Tim may indeed have been modestly intimidated by Larry's linguistic expertise. Beckett's suggestion that Tim chose to reject Larry and write his own lyrics in order to top Larry and prove himself, seems to me a bit of a distortion, especially in light of Buckley's evolutionary temperament. If he truly believed "the worst" about himself, would he have had confidence enough to grow? Unlikely.

Buckley neither accepted nor rejected people because of weakness or self-contempt —the "worst" in himself—but because of strength and self-confidence. As we saw earlier, far from being intimidated by other people's finer qualities, Tim *surrounded* himself with brilliant and often well-educated individuals every step of the way, precisely so he could gather information that would help him actualize his enormous talent. He did not have to prove himself *against* their talents and accomplishments, nor did he give himself up to them and withdraw. He enlisted them as mentors and catalysts for his own evolutionary development. That is very different from what Beckett perhaps self-servingly suggested to Isler. *Of course* Buckley had confidence enough in himself to write his own lyrics—and that is exactly what he did.

Larry Beckett tended to resemble Descartes—"I think, therefore I am"—whereas Buckley was a true musician—"I am, therefore I love." The rift had nothing to do with "believing the worst about himself." Buckley had outgrown Larry and left Larry's intellectual posturings and divisive politics behind, that's all. In their place, he embraced the heart-connection.

New York Times writer Mike Jahn, in his review of our Philharmonic Hall concert, pointed out that on *Goodbye and Hello* and in previous New York performances Tim had "spent too much time trying to be a sensitive, alienated poet and not enough time exercising his voice." On *Happy Sad* and in the Philharmonic performance, however, Buckley "left poetic sensitivity behind and just sang his head off." Jahn thought that was terrific. So did I.

As for "success," well, *Tim Buckley* never made the charts and *Goodbye and Hello* peaked at No. 171, fading in five weeks, while *Happy Sad* became Buckley's biggest hit. It reached No. 81 and stayed on the charts for three months. Undoubtedly, some of the initial sales were carryovers from *Goodbye and Hello*. But the album's long-term success was all Buckley.

In a Buckley Album Poll taken online by Jack Brolly on October 4, 1999, *Goodbye and Hello* placed fourth and *Tim Buckley* placed tenth, while *Happy Sad* placed *first*.

So much for whose lyrics did what.

It is to Larry's credit that he eventually altered the view he had held for decades. In 2000, he told writer Ben Edmonds, "For years I wondered if [Tim decided to write his own lyrics exclusively] because he attributed the success of *Goodbye and Hello* to my lyrics and wanted to see if he could do it all on his own. Tim genuinely cared so little for acclaim, though, that I no longer think this theory holds water. I can see how he might have felt that my more literary approach was not gonna work with the jazzy, melancholic feeling he was going for, where his voice was another instrument."

THE SOUNDS OF JAZZ

Tim shifted gears all the way, not only lyrically, but musically too. He moved out of folk and rock styles, into jazz. The sounds of jazz were not new to him. His mother had enjoyed instrumentalists and vocalists of the forties and fifties, notably Stan Kenton, early Miles Davis, Nat King Cole, and Johnny Mathis. And in various forms, jazz had been the pop music of several previous generations—the twenties, the Depression era, World War II, the Beats—and all of it remains in our cultural atmosphere to this day.

In another sense, in terms of fundamental psychological and improvisational *principles*, jazz knows no time or place. It remains undated and ageless. Styles change with changing times, obviously, but in principle the genre remains a music of the moment, spontaneous, improvised, free, forever growing and developing and renewing itself from generation to generation.

There were dozens of first-rate popular musicians in the sixties, and Tim liked many of them—notably the great singer/songwriter Fred Neil, folk singer Richie Havens, the inimitable Ray Charles, and guitarists Hendrix and Clapton. He felt that these and certain others sang and played from the heart. They had depth, they were *believable*, and they moved him.

However, much of sixties and early seventies pop music sounded rhythmically stiff. Much of it was rooted in ripped-off blues clichés. It had the vitality of a new generation's sparkling optimism and youthful passion, and a heck of a lot of noise and enthusiasm, but not much improvisational daring, technical skill, and emotional depth. Tim once walked out of a Doors concert, utterly disgusted with the way in which Jim Morrison "confused drunkenness with entertainment." On another occasion, he spat and called Neil Young a "whiner."

Perhaps remembering one of our own drunken nights in New York, not onstage—we didn't do that—but in Louie's bar, Tim embellished one of my remarks when telling a writer, "The hard thing about writing within a rock and roll beat is that it's difficult to write a good chord pattern. . . . It's so rigid, it's like a march. I think Beatles songs are really great for playing at half-time during football games. They wrote a lot of great marching songs."

Jazz wasn't stiff, it swung, and it was fun. At Big Pink in Venice one day in early 1968, Tim said, "Let's shift the tides, ol' buddy. Play me some music."

He wanted new musical substance and new information. I did what I could to provide that. During the course of the next year or so, we spent hours listening to certain artists in particular, including:

Miles Davis—*Kind of Blue, Sketches of Spain*, and *Porgy and Bess*.

Bill Evans—*Nirvana, Town Hall, Trio with Symphony Orchestra*, and *Intermodulation* and *Undercurrent* (both with guitarist Jim Hall).

Jimmy Giuffre—*The Jimmy Giuffre 3* (particularly Tim's favorite track, "The Train and the River").

Gabor Szabo—*Sorcerer, Spellbinder, Bacchanal*. (This haunting, lyrical Hungarian

On the wings of jazz—Lee, Tim, and David Friedman performing in Europe.

guitarist was one of my major influences. For Tim, the atmospheric ambience Gabor cast became quite influential.)

Roland Kirk—the phenomenal multiple-horn player (particularly the title track of *Volunteered Slavery*).

Among dozens of others, we also listened to baritone saxophonist Gerry Mulligan, the Modern Jazz Quartet, and more of MJQ vibraphonist Milt Jackson in a variety of settings. At a later time, approaching *Lorca*, we moved into complex, demanding forms of avant-garde jazz.

Tim was deeply moved by these fresh sounds, styles, approaches. They touched his heart and stimulated his mind. *Happy Sad*, a mellow jazz-flavored album, emerged from this context. It warmed my heart when, just as we were setting up in the recording studio, Tim said, "Play all of your influences, Lee. This is your album."

Two posthumous CDs emerged from this same period: *Works in Progress* (our first *Happy Sad* efforts), recorded in March and June of '68; and *Dream Letter: Live in London*, a well-performed presentation of the *Happy Sad* period, recorded in October, 1968.[1]

1. I owe an apology to journalists and other listeners regarding the date of *Dream Letter*. In my liner notes to that double CD, I stated it was recorded live in Queen Elizabeth Hall on July 10, 1968, during our first visit to London. I was mistaken. The date written on the tapes I was given read 7/10/68, which to me, an American, meant July 10, 1968. I went with that July date, and thus misinformed all who noted it. The date on the tapes was undoubtedly written by the English recording engineer, and meant, of course, the 7th of October. In short, *Dream Letter* was recorded live in Queen Elizabeth Hall on October 7, 1968, during our second European tour. *Happy Sad* was released in the spring of 1969.

Inspired by the sounds of jazz, Tim hired vibraphonist David Friedman and acoustic bassist Johnny "Bongo" Miller, both well-schooled musicians with a great love of improvisational music.

Friedman was one of the more interesting musicians Tim worked with. Fresh out of Juilliard, a proud, intelligent young man with black hair and black eyes, a master vibraphonist as lion-like in his presence as he was subtle and original in his playing, David joined Buckley on short notice. Tim called him the evening before opening for the Byrds at Fillmore East. The next day, they rehearsed 16 tunes for seven hours, with no written music—and went onstage that night and played.

David remained with Tim for more than a year, touring Europe and recording on *Happy Sad* and *Blue Afternoon* (also appearing on the posthumous *Works in Progress* and *Dream Letter: Live in London* CDs).

Along with John Miller's acoustic bass work, it was perhaps especially Friedman and his vibes during this period that gave Tim's music its distinctive jazz flavor. It was Friedman who playfully dubbed Tim's group at this time, "The Modern Jazz Quartet of Folk."

Happy Sad was a good album, with several engaging stories about its realization.

One day, Tim walked in and heard Friedman and Miller playing a piece he was already familiar with—Miles Davis's "All Blues," from *Kind of Blue*. He played along with them, and out of that impromptu session was born "Strange Feelin'."

One night in New York, Tim and I dropped Owsley acid, zipped back to the Albert Hotel (rushing on LSD as the elevator ascended), and spent the night writing "Buzzin' Fly," one of Tim's best-loved *Happy Sad* songs. He strummed and sang. I played guitar. The walls and curtains breathed. Glistening orange velvet lining in open guitar cases undulated like red-orange seawaves. (Elsewhere, Beckett has said this was an old song carried over from earlier days. Not so. A line or two may have been carried over, but the total song was born that night in the Albert.)

Germinated in the "lost" *Works in Progress* sessions, gestated in the *Dream Letter* stage, and restructured and re-recorded on *Happy Sad*, "Love from Room 109 at the Islander (On Pacific Coast Highway)" became one of Tim's most accomplished compositions—five sections, multiple tempos, beautifully flowing lyrics, extraordinary intimacy.

I should note that Manda Beckett has said some of the lyrics on "109" were extrapolated from letters she had written to Tim. . . . And those gently sighing seawaves are real, not electronic.

Tim and Jainie had moved to a beautiful house at 19550 Pacific Coast Highway overlooking the ocean in Malibu. In the recording studio, when engineer Bruce Botnick blew the "109" take by failing to turn on the Dolby sound processor—thus leaving all kinds of hiss on the tape—producer Jerry Yester suggested they drive out and record the sea under Tim's front porch. That would cover up the hiss and create a nice ambience. They did that, and it worked.

Tim said he recorded "109" in the Islander Motel on the Pacific Coast Highway; he simply hooked up a little tape recorder in the morning, just when he woke up, and the waves came in right under the room. Well, yes, but according to writer Bob Niemi, the Islander was in the commercial district of Seal Beach, not on the ocean. And Tim recorded the song in Hollywood. Personally, I like Buckley's vision better than the truth. It has more truth in it.

Lee and Tim—friends and musical comrades tuning guitars, regrouping between songs.

"Dream Letter," one of Tim's most intimately touching songs, gently and loving-ly celebrates his son, Jeffrey Scott. His voice aches with care and concern and heart-touching emotion for both his son and himself. Is his little Jeff a man of action or is he an artist? Does he help his mother with work? And, most poignantly, does he ever ask about the vagabond father who misses him?

During this period of Tim's career, I had been inventing and exploring innova-tive impressionistic technical approaches to the guitar—both hands on the finger-board, tapping, sliding, rubbing the strings, sometimes playing chords with the left hand, sustaining melodic lines with the right, creating washes of textural sounds, sonic effects, unusual atmospheric colorings. In its nascent forms, this approach showed up for the first time on "Dream Letter." I later developed the techniques more extensively and showcased them in modest ways on *Lorca* and *Starsailor*.

Well before recording "Gypsy Woman" for *Happy Sad*, Tim had been using that song as a springboard for increasingly complex vocal improvisations. Utilizing part of a guitar riff I had shown him that first day in Greenwich Village, he strummed with abandon, creating thunderous rhythmic momentum, over which he sang words, yes, but also nonverbal *sounds*—the early leaps, moans, groans, shrieks, and howls that would eventually evolve into the vocal pyrotechnics of *Starsailor*. It was during this *Happy Sad* period that he started evolving from being strictly a singer who used the voice solely as a vehicle to carry words and showcase emotionally charged thoughts (the way he was in, say, the first album), into a combination singer and vocal improviser. These were *Starsailor*'s beginnings, around mid-1968.

"Gypsy Woman" worked much better in live performances than it did on *Happy Sad*. Unfortunately, the rhythms didn't jell on the album and everything seemed rather out of whack, for which I must admit and accept my share of responsibility.

Although Buckley seemed to be reasonably comfortable in a recording studio, especially as he gained experience, I never managed to feel relaxed. As a conse-quence, I rarely loosened up in the studio as much as I could and did onstage (as in *Dream Letter: Live in London 1968*, and the unauthorized CD of the *Santa Monica Civic* performance). There were dozens of unrecorded concerts in which I felt totally relaxed and confident enough to play with complete abandon everything I heard in my head. I never considered myself to be the greatest guitar player in the world, but neither was I the worst, especially if we consider the fact that Buckley asked for originality, uniqueness.

He did not approve when I played chords or rhythms shared by others in the pop arena. That meant I had to avoid convenient clichés and easy musical solu-tions—the licks and tricks that most guitar players use on a regular basis, often to great acclaim—and come up with melodic, harmonic, and rhythmic forms that (hopefully) were previously unheard. Not easy. And not always effective. Sometimes I got it. Sometimes not. Or I got it, but it didn't work well. To Tim's credit, he valued my efforts to learn and grow more than he censored my failures or partial successes. And he heartily appreciated everything that did work. He almost never directly praised with words. But when he turned and smiled his approval and appreciation onstage, he vitalized and strengthened the bonds of our musical friendship enormously.

"A lot of the reasons things sound tight on recordings," Tim told Anne Marie Micklo, "is that people get you so uptight in the studio that you do things because they're the only things you know you can do. You don't ever stretch out to things you could create spontaneously."

Although "Gypsy Woman" didn't quite come together on record, it remained a big gun in Tim's expanding arsenal. It carried weight in concert and served as one of his most thrilling and expansive showcase pieces.

The tune that follows "Gypsy Woman" and concludes *Happy Sad* is a jewel originally recorded in the *Works* sessions, often overlooked because it is so quiet, gentle, and brief. It is one of the loveliest songs Tim ever wrote, both lyrically and musically, entitled "Sing a Song For You."

Goodbye and Hello and *Happy Sad* were produced by Jerry Yester. On *Goodbye and Hello* he did a sterling job lining up studio musicians, writing some of the arrangements, directing Tim in the sessions for as many takes as it took to get the job done, and more or less co-creating *G & H* as a first-class marketable product. Tim (and Larry Beckett's) musical vision smoothly and naturally mirrored the times and various business interests—and Yester's view of what quality commercial popular music should be. It was a good match.

By the time the day arrived to record *Happy Sad*, however, Tim and the music and Tim's creative process had changed. The sessions proved difficult for Yester.

Several journalists have spoken to Yester about the *Happy Sad* sessions, including, among others, Scott Isler (*Musician*, July 1991), Ben Edmonds (*Mojo*, June 2000), and author David Browne (*Dream Brother*, 2001). In each of those cases Yester stringently criticized Tim and his musicians, saying things like, "Tim was tight with his band to the exclusion of everyone else. His musicians couldn't have been snottier," (*Mojo*). Or accusing Tim of not being his own person and of being unduly under the influence of his band; Yester's muttering to himself, "Who are these guys? They're good, but this kind of shit is a pain in the ass," (*Musician*). Or telling David Browne, "It was so cliquey, as if Tim and the others were saying, 'You guys behind the glass, you don't understand what an *artist* is going through.' Co-producer Zal [Yanovsky] and I were 'the suits.' I thought, "Who are you snot-nosed fucks out there?'"

Personally, I am not sure why journalists give Yester's perspectives and opinions credibility in the first place. He had virtually nothing to do in the studio on these sessions except tweak a few knobs and dials—Tim and the band already knew the music, and no studio musicians were utilized. On *Goodbye and Hello*, Yester's views, values, and processes fit perfectly. On *Happy Sad*, however, he was merely a functionary who could have had a wonderful time, but he missed.

Simply stated: Yester's problem seemed to revolve around the fact that he wanted to dominate the sessions and co-create *Happy Sad* the way he had *Goodbye and Hello*, and Tim refused to let him. It is my perception that by nature, experience, and temperament, Yester wanted us to do multiple takes and to perform clean, slick, well-rehearsed, reproducible, formulated pop songs that would fit radio timeframes and appeal to the musical tastes of the 18–25-year-old business demographic. That is what "commercial" is, and as a representative of the Elektra corporation it was incumbent upon him to do everything he could to accomplish that goal. In this light I can understand Yester's discomfort and confusion, although I see no reason for him to get nasty about it.

With *Happy Sad*, we were going for something else. We were going for the honesty and magic of spontaneity—thrilling, imaginative, unpredictable, irreproducible, dangerous, but real and honest and true: not a cover band casino act, but authentic music, recorded live, all of us playing simultaneously with no overdubbing—like walking a high wire without a net. I can sympathize with Yester's plight. Our aesthetic perspectives clashed with his, so of course we felt it was inappropriate of him to try to superimpose his values on top of ours.

Ultimately, of course, Yester has nothing to complain about. *Happy Sad* stayed on the charts longer than *Goodbye and Hello* and topped it in sales. As far as I know, it is still Tim's best seller after more than 30 years.

I feel proud of *Happy Sad* and assume the other musicians do, too. Rough spots and all, its heartsong flies in spring's blue skies outside of time. Some of the music on it will last for decades to come.

The shift from the orthodox showbiz values of rehearsing, memorizing, and performing to the more demanding, adventurous and dangerous value of improvisation was central to Tim's aesthetic during these years.

In the earlier *Tim Buckley* days, Tim and I worked on material together. I wrote chord charts, memorized his songs, came up with guitar parts and played them. That was our usual way of doing things, *and* it happened to fit music business values. We were happy. They were happy. But all that changed.

During the course of the *Happy Sad* years (all the way through the *Starsailor* period), Tim stopped rehearsing, intentionally so. He wanted the immediate environment and the fresh, new, vibrant, pulsating moment to express itself onstage and

Lee onstage, listening intently. Sometimes an astonishing energy gave the music transcendent beauty.

in the studio. That meant improvisation. He'd launch into something new onstage and say, "Lay out for a while. When you get it, come on in."

He didn't want preconceived mind-music, rehearsed art, static museum pieces. He wanted expression-music, living emotion in sound. That meant a complete shift of creative *gestalt* for us musicians. On the one hand it made playing incredibly thrilling, challenging, exciting; On the other, it made things more difficult. For Tim it was easier—it was *his* music. But it placed additional weight on our shoulders: where were we going? We didn't memorize anything, and there were no charts. What was next? Every time was the first time. How to react and respond? Sometimes the music worked in performance or on record, and sometimes it did not—but at least it was radiantly alive. It did not merely give the *appearance* of spontaneity. It truly was. And *that* was its greatest value.

One sunny Los Angeles afternoon in early 1969, Tim and writer Paul Eberle sat in the Troubadour bar and talked about this very subject. In the adjacent performance room, a rock group rehearsed.

"We don't rehearse songs," Tim said. "Instead, we get our personality together with our musical ability. . . .

"We start from scratch every time we go onstage. What progressions are you going to think of? And, like, maybe we'll think about it in the room a little bit and then we'll go out and just do it. We take what's happening in the moment and work with it, and explore it . . .

"And it's a very great thing to do that, because there are, man, some very miserable moments, right? But then on the other hand, there are some very beautiful moments. That band in the next room is really great, but they're not gonna grow unless they let it all hang out when they play—and that takes a lot of musical ability."

He said to writer Michael Davis, "People like Duke Ellington, John Coltrane, anybody—I mean, they discovered the fact that musicians could communicate. Jazz was probably the first form of group communication in this country. I know, some of it is painful to listen to. You can't listen to all of it. A lot of it is very tedious, and a lot of it wastes your time. Still and all, there's a lot of beauty involved in it."

With writer Sam Bradley, Tim emphasized the spiritual nature of spontaneity. "When you stack Miles Davis, John Coltrane, and Roland Kirk up against rock and roll, rock is a total prefabrication. The reason I like the people I've mentioned is because the music comes out of ensemble playing—trios, quartets, quintets, sextets—communication between the men playing.

". . . But in rock, everything is so rehearsed that nobody knows what to do. They say, 'That's a wrong note,' when in fact you're playing a kind of music that is *spiritual*. . . . It's spiritual, because when a man plays something, and you hear it, and you know him so well that you can follow it and take it someplace else, whether you're singing—I regard myself as a horn—or playing on your axe, then it's spiritual. . . .

"It has to come out of your heart. You just can't just be like the professional English musician, who comes over here, buys all the old blues records he can, learns all the licks, and makes a lot of money. You can hear the difference. I mean, they're never gonna be B. B. King, so why try?"

With a new perspective—and a wing and a hope and a song—we took it on the road.

CHAPTER 8

ON THE ROAD

HI JINX & LOW JINX

It was up, it was down. It was serene, it was chaos. It was happy, and sad, and beautiful, and ugly. It was tears, laughter, pain, joy. Best of all, it was alive.

In early March of 1968 Elektra stuck us in the Mayfair studio, a cold cinder-block room in New York, and told us to record beautiful music. We got several fairly good takes of "Song to the Siren," but used none of them. Takes of other songs were reasonably good and probably could have been used, but much of the material itself seemed embryonic and needed further development. During a few other sessions in June in Los Angeles, "Sing a Song for You" and "Dream Letter" were recorded, and eventually included on *Happy Sad*. These March and June sessions were set aside and became known by insiders as "the lost tapes." Relocated over thirty years later, they appeared posthumously in 1999 as *Works in Progress* (for which I wrote the liner notes, and for which my photo of Jennifer's portrait of Tim was used as the CD's cover).

I remember Tim slouching in an armchair in that chill Mayfair room, hands tucked inside his navy-blue winter jacket, depressed that the sessions had not gone well. While the engineer finished packing up, I played piano for the first time in many years. The engineer liked what he was hearing and spun a tape. He caught some of the improvisations before I became self-conscious and stopped. I still have that fragment on a cassette. The music I played helped Tim feel better, and he remembered those brief moments. Later, on *Blue Afternoon*, *Lorca* and *Starsailor*, he asked me to play keyboards in addition to guitar.

We toured like madmen during those years, not only New York, which showcased much of the music of that era, but outlying cities as well—Boston, Detroit, Cincinnati, Chicago, Cleveland.

At a club in Boston, I met Jacqueline Klein, a nineteen-year-old young woman who became a lifelong friend. So many of the people we met on the road were loud, coarse, harsh, orthodox, unintelligent. Jacqueline was none of those. She listened to music, not for sexual intoxication or adrenal rushes, but for beauty, tenderness, aesthetic brilliance, emotional depth. That's why she came to hear Tim and me in a duo performance. She was a beautiful human being, exquisite on every level—her gestures, her quiet voice, her shy dark eyes, her subtle and complex mind, her delicate emotions, her refined tastes in literature, classical music, art, poetry.

Together in Boston, then in John King's New York apartment, we made love without having intercourse, as she wanted to save that moment for whomever she married. We walked in parks by lakesides, visited art galleries, kissed each other in front of Monet's water lilies, enjoyed healthy food. With her I drank little or not at all. She gave me understanding, emotional and spiritual energy, and profound relief from the tawdry, raucous vulgarities of the road. Her inner and outer beauty, her intelligence and quiet, gentle ways, lifted my soul, gave me life and hope, and remain a vital part of my being to this day.

When the road called, Jacqueline and I went our separate ways with different people, but later reconnected through the mail and corresponded for several years as the closest of friends. She was one of the shining lights of my life.

There were moments that weren't so shining, of course, even with light at the end of the tunnel. One night drunk and alone in John King's basement apartment, I crawled on the floor over to his bookcase, checked it out, and saw Karen Horney's book, *Neurosis and Human Growth*. Looking through it (with one eye closed for focus), I was amazed—there I was, me and my misery on every page. To my astonishment, here was someone who understood. And there *were* ways to get out of this mire. There *were* ways to heal. I made a mental note to myself about the woman and the book, and about psychoanalysis in general—and then crawled back to bed and drank some more.

In Cleveland that spring, Tim, Carter, and I were being interviewed on the radio. Carter jumped into his black protest trip, talking about Martin Luther King Jr. and Malcolm X and the Black Panthers, saying, "It's time for the black man to stand up and be counted. No more political procrastination, no more broken promises, no more exploitation. All Whitey does is smile and promise reform, then turns around and steals our money, our dignity and our life. Nothing *ever* gets accomplished doing it Whitey's way—enough! I'm in perfect sympathy with kidnappings, bombings—whatever it takes. If that's what's necessary, then do it!"

I disagreed, saying, "Nobody can ever attain peace, love and mutual respect by using violent means. That's what the real revolution is about—learning how to transform anger into wisdom, how to use higher-consciousness and non-violent activities in politically effective ways. Fire creates more fire. Violent means cannot create peaceful ends. Violence only creates a cycle of more violence. The only way to bring about effective change is to have reasonable people discussing the issues in good faith. It's the good faith that is important—and the willingness to keep one's word."

Carter spat back, "Give me one instance when Whitey has kept his word! With Native Americans? With Kennedy and his laws? With Martin Luther King? We want freedom and respect, and we want it now!"

I don't recall Tim taking sides, perhaps because he didn't want to be caught in an either/or dilemma between me and Carter. However, I knew his heart was strongly in support of Black America, if not of every tactic being used. His empathic connection with the black experience in America was becoming an important element of his thinking and his music.

Although I disagreed with Carter's support of all available means, especially violent tactics, I found him to be magnificent in his urgency, conviction, and pride. At the same time, I again felt a kind of sickness, a deep-seated frustration, a profound discontent, even rage, at being unable to get my views across, unable to connect, unable to establish love and harmony either with people I knew, such as Carter, or with strangers. The bottle was my only solace.

The next morning, I woke up shivering in a hotel room that was so cold it turned my breath to mist. Outside, the sky was gray. Couldn't tell if it was morning or evening. Didn't know what town it was, or what time, or what hotel I was in. I listened, but couldn't hear anything, no people muttering in hallways or other rooms, no cars on the streets far below, no clanking radiators. Utter loneliness, cold silence, like a grave.

Worse, I couldn't feel anything within myself. I could feel the surface of my skin, but inside—nothing. Emotions extinct. Mind numb, spirit a void, dark, hollow, vacant, no care within, no joy, no memory, no hope, just bleak dread and benumbed emptiness, zero absolute. Totally disconnected. Dead.

I lay there staring up into the shadows of the ceiling, holding the covers to my neck, watching my breath turn to mist, wondering if this would ever pass.

In the fall of '68 we toured Europe a second time, but without Carter or bassist John Miller, due to lack of travel funds. In London, bassist Danny Thompson of

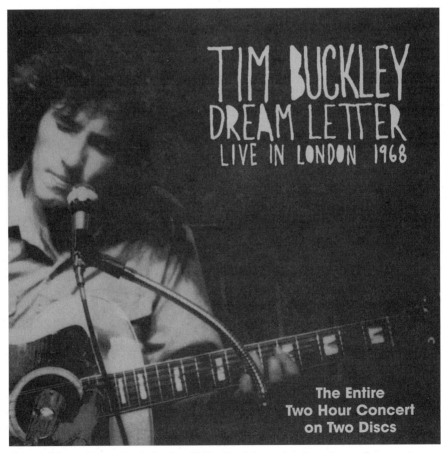

Cover of *Dream Letter: Live in London, 1968*—"real fire and real tenderness."

Pentangle joined Tim, Friedman, and me. One of the highlights of that tour was Queen Elizabeth Hall. I was not aware of it at the time, but the concert was being recorded. Long after I had forgotten about that performance, it appeared in 1990 as *Dream Letter: Live in London, 1968.*

I wrote in the liner notes, "It seems to me that this concert transcends nostalgia. Many listeners will experience the intensity and beauty of the music immediately and directly, not through the rosy mists of memory, but here and now, in the living present, as if it were recorded only yesterday. In a sense, of course, it was. All time past is yesterday.

"One of the reasons this music sounds so fresh and hits home so directly is because, by 1968, Buckley was insisting upon improvisation, not just for himself, but from all of us. . . . As a result, *Dream Letter* is not a glossy, money-based, Top 40, manufactured, MTV, product-imitation of emotion. It is not a corporate sham, and it doesn't date itself, because it's the real thing, with real fire and real tenderness. It's alive in this moment, right here, right now."

Indeed, I think that is the reason why so many people have stayed in love with Tim all these many years, why there is still a demand for his music, why so many new listeners are discovering him, and why there continues to be so much interest in him—truly, he is the real thing, with real fire, alive right here, right now.

To writer Paul Eberle he once talked about music "with a touch of madness in it, like Orson Welles gets in his films . . . The insanity is like daring to take it into ultra reality." I think that's what Tim did, and why his music lasts. With a whisper and a kiss, a whip and a teardrop, he dared to create music with a touch of madness in it. The levels of ultra reality he gave to the world while he was with us shimmer in our lives to this day.

This was our first and only European tour with Friedman, and it was interesting getting to know him. Although he was extremely sophisticated in terms of intelligence and musical knowledge, he was but a babe in the forest when it came to those time-honored vices held sacred by so many musicians, poets, and writers—booze and pot. He tried, but alas, and perhaps to his credit, he remained forever straight. He treasured his mind, and rightfully so. In a way perhaps similar to Larry Beckett, David was a "head" guy. Lots of brains, but artistically uninterested and unavailable when it came to intoxication, the madness of flesh and passion, the maelstrom of out-of-control emotion. Control, in fact, seemed central to David's aesthetic, even as it was to Beckett's. In spite of Friedman's ignorance of the Dionysian way of life— or possibly because of it—he was perfect for Buckley at the time.

It seemed to me that Friedman valued conscious artistry above all. His own music was interesting, clean, tidy, well conceived, often intricate in its well-executed complexities. By way of contrast, Buckley played without academic knowledge or training, relying entirely on instinct, heartfelt emotion, searing passion. Buckley's approach was not objectified and contained within rational boundaries. It had that "touch of madness" in it. His music was intuitive, urgent, organically realized, often quite untidy, very sweaty and sensual, and driven by a sense of mortality—so much to do, so little time. Tim's impassioned vulgarities and purposeful lack of restraint had to be difficult for Friedman at times. David was an academician, much like Beckett. Buckley was a madman passionately exploring his own musical demons and angels, searching for discipline and direction within firestorms of excess.

I found the contrast between them to be as stimulating as it was well balanced and beneficial. Friedman brought a flavor of order and reason to Tim's music and helped Tim develop a sense of form and structure within increasingly expansive improvisational contexts. In turn, Tim injected flames, fury, and ferocity into Friedman's psyche, sometimes screaming at him onstage, "Wake up! Get off your ass! Play!"

Later, after recording *Happy Sad* and playing gigs to promote that album, David felt Tim dropped him because he was "too strong musically." In fact, Tim needed to stretch out beyond rational confines, and found Friedman's temperament and point of view constricting.

Tim played a duo gig with me in Boston, which infuriated Friedman, who confronted Tim about his being left out. Tim was forced to defend himself, ultimately by asserting his right to do whatever he wanted—and he wanted to move into new dimensions (namely the *Lorca/Starsailor* realms), which did not include Friedman. Friedman complained in print that Tim "had absolutely no integrity," and to this day on his web site refuses to list Tim among his credits.

Things were becoming crazy in Europe. Warm beer. Strange places, incomprehensible languages, cars, traffic regulations. Odd-looking buildings, streets, people. Everything seemed so . . . well . . . *foreign*. I don't know how Tim and Dave felt, but I desperately needed someone like my bawdy Jennifer with her heart of gold and her way of bringing sunshine and laughter into everyday life, or exquisite Jacqueline and the empowering beauty of Monet, Utrillo, Modigliani, Van Gogh, uplifting spiritual energy, grace, something, anything, to get away from environmental noise, harshness, vulgarity, superficiality, and my own corrosive sense of alienation.

One afternoon in Copenhagen Tim said, "Come on. There's a good movie in town. Let's go."

That sounded like fun, so we took a cab to the theater and watched Tim's movie— *The Wild Bunch*, directed by Sam Peckinpah. William Holden, Ernest Borgnine, and their buddies played doomed turn-of-the-century cowboy outlaws on the run and plotting to rob a U.S. Army train—one of the earlier American films to glorify hideous violence and unmitigated slaughter. It was exactly the kind of brutality, bloodshed, and horror I did not need. Tim loved it.

"*The Wild Bunch* is great, man!" he told writer Anne Marie Micklo. "You gotta see it. It's really great. It's beautiful, man. They kill more people in six minutes— WHEW! And every time they shoot somebody, it goes in slow motion, and the blood spurts out—it's beautiful. You gotta see it, it's such a good movie. It's like going to see Mifune—you know, samurai stuff, *Throne of Blood*, 'cause that's what it's all about."

This side of Tim's character disturbed me. He may have been putting Micklo on, of course. He loved to shock flowery hippies and idolaters, and perhaps he was pulling that stunt with her, although I doubt it. I don't think Anne was a hippy-dippy type, and I don't think Tim's enthusiasm was feigned. In fact, I'm sure it wasn't.

This was a side of Tim that came down through his physically and emotionally wounded father—the war hero, the fighter, the macho man, the John Wayne–World War II–good-guys/bad-guys-kill-or-be-killed mentality. Sometimes when Tim felt weak or unsure, he turned to the only source of power or strength he knew as a child—father energy. *The Wild Bunch,* a vicious, unstintingly brutal bloodbath, reconnected Tim with his father and gave him that sense of power, a connection that became more pronounced as time went on. Tim felt *The Wild Bunch* was thrilling and *uplifting*.

As for myself, I felt sick afterward, headed for the hotel bar, passed out in my room, and didn't come out for two days.

March 1969. New York City. Philharmonic Hall. Lincoln Center. Those words sparkle. What a great gig. This was the concert for which Tim missed the afternoon sound check. Turns out he decided to take his clothes to the laundromat. It soothed his nerves to watch them spinning around in the dryer. It never occurred to me at the time that he might be nervous about that evening's concert, and so, like some old lady, I was upset with him for standing us up.

He may have missed the sound check, but he sure didn't miss the performance.

Backstage, warming up, David Friedman played piano and John Miller played bass while Tim sang excerpts from a few great standards, including "Angel Eyes," "September Song," "That Old Feeling," "What's New" and "One for My Baby (One More for the Road)." Then he leaned over the piano in a vampy chanteuse pose, bent his wrist, clouded his eyes, smiled, and swished through "Mad About the Boy." Hilarious. And musically excellent. With his eyes bright and happy, he pulled the guitar strap over his shoulder, cinched up his guitar, and chortled that old Judy Garland line, "Hey, ya babies! Get ready for the dream sequence! Show time!"

He surprised me to no end. I hadn't known he knew those tunes (rather like his son, Jeff, who also knew words to songs perhaps generations old, even tunes he might have heard only a time or two). In the years since then, of course, Linda Ronstadt, Willie Nelson, Michael Bolton, and others have released albums of classic jazz standards. They were good. But Tim was great. He would have blown all the pups away. And that was just a backstage warm-up.

When we trooped out people cheered and rushed the stage. Girls tossed bouquets of flowers, passed paper valentines and notes up to him, squealed with delight. A tall blonde stood up and handed him a single red rose, as I recall (not a carnation as reported elsewhere). Tim graciously accepted it, smiled at the girl, put the flower in his mouth, and chewed it up! Spitting the crunched petals out, he said, "Yeow—that really tastes terrible!"

He later told me he had met Salvador Dali in an elevator that afternoon. Tim had mentioned the concert coming up that evening, and Salvador attended. Tim saw him sitting in the audience. "What could I do that would be audacious enough to get a laugh from a master comedian like him? I ate the flower!"

We played well, the crowd loved us, reviews were good, and we stood on top of the world. It was a shining moment of glory.

After a gig someplace in Toledo, Tim, David, and I were invited over to a very pretty redhead's house by her girlfriend. Toledo Red smiled at us, went into her room, closed the door. Her friend said, "She wants to make love to all three of you, one at a time." Tim and David smiled. I felt uneasy. "She doesn't need your name, just you. She knows her passion is mad, but she can't help it. Be gentle when you go to her, but please be a man."

Tim entered the bedroom first while David and I sat on a bench in the living room, as if waiting for a bus. Tim took forever. Jesus, what was keeping him. He finally came out, smiling.

I went in. The room was dimly lit in blue Day-Glo light, a mattress on the floor, Toledo Red on her knees, naked, hot. I didn't want anything to do with this whole situation. I even resented being more or less pressured into it. So I intentionally got off as quickly as possible, went back out—Tim looked surprised, as if saying, "Hmmm, I see ol' Lee can't last long." Annoyed the hell out of me.

I don't know why, but the situation didn't excite me. All I felt was lonely and used. However, as I thought about Toledo Red in years to come, she and the situation turned me on tremendously. She was sexy, and in need. God knows, I understand need. Today, that sweet desperate young woman occupies a warm spot in my heart. I was selfish and should have treated her better—more compassion, more heart, more lust, more me.

We were late for the flight to Denver. Laughing and stoned on reds (Seconal), Tim and I staggered as fast as we could toward the airport's gate. Tim lurched and fell. I got him back on his feet. We kept running down those shiny, endlessly long halls, barely making it to the plane. It was waiting for us, engines idling. The door was open. A stewardess was reaching out to close it just as we made it to the tarmac, yelling and waving at her. "Stop! Wait! Not yet! Don't go! Hey!"

The next day around noon, sober and straight at Mile High Stadium, June 27, 1969, we admired Tim's name on the giant marquee beside those of Jimi Hendrix, Mothers of Invention, Iron Butterfly, Creedence Clearwater, Crosby, Stills & Nash, and several others.

That afternoon, Tim and I stood on a platform in the middle of a baseball diamond, looking up at thousands of people, just the two of us playing our hearts out. Suddenly, from our left, after only four songs, a great roar erupted from the crowd. Wire fences crashed down. Hundreds of fans who had been denied entrance to the sold-out festival rushed in. People screamed, ran, fell, tried to get away.

Cops pulled on gas masks and attacked the crowd with billy clubs. Other cops set off tear gas bombs. Great clouds of smoke rolled up into the stands and billowed out on the field. Tim and I heaved our guitars into cases and ran down the stairs at the side of the stage, out into right field.

People screamed, yelled, coughed and cried while cops attacked them wherever they could. Tim and I got separated. Whenever a wave of smoke came my way, I lay down on the grass, covered my head, buried my face in soil, then got up clutching my guitar and kept running for the rest rooms, coughing, crying, eyes stinging, lungs hurting.

Inside, safe from the smoke, I watched a cop taking a leak. He propped his gas mask up on his forehead, chuckled, smiled a big grin, and said to the guy standing next to him, "More fun than shootin' bunnies, ain't it?"

The night before the Seattle Pop Festival in July of '69, Tim and I had a few drinks in the hotel bar. I figured I would try a mixed drink instead of my usual beer, so I ordered a Manhattan. That didn't get me high, so I ordered another. Then a couple more. Still not feeling much zing, I said good night and went to bed.

The next morning, I couldn't move. I struggled to the edge of the bed, took out my guitar, tried running a few scales to see if I could get my fingers in motion—no go. Couldn't get them to work *at all*. Frightening.

By the time the gig rolled around that afternoon I was a little better but not much, still so hung over I could hardly play. Muddling through everything, I swore to Tim onstage that this would never happen again. He laughed and said, "It's okay."

Bless him—neither condemnation nor contempt, but acceptance, understanding, forgiveness, and cheerful love. I remembered that long-ago day in London when he had not wanted to visit the Tate Gallery, "Don't mock the afflicted," he said. Well, it seems to me each of us is afflicted one way or another, but only some of us know it. Tim had heart. "It's okay."

Later, he told me Herb showed him a review of that concert, in which the writer slashed me to shreds. I felt horrible, knowing full well I deserved the criticism.

It never happened again. I played straight, no hangovers, and no booze before performances.

For a while, it looked like Tim was going to be a movie star. He was to get 100% top billing in the role of Fender Guitar, an American Indian, in a feature film called *Wild Orange*, directed by Robert Cordier. It was slated to begin production in New York on May 1, 1969, but fell through.

However, Tim did contribute three tunes from previous albums and three new songs to a movie entitled *Changes*, directed by Hall Bartlett (*Jonathan Livingston Seagull* and *The Children of Sanchez*). Tim gave them "Morning Glory" and "Once I Was" from *Goodbye and Hello*, and "She Is" from *Tim Buckley*. The new songs were "Wildwood," "The Prize" (at this writing unreleased), and "The Father Song," (released on *Works in Progress*).

Changes starred Bartlett's stepson, Kent Lane, as a troubled youth growing up in the sixties, searching for identity, love, truth, and meaning. I enjoyed the movie when I saw it years later. Noted film critic Judith Crist liked it too, calling it "A beautiful film! Even in this age of beautiful films—subtle, perceptive, alive."

However, the experience was mixed for Tim. "It was a fifty-year-old concept of what young people should be," he told writer Michael Williams. "I told them I hated it from the beginning, but I felt obligated. I also wanted to learn something about movies. I wrote a very subtle, alive score for guitar, vibes, congas, things like that. . . . What a bummer. Mess up my body, man, but don't mess up my music."

"It taught me not to trust anyone," he told journalist Mal Karman. "I wrote most of the stuff for it, and then Bartlett changed it around and took some of it out. I hate to be used like that. I'll never do another film score again, unless I make the film myself. I want to do a kung fu karate ballet. And I think I can probably get the money for it."

Although Tim suffered disillusionment about the film process—good work gets lopped off as a matter of course—he nevertheless knew he looked great on film (I assume he took a screen test for *Changes* and it had been magnificent), and he retained his interest in movie making. In 1970, he was up for a role in Lawrence Kubrik's *Zachariah*, which he didn't get, and in 1970–71 he acted in a film called *Why*, with none other than O.J. Simpson—more on that later.

AMERICA BLACK/AMERICA WHITE

Tim had four heroes in those days, all of them black. One was Muhammad Ali. The other three were musicians—Miles Davis, Charlie Mingus, and Roland Kirk.

Most of the photographs of Tim during this *Happy Sad* period show him in a kind of poetic, soft-focus, rainbow haze, a sweet pretty-boy, sensitive, vulnerable, androgynous, incredibly lovable.

But Tim was also a fighter, a young man of high ideals, fierce integrity, and angry passions when it came to liberation and justice, perhaps especially in the case of the black man in America. Carter was a part of that broad-based liberation process and so were Tim and his heroes.

He gave up on white politicians. It was his view that politicians lie their way to the top, and by the time they get there they owe so many other politicians and Mafia gangsters that "even if they had anything good in them, they can't do it anyway," he told me. And when somebody worthwhile comes along, like Jack and Bob Kennedy, the right-wingers kill them. As for those who survive—Nixon, Johnson, Humphrey and their ilk—"They're all the same person."

White businessmen were just as bad. "A white businessman pulls into the city, sucks out all he can, and leaves the city a shell, never puts anything back."

College kids meant well, wearing flowers in their hair, tie-dye t-shirts, long hair, rebelling against their parents by sticking daisies in gun barrels, but Tim was skeptical about their sincerity and commitment. More than once he said, "As soon as college is out, they won't do it anymore."

In the burning streets of urban America, the black man stood strong and proud, the Black Panthers in particular. The white man praises the Panthers, Tim observed, not because he likes them, but because he's afraid of them. When it comes down to it, the cops will protect the white man, not the Panther.

Between businessmen, politicians and cops, he told Anne Marie Micklo, "It's impossible to do anything. There's nothing that you or I can do to change what the government is or what all the monopolies are. You can't, you know, you just can't. The only thing you can do is to expound to more people . . . give them hope . . . give them love. . . ."

And so Tim "expounded to more people" about the problems America faced, sorting out his own thoughts about America's dream and America's reality—and where he personally and musically stood in relation to it.

Over in London, he told British journalist Norman Jopling about some of America's racial problems—"America is very frightening right now. People are building up arsenals to protect themselves. You're attacked in the streets just for being what you are. There's prejudice and fear everywhere. People really *hate*."

But he affirmed America in spite of those problems, and for good reasons, exactly the kinds of reasons Buckley the warrior would come up with:

"I think my main message is trying to break down prejudice between black and white. Everywhere I go in America, I meet prejudice. This is often aimed towards me too, prejudice towards my hair, my clothes, the fact that my conga player is a black man, every possible kind of prejudice . . . But living in America makes me feel as though I'm alive, you see? It's something happening, this continual state of prejudice."

Like his Irish father and grandfather, Buckley regarded the British with disdain, "white bread dipped in water," he once told me. With American journalist Paul Eberle he was frank about his attitude toward Europeans in general and "emasculated Limeys" in particular:

"For all of its problems, America's a lot better than Europe. Europe's dead, burned out, like they don't really want to try it again. . . . You don't feel the energy that you need in order to create."

White America was rife with indecision, lack of commitment, and hypocrisy. "When we go to Chicago," he told Eberle, "we go to the spade bars and we live in the spade section of town, because they're the only people who treat each other human."

I noticed that Carter was a black man who, in Tim's sphere, lived and worked in white society, even as he railed against it. And that Tim—"brown-eyed, blue-collar white trash from Anaheim," as he once called himself—sympathized, not with his "white roots" background, but with Carter and the Black Panthers, even as he freely used racist terms in conversation and interviews and got away with it.

In America's so-called "real" world, where insanity was the coin of the realm, the black man's commitment to freedom was not a superficial collegiate "peace and beads" indulgence funded by Daddy's checks from home. It was authentic, impassioned, and blazing with spirit. The streets of urban America blew up in flames.

Onstage, James Brown led the way: "Papa's Got a Brand New Bag," "I'm Black and I'm Proud." Tim's personal heroes led the way too: Miles, Mingus, and Kirk—musicians who brought the freedom song out from a place as deep as despair, as high as hope, as fierce as rage, as strong as pride, as beautiful as indomitable courage.

Tim had stopped listening to pop music by this time. He felt he couldn't learn from it anymore, "and that's the main thing—to learn. That's what life is all about," he told me. The music that now nourished, educated, and awakened him to new ways of creating was jazz.

Tim suddenly found himself an outlaw in disguise, moving parallel to a white hippie populace awash in sunny Beatles songs, performing for audiences that still thought of him largely in terms of folk music and those early "paper hearts and Valentines" tunes. Now an outsider, he moved progressively further from the youthful incense and patchouli oil culture that still adored him.

Tim didn't care if he found himself outside the mainstream. He was on a musical odyssey. It was vitally important to learn about the sources of black music that had energized so many white pop musicians. Janis Joplin, Mick Jagger, Johnny Winter, and Eric Clapton wouldn't have existed without black music.

And so Tim's reference points changed—where once he spoke of gifted and musically responsible musicians such as Fred Neil and Bob Dylan, he now spoke of Miles, Mingus, Kirk and other jazz giants. He wasn't a jazz fan per se. Nor was he sentimentally locked into any particular time zone like the forties or fifties, and he didn't listen to just anybody; he searched for innovators.

"Right now in New York," he told Micklo, "You have about [three] geniuses as heavy as Stravinsky, Mendelssohn, Bach, Bartók. . . . You've got Miles, you've got Monk, you've got Mingus. . . . By the time people come up to where *these* dudes are at, all three will be dead."

Then Tim told Micklo a story about Charlie Mingus that he never told me. It may or may not have happened, but it is absolutely true to Tim's character—his respect for genius, his respect for the black man, and his willingness to fight for human dignity. He explained to Micklo how too many people in New York "don't even know who Miles Davis is, or who Charlie Mingus is. Like, I sat down in the Village Gate last night and Charlie came on and he was writing out some music before the set.

"So what happens? This dude up in the sound booth puts on a record of some group playing this loud music all through the thing, while he's trying to write out a score, man. This thing Mingus is doing is beautiful, so I asked the waiter, long-haired cat, 'Hey, man, could you tell the dude up there to cut out the music? Mr. Mingus is trying to write out a score.' And he said, 'Well, uh, ah. . .' So I said, 'Look, schmuck, go up there and tell him. I'll give you five dollars if you go up and tell him to turn off that music.' So he comes back and says, 'Uh, there's a lot of bureaucracy, blah, blah.' So I said, 'Well *fuck you*, man,' and I went up and ripped the record off. . . . Mingus never knew, but at least he got the fucking score done."

That story reminds me of the time in Hollywood when the neighbor hollered at me to stop singing "There Ain't No Such Thing as Hard Times," and Buckley ran out of the house and yelled at him to shut up or he'd bash his face in.

Indeed, Buckley supported the people he liked, stood face-to-face against those he did not like, and never backed down from a one-on-one challenge, even when he was at risk. Some might call this pugnacious characteristic noble. Others might call it stupid. But when he got away with it, it was glorious.

From the moment Tim listened to Roland Kirk at Big Pink, he did whatever he could to support Kirk's name and music in public. He regarded Kirk, a blind man who played as many as three reed instruments simultaneously, as a supreme exponent of "American music and American expression." He felt that Kirk's use of the appellation "black classical music" for jazz was both accurate and insightful. To a number of journalists, he celebrated Kirk's music, insisting that Kirk himself was worthy of being documented by the media.

He told writer Frankie Nemko, for example, "Roland Kirk is a man who knows America. He knows, from a musical thing, and also from the sound of the voices. His memory is incredible, and his information on black heritage is amazing. He knows who stole what from what apartment building from what musician who copped what lick from what clarinet player down the street from Paul Robeson who copped it from Othello who lifted a line from somebody else. . . . That man can go on for days talkin' like that, and then go out onstage and aspire to the heights that he does . . .

"When Roland came to Concerts by the Sea in Redondo Beach, Muhammad Ali had just knocked out Foreman. [My wife] Wu and I were up in Hollywood watching that fight in a closed-circuit theater. I remember it well. It was October 30, 1974, and Ali took him out in the eighth round. Foreman was 25 years old, Ali 32, and nobody in the place could believe that Ali knocked him out. I figured, 'This is a perfect time to go down to see Roland Kirk.'

"So we're barrelin' down the freeway to Concerts by the Sea, turn on the radio, and Roland is talking everything about the fight, that it's religion also. He was talkin' about how the old man beat the young man, and about how experience is sometimes a lot better than youthful piss and vinegar.

"And we got there, and for the first time since the time I had seen him seven years before that, for the first time people were actually listening to every word he was saying—and not becoming uptight—because Muhammad Ali had just proven it. So the white folks there were saying, 'It's all right to listen to this crazy nigger talkin' like this onstage.'

"He talks a lot between songs, and it's real hard for a white audience to sit there and listen to this black discourse without feeling alienated. That's not his purpose, not his reason for doing what he's doing. He's trying to tell you what American heritage is—and he's a walking museum of information. He's amazing. If I had the bread, I would do a documentary on this man, on his terms, whatever he wanted to say. They should just let Roland talk, let Roland interview Roland on film   ."

Tim talked to journalist Sam Bradley about the time he listened to Kirk play in a Montreal nightclub, after which he visited him backstage.

"I've never done that with anybody, gone backstage. But two guys from the record company were taking some cassette tapes to Roland. They had met me at the airport—which rarely happens. I told them I had a day off and asked who was in town. They said Roland Kirk, and I said, 'Can we go tonight?'

"Well, I didn't know they were his record company people too. They got up from the table after the set. I was ready to leave, but they said, 'Come on back and meet him.' I said, 'No, man, no.' They said, 'Aw, come on. You gotta come back and meet Roland Kirk. He'll love to meet you.' I said, 'You guys don't understand—you don't meet idols!'

"But they insisted, so I walked in and sat down. These two guys were talking to him. I don't want to speak for Roland Kirk, but this is my observation of the situation—total plantation. That's how they treated him, for about half an hour. He handled it very humbly.

"The point came up about the time he did *The Ed Sullivan Show*. These guys mentioned that some people didn't like what Roland had done, because he had used Charlie Mingus, Roy Haynes, Archie Shepp, and somebody else all at once. They said he should have let them bring on their own groups.

"I stepped into the conversation and explained to these guys for about 15 minutes that that wasn't going to happen. Television executives weren't going to give a black musician *five* chances to get on nationwide TV. *And* those eight minutes that they played on TV was the greatest jazz I had ever heard.

"Roland had said, 'This is *black* man's music!' And Mingus tore into the goddamned bass. And I was in tears from up-front, from the get-go, all the way out. Only an idiot could have sat in front of that TV and complained about anything at all.

"I had to explain that to them.

"Then Roland started talking to me. I didn't tell him anything about myself. I said, 'I'm just a musician.' I don't think he knew anything about me or many other white players. But I didn't want to get into my story. I wanted to know what he did. Afterwards, Roland dedicated the next set to me, a really nice gesture on his part.

"Over the last five years, he has been moving toward playing by himself, without the band backing him. That night he did about ten minutes. It's really coming along. He's moving toward doing a whole album by himself . . .

"Roland knows so much about America, what relates to what, and how it all ties up. He's got to be documented. He's gotta be given a chance. He has a hell of an understanding and a huge heart, and he's a phenomenal player. He is still an idol of mine and an inspiration, and probably always will be."

THE JOURNEY OF ART AND COMMERCE

As we traveled the country or hung out together in California, Tim unfolded layers of his character that revealed why he so often had difficulties coping with the business aspects of music. Later, his mother, Elaine and his sister Katy also shed light on this important dimension of his nature.

Right from the get-go—in fact, from childhood's hour on—his struggle with the business world was made doubly difficult by the very people who loved him. In light of conditioned attitudes ingrained in him by his parents, it is something of a wonder he ever set foot out of the house, much less into the recording industry and onto international concert stages. His parents meant well, as parents often do, but they had no idea what they were instilling into their talented son.

Elaine lovingly recalled to me how, "Oh, yes, we used to talk about how corrupt business is, private industry, corporations, monopolies, big money, people merging. . . . In private industry, the little guy is no more . . . And I would talk about the corruption, and I would always say, 'What we really need is a good revolution in this country, to really bring people back to their senses. . . .' We don't know what the hell's going on in this country. . . . Money is great, but it's not that great, not when you start squashing people. We used to talk about things like that. Tim and I used to talk hours and hours on the phone about things like that. He'd give me feedback, and he'd talk too."

Even as Tim's father told his sister, "You're never gonna fit into this society, because you're artistic, and that's worse than having leprosy," so he pounded the same thing into Tim. Of course, Tim protested, "No, it's gonna change." Nevertheless, during years of day-to-day life, that idea was driven home again and again, like a spike in the skull.

On the surface, the notion behind anti-business attitudes nearly always seems moral and righteous. The argument goes something like this: Because of all the ruthless bad things one has to do to earn money, business is corrupt. You are a good person; therefore, don't become a part of the business world or you will be corrupted. Even worse, your sensitive artistry will be destroyed.

Underneath the surface, however, moralistic views against business often conceal a deep-seated fear of success, a profound sense of inadequacy, as it did in the case of Tim Jr. ("Buck"), who passed it along to his son, Tim.

Almost always within an unconscious subtextual flow, the *underlying* argument goes something like this: If you don't try to win, you won't have to fail. You can remain outside the business world and not have to face your own inadequacies. Not only that, you can retain your moral purity and enjoy all the egoistic rewards of criticizing from the sidelines. Society hates artists and sensitive good guys. You are an artist and a sensitive good guy—that makes you a vulnerable freak, a leper doomed to destruction. Better to not even try. If you do try, you're a fool. Don't play the game. Not playing makes you superior.

Such deeply ingrained attitudes debilitated the father and made it extremely difficult for Tim to make the effort to succeed. If Tim did not try, he would have pleased his parents by adopting their views, but he also would have felt like a coward, unworthy as a man, unworthy as a human being. Conversely, if he did try to succeed, he would be violating his parents' credo, and transgressing against the loved ones to whom he owed his very life. Either way, guilt, shame, and perhaps even potentially suicidal rage could result—and they did.

It was a no-win situation. Whichever way he chose, he lost. Success beckoned alluringly, like a Siren. And yet, even as it beckoned, it was leading him into pits of self-destructive shame. If he did not try, he wasn't a man. If he did try, how could he bear to defy his father, and then psychologically slay his father by succeeding? Hence those lines in "The Father Song" in which he recalled the battle between them when his father said he felt ashamed of Tim and cursed the day he was born.

In this painful dynamic, there would be shame in his father's heart because his son dared to succeed. He would curse his son because his son succeeded where he himself dared not try. If Tim made the effort, and especially if he succeeded, the father would be forced to face his own fear and inadequacy. He would be forced to confront his own self-betrayal, his almost total inability to live up to his own talents as a writer.

And from Tim's side, how could Tim dare to inflict that kind of shame upon his father? Clearly, the shame was lodged in Tim's heart, too, for audaciously going against his father's weaknesses and beliefs, and for insolently trying to succeed where his father could not. The curse had to be his, as well—his curse on his father, for the guilt and rage and shame he felt because of his father's condemnations.

Shames and curses. Neither father nor son was spared.

At first, everything in the business sphere was rosy for Tim. Herb Cohen and Jac Holzman fell in love with him and his music. As men with good ears, they appreciated his songs and voice. As businessmen, they recognized his commercial potential.

Jac has often been quoted as saying, "Herb called to tell me that he had a new artist. . . . I didn't have to play the demo more than once, but I think I must have listened to it at least twice a day for a week. . . . Whenever anything was bringing me down, I'd run for the Buckley. It was a restorative."

Tim liked Herb and Jac personally, and liked the fact that he could speak directly with Jac, one-on-one. He didn't have to be an anonymous cog in a manufacturing product-machine—he could be acknowledged and respected as an individual.

When the first album came out, however, Jac evidently did not express the kind of enthusiasm Tim had hoped for. Hence, Tim's discussion with writer Bob Garcia, in which he made several generalities about the business mentality in the music industry:

"There are an awful lot of playboy-business types in the record business. They dig the Hollywood–New York hippie scene. They do this super-sophisticated bullshit thing that I can't stand as far as being hip is concerned. The people in record companies never understand what their performers are actually doing. It's ridiculous. . . .

"They think they know what the kids want. I think that's bullshit. Most of the kids will eventually wade through all the commercial crap to find what they really want. DJs and record promoters have no taste. They don't know what they like until it's number one."

In later years, Jac expressed his appreciation of Tim in his book, saying, "The pain and purity of the songwriting, the plaintiveness of his melodies, the nakedness of his vocals, the artistic risks. I had believed in Tim from the beginning, and the enchantment of *Goodbye and Hello* exceeded anything I could have hoped for."

In 1967, however, Tim didn't see it that way. In a second interview with Garcia, the one in which he related how Holzman couldn't connect with *Goodbye and Hello* until he listened to it stoned on acid, Tim pointed out how the business mentality in general and Jac's mentality in particular was divided, which created problems for the musician:

"Jac is 36 years old, and televisioned in a lot of ways. He's done a thing business-wise, without any respect for the people he's worked with or done recordings with. He has certain tastes, but they are superficial at times.

"He's not a musician. There are things that only musicians can feel, certain textures, subtleties, and things like that. And there are certain other people who do a big listening thing all the time . . . and they respond to it like a musician. . . . But when you have people that are doing a split-up thing, well, man, like they're doing a half-business thing and not that much of a listening thing, and of course the balance is going to get mixed up."

In the beginning, Tim felt pleased that Jac looked forward to evolving with him.

"I explained to Tim that Elektra was growing in a new creative direction at that time," said Jac in an Elektra bio, "and that he was exactly the kind of artist with whom we wanted to grow: young and in the process of developing, extraordinarily and uniquely gifted, and so 'untyped' that there existed no formula or pattern to which anyone would be committed. Tim understood that *we* understood, and he knew we wanted him for the right reasons."

Yes, Tim was pleased Jac viewed him in that light. For a while, he also understood the mutually beneficial, though symbiotic, relationship that can exist between a company and an artist.

"I realize there are two sides to every coin: artistic and commercial," he told Garcia. "I know that I must have money rolling in so that I can keep recording and growing. I want to do many more records."

But as Buckley pulled away from the fragile, vulnerable poet image of the earlier years, his musical direction was becoming more and more distant from mainstream commerce. The relationship between Tim and the business world was no longer hearts and flowers. Business people did not want him to stray off the commercial path, and Buckley did not like being told he should exploit his music to serve business interests.

In a quote that has become widely circulated since my 1977 *Down Beat* article, Buckley told Anne Marie Micklo, "America is a business, and if you have to be an American, no matter what you do, you are first of all a businessman.

"So any show that I go on, they ask me, 'Well, you make albums, and so you must make them for money.' And I got to go through the whole thing, gotta tell them, 'Man, you people are the same people who when Monet or Modigliani were starving for 40 years and they finally sold a painting, said that they sold out.'

"I said, 'Like man, what have *you* got to worry about? You got all the money you want, all the fine suits—why do you have to pull me down to where you are, man?'"

After *Happy Sad*, Tim recorded *Lorca* in late 1969, his first step into avant-garde dissonance and odd-time signatures. By then, he had lost all connection with business mentalities, record companies, hit singles, mainstream popular values, and musical tastes conditioned by AM radio. With *Starsailor*, his magnum opus, the gap grew even wider.

In Tim's world, key words included creativity, change, evolution, and quality. In the business world, key words were numbers: sales, charts, dollars, quantity.

As Holzman expressed it, "He was really making music for himself at that point, which is fine, except to find enough people to listen to it." Numbers. Quantity.

Tim didn't care. He was an artist, doing what a serious multidimensional artist does: create, don't look back, take it someplace new. As he expressed it to Micklo, "I mean, someone like Miles Davis, he's been in the business a long time, but he never stopped learning, man. He's always managed to take it and bring it all back to himself." Growth, development, quality.

The gap widened. Tim started calling DJs on their superficial, pseudo-hip veneers, performing songs on television that were too long for the time-slots, bad-rapping industry executives, insulting journalists. He was not winning friends in high places.

Angry with the growing lack of response to his music on the part of music business professionals and increasing numbers of listeners, he had begun lashing out. He led the way, and I did not often discourage him. Even when I tried, my efforts were not successful. And I did not always try, because in many ways I felt the same.

We were playing some college gig, for example, and backstage after the show two journalists showed up, aspiring kids with stars in their eyes, one from town, the other from the college. Both wanted to interview Tim. I suggested they pitch pennies against the wall the way we ourselves did when waiting in airports. Whoever got his penny closest to the wall two times out of three won the interview. Tim laughed, thought that was terrific, and made them do it. One kid got the interview. The other departed, practically in tears. Not exactly a way to woo the press.

In another incident, in Buffalo, as I recall, Tim was told to go over to a TV studio and lip-synch "Pleasant Street" for a video shoot. Back then, videos were just coming in. They weren't taken for granted as part of the music business the way they are today. We regarded them with skepticism.

Tim asked what I thought. Should he do it? I wasn't sure. On the one hand, it might be a good career move. On the other, did they really want him to *pretend* to sing? What kind of commercial fraudulence was that? Tim skipped the date.

Of course, I kick myself today. He bore the responsibility for the decision, but I bear the blame. If I had told him that it might be fun and go ahead and do it, he surely would have taped the song. Today we would have a visual artifact from that time and place, probably a good one too; he photographed as magnificently as he sang.

On the one hand, psychologically speaking, Tim was taking on the business structure, defying its mentality and showing his war-oriented dad he was capable of fighting battles. It was essential for him that he prove his manhood both to himself and his father. He would step into conflict with those "corrupt" powers and give it the good fight, saying, in effect, "Just wait and see, Dad. I will courageously live up to the best in myself, in spite of your insistence that it can't be done. If I win, you're wrong. If I lose, I still win, because at least I have guts enough to try."

On the other hand, he was intentionally, albeit unconsciously, withdrawing from the only arena where any sort of worldly success was possible for him. You can't insult executives, DJs, and journalists and expect their support. But that's what he did, precisely so that he could say to himself, "See, I tried. Business is corrupt, but I maintained my integrity. I may be a financial failure and no longer a pop star, but I stand proudly on the musical and moral high ground."

By defying business in the name of art, Tim could assert his integrity, wage his war, triumph over his father. And by losing everything in the process, he could wage

that war without vilifying his father's values. From both positions—defiant asser-
tion and noble failure—he could lose with honor.

These kinds of neurotic psychological dynamics can be devastating. Many people in their grip cannot move even a single step, much less take wings and fly. In
such cases, creativity becomes emotional torture, because, as suggested above, it
inwardly challenges the deeply rooted conditioned psychological forces that fear
success and resist it.

It was a paradox. On the one hand, desperately wanting to succeed as an artist
and a pop star, Tim fought the good fight to be creatively free in the marketplace.
That was the external level. On the other hand, inwardly, psychologically, he felt
severely inadequate when confronted by potential demands that great success might
place upon him. That sense of weakness generated anxiety and resistance, that in my
opinion caused him to make numerous problematic choices in both music (the
warrior stance) and life (substance abuse). His inner conflicts, his fear of success,
and his anger at the rejection of *Lorca* (and later, *Starsailor*) plunged him into a
black hole.

I stand in total admiration of what Tim managed to accomplish in spite of these
problems. But the price he had to pay was pain: Burdened with conflicts, he managed to create anyway. On a daily basis, he suffered enormous fears, doubts, and
guilt, and yet over the long haul courageously summoned enough wherewithal to
struggle through them. More than once, he found light on the other side of self-
destructive darkness, however dim or clouded that light may have been. As years
drifted on by, he suffered sometimes terrible rejection—from friends he had outgrown, from audiences, from the recording industry—yet managed to sustain his
faith in his music and his heartfelt message.

On this lonely journey, Tim Buckley showed the courage and strength of a van
Gogh, an Antonin Artaud, a Muhammad Ali, a Miles Davis. I am not comparing
accomplishments. I am saying that, like them, he kept on keepin' on, no matter what
the odds or the popular climate of the day. When he had to walk in dark isolation
because of his choices, he went ahead and walked in dark isolation, sometimes for
years on end, as in the *Lorca/Starsailor* period. And he didn't let fear or alienation
stop him. Until the end of his life he kept creating.

There is a key point in here. In fact, I see it as the definitive point.

Millions of people suffer psychological conflicts, and so did Tim. But Tim was
much more than merely neurotic. Above all, he was an artist. Music flowed
through him like ocean currents. Above and beyond his neurosis, his talent
demanded that he give expression to that music. Like every authentic creator,
whatever their mindset—and who can claim absolute psychological health?—he
enjoyed the delights and benefits of his art, but he did not cynically exploit that
art for its by-products and perks. He served it. His particular brilliance demanded that he give himself to music in as many forms and modes of expression as he
could. In spite of neurotic conflicts, he felt a profound responsibility to music
itself, wherever it may take him. Even as he transcended the seductions of commercial success, so he transcended the pain of its loss. It was not neurosis that
ultimately drove him, but selfless service to music as a living force of nature. He
did not create to destroy himself, as some people maintain. He created to serve
music and fulfill his talent.

He was not just some selfish simple-minded adolescent playing rock 'n' roll to get laid. And he did not allow himself to fall into the business trap of allowing previously successful expressions of intense feeling to take precedence over feeling itself. Genuine feeling always takes place in the *present moment*, as does authentic creativity. That is why he refused to betray himself and music by copying and repeating commercialized formulaic song forms, as many industry musicians so blithely do.

At each turning point in his journey, Tim felt new feelings and conceived new visions in the present—the living moment—and dared to serve those feelings and visions with all the passion, intelligence, skill and commitment he could muster. Music is forever alive, and he gave his energies to it selflessly.

Tim Buckley did everything he could to live up to the best in himself, even against heavy opposition from three fronts—1) the stratum of listeners who claimed to love him and yet would inhibit his artistic evolution into new and unfamiliar forms by insisting that he provide them with conceptually repetitive song stylings that more closely mirrored their own tastes; 2) vested business interests who measured musical effectiveness exclusively in terms of profit and *Billboard* chart positions; and 3) his own neurotic conflicts and self-defeating inadequacies.

He deserves respect for that courage, particularly in light of various caviling critics who condemn him because they either cannot understand or do not like some of his music. Or think he should have catered to *their* tastes instead of aspiring to realize his own visionary explorations in new musical domains. Or who never had guts enough themselves to step beyond the comfort and security of the familiar, the orthodox, and the profitable.

There are still those who refuse to see a certain point clearly: If Buckley did not deserve all of this attention, he would not be getting it. Whatever his mistakes and psychological flaws, he gave his all and did it so truly and so well that we are talking about him to this day. How long does a guy have to last before he's proven himself? Seems to me a little respect might be in order.

As for myself, a tip o' the hat to my old friend Tim Buckley.

CHAPTER 9

CARNEGIE II—1969

Meanwhile, back in Venice, "our little Bowery by the sea," as Tim called it, things kept rolling along—laying on the beach, body surfing, hanging out at Big Pink, enjoying more of those great conversations with Tim and Larry about art, life and love, drinking beer and wine, smoking pot. Tim and Danny kept us laughing, while Larry's intelligence kept our brains churning. During the day, Tim and I listened to jazz. At night we returned to Dr. John and the Night Trippers, Aretha Franklin, sometimes Jimi Hendrix. Jennifer and I tried acid a couple of times. Nothing much happened, wiggly patterns on the rug, big deal. I said I'd rather drink beer.

Jennifer's son, Michael, came home on vacations from Happy Valley. On one of those visits we discovered he had started smoking cigarettes. I told him not to do that, even as I lit one of my own. He laughed and showed me some new piano chords he had learned. This was the period when Jennifer painted a portrait of him playing upright piano, stylistically reminiscent of Picasso's blue period.

Then life's kaleidoscope spun a little faster.

Tim, Carter, and I played the Cheetah down at Pacific Ocean Park two blocks away. Shortly afterwards, the place burned down. Not long after that, POP shut down, and we didn't hear kids laughing and screaming on the roller coaster any more. We didn't see the top of the Ferris wheel spinning. We didn't hear calliope music from the merry-go-round.

Right next door to Big Pink on the east side, contractors built a liquor store. Convenient for buying beer, but the noise of it going up was not pleasant, especially in the morning. Not long after that, a construction crew started building an apartment house next to Big Pink on the west side. Pretty soon, we wouldn't be able to see across the vacant lot down to the ocean.

Larry got drafted and went away. Dan started drinking too much red wine and wasn't so funny any more. Tim drank beer, and for a while he was funny, intentionally exaggerating the slur of his words, physically turning to rubber, pretending to be drunker than he really was. Because of his shenanigans, I drank a little more beer than before and started allowing myself to stagger and slur my words too. Fun for a while. But then I began losing my cool and feeling irritated or getting angry or depressed about little things, not understanding why.

One warm spring night, with gloriously clear black skies and a billion shining stars, Jennifer and I stagger-walked barefoot down to the beach, me carrying half a six-pack, lurching, laughing, wearing jeans and a white T-shirt. We crossed the sands to the water and tumbled into the ocean.

I gave myself up to the sea, relaxing, floating, no resistance, letting the currents carry me slowly away from Jennifer up toward the old POP pier jutting out into the ocean like a wrecked ship's ancient skeleton.

Jennifer looked out into dark waters, couldn't see me. She called, but I didn't answer.

I floated easily on my back, arms outstretched, letting waves roll me over, relaxed, yielding up my soul in bliss, breathing when my face surfaced, opening eyes, looking up at the stars in the mighty nightsky, hearing Jennifer calling frantically, "Lee! Leeeeee! Where are you—Leeeeeee!"

She in torment, calling her lost love. Me in bliss and surrendered joy, at one with the cosmos, floating in God's ocean, starsailing up into the vast black and glittering heavens above . . . "Leeee—answer me! Where are you—Leeeee!"

I stood up, waist-deep in water, yelled to her. She heard and ran to me, desperate, relieved, frightened, crying, splashing water. The two of us hugged in waist-high shoreline waves, the slow ocean gently sighing all around us, she and I in love in the sea, forever-stars twinkling all around us.

Jennifer's painting of her son Michael playing piano at Big Pink.
Michael went on to become a professional musician in Hollywood.

118

Lee and Jennifer's house at 136 Park Place in Venice,
just down the walkway from Tim and Jainie's place.

Then our landlord raised the rent. Well, that was it. We had to move out of Big Pink. A little sad, but okay. With the construction going on, it was time to leave anyway.

Jennifer and Michael found us a house at 136 Park Place, still in Venice, in a comfy neighborhood near the corner of Brooks and Main. A cement sidewalk lined with trees, bushes and flowers ran from Main Street toward the ocean between our row of houses and the row of houses facing us. We had a small front yard with grass, a large living room with wood floors, two bedrooms. When Michael left Happy Valley and started attending Venice High School, we moved him and his piano into one of the bedrooms. There we were, a family again.

Our landlady owned the house behind us, too—134½ Park Place. A certain fellow who eventually played a major role in this story lived there in the ground floor apartment with his wife, Gloria, and her young son, Gregory. His name was Richard, and he was cool, so Tim nicknamed him "Cool Richard," CR for short.

Cool Richard was good looking: black hair, high forehead, high cheekbones, pockmarked skin, well-muscled body, and ruggedly handsome. He was a self-possessed, intelligent, independent young man—a bit mysterious, which made him even more attractive. He looked almost exactly like Tommy Lee Jones in *The Executioner's Song*, a movie made years later about the execution of murderer Gary Gilmore.

CR attended UCLA, studying world music in the Ethnomusicology Department.

Tim and he got along well, and Jennifer and Gloria and Jainie liked to hang out in our kitchen, laughing, gossiping. Everybody liked each other.

Tim's mother, Elaine, however, felt differently. "I never liked Richard," she said. "From the first time I met him at Tim and Jainie's place I didn't like him. It was Mother's Day and they were having a steak dinner. When Richard came in, he was the weirdest character I had ever seen—and I've seen a lot of weird characters in my life.

"He had this white paint all over his face, white makeup, and he was stoned out of his gourd. He was just *white*, and I was looking at this *thing*, like it was a ghost at the table. Tim said he was gonna be in a mime show that night. He said Richard played piano and was a bright guy. Still, there was something about him I did not like. He looked so weird, like death.

"Every time he came to Tim's house when I was there, there was something about Richard I never cared for. And I didn't think he was a friend either, even though Tim said he was. I just couldn't get that feeling that he was a friend."

Tim wasn't working for a while, so I auditioned for a big band called the Mariachi Brass, a spin-off from Herb Alpert's Tijuana Brass. John Balkin, the bass player, liked me. He put in a good word to the director, Buzz Gardner, a trumpet player formerly with Zappa's Mothers of Invention. I got the gig, and we traveled to Edmonton, Canada.

John and I got along well. He was from the South Bronx and some ten years older than I, a graduate of the Manhattan School of Music (B.A., M.A.). He appreciated nearly every generic type of music, particularly jazz and avant-garde classical. He also enjoyed drinking beer, or "tippling goldies," as he called it, and was an intelligent fellow with a good sense of humor, which made conversation easy and fun.

Tim had been looking for new directions, and I felt John might be helpful. Near the end of the summer, I introduced them. The three of us made music together in my living room at Park Place, and before long, John came to play a major role in Tim's musical evolution.

Tim and Jainie still lived in their Malibu house by the ocean, where the waves for the "Love from Room 109" background were recorded. They often drove down to our place to hang out. A young woman named Daniella Sapriel joined our little group, a kung fu practitioner, long dark hair, bright eyes, intelligent, studying to be a lawyer, fun to be around. She lived in Topanga Canyon. Every once in a while when things got too tough for Tim in the days ahead, he visited her house in the canyon, got away from his problems, escaped the madness. He also met his ex-wife Mary and his young son Jeff there on occasion, to visit with his son and avoid Jainie's potential jealousy and/or resentment.

I bought Miles Davis's great new album, *In a Silent Way*, which included John McLaughlin on guitar. Both sides of the LP were based mainly on one chord and a smooth rhythmic groove—a far cry from bebop with a thousand chords, frenetic tempos, superspeedy improvisations. Each side of *In a Silent Way* was sexy, rhythmic, sensual, intimate—not a series of short, fast tracks either, but one long flowing track, great to dance to. Today, many musicians follow this format. Back then, it was an innovation.

Jennifer, Tim, Jainie, Michael, and a few other friends would light the candles, get high, put on *In a Silent Way* and dance to the music in our living room. This particular album was another important influence in Tim's conceptual development. He made a tape of it, as I recall, and took it home with him.

One night I flipped out, something I had never done before.

It was late, and Jennifer, Tim, Jainie, and I had been drinking. Michael slept in the other room. I had an undeniable urge to hear something fierce and fiery, something raw, searing, so I grabbed Jimi Hendrix's *Are You Experienced,* put it on, turned it up *loud.* Jennifer angrily rushed out of the kitchen, ripped the needle off the record—scratching it—and said, "That's way too loud—Michael is sleeping!"

"Fuck Michael! Fuck sleep!"

That moment—that rejection, that denial of my wishes, that simple affront—tapped into everything I had been denied from earliest childhood. A lifetime of bottled-up rage exploded like a volcano. As Tim and Jainie sat on the couch and watched, I heaved books, records, candle holders everywhere. I shattered living room windows, toppled lamps, threw ash trays, dumped bookcases and record collections to the floor, howling in anger, exorcising decades of pent-up fury—rage at not being as good at anything as I would like to be, rage at my parents and their total inability to understand my nature, rage at unbearable years of hurt, pain, withheld love, exploitation, manipulation, resentment, frustration, need.

It was awful. It was wonderful. It was frightening. It was cleansing. It was Janov's Primal Scream in living color. Baby Narcissus on a rampage.

Tim and Jainie witnessed my tantrum without interfering. And in the core of my psyche there was a quiet observer that made me careful not to hit them with anything. Interesting how one can be lost the throes of emotional upheaval and still be centered in that still-point inner eye.

Michael staggered out of the bedroom, rubbing his eyes, afraid—"What's going on?" Because of that same quiet center of awareness, I lowered my voice and very gently and rationally told him I was upset but nobody was going to get hurt, everything was all right, and he should go back to sleep. He returned to his room. I returned to my cathartic rantings. It felt so odd to be absolutely *in* the drunken rage while simultaneously being nonjudgmentally aware of each nuance of feeling and every external gesture.

Jennifer called the cops. They arrived, walked me around the block, brought me back. I started throwing things again, just to show everybody no fucking cops were going to cool *me* out.

Throughout this ordeal, Tim seemed to understand my misery, those ancient hurts erupting, that need for love that never came, perhaps especially from the father. He didn't show fear or condemnation, only sympathy and compassion, the kind of empathy that could embrace the enraged destroyer in me just as lovingly as he could embrace the creator.

Jainie felt extremely anxious during the ordeal, of course, but stuck it out. She later said I wasn't "convincing" after the cops brought me back. Ah, well . . .

As the sun rose, we left Jennifer at home and headed for the liquor store. On the way, a police car pulled up, two different cops jumped out.

"Okay, hands against the wall."

I didn't want them to bust Tim for having long hair or being good looking, so I drew attention to myself as they searched us—"What the fuck are you hassling us for? We haven't done anything. Jesus, don't you have anything important to do?"

"Shut up, buddy, or your ass is fried chicken."

Tim and Jainie remained quiet. The cops made me show my ID, then departed. We continued to the liquor store and sat on the lawn in the park sipping beer until I had finally cooled out enough to go back home. After sleeping a few hours, I cleaned up the wreckage in the house.

Jennifer asked me if she had done the right thing by calling the police. I said, "Yes. Don't feel badly about that." Michael didn't say anything about the matter, nor did he hold it against me. I don't know how, but he seemed to understand.

Tim and I flew to Atlantic City to play the Pop Festival on August 16, 1969, at the racetrack outside of town. The day was bright and sunny, the stands packed with people—50,000 of them, the largest crowd we had seen up to that time.

Scheduled to go on at 2 P.M., we waited our turn, hanging out among parked cars beside the stage, meeting and talking with people, one of whom was a lovely nineteen-year-old I'll remember as Meneli. Tall, well-built, with long blond hair, high cheekbones, full lips, hazel eyes, white teeth, a saucy, flirtatious smile. She was a beauty, thrilled to be in Tim's presence.

Tim and I got hot just talking with her. The three of us lay back on the hood of a car and started necking, Tim on one side, I on the other, Meneli laughing and

Tim and Lee in a duo performance at the Atlantic City racetrack, August 16, 1969. When Tim started singing, thousands of people broke down the safety barriers, crowded up to the stage, and kept on cheering.

giggling in the middle. Ah, she could hug, she could kiss fantastically well, she was a little kinky, like we were, and she felt oh-so incredibly good.

Before we knew it, just as we were getting stiffies, somebody called, "Buckley! You're on!" We grabbed our guitars and hopped up onstage. Shaded under a high roof, we looked out across the racetrack that separated us from the stands. Behind a high fence barrier, 50,000 teeming people filled the bleachers all the way up to the top balconies on the other side of the track. At the sight of Tim, they started clapping, cheering, whistling in anticipation. We could hear the excitement growing.

Tim said to me, "Lay out a while. Gimme some time."

He started strumming those rolling-thunder rhythms for the opening of "The Train." Giant speakers on both sides of the stage amplified the sound louder than anything we had ever heard. People cheered and clapped and whooped while Tim strummed hard and fast, mixing in fast double-strums as he rolled on, like whiplash lightning flashes. Then he threw back his head, opened his mouth, and sang a high-pitched banshee wail that literally shivered my spine.

The crowd roared, stood on its feet cheering and yelling, and ran at the fence-barrier en masse. The fence crashed down in an enormous cloud of dust, and thousands of fans surged toward the stage, running across the track and filling the gap between us and the bleachers.

Tim hollered at them, "Yeow!—I think I'm starting to feel like a pop star!"—and kept on strumming, his voice soaring up and down the register, working the crowd to a fever pitch. I had never heard anything like what he was doing—and had never seen anything like what was happening.

"Come on!" he motioned to me. I jumped into the music, screaming high notes on the guitar like a rock 'n' roller, astonished at how loud they were through the massive speakers—the power of it, the wing-zinging thrill of it—and we were off and running: Tim wailing, me playing, the crowd cheering and clapping, all of us riding waves upon waves of music together.

Summer in America, 1969. Music, sunshine. Communication, communion, community. Meneli stood beside the stage looking up at us, beaming and smiling, her eyes dancing, excited, clapping her hands, thrilled by the passion and magic in the air. And the music, ahh, the music, wings of golden light all the way to heaven's gate. . . . Unforgettable moments.

Meneli had come to the concert with Joey Stevens, a photographer friend of Tim's, so we didn't get to spend time with her afterwards, plus we had to move on to other gigs, notably the Schaeffer Music Festival in Central Park. But she re-entered our lives later and played a significant role.

One night at Max's Kansas City in New York, Tim and I sat with Janis Joplin and her lead guitarist, Sam Andrews, hanging out, getting drunk, snorting coke on the side. Janis was in great form that night, loud, funny, expansive in her gestures, affectionate to Timmy, practically smothering him with boa feathers and kisses. I finally had enough and took a cab back to John King's place in the Village.

A couple of hours later, the door burst open. Some large, fat, blond girl helped Tim lurch through the door, practically carrying him. He was as smashed as I had ever seen him. The girl took off his shoes, turned out the light, got into bed beside him.

A few minutes later, Tim leaned over the edge of the bed and puked all over the floor. The poor girl got out of bed, cleaned up the mess with towels, and left the next morning.

I asked Tim, "What happened? I thought you and Janis were gettin' it on."

"No way I could handle a voracious tiger like that. No way."

Not long after we recorded *Blue Afternoon*, Tim and Jainie invited Jennifer and me up to their Malibu place. It was a large one-room, glass-walled house overlooking the ocean, with a wooden balcony under which the waters rolled in and touched the shoreline.

Tim said, "Let's get high." He gave me a block of orange acid. "Take this."

"I don't know, Tim, it looks like a lot."

"Take it."

I did. He swallowed mescaline and orange juice. We sat with our guitars and played.

Before long, the acid started rushing—with such power that I was overwhelmed, had to set my guitar aside—"Sorry, Tim, comin' on." I wobbled over to the mattress on the floor to lie down. Tim kept playing, then set his guitar down too. Jennifer and Jainie hung out in the kitchen, relaxed, chatting, casually enjoying each other's company. I lay on the bed, for the first time totally caught up in the LSD experience.

"My God, Tim, this is fantastic!"

He smiled. "You've got a strong will. That's why it couldn't happen before."

"This is magnificent!"

All reservations, criticisms, egoistic judgments, psychological fragmentations, fears, and hostilities vanished. Finally, and for the first time, I felt the profound bliss that comes when one transcends the ego and experiences unity-consciousness. No longer separate and alienated, I loved people, I loved nature, I loved my life, my friends, strangers, animals, plants. I merged with existence, felt the power-flow of divine energy, became Love itself. I finally understood what the great mystics were talking about—not to mention Jimi Hendrix, the Beatles, Timothy Leary, Ram Dass, and millions of hippies throughout the world.

While I was moaning and muttering ecstatically about how much I loved everybody, Jennifer sat down beside me, held me in her arms, and asked, "And do you love the middle class too?" "I do! I do!" I laughed. "I finally broke through!"

Tim put on a Bill Evans album. I watched him as he did so. He glowed in a green aura, which phased into purple haze. His beauty took my breath away. The piano music sounded tinny to me, artificial. Tim took the needle off, let the gentle hush of ocean waves return. "Kind of irrelevant, isn't it," he smiled, slipping the album back inside its cover. Although he was very young, he seemed to know and understand so much about big things, little things—about nearly everything that mattered—music, love, suffering, pain, pleasure, anguish, yearning. . . .

Someone knocked. I sat up sharply. "It's okay," Tim said. "Relax." Jainie answered the door, talked to somebody, called to Tim, "Did you have a photo session scheduled today?" "Oh. Yeah. I forgot." I looked at him, anxious. "It's okay," he assured me. "No problem. I'll be back soon." He grabbed two or three shirts from the closet and left the house.

"Can he handle it?" I asked Jainie.

She chuckled. "He can handle anything stoned," she said. "Sometimes he amazes me."

Four of the twelve pictures that appeared on *Blue Afternoon* were taken that day: the back cover, with Tim underneath the Santa Monica pier, straightening his jacket collar; two photos inside, also under the pier, one in a cowboy shirt with black and white designs (originally CR's shirt), one in a red shirt; and a fourth one, Tim sitting next to a log among trees, wearing a white pearl-button shirt.

Later, after taking a shower, I looked into the mirror and smiled a huge smile. For the first time in my life, I loved myself and found myself beautiful. When Tim returned, the four of us drove up the Malibu coast and walked at sunset on one of those gorgeous beaches that make Malibu famous. I thank Tim for the best acid trip I ever had.

Tim and Jainie decided to throw a party. They invited me and Jennifer, Danny Gordon, Daniella, CR and Gloria, Bear, and a dozen other friends. Jainie played rock 'n' roll in the living room: Rolling Stones, Beatles, Eric Burdon and the Animals, the Who.

It was a glorious night outside. The sky was unusually clear, vast, dark. Sometimes a blue-white star gracefully arched down into the sea. Far out on the ocean we could see gold lights twinkling on passing ships, and hear the poignant

The front porch of Tim and Jainie's house at 111 Park Place. A high wooden fence was erected after Tim left, to prevent people from peering in.

sound of bells ringing on buoys. Easy waves rolled in that night, gently tumbling over themselves, slipping in up under the balcony.

Pleasantly tiddily, nothing heavy, we stood outside on the balcony enjoying cool breezes. Danny Gordon raised his glass and started singing that great old Gene Raskin song, "Those . . . were . . . the days, my friend. . . . We thought they'd never end. . . ." We raised our glasses and sang along with him, "Those were the days, my friend. . . ."

But of course they did end. Tim and Jainie moved back to Venice, into a house at 111 Park Place just up the walkway from Jennifer and me. Not long after that, the place they had rented in Malibu burned down.

Then things weren't good between them anymore, and they broke up. Tim was evolving toward stardom and a different type of woman, while Jainie needed a loyal man to be home with her instead of out on the road all the time. She moved out, leaving Tim in the house by himself.

Although Jennifer and I got along well, I had been inwardly pulling away, needing time alone. Before long, she and I broke up too. I remained at 136, while she and Michael moved to her mother's house in Laguna Beach, eventually returning to Venice. Her farewell words to me: "You won't last a year before you'll fall apart."

Now that Jennifer and Michael were gone, I didn't need a two-bedroom house and did not want to pay for one. CR's place in back was too small for him and his family to live in comfortably. So he and I traded places. Jennifer had bought some lightweight bright-orange blankets. I hung them over the bedroom windows and settled into 134½ Park Place for the next three years.

The phone rang. Without saying hello, Tim said, "Herb booked us into Carnegie Hall."

"Carnegie Hall! Wow, Tim—congratulations!"

"We'll gig our way across the country, then stay at John King's farm for a week before the November 2nd concert—bring a warm coat."

"I'm ready!"

Bassist John Balkin had played Carnegie several times during his classical music days at the Manhattan School of Music, plus he was from New York to begin with, so he didn't feel as impressed as we were. For him, Carnegie was more or less just another place to play. For us, the very idea of playing Carnegie—our own show, not a hootenanny with other people—was intimidating, exciting, thrilling, a major event.

We hit the road with John and Carter, working clubs across the country, getting ourselves into shape for the big one. At John King's farm, the lovely raven-haired Hope Ruff joined us, along with Bob Campbell, Bear—and Meneli, who took a train up from New York by herself. We picked her up at the Craryville station in John's fabulously decadent Excalibur car. Her cheeks were rosy in the winter chill, her eyes sparkling, a vision of loveliness.

We hung out for a couple of days, then John King called a few girls at the nearby private school. Sure enough, about ten showed up, eager to meet Tim. We got high on pot and a few goldies. Somebody pushed aside the living room table, laid out a mattress, said, "Let's have a group grope!" We had read and heard about such things, but had never done it.

Tim couldn't back out, because he was the star. I couldn't back out, because this was the hip thing to do. So we found ourselves rolling around naked on the mattress with four or five girls, including Meneli. Some of the other girls stood around in a circle and watched, giggling and laughing with us, while a few others stayed in the kitchen drinking wisdom from John Balkin's eyes and listening to Bob Campbell expound on the virtues of good wine, good music, good sex.

Far too self-conscious, I couldn't get it up. So I buried my face in Meneli's sweet muff, hoping I would get turned on, making sure my limp pecker faced the mattress out of view. Tim was humping some girl, so I figured he was up and happening. Response to challenge. Lucky guy. Everything he did was right. God bless him, the little twit.

Suddenly, Hope strode in from the kitchen, visibly upset, gnashing her teeth. She grabbed Timmy by the hair, yanked him up—"You son-of-a-bitch! How dare you invite me here, then screw around like this! Get your ass outta here, you fucker!" She hauled him out of the room and upstairs by his hair, like an angry mother chastising her wayward brat-son.

Well, that rather took the wind out of a mostly windless sail anyway, so we cooled it. Meneli and I made love upstairs, but I wasn't very good. I could tell she wanted Tim. Oh, well. Showbiz.

Later, I told Tim I couldn't get it up in the living room with all those girls, but he had looked like he was doing fine, humping away. "Me?" he laughed. "I couldn't get it up either! And boy, was Hope pissed—ha!" The entire scene tickled his pixie sense of humor.

Certain people have characterized the farm as a kind of Bacchanalian flesh pit, which was simply not so. Even this incident with the girls was playful, innocent, a childlike aspiration toward a decadent intoxication quite beyond us.

Usually when we spent time there, no lovers were present, and certainly no strangers, male or female. For the most part, John King's farm was a retreat from the city, a place to get away from so-called "friends" who later characterized the farm in sensationalist terms and irresponsibly celebrated Tim's tormenting fears and needs and periodic self-destructive excesses in New York and elsewhere as romantic hedonistic whimsies.

Tim and Hope enjoyed each other's company and got on well. This was the period during which he said he thought he might like to marry her. Meneli pretty much ignored me, constantly smiling at Tim, letting him know she was ready and willing, which of course left me outside the circle again.

More than that, although I had no idea of its effect at the time, Carnegie was looming, a gig so big I simply could not handle the weight. The prospect of it aroused all of my inadequacies, insecurities. Unbearably painful anxiety.

And so one night I kept drinking until I was bombed. I called Michael Cavanaugh back in Venice, and said, "Michael, I'm disappearing forever. Leaving all this music bullshit behind, all this ambition crap, and heading out to New Mexico. There's a place called Eagle Nest, a teensy town high in the northeast mountains. I'm gonna hitch-hike there, drop off the edge of the world."

"That's great, but what about Carnegie?"

"Fuck Carnegie. It's Tim's trip anyhow. I just wanted you to know I'm disappearing and I love you."

I staggered out of the house—it must have been 2:30 A.M.—and lurched down a dirt road toward Craryville. Before long, unable to walk any further, I lay down off the side of the road in a cornfield—"Jus' for a few min . . ."—and fell asleep. Woke up at sunrise, chilled, sick, horrendously hung over, staggered back to the house.

Tim was visibly relieved to see me. "Where were you? Where did you go?"

"Spent the night in a cornfield," I muttered, embarrassed, shamefaced.

"I came after you in John's car, tried to find you."

"Thanks, ol' buddy. Thanks for caring."

"I looked everywhere. Glad you're back. You could have frozen."

"Thanks, Tim. Sorry 'bout that—lemme go upstairs and crash."

The four of us took the stage at Carnegie Hall and played exceptionally well. Tim was in magnificent form. He wore a gauzy white cotton one-piece shirt with wide sleeves, black corduroy pants, shiny black boots. The people in the audience were ready for us—bouquets of roses, love notes, cheers. All those good vibes—respect, admiration, appreciation, adulation—hummed in the air. This was Tim's night. Our night, too. Carter looked great, played fantastically well. John Balkin was right-on, thumping out first-rate bass lines. I had recovered from the binge, felt good, had everything together.

We looked up to our left, and there sat Hope and Meneli and Bob Campbell and big ol' Bear in the Numero Uno front balcony box, almost within reach, beaming down on us with love and pride and excitement.

We played the great tunes that had brought us to that point, including "Buzzin' Fly," "Pleasant Street," "Once I Was," "Love from Room 109," "Morning Glory," Fred Neil's "Dolphin Song," and finished with a rousing rip-roaring extended version of "Gypsy Woman."

Throughout the concert, and especially in "Gypsy Woman," Tim gave people a taste of the extraordinary vocal pyrotechnics that were beginning to define his relationship with music—the hoots and hollers, the snarls, growls, yips, yodels and animal sounds that eventually made his singing so powerful and ultimately inimitable. His conceptual evolution displayed the brilliant imagination and amazing technique for which he was already famous. It now showcased as well, and in often dazzling ways, his amazing ears—an unerring sense of pitch, coupled with unmatched control.

After "Gypsy Woman," we walked backstage, stood in the wings breathing hard. "Gimme a $B\flat$," Tim said. I played the chord for him. He hummed the key-tone, walked back out, and sang "Anonymous Proposition" a cappella, perhaps remembering Roland Kirk's unaccompanied performance in Montreal.

To this day I have not heard another performance that matched the intimacy, melodic range, and musical beauty of that song and the way he sang it. "Anonymous Proposition" had appeared on *Lorca*, but at Carnegie he sang it by himself, no group, no 12-string guitar, just him and his voice, radiant in the spotlight on one of the world's most revered stages, holding notes higher and longer and with greater strength and conviction and beauty than I had ever heard. He lived up to the spirits in that hallowed hall, the unnumbered great artists and composers who have set foot on that stage and given their all. Tears came to my eyes as I watched from the wings. He did it, he did it on his own, and he did it right. It was one of the highlights of his life. Mine, too.

I also felt pleased with my own playing, and was flattered to see in a positive *Times* review the next day that writer Nancy Erlich thought I had done well. She said I shone as the outstanding musician of Tim's group, that my solos were "consistently exciting and original," and that if I hadn't worked at being unobtrusive when Tim was singing I might have "walked off with the show."

That was exaggerated praise, of course, but it was nice to see that I had connected with a professional listener as an individual player, not only as an anonymous member of a backup band. Indeed, throughout these years, Tim gave all of us room in the spotlight and welcomed our contributions. We weren't merely faceless cardboard props. We were his friends in life, his compatriots in music. He welcomed our music as a vital part of the sound that made him a distinctive artist.

CHAPTER 10

LORCA'S BLUE AFTERNOON

While still playing mellow jazz-flavored *Happy Sad* music and including a few crowd pleasers from *Goodbye and Hello,* we began improvising music that flew further into the stratosphere, leaving many fans behind. More and more frequently, crowds grew restless as Tim started wailing and howling nonverbally. We still got cheers, but now interlaced with boos.

Tim did not back off. He kept exploring, developing, growing—but he also started wearing combat boots every set, even as his father had worn combat boots in public while celebrating World War II.

By the time we started moving out of *Happy Sad* into the experimental early *Lorca* period and played the *Live at the Troubadour* gig on September 3 and 4, 1969, the discomfort some listeners felt started appearing in reviews. Defiantly, Tim came up with a term for a certain kind of rigidly conditioned consciousness—"lobotomized." And there he was—wearing combat boots, shrieking at audiences instead of cooing and wooing them, fighting the ubiquitous "Lobos" wherever they surfaced.

Live at the Troubadour featured John Balkin on bass, Art Tripp on drums, (I think Carter was with us on congas too) and me on guitar and electric piano. It was our first effort to play "Lorca" onstage, a piece written in the odd time signature of 5/4, unheard of in pop music (although not in jazz or contemporary classical music). On the whole, that Troubadour performance was an extended exploratory jam session and not one of our better outings. "Driftin'" worked well, but otherwise we were moving forward into new and unknown territory and did not yet feel comfortable or secure in what we were attempting. Having embarked, however, we sailed on, undaunted.

A sort of war was brewing, and Tim embraced it. It gave him an opportunity to prove himself on two different levels. Consciously, the conflict was a matter of artistic evolution and commitment to transcendent aesthetic principles. On an unconscious level, he didn't have Hitler for his war like his Dad did, but he did have the Lobos. Maybe his father would be proud of him. And avant-garde artistry was a mighty weapon. If necessary, Tim would take on the world. In some ways, that is exactly what he did.

For several months preceding *Live at the Troubadour*—since mid '68 or so—Tim had been extending and expanding his improvisational vocal skills, experimenting with new concepts that were in fact the seeds of what would become known as "the Starsailor period." *Live at the Troubadour* marked the first recorded explorations of that period.

Then, with *Lorca* and especially with its successor, *Starsailor*, Tim ascended the highest creative peaks of his career. He also descended to the commercial arena's darkest valleys. As a visionary innovator, he soared to the mountaintop. As a hit parader, he bombed. Fans who claimed to be his greatest supporters commercially crucified him, insisting it was his fault, not theirs.

Of the five stages of his artistic development, this was far and away the most exciting, challenging, adventurous, complex—and devastating.

One day at Big Pink on Navy Street in Venice, before we had moved to Park Place, Tim indicated to me in his usual dramatic fashion that he was ready for new directions. When I told him Gabor Szabo had come out with a new album, he replied, "That faggot! What else you got?" So much for Gabor. Something new was needed.

Music is not monolithic, although many musicians, listeners, and business people would like to think its relevance and validity begin and end with Top 40 radio music. However, starting with country and folk and moving up through pop, soul, and rock, mainstream jazz, avant-garde jazz, and then into Euro-American classical and East-West higher-consciousness realms, Western musics vary enormously in terms of aesthetic style, psycho-spiritual content, and motivational intention. They also ascend a spectrum of consciousness from simple to universal, from flashy to subtle, from sensual, sentimental and personal realms to radiantly transpersonal domains.

By this time, Tim had absorbed and transformed all he wanted and needed from folk, rock, and mainstream jazz. He was searching for new ideas, new concepts, and new directions. Answering his call as well as I could, I trotted out several innovative avant-garde musicians, notably saxophonists John Coltrane and Eric Dolphy, and pianist Cecil Taylor—three of America's greatest creative forces.

If they had not suited his needs at the time, he could and would have rejected them. As it turned out, he was thrilled by what he heard. Unmatched musical spontaneity. Freedom organically structured from within by creative brilliance. Clashing dissonant intervals. Criss-crossing melodic lines. Fluid and flexible rhythms. Vivid sonic tapestries. Fierce emotional climates. The rushing river-rage of inspired creative energy—all of these dynamic musical principles stimulated his imagination and contributed to the next stage of his evolution.

Larry and I always took great pleasure in talking together. It was a way of entertaining ourselves, juggling philosophical ideas, frolicking on intellectual playgrounds, testing each other's wit and skill, laughing, enjoying each other's company.

Tim and I also enjoyed each other's company, and we, too, transported each other up into the highest realms of thought, laughing and playing and enjoying ourselves along the way. But the journey with Tim was personal and intense as well, and life-or-death sincere. Conversational content had profound relevance to our lives. It had to do with identity, meaning, creative direction. We weren't playing with cerebrally titillating philosophical toys. We were exploring the depths and heights of ourselves, identifying who we were, and finding out what we wanted and needed to do with our little handful of years.

In the past Tim and I had talked intensely about jazz. Now we talked about avant-garde ways of approaching music both psychologically and formally—releasing and trusting streams of consciousness, such as Cecil Taylor, or moving into odd time signatures, where rhythm is not contained within four metric beats, but within five, or seven, nine, ten, like Dave Brubeck, Don Ellis, or Bartók. Or free rhythms, natural, like ocean waves, unrelated to time signatures. We talked about utilizing a fundamental root-chord pedal point, like Bach or Miles Davis, over which could be played any number of chromatic harmonic and melodic variations. We talked about emotional spontaneity, liberation from conventional song forms, freedom from orthodox melodies and harmonies, the creative responsibilities that came with such freedom.

We talked about several fiery and affirmative dark-side poets, including Lorca, Brother Antoninus (a.k.a. William Everson), Delmore Schwartz, and Dylan Thomas. Tim had heard Larry Beckett speak glowingly of Thomas, but had not read much of him, and the other names were new. I also suggested he check out the higher-consciousness poetry of two Western mystics, William Blake and Rainer Maria Rilke. Somewhere between Lorca and Rilke, surely he would find aesthetic stimulation and sympathetic literary friends. Writers and musicians do not have to be alive to be one's friends. Their genius lives in the present through their works. Sometimes, in fact, one's *only* friends are found in the writings and music of those who have gone before or who are struggling to create something fresh and new in the Now.

To help him along, I loaned him four New Directions paperbacks—the *Collected Poems* of Dylan Thomas, with a white cover and blacks letters; *Flowers of Evil*, by Baudelaire, and a book of Lorca's poems, both with black-and-white photographs on their covers; and *Nightwood*, by Djuna Barnes, prose fiction written in 1936 by a woman who had intensely poetic sensibilities. Tim returned the Baudelaire and Barnes books, but kept the Thomas and Lorca poems. When I asked him about them a year or two later, he said he had loved the poetry and taken them with him on the road, but lost them somewhere along the way.

Continuing our explorations at Park Place soon thereafter, we visited record stores and checked out electronic music. Since neither of us knew anything about this domain, we bought things that looked modern in the cover photos and ultra-abstract in the paintings, and any name that sounded foreign—the more consonants, the better.

Four significant compilations—*Images Fantastiques*, two entitled *Electronic Music*, and one entitled *Electronic Music III*—included works by Xenakis, Berio, Ilhan Mimaroglu, John Cage, Tzvi Avni, and several others.

At home alone, I lay down on the floor with a speaker on each side, and was blown away by the extraordinary sonic dimensions these composers brought to music. They soared a million miles beyond traditional Western classical concepts of melody/harmony/rhythm, into spatial dimensions, sound-flows, and psycho-sonic electronic permutations like nothing else I had ever encountered. Talk about innovators!

This was not "body" music, in which sexual intoxication plays a paramount role. Nor was it pop-oriented "heart" music, rooted in love, loss, hope, pain and other personal sentiments. I would have to characterize it as "mind" music, in which the impact and significance had to do almost entirely with non-referential transpersonal aesthetic pleasures—intellectual stimulation similar, perhaps, to mental pleasures derived from brilliantly conceived non-representational abstract paintings.

Perhaps it is no wonder that when I excitedly told Tim about my research, he listened to some of the electronic music briefly, then turned away and said, "No, it doesn't touch my heart."

However, when I played several electro-acoustic pieces by Italian composer Luciano Berio, featuring vocalist Cathy Berberian, particularly "Visage," "Sequenza III" and "Thema (Omaggio a Joyce)," his eyes lit up.

Berberian usually did not sing words. When she did, she held on to vowels and extended their sounds indefinitely. More often than not, she chirped, beeped, cheeped, clucked, cooed, squeaked, gurgled, peeped, yowled, howled, growled, whispered, cried, wept, laughed, wailed, utilizing her voice, not as a vehicle to carry words and concepts, but as a multifaceted sound-source that created pure, direct emotion—like a new instrument. Her approach was not verbal, but sonic; not conceptual, but aural; not linear, but abstract; not metered, but flowing; not artificial, but natural; not decorative, but primal.

Delighted, Tim clapped his hands and listened to these pieces several times. In Cathy Berberian, he had found a friend. Her work with Berio affirmed his own nascent nonverbal vocal explorations. Tim no longer felt lonely, isolated, freakish. He had intuitively suspected he was on the right track. Now he knew it, without doubt, and chose to pursue it to the end.

I did not know enough to continue nourishing Tim's hunger for new information—but John Balkin did. He had a ton of information about avant-garde jazz and contemporary classical music, exactly the domain that now interested Tim. It was at this time, late summer of '69, when I brought John over to my living room at 136 Park Place as a kind of gift to Tim, and the three of us played together. As Tim and John got better acquainted, they began appreciating each other's intelligence, sense of humor, and considerable knowledge. Before long, they were friends.

Balkin lived in North Hollywood, where he built a small music studio behind his house, complete with gongs, bells, shakers, metal pipes, a variety of basses, guitars, whistles, horns, drums, a piano stacked high with dusty sheet music, and several microphones, amplifiers and tape recorders.

He invited Tim over, and sometimes I was included. Our music-making process was fascinating, initially starting from nothing. Then perhaps a single bell or one scratch of a bow across the bass, or maybe Tim's humming a note out of the blue and holding it. Then, slowly, slowly, we built harmonic layers with interweaving notes, tones, or atonal chord clusters—creating music, not in conventional song forms, but as a flowing, ongoing stream of sound-colors. The dissonance had intensity. The flow generated its own forms. Tim sang either words or nonverbal sounds, using his voice to create horn lines or sonic effects. The atmospheres and contexts produced through these means eventually became extraordinary in their intricacy and beauty.

John brought over two of his best friends from the Korean War days: Buzz Gardner (trumpet) and his brother, Bunk Gardner (various horns), both former members of Zappa's Mothers of Invention. John, Buzz, and Bunk had been improvising together for years.

"As I recall," John said, "Tim had some difficulty jumping in at first. Not his fault; just the nature of what we were doing. Our backgrounds were different, and the genre was completely new for him. Educated free-form stuff is a bit of a walk on the wild side, with no road map.

"For many years, Buzz, Bunk, and I had done free improvisations with our trio, but we didn't do it haphazardly or arbitrarily. We were trained musicians. Buzz went to Manhattan [School of Music] with me. He didn't graduate, but he studied there. Bunk went to school in Cleveland. And they had been playing since they were sixteen. They were both excellent jazz players, and they were in the 7th Army Band with Herbie Mann, among others. A couple of mornings a week, we would play chamber music together too. We'd write out Bach trios, fugues, play them with trumpet, flute or clarinet, and bass.

"So when we improvised, we had this panoply of sounds. We knew each other's sounds, and we listened to each other. It was not just picking up an instrument and playing 'free.' It was more than that."

With Tim and sometimes myself in the group, musical inventions sailed further and further out. As exploratory experimentation continued, Tim became more adept at listening to subtleties and more confident in creating within spontaneously structured contexts. It didn't happen overnight, of course, but work done sporadically over a period of months generated many of the concepts and ideas that led to *Starsailor*.

In addition to being an accomplished bassist, John was well-versed in the history of Western classical music, which gave him depth and scope, while his per-

John Balkin and Lee at Balkin's place in Colorado, circa 1997. Still alive, still caring, still strong, still creating.

sonal tastes inclined toward the avant-garde. I had brought Cathy Berberian to Tim. Now John brought Krzysztof Penderecki, Arnold Schoenberg, Werner Henze, and Olivier Messiaen.

Tim devoured them all. He came to especially love Penderecki's *To the Victims of Hiroshima* and Oliver Messiaen's *Quartet for the End of Time.*

When John met Tim, he realized right from the get-go he was in the presence of a very special, very talented person, not just another pretty-boy pop star. He saw the diamond-in-the-rough, so to speak, and appreciated what Tim might do if given a few skills and proper musical nourishment.

John participated in Tim's music with enthusiasm, becoming a teacher, helper, and confidant whom Tim deeply valued. He gave Tim knowledge, courage, and friendship during the *Lorca/Starsailor* period, a time in which Tim needed all the help and encouragement he could get. When almost nobody else was there, John stood by him.

John participated with full awareness of the significance of what was going on musically, and did not let the intensity and vividness of the experience fade away and vanish into extinction when the years rolled by. His capacity to see, to feel, to be conscious of events as they took place, and to distinguish between diamonds and glass, speaks well for him. His conceptual and musical contributions to Tim during the *Lorca/Starsailor* period were invaluable.

Tim owed Jac Holzman another album. We went into Whitney Studios in Glendale and recorded *Lorca*. Balkin played pipe organ and bass. In addition to guitar, I played electric piano.

The title track is nearly ten minutes long, written in 5/4 time over a single C-minor chord, and showcases Tim's emergent avant-garde vocalizings—nothing harsh, but certainly unconventional and comparatively abstract.

Tim felt that with this song, "Lorca," he had finally attained his own identity—no influences from vocalists of the past, whether Nat King Cole, Johnny Mathis, Pete Seeger, or Fred Neil. Cathy Berberian had opened a door that he was already halfway through, but it was he, not she, who recorded the album, *Lorca*. With her help, he had finally discovered and expressed his unique creative voice, in a new and original context. Tim felt proud of himself, justifiably so. Thousands of artists slave a lifetime without finding their own identity. The realization of self is the gateway to artistic authenticity. Years later, his own son, Jeff Buckley, raved about *Lorca* in his notebooks, celebrating it (along with *Starsailor*) as one of his Tim's greatest accomplishments.

As Tim told writer Michael Davis, "I decided it was time to come up with something new—a voice capable of five-and-a-half octaves certainly can come up with something else. And I was getting real tired of writing just standard songs, adhering to the verse-verse-chorus-verse form. With *Lorca*, it was finally me, beyond influences."

Tim often said "Anonymous Proposition," the gorgeous ballad he sang a cappella at Carnegie Hall, was written for sultry Marlene Dietrich. Many writers later commented on the sheer *intimacy* of that song.

"The real advance with *Lorca* was in 'Anonymous Proposition,'" Tim told Davis. "It's the physical presentation that makes it so personal. It has to be done slowly. It has to take five to six minutes. It has to be a movement. It has to hold you there, and make you aware that somebody is telling you something. He's telling you something about himself in the dark. That's what music is all about on record. It is *very* personal. There is no other way to deal with it."

One of the most accessible tracks on *Lorca* was the intimate, sensual, heart-touching "Driftin'," neatly lifted out of context from the *Live at the Troubadour* performance. Nothing was mentioned about it on the *Lorca* jacket, but if one listens carefully a few background club sounds can be heard. The other two tracks on side two, the gentle "I Had a Talk with My Woman" and the upbeat "Nobody Walkin'" (also extrapolated from *Troubadour*), are very touching love songs, easily accessed, easily enjoyed.

Lorca was a first step, hesitant, flawed, initially a little difficult to understand. The second side was rooted in Tim's earlier familiar folk-jazz mode, but the first side (with "Lorca" and "Anonymous Proposition") was extending beyond the familiar, into new conceptual domains. Much of Tim's previous audience couldn't get through the first side, didn't like the album and didn't buy it, and a majority of critics denounced it. A typical review might describe the title track as opening with a "doomy, menacing organ sound, morbidly reminiscent of *Phantom of the Opera*," while "Anonymous Proposition" was described more than once, not as "intimate," but as "deathly slow." The other songs, at best, were "not completely satisfying."

Larry Beckett found *Lorca* (and later much of *Starsailor*) repugnant and utterly beyond his grasp. He shook his head sadly and felt so "disheartened" that he wouldn't even listen to the second side. I can only assume he soothed his dejection by retreating to familiar Bob Dylan folk songs and perky Beatles tunes.

On the whole, *Lorca* got a bad rap. It holds up extremely well under the test of time and is, in fact, a work of which some is challenging and some is eminently accessible. It is by no means a "perfect" album, whatever that might be, but it definitely rewards receptive listening, which is why not all critics missed the point—some understood *Lorca*, and liked it, and said so.

The New York Times, for example, praised Buckley's search "for primal colors, fundamental rhythms and pure, direct melodic lyricism." The writer (uncredited on copy) said "Driftin'" and "Anonymous Proposition" have an "almost Coltranesque modality," while "Lorca" is "a stunning *tour de force* that has a sensual involvement with sound for its own sake." The writer perceptively concluded with the observation that the label "jazz" is too limiting for *Lorca*, that Buckley is his own man, and that *Lorca* "is simply Tim Buckley music—and damn good music at that."

Following one of our live performances during this period, at Edwards Auditorium at the University of Rhode Island, writer Gerry Boudreau observed that Buckley was by no means a "folk" singer and that the audience reaction was one of restrained dissatisfaction in the face of Buckley's "new style." Perceptively, he did not blame the music, but attributed the reaction to the listeners' "failure to adjust their preconceived image of Tim Buckley [as folk singer] to the Tim Buckley [of *Lorca*] that appeared onstage."

When Jac Holzman sold Elektra, Herb Cohen shifted Tim over to Bizarre/Straight, an independent publishing and recording company he had formed with Frank Zappa. Herb knew *Lorca* was not going to be a big seller in the marketplace, and hoped for a commercially viable album with which to make Tim's debut on the new label.

Recorded almost immediately after *Lorca*, *Blue Afternoon* was a collection of unrelated older songs that had not found homes on earlier albums.[1] Tim brought vibist David Friedman and bassist John Miller back on board, along with me and Carter and studio drummer Jimmy Madison, thus extending the mellow jazz orientation of *Happy Sad*.[2]

With the first side of *Lorca*, we had been moving adventurously forward into ever-greater freedom and abstraction. With *Blue Afternoon*, which Tim produced himself, we moved back to concepts explored on *Happy Sad*. It seemed odd, regressing to a prior aesthetic. It was also a "rush job," as Friedman described it, and because it was unrelated to the avant-garde direction in which we had been evolving, it felt a little distant, which made it somewhat difficult to muster the kind of enthusiasm the project called for. At the same time it was fun, and Tim never did anything in a lazy or half-hearted way. We worked as hard and as well as we could, and hoped the album would make a satisfactory debut on the new label.

It is important to note that while Tim and I regarded *Blue Afternoon* as a conceptual step backward (which it was) and motivated in part by Tim's recognition of Herb's need for commercial product, in no way did Tim—or I—"dismiss" the album as being "bad" music or unworthy of our time and effort. In fact, some of Tim's all-time best songs appeared on *Blue Afternoon*, and he wanted to get them recorded, including "Blue Melody," a gorgeous ballad that he sang in live performances to the very end.

That particular song has remained a personal favorite of mine. Its sensitive lyrics and melodic grace seem to distill Tim's yearning heart, courageous integrity and quiet power into a singular moment of teardrop intensity. On stage whenever we played it, the elegant flow and gentle beauty of that song inevitably touched my heart. These are some of the reasons why I named this book *Blue Melody*.

Although I had played electric piano on *Lorca*, I had not played acoustic piano on any of the albums. As we were driving to the session, Tim said, "I want you to play piano on 'Blue Melody.'" That shook me up. He was remembering those piano improvisations after our first and somewhat disappointing *Happy Sad* sessions in New York at the Mayfair studio. But I had not really *played* piano in a thousand years—and had *never* played any kind of keyboard instrument on "Blue Melody." I did it anyway, and felt good about it.

"Cafe" was another extraordinarily intimate song, one of his most beautiful creations (which he later said he hoped to re-record so it might get greater exposure). This piece also includes some interesting guitar techniques on my solo, primarily a way of sustaining melodic lines, like a violin, by rubbing the tip of my right index finger on the treble strings. It is a song and a performance perhaps best listened to in quiet, intimate surroundings, maybe by candlelight, deeply relaxed, eyes closed.

---

1. *Lorca* was recorded first, but *Blue Afternoon* was the first to be released, hence the confusion among journalists. In a 1974 interview with Steve Lake, Buckley himself said, "That was a complicated time between labels. But *Blue Afternoon* was done immediately after *Lorca*."

2. Guitarist Steve Khan, son of songwriter Sammy Cahn, appeared as an accompanist on two tunes, "Happy Time" and "So Lonely," but was not given credit on the album. Nothing personal, probably just a snafu in the office.

Tim originally wrote the poignant "I Must Have Been Blind" in 1966, but had no place to put it until this album. "The River" is another classic Buckley song from the folk era, a powerful anthem of loneliness and creative freedom.

It was appropriate that *Blue Afternoon* came out before *Lorca*, if only because, artistically speaking, *Blue Afternoon* was an aesthetic extension of *Happy Sad*, while *Lorca* introduced a new conceptual dimension, particularly in the title track. Releasing them in reverse order would only have muddled the picture even further.

Ironically, *Blue Afternoon* was not the hit Herb and the rest of us hoped it would be. It received decidedly mixed reviews. Debbie Burr felt that it was "not even good sulking music," for example, while Don Heckman of *The New York Times* called Buckley "one of the most gifted of today's young songwriters" and celebrated *Blue Afternoon* as "far and away his best to date." Today, more than thirty years after we recorded it, many listeners regard *Blue Afternoon* as one of their all-time favorite albums.

Tim did not let any of the commotion stop him. He returned to the direction launched with *Lorca*, and immediately resumed work on *Starsailor*. No looking back this time.

CHAPTER 11

MADAME WU

With Jainie and Jennifer gone, Tim and I sank into a funk that got a little crazy for a while. Even as Tim had written in "So Lonely," we didn't get letters, nobody called, and hardly anybody came to visit. Loneliness began eating our insides.

We lived on Park Place, in separate houses. For a while we had a ton of work to keep us occupied—recording *Lorca* and *Blue Afternoon* and starting *Starsailor*—but I was withdrawing more and more, lying in bed all day sipping beer, watching black-and-white TV. He was drinking a little too, and moving into barbiturates to ease the pain of loneliness, on the one hand, and *Lorca*'s rejection on the other. I had given Tim everything I had in terms of knowledge and insight and new ideas, and now felt empty and useless—which, of course, did not exactly make me a thrilling guy for Tim to visit.

Even when we got together, realities tilted. One afternoon Tim said, "Come on, let's go play pool." We drove to a bar on Lincoln Boulevard. The juke box was great—B.B. King's "The Thrill Is Gone," Peggy Lee's "Is That All There Is?" As B.B. sang, Tim chuckled and sang along with him, "The thwill is gone, you cwazy wabbit." It was a hot day, the beer was cold, and we were having fun simply being together. Feeling good felt good for its own sake.

About five o'clock, pleasantly loaded, we hopped into Tim's car, headed for home. He turned off Lincoln onto a side street. We approached a left turn curve in the road. Tim didn't slow down to make the curve, or even try. Instead, he stomped hard on the gas, steered straight ahead, whacked into the curb, jumped it, roared halfway up the steep hill of a vacant lot—wheels churning, dirt flying, engine squalling and grinding—until the car hit a bump, lurched up into the air, crashed down in a bang-clanging halt on top of a rock, stalling out in a swirling cloud of dust and steam.

"You all right?" I asked.

"Yeah. You?" His eyes twinkled gleefully.

"Yeah. Get outta there—change seats with me."

Down below, people standing in front yards looked up at us, pointing fingers. Somebody called the cops. I knew that if Tim were busted for driving drunk, they might throw him in jail. Better me than him—because I loved him, because a person of his talent and beauty should never have to endure jail, because my greatest purpose and joy was to serve Tim and the music, because he was my friend. No way would he go to jail if I could prevent it.

But why had he done this? A mad whim? He might have injured or killed us. No time for questions. I jumped out, ran around to the driver's side, pushed him into the passenger seat, took my place behind the wheel. He was laughing.

Cops arrived, grilled me. I insisted I had downed only a couple of beers and was perfectly sober. Just a mistake, a lark, I thought I could make it over the top of the hill. A nearby observer told the cop Tim had been driving, but I denied it. The cop couldn't do anything. And it was public land, nobody hurt, forget it, call a tow truck.

Tim once said of our relationship, "We didn't have sex, but we were married." And that was true. We loved each other and were intensely close. There are those who might say, "Then why not have sex? What the hell?" For one thing, neither of us was gay, plus "No fuckin' in the band" forever remains a good motto under all conditions.

On one occasion, however, things veered close. After playing music in my living room, we sat at the table around midnight. Candles burned low as we finished off the last beers. He burped and said, "Here, take these." He reached into his pocket, pulled out a small film container, opened it, tipped four red barbiturates into his palm, handed two to me, washed his down with beer. I did the same.

"I might try heroin someday," he said.

"Don't do it, Tim. Look what it did to Fred Neil, man. Stay away from that shit. I have followed you with grass, booze, acid, reds, but I won't follow you into heroin. If you start with heroin, you gotta find yourself another guitar player."

He didn't reply, just nodded his head, burped again, smiled, said, "Let's go to the beach."

Midnight on the boardwalk. The day crowd had disappeared. Music, noise, skaters, and tourists had faded away. Widely spaced street lamps cast an eerie golden glow across the walkway, out onto the sand. Beyond the lights down to the sea, darkness descended. Where water met sand, easy waves whispered siren songs.

With the reds coming on, we turned off the boardwalk, tripped across the beach to the shoreline and turned north toward the ruins of the old POP and Cheetah piers.

At the pier Tim whispered, "Follow me. Shhhh." Shoulders hunched over to avoid the overhanging beams, he made his way underneath the pier. I trailed close behind. Darkness intensified. We could hardly see the pilings until our eyes adjusted. Ocean waters slowly rolled in as we groped our way from pillar to pillar, feeling the cold, wet surfaces of the wood beneath our fingertips. "This way," Tim whispered.

He dropped to his hands and knees, crawled to the top of a heap of sand. So did I. Lying on our bellies side by side, shoulder to shoulder, stoned on beer and downers, we peeked over the rim. On the other side we saw two dark forms, hardly moving. I squinted, looked more closely. Two men stood face to face in the shadows, whispering to each other. The dark-haired man leaned his back against a post. The blond fellow facing him unbuttoned the guy's shirt, running his hands over his chest and abdomen, down to his crotch.

"See that?" Tim whispered.

The blond unbuttoned the other man's jeans, pulled them halfway down. The dark-haired guy leaned his head back and closed his eyes, held his hard cock straight out. The blond sank to his knees, worked the man's cock with his hands, opened his mouth, slowly took it all the way down.

Tim nudged me with his knee. "Look at that," he whispered.

"Yeah . . . Jesus . . ."

My own pecker started swelling, confusing the hell out of me. I didn't know what to do—or not do. I didn't mind watching two guys getting it on. It shocked me, yes, but it turned me on too. I felt uncomfortable watching with someone I knew. Porny zones were *secret* zones, it seemed to me, personal voyeuristic realms too private and volatile to be shared, even among friends as close as we were. But hey, this was sexy, and the booze, and the reds, and these guys gettin' it on . . .

"Come on, man. Let's get outta here," I whispered hoarsely, slowly backing down the sand slope.

Running out from underneath the pier ahead of me, Tim whacked me on the ass and laughed aloud, dancing in the white-foam surf along the shoreline like a little kid who had just played a funny trick on his buddy.

Living alone in that two-room apartment on Park Place in Venice a couple of blocks from the beach, I hardly ever went out. I stayed home in bed. Booze and black-and-white TV kept me going. When I woke up in the morning, I ambled to the fridge in my pajamas, cracked a tall cold can of Budweiser, ambled back to bed, turned the TV on exclusively to old movies, crawled under the covers, and didn't move except to sip beer, take a leak, change channels, or walk to the fridge again for another goldie.

I remember the day I decided to disappear—to pull the curtains closed, lock the door, and never go out again. An incredible sense of relief. A big sigh, and into bed. That very day, Daniella Sapriel knocked on the door. I peeked out, saw her, didn't open the door, and soon she went away—the last acquaintance I saw at all except for Tim.

Once in a while, Tim would drop by, say hello, or roust me out for a gig. For the most part, I spent late 1969 and the whole of 1970 alone, in isolation, living on the recording money, unemployment, and an occasional outside gig. It wasn't serenity. There was no clarity in it. It was only the best I could do at the time—escape, oblivion, no hassles. The Big Fear had gotten to me. I drifted lost on those shipless oceans Tim sang about. . . .

Non-life, non-existence, non-being, got so trippy that even an occasional short drive to McDonald's for a hamburger became an adventure. That was good. Most adventures are expensive. McDonald's was cheap. Especially when I drove there only once every two weeks or so. The other big adventure—sporadic late-night walks to the liquor store a couple of blocks away for beer and cat food. Opened a can a day for the cat, set it on the ground outside the back door. Almost never saw her. Didn't care.

I had only one rule: When drunk or tired, never answer the phone or make important decisions. That simplified things. A lot. I sank into the mattress, quiet as stone. Fuck Rolaids. Total isolation—now *there's* relief worth talking about.

On Christmas Eve, about 10 P.M., I heard someone knock. Didn't answer. Tim quietly called my name. I still didn't answer. Didn't want to see anybody, not even him, not even my best buddy who lived just up the street, the person in the world I loved most.

I turned down the TV sound. Tim stepped off the front porch, moved over to my window. I knew he could see the blue TV light around the edges of the shade. He did. He knocked on the window and called again, figuring I was asleep. I didn't answer. He walked back toward the front door, stopping at the living room window next to it. He pushed the window up. Rattling a plastic sack with something inside, he crawled in. He stood silhouetted at the door separating the living room from my bedroom, peeking in to see if I was awake. Not raising my hand, I wiggled my fingers at the edge of the covers, staring into the TV without looking at him or speaking to him.

He turned a lamp on to its softest, dimmest amber setting, flicked on the stereo, pulled a recording out of the plastic sack and put it on the turntable.

Avant-garde harp and choral music, Hindemith, in gentle ways reflecting our *Starsailor* music. Although Hindemith's music was melodically angular, it also had a flow to it, and a high, adventurous spirit, with radiance, optimism, strength.

With the sound of that music softly filling the apartment, Tim slowly danced in the living room. He gracefully raised his arms and hands over his head. He made turns and glides. He crossed back and forth in front of the bedroom doorway, passing in and out of view, sweeping his hands up, swooping his body down in an arc.

He danced for me, for his stricken, lonely friend. He danced for the two of us, for our abiding friendship. He danced for our suffering. He danced for the love he and I shared through music. I lay on the bed, awash in television blue, watching him express his love and empathy and compassion. In those moments, one of my bleakest hours, I was not alone.

He was there with me, a friend, and more: a visiting spirit, a Christmas vision, a beautiful boy-man, an angel imbued with wisdom of the heart. He came to wish me well and help as best he could. In his gift of silent dance, natural beauty expressing itself honestly, without self-consciousness, with love and strength and concern and grace in each innocent gesture, he imparted vitality enough for me to continue.

Without saying anything, he gently smiled, waved, climbed back out the window, quietly closed it behind him, and vanished into the night.

CAPTAIN EDDIE MEETS MADAME WU

She had her beauty. She had her pain. She had womanly ways, beguiling beyond anything Tim had ever known. A young widow. Shining raven-black hair cascading down her back to her waist. Wolfen eyes, slate-blue, a sexy black ring encircling each iris. Body thin, lithe, supple. Languorously slow and sensuous moves. Tapered legs, smooth, graceful. Seductive voice, moonlight, jasmine. Laughter, wind chimes. Long red fingernails. Slit skirts. High heels. She had known men. She had known true love. She had known loss. Irresistible.

Her name was Judy Fern Brejot. She and Tim had seen each other numerous times, several years before they connected, usually at her husband Darrell Sutcliffe's studio in Venice, where Tim, "just a shaggy-haired little kid," used to sit and play guitar shortly after his first album. Time passed in summer kites and winter suns.

Then one day Judy and Darrell stopped by Tim's place to pick up her friends, Molly L. and film director Carroll Ballard.

"We were going to the racetrack," Judy told me in our interview. "At that time that's how Darrell and I made our living, so we were really dressed up. We walked into Tim's place. Jainie was doing her grumpy Mother Earth thing. Tim and I noticed each other, but we didn't speak for a long time.

"Everybody was talking, but he was being just this kind of nondescript object in the corner of the room, with everything going on around him. He kicked my dog. Nobody saw him but me. Then he looked up at me with that cute little devil look of his, and motioned me over.

"I had caught him staring out the window earlier, so he motioned me over and parted the blinds a little wider and showed me what he had been looking at. There was this woman, sitting on the steps across the street with her dress up. He didn't break stride, not at all. That's when he won my heart. That turned me on." Tim later celebrated that charming moment in "Come Here Woman."

Judy was not pretty in a standard Hollywood fashion, but she was captivatingly chic. She had style in the way she dressed and carried herself. She was sexy and she had a sense of humor. So did Tim. Made for each other.

She brought her baggage along, of course.

She never got over Darrell, a charismatic painter, sculptor, auto-body mechanic, inventor, traveler. He was the one, just under her skin, the true love who floated in dreams behind her eyes. He died, yes, but his memory lingered on, wouldn't let her alone, wouldn't let her be completely with Tim.

Darrell, Judy, and their blond-haired son, Taylor . . . a car wreck down in Mexico, near Tijuana . . . thrown out of their Jeep, lying across the highway at night . . . drizzling rain . . . car lights shining . . . people standing, staring . . . everybody afraid to do anything . . .

"I was conscious, but completely broken," Judy said. "It was raining and I was lying there. I didn't know if I was dying, didn't know if that's what it was . . . so strange. I knew that I was hurting, because all my ribs—I had all my ribs broken. All I could think was, 'Rip off my clothes,' because they must be binding me. You operate on weird . . . and I was yelling for Taylor. I wanted to know where my baby was. There's a part of you, a different part of you, that just takes over. It was pretty heavy.

"They put us in the Mexican jail. They didn't set any bones. Taylor was broken. I was broken. Darrell was broken. There were bars. We were just on cots, and all they did was shoot us full of morphine. Darrell died for lack of medical help."

Tim asked Judy questions about it, fascinated by the bizarre nature of the incident, and by the pain. In his song "Jungle Fire" he caught those images of the wreck at night and passing traffic, and the rain on the slick black road, and the moans and groans, and curious people gawking.

After Darrell's death, Judy went back to designing clothes, and Tim went on the road. He got in touch with her, invited her to an upcoming gig at the Troubadour, but she didn't go. "I was working and having so much hassle just keeping my existence together that the whole idea of going out to hear what I thought of as some folk singer just didn't turn me on. Really—isn't that cold?

"So I called my sister, Michelle, and told her to go. What the hell. She's young, so I told her to go on over. I didn't want to hear any hearts and flowers and 'mood.' So I didn't go."

Judy traveled back East to visit her father and recover from Darrell's death, missing the recording of *Live at the Troubadour*. Months went by, then her father bought her a plane ticket and insisted she fly back to California and look at the ocean.

In Venice again, Judy was on her way with Molly to visit a friend, but Molly wanted to stop by and drop off a book at Tim's. Judy waited in the car. After half an hour, she walked to the house and knocked on the door.

"Jainie had left and taken everything with her," Judy said. "Here Tim was, staying in this house on Park Place, with nothing but a mattress and his guitar. I told him I thought maybe he ought to change careers. I hadn't seen him in a long time, and it looked like complete poverty, you know?

"I was dressed up. I had on this green velvet outfit I had made, and a mink coat and a lot of pearls—comin' from the city, y'know. Timmy had on bib overalls, a red-maroon corduroy shirt that was too big for him, and tennis shoes three sizes too large that somebody had left at the house—the kind that lace up around the ankles."

While they talked, Danny Gordon ran up the steps, into the house. "Look what I got!" He held out four tickets to a Ray Charles concert at UCLA that night.

"So Tim and I went to the concert together dressed like that—what a sight! He used to walk with his back slumped over, dragging his feet, his heels. He'd do things like cut the heels off his shoes. And if he got a new shirt, he'd tear a sleeve or something so he'd feel comfortable in it. I'm telling you, if you think nobody notices, it's not true!

"He said it felt a little strange, the two of us walking down the aisle to our seats. I said, 'Just walk straight and don't drag your feet—just walk straight!' We saw a great concert."

In talking with her about Ray Charles, Tim began checking Judy out, asking her questions about musical tastes. After all, we are what we listen to. The scope of our music is the scope of our vision. Clearly, she liked Ray Charles. What else did she like?

"He was doing what he later told me he did with everybody, giving me test shots," Judy said. "I didn't realize it. I was just impressed that he cared. He said, 'What's your favorite opera?' Well, I love *Carmina Burana*, by Carl Orff, I told him. It's one of the most sensual melodies ever done. The BBC filmed it in 1964, in a castle in Norway. It's beautiful. 'Well!' he said. 'I didn't think you'd say anything!'

"I was surprised, considering his young age, that he was so aware of different musicians and composers, and the jazz field, and so many different singers, Morgana King, Cathy Berberian. . . ."

It is probably understandable that some of the women in Tim's circle of friends resented Judy's intrusion. She was decidedly not a scruffy hippie. She looked great. And she had won Tim's heart. Oddly enough, I found myself in the position of defending her when they spoke of her behind her back as being morbidly evil looking with her velvets and long black hair and her vampiric black clothes, "always dressed for death," as one of them put it, or when they accused her of being manipulative, vain, untrustworthy, or possibly even parasitically exploitive of Tim's fame and potential earning power.

"How can you say that?" I protested. "It's not fair. You don't even know her." I insisted that so-called "woman's intuition" or "bad vibes" was simply not enough. They should grant Judy a chance, let her prove herself, give her time to show her true colors—and they sure as heck should respect Tim's wishes to be with her. "Good grief," I said. "This is the first time I've seen Tim smile in over a year. Give them a break. They're happy together." I dropped the matter and didn't think about it any more, not at the time.

Not everybody felt envious or hostile toward Judy. For example, Tim's sister, Katy, said, "I remember Mary, who was the worst. How could he love *her*, you know? And I remember Jainie, Miss Organic, but I liked Jainie's eyes. She had good insight too. She could read people really well. She had good intuition. And also I liked about

Jainie the fact she was so masculine. And then Judy came into the circle. I think the reason I liked her at first was because she was the first woman Tim had gone out with that smelled good."

Daniella Sapriel owned Tim's albums, so Tim drove Judy up to Daniella's house in Topanga. They listened to all of Tim's recordings—the only time Tim ever did that. Normally, when an album was completed, he never looked back. This time, he surveyed the entire scope, up through *Lorca* and *Blue Afternoon*.

"He played the albums to show me his music," Judy said. "It was just before *Starsailor*. I remember he played certain cuts for me from the first album. For me, hearing the transition from the first record to the last one—in the beginning, he was like a choirboy. I could just see him in the white gown, with his *Ahhhhh* little voice up so high and pure and innocent."

Judy and Taylor moved into Park Place and a new life began for all three. They often ate dinner at Wu's Garden Chinese restaurant on Wilshire Boulevard in Santa Monica (since torn down) or Ted's Rancho out on the Pacific Coast Highway. Tim started caring about his appearance—hair trimmed, clean-shaven, polished black boots, pressed pants, good-looking shirts. Elegant, sharp. He and Judy looked terrific together. Judy decorated the house, using her designer's eye to create lovely color schemes—black and white screens and curtains, green plants, marble tables, crystal glassware. Classy, beautiful, sensual, polished.

That spring of 1970, Danny Gordon and Tim were invited to a high school class reunion in Bell Gardens. Initially, Tim refused, but Danny insisted—"Come on, let's go. Nobody would ever expect you to show up. Or me either. Why don't we go?"

So, with their urbane friend, would-be writer David Thoreau—"The Baby," as Tim called him—the quartet drove down to Bell Gardens. "Danny, of course, was The Writer," Judy said. "And Tim was The Star. The Baby had on a tuxedo. I wore a long gown with a slit up the sides and boa feathers around my neck.

"We got there, and of course there were couples with their babies, and other couples with babies on the way. There were guys back from Vietnam. What a crowd Tim hung out with! You could really see how and why he had all those punchy things going where he would turn into Stanley Kowalski—Bell Gardens punchy.

"And when he introduced me, he introduced me, not as Judy, but as 'Madame Wu,' who saved his life when he was on a boat. He said he had been on vacation, and the boat had hit a reef, and I was there and saved him. I nursed him back to health, and he was totally indebted to me—to me, Madame Wu.

"That story came from out of nowhere. That's when it started, where he would be talking, setting up this incredible situation, doing it all with a straight face, lying through his teeth and loving it—and then he'd turn to me and say, 'Take it. Your ball!' I couldn't believe it at that reunion. What a test shot!

"But they were all paying attention, and he made it very poetic, very exotic. He created it all, the whole scene—and all I had to do was *just step into it*—ha!

"When I wanted a place to sit down, they got me a chair, brought me drinks, and all the guys stood around and admired me and waited on me.

"He had bought his first electric guitar, a Rickenbacker. All I knew of Rickenbacker was that World War I aviator guy, Captain Eddie Rickenbacker. So I started calling Tim 'Captain Eddie,' and he started calling me 'Madame Wu.' It got to where he mostly called me just Wu. And I got used to the name. It was really neat. It was the only time that I'd ever had a different name."

In his always imaginative way, Tim had transformed the name of a Chinese restaurant into an exotic name for his provocative, tantalizing vision-woman.

(When he bought the Rickenbacker electric, he gave his customized acoustic Guild F-512 to his good friend Bobby [a.k.a. Jesse] James, even as he had earlier given Bob his first stress-back 12-string F-512 when he purchased the customized guitar.)

Judy was all Tim had ever yearned for. Four-and-a-half years older than he, she had the kind of experience of sex and love that he needed. From the beginning of his career to the end, Tim was very much an autobiographical writer, although not exclusively so. To the extent that songs such as "Come Here Woman" and "Quicksand" and others were autobiographical, he appeared to be celebrating Judy and his love for her. She was neither crude nor frenetic like so many younger women he had known, but moved slowly and sensuously, captivating Tim's imagination with her elegance and slate-blue wolf-eyed charm ("Come Here Woman"). Indeed, she was the physical embodiment of his fevered dreams, his phantasy woman in living flesh ("Quicksand"). And once again he felt inspired.

Tim had never been happier. He was in love again, with an exotically attractive woman who made him laugh and turned him on. Sometimes she gave him a certain quizzical look, which occasionally inspired him in conversation to affectionately call her his "cross-eyed flamingo."

He didn't necessarily know her in an inner, essential way, even as she didn't necessarily know him. But their images matched their respective needs and fit together well. Their laughter matched too, and so did their craving for attention. Each vied for the eyes and smiles of the other, a kind of mad competition that generated heat, fire, lust, laughter, fun. Look at me. Love me. Be me. The music swirled, wine glasses tippled over with Harveys Bristol Cream, life was good again. Both had been shipwrecked, and each had saved the other's life.

On April 19, 1970, they married at the Little Red Chapel in Santa Monica. With unspent money from *Goodbye and Hello* and *Happy Sad*, he bought a fire-engine-red Volkswagen van and a large house in his childhood dreamtown, Laguna Beach. It was a three-bedroom house, as I recall—$40,000, a lot of money in those days—at 2972 Rounsevel Terrace, an upscale suburban neighborhood. He whimsically bought a snazzy 1940s tan Cadillac sedan as well.

"When he lived in Bell Gardens as a boy, Laguna was where he'd go," Judy said. "They had the art fairs there, the ocean, that great beach. He thought Laguna was really the way to live. The house we got was the house that he had loved when he was young. It was important to him. He had never bought a house before. He was really getting off on getting married, having a home, a family, the whole thing."

Just to outrage his straight neighbors, Tim plucked a leaf from the Rolling Stones songbook and painted the entire outside of the house black. Inside, he draped the ceiling-high windows with black velvet curtains, closed day and night. The neighbors must have loved him madly.

Having already begun work on *Starsailor*, Tim continued creating music in

Laguna. He knew *Starsailor* would be a marketplace long shot, but that didn't matter. "Sometimes you're writing and you're just not gonna fit in," he told writer Bill Henderson. "But you do it, 'cause it's your heart and your soul and you gotta say it. It's the foremost thing in your mind. . . ." Judy didn't necessarily understand the avant-garde aspects of the music, but to her credit she supported Tim's desire to do it.

Tim took a break and visited Larry Beckett in Portland. Hashing out lines together one by one, they accomplished a certain amount of work, but failed to get along. Tim left after only two or three days.

Being something of an emotionally timid intellectual, forever the mathematical physicist inwardly divided between head and heart, Larry apparently had no grasp of the searing emotional intensity Tim was feeling, nor did he seem to understand the fierce and fiery nature of the aesthetic zones Tim had been exploring since *Happy Sad*. Neither did he have any indication of the avant-garde musical context Tim would be creating for some of Larry's lyrics. Larry was still into orthodox song forms, still reading Bobbie Burns, and was busily writing an extended poem about Paul Bunyan, while Tim had been moving into avant-garde jazz, contemporary classical music and *Starsailor*.

At one point during that visit, Larry boasted that he continued writing on his Paul Bunyan epic, even though he had no prospects of publishing it. He was an artist. He wrote for the love of writing itself. Did Tim think he would keep composing music if he didn't have a recording contract to goad him on? Was Tim as strong as Beckett? Was Tim a "real artist"?

That toxic question instilled doubt in Tim's heart—and at a most inappropriate time, just when *Starsailor* was getting launched. Tim was still thinking about that question when he dropped in to see me in Venice. He seemed troubled by it. "I don't know, man. Maybe I *wouldn't* keep on writing if I didn't have a contract, you know?"

"Sounds to me like Larry's messing with your head," I responded. "Do you think he might be feeling a little envy? The old 'sour grapes' syndrome? Has he ever had courage enough to submit his poetry for publication? Even if he has, I doubt if he will *ever* be able to step into the marketplace and risk the kind of criticism you have already experienced and absorbed and transcended. You can cut it in the public arena, but maybe he can't, so he puts you down for having a contract. Does that not sound like 'sour grapes'?

"And what is he writing, anyway— archaic language about an irrelevant comic book folk hero and a blue ox named Babe? He's not writing about anything real, Tim. It's an abstraction, an intellectually concocted fantasy. It's mind-game masturbation, and he's calling it art and then bragging about it—the worst kind of self-deception. I may be wrong, but it sounds like the only way he can build himself up is by criticizing you. Doesn't he know it yet?"

"Know what?"

"You are an authentic musician. You've been playing music all your life, long before you got a contract. And you don't merely play it. Music plays you. You devote your life to it. In your deepest being, you *are* music. Contract or no contract, you can't stop, even if you want to. You are a true artist. And *that* is a noble calling.

"I'm not sure Larry has any idea what he's talking about, Tim, and I'm not sure I trust his motives either. He abandoned the artist's life years ago, when he copped out for computers, money, and security. Don't get me wrong on this point. There is absolutely nothing wrong with making money and earning a living. But the cop-out to money is hardly a focused commitment to art, is it? I suspect poetry is a word-game for him, an ego-tripping hobby, although it's unlikely he thinks so himself. It's not like he's putting his life on the line to serve the muse, is he? More power to him on the money front—but where does a dilettante technician derive his authority to question *your* sincerity, dedication, and talent as a musician?

"With or without a contract, you will be singing, writing songs, playing guitar and making beautiful music until the day you drop, man. Take heart. Follow the music wherever it leads you. Everything will be all right."

Back home in Laguna, Tim was listening to Olivier Messiaen's *Quartet For the End of Time*, and thoroughly enjoying family life and healthy creativity.

"He set up a work area at one end of the house," Judy said, "and that's where he wrote his *Starsailor* stuff, in the bedroom where the steps went up. It had a big window where you could look at the sunset behind Catalina. He had a table and a chair, and he would sit there and look out the window and write. I was doing a lot of leather work for people, so I had my area at the other end of the house."

They didn't have any furniture, so Judy made a couch. She also painted walls and did other work around the house. Tim had never been with anyone who enjoyed doing things like that, and he got into it with her. He bought two giant cable spools, sanded them, brushed on several layers of lacquer, and made them into tables. Next, he wanted to plaster the thirty-foot ceiling in one of the studios and stain the wood floors in another section of the house. So far, so good. For the ceiling, he checked everything out, put up black tar paper, chicken wire—and real plaster, for quality sound.

"Poor baby," Judy said. "He did everything the way the directions said, except when he mixed it he didn't put in a special alloy or catalyst it needed, the sand or something, which makes it turn into stucco. So he plastered the whole thing with just the regular plaster.

"We went to bed. He got up the next morning and was just in tears, because if you touched any place on that thirty-foot wall, all the plaster came falling off the chicken wire. The whole room. We had to hire people to take it down and redo it."

Undaunted, Buckley cinched up his belt and started on the floors. "He sanded them and worked hard," Judy said. "He stained them with a teak stain—he had really good taste. But he didn't want to varnish them. He thought it would be better to put resin on the floor. He put it on, but it didn't dry. Two rooms. Wherever you walked, you stuck to the floor and left footprints. We had to have the floor redone."

Life in Laguna as he worked on *Starsailor* was probably the sweetest time Tim had ever known. "We took walks on the beach every night and watched the sunsets," Judy recalled. "We checked out Mexican restaurants. Capistrano was right down the road, and they had a great Mexican restaurant near there. We used to go over to the Mission all the time. There was also a wonderful gay piano bar in Laguna called the Little Shrimp. A lady played piano—'Mad About the Boy'—and had a wonderful voice. Sometimes we'd drive to Newport Beach and hear jazz. While everything was working, before things got bad, Laguna was a wonderful place to live. It was really private and good for being productive.

"He had been working so hard for so many years before that—just put out, put out, put out. And I had had problems of my own—the death of my husband. Being in Laguna was so nice, just to be able to get our heads into our work and to have a relationship that was working too. A big sigh of relief.

"I didn't want to know too much about his past, and he didn't talk about mine. It was just comfortable there. It was of the moment. He had the freedom to do what he was doing. I did too. We didn't have to worry about other things. It was good then. Life was good."

CHAPTER 12

STARSAILOR

With *Starsailor*, Buckley pulled out the stops. He wrote the music to all nine songs, the lyrics to five. He cowrote four new songs with Beckett. He included two very accessible pop-oriented pieces that he hoped might balance the avant-garde material—a resuscitated "Song to the Siren" and a charming quasi-French song, "Moulin Rouge." In a sense, he included something for everybody on *Starsailor*.

No question about it, however—this was not an "everybody" album. As I wrote in *Down Beat*:

> With the exception of "Moulin Rouge" and "Song to the Siren" . . . *Starsailor* was a pop monster of odd time signatures ("Come Here Woman"—5/4; "Healing Festival"—10/4; "Jungle Fire"—5/4); bizarrely dissonant crisscrossing shrieks, wails, and moans; surrealistic overdubbing (the title cut is Buckley singing 16 tracks with himself); freely improvised instrumental madness (trumpet, saxophone, pipe organ, timpani drums, etc.); a virtually unparalleled exoticism and sensuality in the lyrics [e.g. "Come Here Woman"] . . .
>
> "I was as close to Coltrane as anyone has ever come," Buckley later said in Warners and DiscReet bios. "I even started singing in foreign languages— Swahili, for instance—just because it sounded better. An instrumentalist can be understood doing just about anything, but people are really geared for hearing only *words* come out of the mouth. . . . The most shocking thing I've ever seen an audience come up against—besides a performer taking off his clothes—is dealing with someone who doesn't sing words. I get off on great-sounding words. If I had my way, words wouldn't mean a thing. It shocked hell out of the people. It was refreshing." [1]

Buckley brought in the free-improv trio he had played with in John Balkin's North Hollywood studio—Balkin, bass; Buzz Gardner, trumpet and flugelhorn; Bunk Gardner, alto flute and tenor and alto saxes. Balkin's trio added immeasurably

---

1. Tim talked about singing in "foreign languages," including Swahili. That gave the impression he knew languages other than English, which he did not. He learned Beckett's French lyrics to "Moulin Rouge" by rote.

It is interesting to watch the development of Tim's English linguistic skills as he matured. In his earlier interviews, he swore a great deal and paid little attention to sentence structure. As he evolved, he all but eliminated swearing and paid close attention to the ways in which he structured thoughts, clearly making an effort to speak as cogently as possible. That Alan King incident on the *Tonight Show* woke him up to the value of language and quick thinking—from there, he followed through.

to the dissonance on the album, a mad freewheeling series of counterpoint horn lines that created exciting tension and vivid timbres.

A bright new face appeared on this album: drummer Maury Baker, who became an important member of Tim's groups throughout the Starsailor period.

Shortly before recording *Starsailor*, I played a gig with British musician Zoot Money, a former keyboardist for Eric Burdon and the Animals. Zoot had come to L.A. to start his own career. He had a gig at the Experience in Hollywood and needed musicians. I got the guitar slot. Maury played drums.

Baker was not just any drummer. He included two orchestral timpanis in his outfit, which he played with intelligence, taste, and precision. He also had a bass drum, a snare drum, a variety of cymbals, and an enormous assortment of drumsticks.

Unlike orthodox drummers, Baker did not simply lock into stock 4/4 rhythms and whack monotonously on the second and fourth beats. In fact, it was the extraordinarily elaborate contrapuntal rhythms that he played *within* metric structures that got him fired from Janis Joplin's Kozmic Blues Band. She used to holler at him, "Keep the groove, you asshole! Hit the damn second and fourth beat, and hit 'em hard, see? Nothin' else—just two and four, got it?"

Maury was simply too intelligent and far too multifaceted a personality for the rigidly stylized simplicities of rock 'n' roll, so Janis threw him away. Maury needed intricate complexities along *with* fire and brimstone, which is exactly what Buckley wanted during the Starsailor period.

A classically trained musician, Maury could talk about Charles Ives or Bach with alacrity. He could play in any time signature—5/4, 7/4, whatever—without feeling the least bit awkward. Within conventional 4/4 meters as well, he brought color with his timpanis and cymbals, and depth with his multilayered contrapuntal improvisations—all of which can be heard on *Starsailor*. (Tim and Maury performed "Monterey" as a duo on the album, an excellent showcase for Maury's drumming. I did not perform on that track, as was mistakenly reported elsewhere.)

Not only was Maury a unique and talented percussionist. He was also a delightfully eccentric fellow. He loved the color purple, for example—wore purple shirts, purple pants, purple shoes . . . and even lived in a purple van. As well, he had a marvelously intelligent sense of humor.

As he and I got to know each other on Zoot Money's gig, I realized he would be perfect for Tim's *Starsailor* music. As I had done with bassist John Balkin before, I brought Maury to Tim as a musical gift. They hit it off immediately. Maury performed with Tim on *Starsailor* and on gigs throughout the following two-and-a-half years. He and Tim remained close friends until the end.

Perhaps the great unsung hero on *Starsailor* is bassist John Balkin. Not only was he instrumental in turning Tim on to several contemporary composers and in exposing him to the ear-opening, mind-expanding delights of creating intelligent, spontaneously structured improvisations, but he played a major role in several significant pieces on *Starsailor*, including the brilliant title track, which is often overlooked because it is so quiet, spacious, and ethereal.

John told me the story of how "Starsailor" came about. . . .

"I was composing a piece in my studio, working with *musique concrète*, rather than electronic music.[2] I laid down some vocal tracks myself, then did a few over-dubs and tape manipulations, and ended up with a three- or four-minute piece which I called 'The Nunnery.' It sounded to me like a wall of nuns singing.

"Tim came over the next day and I played him the tape. He liked it and said he'd like to do something like this on the album. So we went into the studio in Glendale with Timmy and myself and the engineer [Stan Agol].

"I started with Timmy's musicality and his voice to create this wash of sound. I already had the sound in my head, because I had just put together 'The Nunnery.'

"I'd tell him to go out and sing in a certain manner: 'Do a thing from low to high.' I'd mimic the sound, or indicate with my voice the direction I wanted it to go. Then I'd tell him to go out and sing counter to that. I began structuring the piece. I'd say, 'Now I want you to sing below it. Now sing above it. I want you to sail through it. Now sustain long tones.' I kept building the piece. Pretty soon, this incredible thing was happening and we were really getting into it, even the rather staid engineer.

"After we had done four or five tracks, Tim had a basic sound to work with, to play against, and he started getting ideas and doing things on his own, and we kept laying tracks down, at least sixteen, maybe more. I'm pretty sure it was more.

"He gave me a short poem, maybe six lines, something about 'Here I am, a buzzing bee.' I said, 'It sounds like a haiku poem to me.' So with this sound we had created, Tim, me, the engineer, I heard a haiku, this ancient Japanese mystical thing, you know? The beeeee, the buzzzzzing, so we got to working with the sounds of the poem.[3]

"I told the engineer that I wanted to pan sound from one channel to the other channel—this wasn't done very much back then. I conceived of the voice-stretches going around in the circle in such a way that the listener would be in the middle of the vortex.

"The engineer suggested we use a trick the Beatles used, where you run two tape decks out of sync. You record one at a certain speed, say 15 IPS [inches per second]. Then you lay out the same thing on another deck, but change the speed a little bit, and get a sound that's slightly out of sync, so we did that, too.

"There were no electronic gadgets used on this album, no synthesizers, no electronic stuff superimposed on top of natural sounds. We worked only with Tim's voice and the tape recorders.

"When we finished Timmy's voices, the piece seemed just a little harsh to me. It needed something to soften it up, so I wrote out a few sketches for alto flute, and had Bunk Gardner come in and play underneath the vocal tracks. It's very subtle, but it's on there, two or three layers of alto flute that sweeten the piece. I told Bunk, 'Go out, follow the flow of the music, and do long, soft, low tones.'"

For some of the other songs—metered, faster pieces such as "Come Here Woman," "Jungle Fire," and "Down by the Borderline"—Tim turned to John and said, "What do you hear on these?"

2. *Musique concrète*—natural sounds, such as the voice or wind or traffic noises, recorded live, then manipulated on tape. As opposed to electronic music, in which the sound is generated by an electronic source, such as a synthesizer.

3. The poem used as lyrics for "Starsailor" was written by Larry Beckett. With his typical sense of humor, Buckley told writer Susan Ahrens, "Beckett and I wrote the whole song as a view of the universe through the eye of a bee. It's a great cartoon."

"I'd like you to come in screaming over the top. Think of a lot of brass horns going through there. We'll lay down four or five tracks of that, arching lines wailing in from the top, sailing on out there, and then put them on top of the rhythmic and vocal tracks we already recorded."

During the course of recording the title track Larry Beckett showed up. He had written his "Starsailor" poem to be used as a straight-ahead song. The last time he had written with Tim prior to *Starsailor* was on *Goodbye and Hello*. By now, Tim's idea of what constituted song forms had evolved far beyond conventional structures. Apparently, the music Beckett heard developing around "Starsailor" sounded a little too unearthly for him.

"I got the feeling that Beckett was very unhappy with what we were doing," Balkin said. "We were formulating and laying down the fundamental textures, the foundations for 'Starsailor.' Larry sat there and listened for a little while, but didn't stay to hear the completed piece. In fact, he just shook his head and got up and walked out. He seemed really upset with what we were doing. As I recall from Tim, his parting message was, 'They're ruining my poem.' But Larry didn't slow us down. We just kept on working."

I played electric guitar on *Starsailor*, utilizing some of my new techniques along the way. Perhaps especially on "I Woke Up" a listener can hear both hands on the fretboard, tapping, thumping, sliding, sustained notes, sonic shadings, enharmonic soundwashes, colorful atmospheres. I developed this style of playing extensively after *Starsailor* and wish more of it had been recorded, either on Tim's records or elsewhere. That was not to be. In "Down by the Borderline," I played a superb straight-ahead solo that unfortunately got more or less submerged in the mix beneath Buzz Gardner's toot-toot-toot trumpet. During the course of the album I also played electric piano and a smidgen of pipe organ.

Although the credits list only Buckley as the composer of "Song to the Siren," Tim wrote the music, while Beckett wrote the lyrics. After performing the song on *The Monkees* show in 1967, Buckley retired the piece, unhappy with the line, "I'm as puzzled as the oyster."

Beckett later told interviewer Scott Isler that Judy Henske had laughed at that line, and that's why Buckley had given up the song, even though it was one of Buckley's favorites. In Beckett's view, Buckley had been too sensitive. Henske, however, categorically denied the story, in which case Buckley's rejection of the line and the song was probably based on aesthetics alone. I suspect that was the case. At any rate, Buckley (not Beckett) finally changed the offending line to "I'm as puzzled as the newborn child," and recorded "Siren" on *Starsailor*. (Meanwhile, of course, that line has gotten more publicity for *not* being in the song than all other Buckley-Beckett lyrics combined!)

When Buckley asked me to play guitar on "Siren," I declined, thinking it odd that Tim would want to include such a conventional piece on *Starsailor*. It was a nice song, but its charming simplicity seemed regressive in light of the extraordinary evolutionary developments that had taken place since its inception back in the folk days of 1967 and the recording of it in earlier sessions eventually released posthumously as *Works in Progress*.

Ironically, it was this song that eventually became a hit, while the spectacular innovations on *Starsailor* received kudos only from the intelligentsia.[4] To this day "Song to the Siren" remains perhaps the most popular of all of Tim and Larry's many excellent works.

Although Tim gave his heart and soul to *Starsailor* and fulfilled his talent and creative genius and exceptional vocal capabilities more magnificently than ever before, neither the album nor his live performances were well-received. The "Lobos" sat on their wallets. However, some of the critics appreciated what was happening, notably Michael Bourne of *Down Beat*, who gave *Starsailor* the magazine's highest rating, five stars, and said, "Where at first Buckley offered only a somewhat pleasant high-pitched croon, now he has proven himself a consummate vocal technician, from shimmering coos on 'Song to a Siren' to primitive wailing on 'Jungle Fire' to distorted chanting on the title cut. . . . I rejoice that such spirit as that of Buckley and his cohorts is available on record."

Lester Bangs of *Creem* magazine departed from his usually scathing, contemptuous, cynical point of view and gave Buckley and *Starsailor* an unqualified rave review, saying in part:

Yet another album by the elliptically rousing Tim Buckley—who I steadfastly maintain is one of the most under-rated and misunderstood musicians ever to develop out of the dead-end of rock and roll into the free-form freedom fusion of rock and jazz coupled with his already original sound. His last album this year, entitled *Lorca*, was a profound example of this rarification, and *Starsailor* is yet another lyric-stung, waterfall-rushing-into-the-night's-combing-of-the-stars manifestation of Buckley's thresholding work in the rock/jazz medium . . . For those who care about what genius can do with lyrics, a 12-string guitar and a windmilling voice, Tim Buckley is to be investigated. . . . An album of universals, absolutes, incantations, and the light of waking dreams . . .

These two critics did not stand alone.

Rich Mangelsdorff, for example, celebrated Buckley's willingness "to burst the bounds," called him a "true vocal poet of the day," and said *Starsailor* "represents one of the more important advances in rock vocalizing which I've run across in some time." Jack Shadoin noted that Buckley was "breaking new vocal ground," "creating new contexts for vocal freedom," and had "a real shot at the sublime." Pete Senoff said Buckley's lyrics were as good, if not better, than anything he had attempted in the past and that the background instrumentation was "uniformly superb, providing musical exploration that readily parallels Buckley's vocal journeys."

---

4. Although I assume Tim's version of "Song to the Siren" did well, it was not until Elizabeth Fraser of the Cocteau Twins sang it in 1984 on *This Mortal Coil: It'll End in Tears* that the song gained significant international popularity. Her version drew attention to Tim, who became known to many people largely because of "Siren" alone. Some of those listeners researched Tim and discovered he had released nine albums before his death, and several other albums have appeared posthumously. Perhaps more than any other single factor, Fraser's version of "Song to the Siren" began the resurgence of interest in Tim that exists today. Others who have covered "Siren" include Cul De Sac, Pat Boone, Beasts of Paradise, the Czars, Laurie Freelove, Damon & Naomi, True Faith, Susheela Raman, and Robert Plant.

Unfortunately, listeners who grasped and appreciated *Starsailor* were far outnumbered by those who found themselves bereft, confused, and dismayed. Their egos, unreflected by the new music, flew into a huff.

In 1999, however, almost 30 years after the album's debut, new listeners were discovering Tim Buckley in general and *Starsailor* in particular. They started asking me questions about it. I wrote a note to Jack Brolly's online site, doing what I could to help new fans get a handle on the music—

It is true that much of the music on Tim's *Starsailor* album is difficult, complex, and far removed from conventional forms of popular music. Listeners who approach *Starsailor* unprepared for Buckley's extraordinary innovations may find themselves a bit confused, even intimidated . . . but only initially. If they give themselves and the music a chance, by listening more than once and by opening their hearts and minds and tapping into their own sense of adventure, they will discover why Tim himself regarded this album as his masterpiece. . . .

Tim had already explored folk music, folk/rock, and mainstream jazz. With *Starsailor*, he dared to move into territory that was completely uncharted in pop music, an unmapped zone somewhere between free-form jazz and avant-garde classical music.

He created new song forms on this album, dove into odd time signatures . . . and combined basic harmonies with dazzling original discordant criss-crossing melodic lines. Tim also wrote some of the most vividly impassioned lyrics he had ever penned.

Interestingly enough, Jeff Buckley was thoroughly enamored of Tim's vocal and conceptual innovations on *Starsailor*. Although Jeff often criticized his father in public, he intelligently and wisely chose Tim as his foremost mentor. He listened over and over to Tim's recorded music, perhaps especially *Starsailor* (and *Lorca*) and incorporated many of Tim's original techniques into his own arsenal of potent and exceptionally beautiful skills. Listeners who love Jeff's music are in many instances loving Tim's music too, often without being aware of it.

Those people who give Tim's *Starsailor* music a receptive, open-minded hearing will find themselves transported into a psycho-sonic inner world that will prove both incredibly exciting and profoundly nourishing . . .

Alas, when *Starsailor* appeared in the marketplace back in 1970, we needed more Bournes and Bangses in our corner. Hard to find them. Clearly, the road ahead was going to have more potholes than a wet back-alley in the Bronx.

CHAPTER 13

STARSAILOR: ON THE ROAD

"It's hard to become a musician,
And it's hard to play the kind of music
That a musician likes to play
And also the audience likes to hear."

Tim, to Bill Henderson

In February 1970, with *Lorca* in the stores and *Starsailor* in the works, Tim took us on the road to promote *Lorca*. Performing *Lorca* and early *Starsailor* music, Buzz played trumpet, Balkin was on bass, me on guitar, Steve Clover on drums. We were the earliest of four Starsailor bands, a transitional group between the *Happy Sad* period and the *Starsailor* phase. We traveled east, in the dead of winter, playing Ann Arbor; Hershey, Pennsylvania; Rhode Island; and several other places.

In Hershey, we appeared on a TV show with *Catch 22* novelist Joseph Heller (a quiet man, reserved, surrounded by our contingent of enthusiastic shaggy-haired hippies playing weird music). We performed at the University of Rhode Island and received that perceptive review by Gerry Boudreau, who astutely attributed audience dissatisfaction not to the music, but to the audience's misguided and now out-dated preconception of Buckley as a Bambi-eyed folk minstrel.

We flew from New York City to Canton, New York, in a small twin-engine plane. It was a tiny airport, and the pilot had trouble landing. Shades of Buddy Holly and the Big Bopper. He tried a second time, barely missing the trees, and still couldn't bring it in. Tried a third time, almost crashed into the trees again, but finally got it down—only to discover that Tim's 12-string guitar had been left behind at LaGuardia. On the way to the college, our bus slid on ice, spun off the road into a ditch. We waited in the cold while the driver went for help. He promised he'd bring a six-pack of goldies upon his return, but he didn't.

At the school—Alfred College, if I recall correctly—Tim refused to play without his guitar. The student body president said there were several 12-strings available on campus, or maybe he could get the local music store to open. Tim refused. Balkin insisted, "Timmy, you gotta go on," and suggested we could back him without his guitar. Tim insisted he could not and would not play the gig without his 12-string. "Just use a six-string," Balkin said. No. And that was that. It was the only time I know of that Tim refused to step onstage and honor the contract.

From Canton, we drove down to John King's farm. The vibes were definitely strained. Tim was furious that his *Lorca* and budding *Starsailor* music was not going over. He complained about audiences and critics, the "stupid Lobos" he had to deal with, music business idiots, asshole DJs. We drank too much. Booze didn't help. He kicked a frozen clay flowerpot and broke it, scuffing his combat boots. Frustration. Disappointment. Pain.

The large crowd packing the Irvine Auditorium at the University of Philadelphia seemed somewhat more receptive than the Rhode Island people. Fueling creativity with anger, Tim sang exceptionally well. By this time, we in the band had coalesced and felt more confident with the music. In addition to *Lorca* pieces and some of the new *Starsailor* songs, Tim relaxed the audience with a funny takeoff on Ken Nordine's album *Word Jazz*.

Although we thought we were doing fine, there were inevitably those listeners who wanted to hear reruns of yesterday's golden oldies. This was the concert where someone hollered, "How about 'Buzzin' Fly'?" And Buckley shot back, "How about buzzin' horse shit?"

I whispered to Tim, "My God, man, what are you doing?"

He said, "Just tryna be a man."

His father flashed into my mind.

During the intermission, Michael Cuscuna of *Rolling Stone* asked me, "Has Tim been influenced by Leon Thomas?" I replied, "Leon's great, but he's got one yodel and that's it. Tim is taking vocal techniques into entirely new realms—exciting stuff, don't you agree?" Cuscuna agreed, smiled, seemed friendly, intelligent, enthusiastic, understanding, supportive.

When *Rolling Stone* came out, Cuscuna's scathing review said, "Buckley's Yodeling Baffles Audience." He talked about "disjointed tempo changes," a "tasteless monologue which consisted of snatches from various Ken Nordine riffs." He talked about the "horse shit" retort and the "wailing, yodeling vocals" that suggested Buckley had "become fascinated with Leon Thomas's avant-garde jazz." Cuscuna nicely capped it off by noting how the audience sat there "baffled and dismayed . . . disappointed and confused."

In April of 1970, Tim took us into our beloved Troubadour once again. Surely, the hip L.A. audience would be thrilled by our fierce and fiery improvisations, the dissonant, innovative, intelligent, and wildly impassioned free-form starsailing excursions we were into.

"Buckley offered a set which was agonizing in its rampant dissonance and deadly dull in its self-indulgent repetitiveness," wrote Michael Sherman of the *L.A. Times*. Sherman lambasted what he called "tortured moaning, high-pitched shrieks, and incoherent muttering" and said, "Only one song, 'Blue Melody,' was really listenable." He quoted someone in the audience saying, "What the hell is Tim into?"

Surely, they would see Tim's evolution from folk, into rock, into jazz, into the avant-garde as being amazing, exciting, extraordinary, and revelatory.

Writer William Tusher dubbed Buckley a "folk singer" and called his "rambling, undisciplined" vocal inventions "caterwauling." He sneeringly said, "Buckley's delivery is more than acceptable—if less than spectacular—until he succumbs, as he does early and often, to his addiction to affecting change of pace with a high-pitched tremolo that comes off like a Siamese cat in predawn heat."

I often recall Anne Marie Micklo's superb interview of Tim, the part where Tim said, "People forever have been afraid and damn near resentful of anyone who truly creates anything. Because you can't talk about it. You really don't know what it is.

You're an instrument of life, and to be that out of control . . . People don't like to know there is really insanity, pure insanity, that takes place in creating. And they don't want to be a part of it."

With the notion of being "an instrument of life," Buckley embraced a way of singing that was totally spontaneous and natural, a kind of Zen no-mind way of approaching improvised music instinctively and courageously, without the safety and comfort of rational filtering. "We're so far away from relying on our instincts," he told Micklo. "That's why animals are so great, because they're just pure instinct. And when you really get into them, you see that birds are even better than animals, because—I mean, they have nothing, they're not even like a cat or dog, they just fly."

During this *Lorca/Starsailor* period Tim was embracing natural music—and learning the hard way about certain perceptions that had so disturbed his talented father, perhaps especially society's perennial rejection of artists, mystics, and other innovators who shatter conventions, step out beyond the known into new realms of beauty, knowledge, and insight, and then attempt to pass their revelations along to others in an effort to lead humanity onward, upward, and forward. It is easy to romanticize explorers and innovators after the fact, but it's tough to actually live the life—although Buckley would be the first to say, "What the hell—it's better than bowling!"

In that same interview with Micklo, Tim quoted a verse written by Moondog, a blind New York street musician/composer/poet:

> *The leaning tower leaned a little farther south and said,*
> *"I wouldn't be so famous if I had a level head."*

"I don't remember exactly when it was," Balkin recalled, "but we had checked into the Ansonia Hotel in New York, a classy place on Sixth Avenue. I remember us getting out of the cab at the Ansonia, and you and I and Tim were pretty loaded—to the point where we could hardly move our legs trying to get out of the cab.

"When we got to the revolving doors, we were trying to look like stars just hitting town, but we couldn't get the guitar cases through the doors. We flung around and around, until Tim finally pushed the doors open and went careening like a stone flung out of a slingshot clear across the lobby, smashing into the front desk.

"And then you came in, dragging your amp and guitar along the floor. I came in with the reservations, and there were the three of us leaning up against the desk trying to convince everybody we weren't smashed.

"We had started out in Cincinnati doing a TV show. We had two hours to wait before going on. The station had a hosting room where they had a bar, so we had a few drinks at the bar before the show. When we got to the airport, we had a three-hour wait for the plane, so we continued having a few drinks.

"When we finally got on the plane, we whipped out a joint, got loaded, and Tim grabbed the stewardess by the ass while reaching over behind her and snatching those little bottles of airplane booze and flipping them to you and me with the other hand. So we had about six more drinks, which he had stolen.

"One time on the plane from L.A. to San Francisco, Tim got his bravado thing happening. 'I'm gonna *get* her—record time!' By the time we reached San Francisco, he had the stewardess in the bathroom.

"I was waiting for him to get out—and I was the only one left on the plane. Meanwhile, the clean-up guy hops onboard, because the plane has to go back. Part of his routine was to check the bathrooms.

"He walks up to one bathroom, opens the door, slams it. Then he opens the door to the bathroom with Tim and the stewardess in it. He looked. He closed the door, shook his head, and opened it again and did a whole double-take. He closed the door again and walked down the aisle shaking his head.

"Then Tim came out with the stewardess and they were both laughing."

John recalled the time he and Tim drove out to a farmhouse after a gig in Boulder, Colorado. "We drove miles and miles out there to this party where they had a rock band jamming in the basement, people tripping all over the place. When Tim got there, he was fairly anonymous. A few people cornered him in the kitchen, and they sat at the kitchen table. He had his little coterie there. In other words, he had to search that night to find a circle of people, because everybody was either juiced or smoking and into rock.

"But we did find this group in the kitchen, and sat down and had a very serious conversation in the midst of the revelry—people stoned and walking around in the woods outside, and the big rock band right below us in the basement going 'thump, thump, thump,' and another smaller rock band with smaller amps in another part of the house. It was like a scene from Fellini's *8½* or something.

"Surrounded by college freshmen, sophomores, juniors, and seniors, Tim would get on literary kicks with them. He had his little upmanship thing going, and his programs for college kids.

"We got into Lorca's poetry, right? And we had an Ayn Rand confrontation, and Tim did the double-dagger thing with them, as only Tim could do, and he could really do it with an Ayn Rand–type chick. Those gals are really out there with their cleavers, ready to go. He just put away Ayn Rand, and the college girls got really uptight. That's the type of thing we were into.

"When he put people down, he usually did it so obtusely, so *hiply*, that they weren't able to pick up on it right away. On other occasions, when he put people down directly, he'd call them assholes right out, face to face. He knew when to shadow-box and when to throw a jab. He could call an asshole an asshole, because he knew it wasn't going to hurt him, because the guy would *be* an asshole, and Tim knew the guy wasn't even going to hear it. You can do that with those people.

"Anyway, at this party, Buckley wasn't putting anybody down personally. It wasn't like that. He was just looking for stature beyond being simply the guy who sang 'Dolphins' or 'Hobo,' so he'd be witty and maybe put Ayn Rand down just for fun.

"He wanted to develop additional dimensions. I think there were areas in his life that were neglected, but that he would have reached into, like literature, maybe as a writer, or maybe just involved in the writer's way of thinking and feeling. Like with Lorca and Ayn Rand, or with that Beat poet-monk you turned Tim on to, Brother Antoninus. So that night at the party, he was being literary, right in there with the college kids on their level, and better, and having a good time with that.

"Tim was very fortunate, in that he could conceivably have remained in Bell Gardens, but he didn't do that. He was able to enjoy things, and get out there and fight through the shit and emerge from it. I don't think he reached his full potential. He still had room to grow. I think by the time he died he was ready to go to another plateau, or needed to. I feel he needed to move in new directions, and writing might have been one of them."

In October 1970, Tim wore the same shirt he wore on the cover of *Starsailor* and brought trumpet player Buzz Gardner, bassist John Balkin, drummer Steve Clover, and myself into the KCET television studios in Los Angeles to tape a show for a youth-oriented program called *Boboquivari*.

Having been trampled by rabid critics, we played a comparatively laid-back, uninterrupted thirty-minute set that included some of the mellower songs from *Starsailor* (e.g., "I Woke Up") and a familiar tune or two from earlier albums (e.g., "Blue Melody"). The set was not lacking intensity or fire, but neither was it harsh in tone nor incomprehensibly complex. It was a good middle-ground show, a welcome introduction for listeners unfamiliar with Tim's new directions.

Perhaps of special interest to Buckley aficionados, one song appeared in *Boboquivari* that as far as I know was not recorded elsewhere. Judging by its linguistic style, Larry Beckett almost surely wrote the superb lyrics. It followed "Moulin Rouge" on the videotape and is a glorious celebration of Venice Beach: the crazy, colorful characters on the boardwalk, summer sunlight glittering on shimmering water, youthful longing, warm Santa Ana winds, sparkling sands—a "swaying day" where the sunrise stings and music boats sing to the "dark slap of conga cries."

After this song in the medley, Buckley shifted into a variation of a verse from "Jungle Fire," then a variation of a verse from what was later to become "Sally Go 'Round the Roses," and finally a variation of another verse from "Jungle Fire" as *Boboquivari* concluded.

Starsailor was released a month later, in November 1970, at which time Buckley put together the most imaginative Starsailor group of this three-year period: Buzz and Bunk Gardner on horns, John Balkin on bass, Maury Baker on timpani/trap drums. Of the four Starsailor bands, the two middle bands, especially this Balkin/Gardner/Baker ensemble, constituted Tim's core Starsailor groups.

"It was great," Balkin said. "You know how people go out and play tunes off their latest album to hype it. Well, we did that. We went out and played tunes off his latest album—*Starsailor* tunes.

"We just launched off. It was fun. Tim was having a ball. He'd pick up horn lines and follow them out. In some tunes, he used his guitar as a baton or a percussion instrument. Sometimes our sets would go for a full hour nonstop.

"He'd lead us wherever he wanted to go. Maybe he'd play the 5/4 'Lorca' bass line, so we'd get into playing 'Lorca.' Then he'd play the 5/4 bass line from 'Come Here Woman,' or the 10/4 line from 'The Healing Festival,' and we'd go into that. He'd sing the tune, and we'd launch off into free improvisations from there. Then he'd shift gears and lead us into the next place.

"He was the leader in the sense that he spontaneously laid out the set as we went. He would use musical signposts as cues—a riff on the guitar or a vocal cue—and then we'd follow him into that zone, explore it for a while.

"Sometimes he'd follow us too. If things were getting bogged down, I might pick up on one of Tim's bass lines and start laying that down. That might lead us into a kind of 'rest area.' We'd play straight for maybe five minutes, clear our heads, then go off again. Over the course of several gigs, he got freer and freer."

LEARN WHAT YOU FEAR: RADIO INTERVIEW, 1970

For the next two-and-a-half years—well into 1972—Buckley did everything he could to comprehensively develop the Starsailor concept. Playing material from *Lorca* and *Starsailor*, improvising at length, often creating new songs on the spot, he worked with his four separate groups, each of which featured different personnel and an impressive array of talent.

On October 17, 1970, he brought Balkin, Buzz, Bunk and Maury Baker into a Los Angeles radio station studio early in the morning, one A.M. The host (unnamed on the tape) clearly was not expecting what he got. He was a perfectly nice fellow, familiar with Tim's first album, but unaware of the many others, a conventional radio music listener who suddenly found himself caught in a maelstrom. This show vividly illustrated not only what Tim was doing musically, but also his patience (and impatience) with the kind of mentality he so often had to cope with in those days.

Buckley opened with the 5/4 bass lines from "Lorca," the other musicians joined in, and the music created its dark atmosphere as Tim sang the song all the way through. Then, with the "Lorca" theme playing behind him, Buckley launched into the recitation of a new poem, which he might have entitled "Learn What You Fear"—a provocative dialogue with an "articulate whore," in which heated sexual imagery illuminates the ultimate emptiness of desire, leaving the protagonist "like the first leper at the equator, without compass or Bible or mirror." The recitation then led back back to the "Lorca" music, with lyrics consoling that "she's your home when no one wants you. . . ."

Disc Jockey: An incredible amount of emotion and strength in that. What was it all about?

Tim Buckley: Well, it was sort of, ah, a tribute to Cassius Clay and his comeback. No? Won't buy it? Actually, it was all a wet dream, the reading part, okay? I figured it would be appropriate this time of the morning. I get censored at the record companies, so I figured I would let it go right here.

After a station break, the music started again, with Buckley and band members barking and howling like dogs, and, in an abstract, melodically angular lyric, Buckley asserting that he never touches cheap booze, the needle, or morphine, and admonishing, "If you're gonna scream, make it like Coltrane."

DJ: What was that?

TB: "You Can Always Tell a City by Its Graffiti."

DJ: Wow, I sure hear a big difference between your first album, *Tim Buckley*, and this music you're playing tonight. You seem to have freed yourself in a lot of ways. How do you relate to that first album?

TB: How do I relate to it? To put it simply, I was only 18 and that was my first shot. I just developed. That was easy. But I didn't *stop* developing. Also, I didn't have any of the fashionable popular influences. [DJ is silent.] Do you understand what I mean?

DJ: No.

TB: Like the Beatles.

DJ: Which influences did you have?

TB: Music. And expression. And reading, and life, just on and on and on like that.

DJ: Anybody or anything in particular?

TB: How about Rilke? Have to start somewhere. I am influenced by a lot of things, a good woman—you don't seem to know what I'm talking about.

DJ: Well, I don't see. I mean, there seems to be a division somehow between the Beatles and . . .

TB: And Stravinsky? Yes, I'd say so. I listen to things like that—timeless. In fact, I'd rather play onstage with Count Basie than the Beatles.

DJ: So you're trying to create something that is a little more timeless now.

TB: I'm just trying to express what I have to express. The more you have to express, the more abstract it gets. If you're not running a campaign for political office, then you're abstract. If you're not laying down facts and figures, if you're not a journalist, then you're relaying human feelings the best way you can. Poetry and music and things like that are very abstract forms. So *understanding* things is not truly the key to relating to it, is it?

DJ: Well, for you, no.

TB: Do you have to understand something before you like it? Do you have to understand everything about a deer before you like to look at it?

DJ: Certainly not. But one can gain appreciation through understanding.

TB: Do you have to know everything about ballet in order to like Nureyev?

DJ: No, but I'm certain that someone who is really into ballet, and can appreciate it on an emotional level as well as on a completely conscious level, can appreciate ballet to an even greater extent by understanding it.

TB: I think that if you understand beauty and what humanity is all about, then you understand what *anybody* is doing, simply because it is being felt and being done.

There is no question about a man playing a saxophone. If he plays his feeling through that saxophone, then what is there to understand, other than hearing what he's feeling and putting out to you and relaying to you, right? You don't have to know everything about the saxophone. That's what I'm saying.

DJ: Okay, no, I mean, understanding doesn't necessarily have to mean that one can't appreciate something at the same time.

TB: That's what I'm saying.

DJ: I really dug the rhythmic figures you were laying down.

TB: I'm talking about *emotional* communication.

DJ: It was almost mathematical, and at the same time you would break from it. Actually, there didn't seem to be any division line between what you had consciously worked out and what you were improvising.

TB: Let's try to relate this whole thing to something else. Do you define differences between reality and unreality? What do you think is unreal to you? And then I can explain to you what this music is all about.

DJ: I wouldn't want to bag anything as being unreal.

TB: Then don't.

DJ: I didn't.

TB: Okay, then everything is real. Everything exists that exists. It picks up and lets go, just like life.

DJ: Well, I enjoyed it.

TB: Thank you. Do we get to do some more, or is that it?

DJ: You get to play some more.

TB: Good. Let's do it.

"YOU CAN ALWAYS TELL A CITY BY ITS GRAFFITI"

To begin the Starsailor tour, Tim and his band flew back to New York and opened at the Academy of Music, heading the bill with Linda Ronstadt and Van Morrison. During his first set, Tim sang "You Can Always Tell a City by Its Graffiti," complete with dog barks.

"With Tim center-stage and the Gardners widely flanking him," observed one writer, "the trio shocked the highly variegated audience with a follow-the-bouncing-ball, three-man barking contest."

"Well," laughed Tim, "we told the people there's one thing we noticed in New York that's been missing: There are no dogs. So we started barking, and the people started barking back. Of course, the promoters were going crazy: 'You're insulting those people's intelligence!' 'Well, hell—they're barking back!' It was fun."

Robin Loggie of *Billboard* magazine didn't think so. She celebrated Linda Ronstadt's sweet but utterly banal warblings of well-worn tunes by Bob Dylan and Hank Williams as "mind-searing renditions," while denouncing Buckley's singing as "an eerie trip into vocal distortion," and criticizing him for "relating mostly to the mike or his electric 12-string." As for the barking dogs, she said, "'You Can Always Tell a Town (sic) by Its Graffiti,' launched with the animal howling of his four sidemen and coiling around Buckley's jazz wails, was the ultimate perspective of the artist's new territory."

I was reminded of Tim's remark to Micklo about Picasso. "What he's doing now is like so far out. And then you watch TV and he'll put up a statue or a painting someplace, and people say, 'Well, that *thing* you put up,' and they cringe, and . . . that's what you're up against."

John Balkin brought considerably more insight to the issue than Loggie. "The dog barking and the howling could have been channeled," he said, "but at the same time it was a search for a new vocal gymnastic. More than that, it also has a lot of philosophical and emotional content if you're sitting there howling like a dog.

"If you're a real singer—and Tim was a real singer—you're not just *imitating* a dog. That was kind of an uncanny thing, if you think about it. You could look at it as being bizarre, and some people did look at it that way. But Frank Zappa howling like a dog is not Tim Buckley howling like a dog. Frank might howl like a dog and take his dick out and piss on the stage. That would be his picture of Dog, right?

"Whereas Tim Buckley was trying to howl *like a dog*—and get into that intensity. When a dog howls, there's a certain passionate thing in the dog that's crying out. It reminds me of that woodcut by Edvard Munch called *The Scream*, you know? That type of thing. Tim was getting into the *essence* of a dog's howl."

The New York Times asked Buckley to write an article in celebration of Beethoven's bicentennial. Buckley stated a profound observation, one of the cornerstones of his outlook: " . . . Man's passioned fear of beauty hasn't changed. Reasons have, technology has, and, in turn, ways of doing things have changed, but what we do hasn't."

He went on to say, "Hardly anybody I know listens to Beethoven, maybe because they can't play him on the guitar." Nevertheless, Beethoven was still relevant because "his majesty engulfed humanity's universe two hundred years ago." It was Beethoven's willingness to be himself alone—deaf, brilliant, unique, authentic— that made him universal and that continues to make him relevant. Authentic music is "not religious or political," Buckley wrote, "but personal . . . alone, only yourself and what you're good for, alone, no banners."

In that article Buckley wrote about music in today's cultural context, saying that we are a business, a marketplace. We want products that can be separated from their creators and sold as items. . . .

"Politics, prime-time TV, Danny Thomas and the game shows—it's all bought and sold and planned out to get a response," he wrote. "But man's music—his bout with the gods—has nothing to do with the latest crimes. It's too personal to isolate, too intimate to forget, and too spiritual to sell."

It is interesting to me that he sang Fred Neil's "Dolphin Song" until the very end, not only because of its beautiful melody, but probably, as well, because of Fred's line, "This old world may never change . . ." (which Tim changed, significantly, to "*will* never change.")

A serious artist such as Tim Buckley simply will not be vanquished by the world's perennial inertia and unrelenting negativity. Whether through anger or joy or both, every artist brings love, beauty and compassion into our lives. All too often, of course, we crucify him or her for making the effort, but that effort is *never* futile. Through its artists, mystics, and athletes, this aching world slowly realizes its own capacity for dignity, creative aspiration, joy, love, beauty, and universal truth. At every level, these dedicated creators lead us upward, toward psychological wholeness and spiritual realization. They themselves do not always attain what they envision, but they light the way toward the gate, and that light forever shines. Their contributions are enormous, and never wasted. The wise and sensitive among us pay tribute to all who have gone before. Even the smallest candle vanquishes darkness. Creativity, authenticity and envisioned beauty count in every form.

For a while, Tim's merry band of Starsailors wasn't very merry. The East Coast lay dark and dreary in the dead of winter—snow, ice, gray skies, barren trees, brown grass. Some segments of audiences responded well to the new music, others didn't. But not everything was bleak. With love and warmth in his eyes, Balkin recalled a very special incident that took place.

"Timmy and I had to get up at five in the morning in the cold, while everybody else was sleeping. I bundled him up with his coat and scarf. We were like two kids getting up and going out and playing in the first snow of winter when nobody else has seen it. We had to take a trip together and drive eighty or ninety miles into Philadelphia for a TV show. It was a very personal thing, being together in the car, making that drive in the early winter morning. While we drove, we decided what to do on the show. We had the cassette tape of the backdrop of 'Starsailor,' without Tim's verbal overlay.

"When we hit the studio, we both felt the vibes of these fucking Lobo assholes. It was six or seven in the morning, and already the producers and technicians were getting juiced on wine. The Philadelphia housewives were sitting out front. And backstage, all these television slickos were getting bombed, sitting there drinking cheap white wine.

"They didn't even relate to us. We could have walked in naked and it wouldn't have made any difference. They didn't even *see* us, you know? We just sailed through the whole thing, carrying our roles off without plotting them.

"My role was to walk coolly into the control room and hand this cat the cassette. He said, 'What is Tim going to do?' I said, 'He's going to do something from his latest album, and this is the background tape to be played under what he will be saying.'

"Tim walked out into the spotlight, didn't take his coat off, didn't even take his scarf off. It was an old dark tweed type of coat. He walked out in front of these housewives who sat in tiers, maybe sixty tiers.

"We cut through the whole thing. We cut through the stoned TV executives. We cut through the stoned cats in the control booth who were drinking a cheaper grade of wine than the executives—they were deciding who's going to bring the wine next week. We cut through the guy who said, 'Well, time to go tame all the animals,' talking about the housewives.

"They put the tape on, and the engineer looked at me as if it was running backwards. I said, 'No, let it go, it's okay. It's not running backwards. Just let it go.'

"Tim took out this piece of crumpled paper from his coat—an envelope with lyrics scratched out on it—and proceeded to read it and improvise on it, with the housewives screaming and chortling, not laughing, but having fun listening to this ragamuffin they were told was a star.

"Nobody listened to the music. Nobody listened to Tim. Everybody backstage was ready for the entrance of the next act. He was just out there. He did his shtick, they gave me my cassette back, nobody said a word. We turned around, walked to the elevator, didn't say anything, got out in the parking lot, and just looked at each other and broke up laughing at the absurdity of it. 'Wow!—where the fuck have we just been!'

"It was an *out-front* experience. It wasn't the 'image' Tim Buckley. It was just two guys doing a thing together."

One night back in Venice, I got a call from Tim. "It's all over, Lee."

"What do you mean?"

"No more roller-coaster ride. It's done."

"What's done?"

"Herb said if I didn't play rock 'n' roll I'd better learn how to drive a truck. No more recording."

"That's outrageous."

"The Cohen giveth. The Cohen taketh away. He can't get me booked anymore, either."

"Why not?"

"Agents and club owners don't want *Starsailor* music."

"What are you gonna do?"

"I'll get somebody to book us under the table."

Balkin recalled that the gig at the Bitter End West didn't come off well. "It wasn't a good weekend musically. There were a lot of different directions in the band. Don't mistake me. It was a good period. It just didn't happen right mechanically. We were still feeling it out, trying to find our way."

Reviewer John Goff of *The Hollywood Reporter* attended the Bitter End West opening night. "Whatever bag Buckley is into these days, it is wished he'd go back to his roots. His music is discordant and rambling both vocally and instrumentally. If he's searching for something, he didn't find it."

Buckley, however, saw the positive side. "I've got some tapes," he told writer Michael Davis. "And they're fun to listen to. It was pretty adventurous. You had heard trumpets and saxophones explore, and that was okay. But never a voice. A voice always had to come up with lyrics, and the voice was supposed to be only a vehicle to carry the lyrics.

"So as a singer, you have to come up with lyrics. You can't just babble on and on and on. You have to write at least *something*, but it is very hard to instantaneously and spontaneously write a lyric and have it make sense. And I couldn't just do a chant, because that's not part of where I'm from, obviously. For Leon Thomas it is, but not for me.

"So it was a challenge. . . . You're still trying to relate something, but in the Starsailor context we were trying to relate something out of a more holocaustic environment. . . . My point is, that when *Lorca* and *Starsailor* were recorded, it was almost sacrilegious to do anything other than sing a lyric. Now, today, more and more people are using their voices for different things."

By the time they headed for San Francisco, the music and the band still had not quite come together, although things were getting better.

"We played an auditorium in San Francisco or Berkeley someplace and played our *Starsailor* stuff, but it was still embryonic," recalled Balkin. "We hadn't yet been into it long enough to have it down pat, and we were kind of intimidated playing a big concert and playing this kind of stuff instead of 'Buzzin' Fly,' which is a great tune. But tunes are easy. You know where they're going. Improvisation is difficult, like walking on a high wire in the wind.

"I didn't think the concert was a disaster, but a well-known critic [Ralph Gleason] came backstage afterwards and said, 'I'm gonna do you guys a favor. I'm not going to review this.' That depressed us. It depressed Timmy, and got everybody saying, 'Aw, man.'

"We drove up to the Lion's Share in San Anselmo around the third week of October 1970, and spent three or four days there. It was a small club, a place Janis Joplin liked to play. She had left money in her will to a string of clubs she liked, and this was one of them.

"We were all feeling pretty dejected because of the critic, so when we got onstage, we said, 'Hey, fuck it, that's it,' and just jumped in with 'Lorca' and tore it up. There was a lot of energy in that club. It was incredible. Everything clicked. The club didn't empty out. The place was still full and we got a lot of applause. A lot of people were into it. We never got booed, and we didn't empty a club after the first set. I've been in bands that have done that."

Feeling better about the music and themselves after the Lion's Share, Tim and the group rested up for a while, then traveled to Vancouver, B.C., where they played the Olde Cellar in January 1971. In a review entitled, "Tim Buckley, We Love You," Casey Burke wrote, "If your mind is open to growth and change, by all means go see Tim Buckley. Personally I think his music now is far superior to his music of the past."

Writer Bob Smith agreed. "Rather than categorize the music, I prefer to describe it as the natural growth of a seriously aware musician."

The Buckley/Balkin Starsailor band landed a few other gigs. One of them was in Escondido, a mountain town northeast of San Diego, on or about October 31, 1970.

"It was one of the few times Tim got accepted, with the barking and all," Balkin said. "The first half-hour, people started to squirm. I mean, if you went to hear John Denver and he started singing Louie Armstrong tunes, it would take a few minutes to adjust to it, right? But once they got it, they really dug it. . . .

"I brought some of our pennywhistles down. We each played a set of three of them together at the same time—got a lot of sound, with three guys playing nine pennywhistles. And we'd sing, and do some repartee. We did stuff from *Lorca* and *Starsailor* and some comedian stuff. It was fun.

"One of the things that impressed me—Tim did just about the whole *Starsailor* album, and he included the tune 'Starsailor' as well. We put a background on it, and he sang it. He used his voice to get that distorted sound that's on the album. He blew me away with that.

"Another thing about Tim that hardly anybody talks about—he was a guitarist in his own right. He did beautiful things on 12-string. He developed a style of playing that was unique to him and that really made it. It was a justifiable way of playing.

"I dig any kind of playing, writing of music, or any kind of poetry, as long as it's justifiable in terms of the craft and the art, content aside. I don't think you can shoot a water pistol full of colors on a wall and call it a painting, unless you can say, 'I'm doing this or that.'

"Tim's 12-string playing sounded good. It had that ring of authenticity. He had his voice and songs together, but he had his guitar together too."

According to John Goff's *Hollywood Reporter* review of the earlier Bitter End West performance, Emmett Chapman was on that gig. I don't know for certain, but I think that was the first gig Emmett played with Tim's group. He was an interesting musician, an inventor who created the Chapman Electric Stick.

I had gone to hear guitarist Barney Kessel at Shelley's Mannehole in Hollywood one night to see if bebopper Kessel had come up with anything new. Emmett was playing his Stick with Barney, just the two of them.

I was dazzled by the sound of Emmett's instrument and by the way he played it—nine strings (later, ten), two hands on the fretboard, tapping out chords and melodies simultaneously, traversing a tonal range from bass to treble several octaves wider than guitar.

After the set, I immediately invited Chapman over to the table, introduced myself, told him he had to meet Tim Buckley. I knew he would find Tim's improvisational context appealing and that Tim would love the scope, depth, range, and sheer originality of Emmett's new Chapman Stick.

Contrary to what one writer erroneously asserted years later, Emmett Chapman did not "replace" me in this third band; there was not a scintilla of "irony" involved in the change; and the change had nothing to do with musical limitations on my part. By that time, my skills were well developed, albeit idiosyncratic and irrelevant to music's mainstream.

Like Balkin and Baker before him, I brought Emmett Chapman to Tim as another musical gift, because Tim needed and wanted to explore *Starsailor* concepts to the hilt and needed musicians with fresh, unique perspectives. I was doing what I could to continue serving Tim, sharing whatever musical knowledge I had, nourishing his capacity to expand and grow.

In fact, it was I who discovered and brought to Tim not only Chapman, but *all* members of Tim's third Starsailor band—Chapman (Electric Stick), Maury Baker (timpani drums), and trombonist Glenn Ferris. Glenn had an imaginative, independent, intelligent love of improvisation, and his trombone added a formidable mid-range sound to the ensemble. This was one of Tim's finest Starsailor groups.

In early 1972, at one of the gigs booked under the table, I heard Tim's Chapman/Ferris band live in Escondido, northeast of San Diego, at In The Alley. They sounded incredible together—loud, fierce, exceptionally complex. Their tonal range was broad, their instrumental textures as rich and cohesive as they were linearly intricate. The guys had fun together as friends and interacting musicians, and took great delight in expressing their creative brilliance in exciting and often humorous ways. Dixieland meets Stravinsky—whew!

Tim and his Balkin and Chapman bands were never officially recorded. That's a shame. For a while, the music was purely exploratory and experimental. Eventually, however, Tim mastered everything he had envisioned. His voice was in better shape than ever before. His compositions, lyrics and improvisational free-flights were as brilliant as they were impassioned. He invented techniques by the dozens and filled them with emotional intensity, utilizing them to navigate his way through conceptual and structural mine fields with grace and strength. His ear for pitch and tone was amazing and impeccable (not perfect pitch [a genetic gift], but virtually infallible relative pitch). Vocal "gymnastics" poured out like waterfalls, shaped and honed by that unerring ear. True, there were no conceptual models, guideposts or maps, and everything was improvised. As a result, the music did not always work. But when it did, it was great.

By the end of that period in his life and music, Buckley technically, conceptually, emotionally and artistically fulfilled *Lorca* and *Starsailor*'s avant-garde concepts in every way. If the economic backing had been there and he had been able to step into the studio in those years between *Starsailor* and *Greetings*, we would have professionally produced recordings to fill in the blanks, not just a few unauthorized tapes.

With neither financial support nor critical acclaim, Buckley heroically pursued his vision to the furthest reaches anyway. He did not hold back. He gave it his all. I don't see how anyone could accuse him of not giving it enough time, or of "selling out" afterwards. Of the five stages of his career, he spent more time with *Starsailor* music than any other. With total dedication he explored the concept's *every* nook and cranny before shifting gears once again.

STARSAILOR: BEYOND THE COMFORT ZONE

Starsailor's conceptual innovations and strange beauties posed challenges that many listeners proved unwilling and unable to meet. To some extent, their reservations are understandable.

As Tim evolved from the mellow jazz stage of *Happy Sad*, he differentiated himself from its basic psychological and aesthetic configurations, transcended them, and identified with the next higher stage, which integrated previous structures into

Starsailor's new framework. The *exclusive* identification with the folk/rock/jazz elements of *Happy Sad* was dissolved, while *Happy Sad*'s capacities and many of its techniques were preserved and included in *Starsailor*'s new and more comprehensive infrastructure. Thus, words, chords, melodies and vocal improvisation were retained, while new song forms, harmonic dissonance, radical new vocal techniques, odd-time rhythmic signatures, and a new array of instruments (sax, trumpet, Electric Stick, trombone, timpani drums) were added. Tim was involved in a totally new way of *hearing* music—and that is what he wanted to share with us.

In other words, Tim evolved into a new psychological and aesthetic worldspace grounded primarily in avant-garde jazz and twentieth-century classical music. Many of his fans could not follow him, because Tim was no longer mirroring their inveterate tastes and values. His new worldview had neither emerged in their experience nor developed in their consciousness. Who could blame them for feeling nonplussed?

Unfortunately, many felt Tim had abandoned them with *Lorca* and *Starsailor*. They felt he had taken disastrous turns both artistically and commercially. They felt offended, not only by the dissonant, avant-garde music itself, but by his unwillingness to apologize, justify, or explain it to them. They felt Tim should be more considerate of the people who had paid money for his previous recordings and concerts. They called his new music a "mistake," denounced him for not giving them more of the kinds of music they loved in earlier albums, and blamed anybody they could—Tim, his fellow musicians, his management. They felt he willfully destroyed his career, throwing away everything he had worked so hard for. They questioned his musical judgment, his sense of responsibility to his audience, his competitiveness in the pop music marketplace. Many of them wondered if he had been led astray by "the jazzers" in his band, if he had given in to their pressures and musical preferences.

It is important to address some of these issues, because there are numerous questions and pitfalls involved with listener receptivity, even as there are unlimited possibilities for growth, expansion, and development.

Pop music audiences are notoriously fickle, often aggressive in their praise and violent in their blame, insisting that performers satisfy and inflate their egos by meeting implicit and explicit demands. Sometimes audiences embrace new musical experiences receptively, and learn from them. On other occasions, however, like customers in a restaurant, they insist the performer cater like a waiter to *their* whims, needs and wants. Entertainers cater well. Artists do not. Artists follow their own vision. When the artist's vision matches the audience's mind-set, there is harmony. When it does not, a power struggle can easily ensue.

Many listeners stayed with Buckley, and admired and worked to understand each new direction that he undertook. But many others abandoned him—and then accused him of abandoning them! Tim was powerfully motivated from within by formidable creative integrity. At the same time, he loved his audience. In fact, he loved and respected them so much that he dared to offer them something brilliant and alive and conceptually new. They could have felt respected, challenged, and astonished, but many did not. Instead of opening themselves and following his lead, recalcitrant listeners shut their ears, pouted, complained, and criticized—and then blamed Buckley instead of themselves for their own shortcomings.

Buckley gave them diamonds. The crowd wanted pebbles. Truly, it is an old story, and it never ends. Philosopher Arthur Schopenhauer once said a man of talent "is like a marksman who hits a target others cannot hit, but the man of genius is like a marksman who hits a target others cannot see."

Today, some of those listeners say they can now appreciate what Tim envisioned then, and that is good—but this "now" is also more than thirty years after the fact. More than once Tim told me he thought he would die young, before age thirty, an idea perhaps unwittingly instilled in him by his mother [see Elaine's interview in Chapter Two]. Throughout history many young musicians, poets, and writers have had intimations of an early death. I know I did. I was wrong. But Tim was right.

In any case, near the end his life as it turned out, he told me, "*Starsailor* is my masterpiece." Would any listener suggest he wait another thirty years for dawdling audiences to catch up before creating that masterpiece? I don't think so. Tim loved his listeners. His was not a "damn the public" attitude. He was not trying to offend anybody when he created *Starsailor*. But he sensed there was no time. He had to get it done while the vision was with him—and while he still had life and breath.

Some people have voiced the opinion that Tim might have created *Starsailor* music because he "wasn't competitive." To the contrary, with *Lorca* and *Starsailor* he challenged the entire mass-mind—the recording industry, radio programmers, concert producers, business people, other pop musicians, and the people who supposedly "loved him" and regarded him as their "friend" (as long as he complied with their aesthetic biases and preconceived ways of thinking and feeling). He dared to pursue a fresh new vision, a unique way of seeing and hearing, and dared to stand alone even after audiences and some of those so-called "friends" turned their backs.

Charlespoet, an online acquaintance, loved *Starsailor*. "It wasn't Tim that left his fans behind," he wrote to me, "but his fans that let him down when so many of them would not even attempt hearing what it was he was creating. It's a shame so many poets end up ignored simply because truth devours any and all comfort zones." Charlespoet has the kind of courage and intelligence it takes to allow "all comfort zones to be devoured." Like every first-rate listener, he has daring enough to shed preconceived "tastes," which blind perception, in order to welcome and experience the new.

Buckley was making a statement, taking a stand for beauty and originality, giving wings to a vision. He never felt better than when creating and fulfilling the *Lorca/Starsailor* concepts. George Bernard Shaw in *Man and Superman* described this feeling of strength and creative integrity when he said, "This is the true joy in life, the being used for a purpose recognized by yourself as a mighty one . . . the being a force of Nature instead of a feverish selfish little clod of ailments and grievances complaining that the world will not devote itself to making you happy."

Manager Herb Cohen was in the business of making commercially viable records. Tim was an artist whose primary concern was to create the new. To his enormous credit, Herb released *Lorca* and *Starsailor* knowing full well they did not conform to commercial parameters. But there came a limit. After Tim recorded *Starsailor* and insisted on further developing its concepts in live performances, Herb finally was unable to record him or to talk agents into booking him. It did not matter whether Tim's music was good or even great. It was not stylistically familiar folk, rock, pop, or Top 40 music. It was purely Tim Buckley music, and decidedly not commercial.

At that point, Tim was stranded but unbroken, alone but courageous enough to follow his own musical vision until he fulfilled it. In fact, from mid-1968 (with initial explorations into improvisation) until early 1972 he gave some three and a half years to it—more time and effort and creative energy than he devoted to any other of the five musical phases he explored during the course of his nine brief years of performing.

As for the question about "jazzers" leading Tim around by the nose, and peer pressure being the reason for his choice of direction, let us remember that Tim was a very bright guy. From day one, as we earlier noted, he gathered and surrounded himself with intelligent, well-educated people. He absorbed their knowledge, utilized whatever he considered apropos, combined it with his own talent, intelligence, and creative perspective, and evolved as a human being and musician. His choices were emphatically *not* the result of peer pressure.

If Tim had been the kind of person to meekly defer to other people during the *Lorca/Starsailor* period, he would have bowed to audiences and Herb Cohen and Jac Holzman and some of the "friends" who abandoned him; he would have catered to popular tastes instead of conceiving and recording *Lorca* and *Starsailor*. He would have recycled *Happy Sad* and *Blue Afternoon* instead of spending the following two years performing *Starsailor* music whenever he could. He was never under anybody's spell. He was his own man. This is not idealization. It is a fact. He had *spine*. For this alone, it seems to me, he deserves respect, even from his bitterest critics.

Larry Beckett made a couple of statements along the way that could use a little clarification.

Addressing my comment that Tim regarded *Starsailor* as his masterpiece, Larry told interviewer Jack Brolly, "Tim was too dissatisfied with his work to think anything a masterpiece, though he was proud of the lyrical, chordal, and time-signature experiments on *Starsailor*."

It is true that Tim was dissatisfied with much of his work, because much of his work was flawed, as is much of every artist's work. Forever there remains a gap between the concept and the attempt to fully realize it.

However, when I have indicated that Tim regarded *Starsailor* as his masterpiece, I was not merely stating a personal opinion or projecting a judgment of my own. I was relating a fact. After recording *Look at the Fool*, glancing back over his work up to that time, he said to me, "*Starsailor* is my masterpiece."

He did not use the word in Beckett's sense of mathematically elegant technical perfection, but in the sense of vision, effort, intensity, imagination, conceptual innovation, daring, and accomplishment above and beyond external technical factors. The goal was wholeness, emotional depth and fire, complete involvement, expanded imagination, moving from the known into the unknown and bringing what he found back to us as musical treasures.

As Larry pointed out in that Brolly interview, Tim was not thinking of sales or popularity, but of music as art. That is true—and in terms of both impassioned innovation and daring artistry, Tim said he regarded *Starsailor* as his *masterpiece*.

Whether or not any of us agree with that assessment is irrelevant. The music stands and endures on its own, its riches available to all who have ears to hear. [The CD may be difficult to locate until it is reissued a second time. Three of its more orthodox compositions—"Song to the Siren," "Moulin Rouge" and "Monterey"—are available on *Morning Glory: The Tim Buckley Anthology*.]

In other contexts I have indicated that the rejection of *Starsailor* by his fans was devastating to Tim. When Brolly asked Larry about that, Larry replied, "*Starsailor*'s poor sales were devastating to the record company, not Tim. He knew it was experimental, and for a select audience."

It is my view that Tim outgrew Beckett after *Goodbye and Hello*, and that although the two remained friends until the end, Beckett was admittedly not deeply or closely involved with Tim's life, thinking, feeling, or creative dynamic. They had taken distinctly separate forks in life's road after *Goodbye and Hello*. They often spoke on the telephone but in my view judging by his interviews, Beckett characteristically remained the straight-ahead rationalist in his own psyche, the detached mathematician, the emotionally timid physicist and computer programmer, while Buckley, rather like Lorca, Baudelaire or Rimbaud, explored the depths and heights of diabolically impassioned emotions. He pushed for extremes. He *burned*. He visited realms of the psyche that the fastidious Beckett would have found appalling. Beckett apparently did not *know* Buckley after a certain point, and to suggest that Buckley was detached and indifferent to the reception of his heart-and-soul *Lorca* and *Starsailor* creations was and is, in my view, a serious misinterpretation.

Buckley was an artist, but not *only* an artist. He was also a professional musician and a human being. As an artist, he pursued his vision without compromise in every aesthetic phase of his career. As a professional musician, he needed the blessings and support of management and record companies. As a human being, he was reaching out to other human beings through his life, his words, and above all through his heartfelt music.

Although the majority of his fans rejected *Starsailor*, Tim persisted in his efforts to reach them. The fact that they abandoned him, hurt him. The fact that they occasionally booed and criticized him, hurt him. The fact that some of his so-called "friends" betrayed him because of lack of understanding also hurt him. I know. I was there for much of it, and in contact with him through the rest of it.

Yes, he knew upfront, going into it, that *Starsailor*'s avant-garde dimension would appeal only to a select group of highly evolved listeners, and not to the predominantly sentimental radio-conditioned pop-music mass mentality. But that artistic awareness was hardly consolation for the pain of being rejected when the album and live performances were held in contempt by business interests, former friends, and hostile nostalgia lovers who could not and would not accept the challenge and take the jump into the new and unfamiliar. Through his music, Tim wanted to breathe life and beauty into listeners' souls. When they didn't care about *Starsailor*, it hurt him.

Without question, the word "devastating" is both accurate and applicable, as anyone who truly knew him during those days could easily see and understand. In other words, Beckett may have known the old Tim well, but he admittedly did not know the new Tim who talked to him on the telephone. To deny the reality of Tim's devastation may not be callousness on Larry's part as much as well-meaning ignorance.

Meanwhile, listeners had to choose between remaining with the herd, or stepping outside into the cold, where Tim (rather like the Beethoven he wrote about) was sailing among blue stars, beckoning listeners to summon up enough fortitude and imagination to follow. Some did. Others didn't. Their loss, not his. What a shame for those who missed him while he was alive. What a joy for those who dared to join him on the journey.

We have looked at some of the pitfalls involved with perceptive listening. It is appropriate that we also offer a few positive suggestions that might help listeners embrace the full scope of Buckley's music.

Every one of Buckley's five stylistic periods offers its own kind of beauty, intensity, and value. It is not that one period is "better" or "worse" than another. Listeners who allow themselves to be touched by at least some of the music within each generic framework will connect with Buckley directly, and joyfully receive what he offered, not necessarily in each and every song, but within the broader conceptual whole. In many people's opinion, including my own, Tim Buckley gave us more variety, imagination, depth and scope than any other singer/songwriter of his day. He was multidimensional, like diamond-light.

There might be some critics who will defend their negative opinions by accusing me of idolatry or of being blinded by friendship, unwilling to face various distorted perceptions that they call "facts." That is simply not the case. I am fully aware of Tim's aesthetic flaws and personal faults. However, his unwavering goal was to give the world the best and most beautiful music he was capable of creating. This perspective helps us liberate our ears. In all of their multifaceted dimensions, that music is still here, still available, still inviting those who are capable of receiving it.

Pianist Bill Evans once said, "My creed for art in general is that it should enrich the soul. It should teach spiritually by showing a person a portion of himself that he would not discover otherwise. That's the real mission of art." I think Buckley did that for receptive listeners in a dozen different ways, among which were the innovations contained in *Lorca* and *Starsailor*.

It *is* possible for people to wake up, grow, and evolve. I think listeners today—far more sophisticated and psycho-sonically experienced than yesterday—will have no trouble understanding and enjoying *Starsailor*'s extraordinary contributions.

As writer Ken Wilber once said, "To understand the art, I must to some degree enter its horizon, stretch my own boundaries, and thus grow in the process: The fusion of horizons is a broadening of self." By opening ourselves to *Starsailor*'s horizons, we broaden our own horizons in the process, which liberates us from the narrow straits of our ideologies and the prison of our isolated selves.

A British woman named Nettie Edwards got the point. After discovering *Starsailor*, she wrote to me, saying, "My immediate impression of *Starsailor* is that it is the most artistically courageous recording I have ever heard. . . . He was way ahead of his time and creatively moving at the speed of light. That's why I think *Starsailor* is such a great title. . . . *Starsailor* totally blows me away with its courage and beauty and innovation."

Maybe the kinds of insights presented above will help some people open their ears to all five of Tim's aesthetic phases. Maybe they will help people give *Starsailor* in particular a full chance over the course of several listenings, embrace the adventurous aesthetic experience, and come away awakened, moved, charmed, and delighted by new discoveries in the music and themselves.

Pitching pennies near Bryn Mawr, Pennsylvania, in 1972 while waiting for
a ride to the gig. Left to right: Tim, bassist Mark Sporer, Lee, drummer
Maury Baker. (Maury won more than everybody else combined.)

HEADING HOME AT LAST

Tim's fourth and final Starsailor group, which featured me on guitar, Mark Sporer
on bass, Carter Collins on congas, and Maury Baker on drums, was not purely a
Starsailor group. Tim had transformed himself again, coming out with *Greetings
From L.A.* We played *Lorca* and *Starsailor* material, but it was mixed in with white-
funk *Greetings* songs, an odd combination. Because of *Greetings* and its commercial
appeal, Herbie was able to get us booked on an East Coast tour in late 1972.

Compared to Tim's groups with Balkin and Chapman, this group was mainstream. The avant-garde pieces were harmonically and rhythmically more contained, while the mixed blend of *Starsailor* abstractions and *Greetings* funk tunes
created a relatively more palatable perspective for listeners. To be sure, Tim soared
on out there vocally, and Maury Baker swirled and churned on the drums, and I was
playing my new style of impressionistic guitar, but, on the whole, the lack of conceptual cohesiveness made this group less musically effective than the
Balkin/Chapman groups. We were another transitional band, moving out of the
Starsailor period into the *Greetings* phase, balanced and poised and relaxed, stretching our wings between the two polarities.

Tim's "pet giant," Barry Schulze, packed and hauled our equipment, operated the sound systems in clubs, and drove the car. When we arrived in New York, we played the Felt Forum—where Zappa's crowd hated us. Somebody even threw a Coke bottle. I saw it flying out of the spotlight, quickly tilted my head; it missed me by less than an inch. Near the end of "Gypsy Woman" Tim threw up his hands in disgust and walked off stage. The only other time I had known him to do that was at the Middle Earth club in London on our first European tour.

Win some, lose some.

Tim and I were riding on a New York subway when I struck up a conversation with a South American fellow. Knowing South America was fertile literary territory, I asked about writers. The guy gave me a list of authors—Neruda, Borges, Carlos Fuentes, Garcia Marquez, Cortazar, Carpentier, Paz, and a few others. I handed the list to Tim, "Here, ol' buddy, you might want to check out these scribblers someday."

He told Judy he'd gotten the list from an old guy drunk on a subway. There was no old guy and nobody was drunk. I think he just wanted to avoid any friction with Judy, as she, too, had recommended a few Latin authors to him.

In any case, Buckley utilized everything relevant that came his way. A couple of years later, he was reading books by South American authors, notably Fuentes and Borges. Some of the lyrics of his last album sparkled with Latin imagery. Shortly before his death, he was planning a trip to Honduras. Musical influences, literary influences, black, white, Latin, Jamaican—everything along the way became potential conceptual fuel for new music. He was a sharp observer. Nothing was wasted on him.

Bear packed up our gear in New York and we headed south for D.C. At the Cellar Door, we played our tushes off and the people loved us. "Either Buckley and his band cook, or I'll be hornswoggled," wrote Alex Ward.

On the last night at the Cellar, Barry didn't work the sound system well. Tim could not hear himself distinctly. The volume was either too loud or too soft. The bass was boomy. The treble was shrill. Nothing clicked.

Outside, after we finished helping Bear pack and load, Carter, Mark, Maury, and I waited in the car for Tim and Bear to get the money and join us. Late at night, nobody on the streets.

When Tim and Bear came out they were quarreling. We couldn't decipher the words. Then Bear, towering over Tim, started yelling. "I did the best I fuckin' could! It wasn't my fault! The fuckin' equipment wasn't workin'—nothin' I could do! Fuck you! Fuck you!" he hollered at Tim.

Barry grabbed Tim by the throat with his huge right hand, lifted him off his feet, slammed him up against the wall. "Suppose somebody grabbed *you* like this and told *you* to sing! How would you like *that*, huh? What the fuck could *you* do? Huh? Huh?"

Tim opened his mouth and started singing! He was being choked the way he'd been throttled in the garage by his father years ago, and he wasn't backing down. Gasping, choking, he defiantly and belligerently sang straight into Barry's face as loudly and clearly as he could. Barry was strangling him and Tim kept on singing!

I banged open the car door and leaped out to charge into the fray, but Barry stopped. He set Timmy down. The incident was over. It happened in a flash. I couldn't believe what we had just seen. Frightened. Appalled. Amazed.

Barry drove us back to the hotel. Nobody spoke.

Weird way to end a tour.

I said goodbye to the group in the lobby the next morning and split with Natasha, a former high school girlfriend, the woman who back in 1966 had steered me to Sean O'Brien in the Village—a lifetime ago.

Natasha and I spent a few days at her beach house in Maryland, north of D.C. She was gorgeous, vibrant, intelligent, full of fun, a joy to be with, exactly what I needed, just when I needed it. A beautiful woman, a beautiful person. Cleared my head, helped renew vitality.

Back in California, Tim and I saw each other on several occasions, hung out once in a while, partied a few times, but we didn't play music together again until mid-1973.

CHAPTER 14

RUNNING
WITH THE DAMNED

I run with the damned, my darling:
They have taught me to laugh.

"Monterey"

When dreams shatter like glass, when hope gets crushed, when the love you have given with all your heart is battered and degraded, miasmic winds burn the brain, scour the mind's dreamscape, poison the very air you breathe. A black rose flowers in the heart's core, chokes the soul unto death. Where once gentle joy played like a child in fields of light, now bitter rage, turned inward upon itself, gnaws its own heart, drinks its own blood, gnashes its own ripped innards in primal lust.

We run with the damned in those howling hot winds, transgressing laws, violating codes held sacred in that world beyond our grasp, where healthy, well-scrubbed gentlefolk live in comfortable security with alarm clocks, appointments, telephones, lawns, tea cups, voting booths, churches, gods, dictionaries, nets, ignorant bliss. Beneath white napkins, scorpions dance, but they will never see them.

We saw them. We giddily danced with them. And we laughed, even as we slid down hell's sleek slopes to join our friends—the desperate, the lost, the frightened, the doomed, the cursed. In their agonized cries, we heard our own blood-songs singing.

Where can pain find peace? When does fire stop burning? What demons writhe unseen inside the shadow-shades of our tormented visions?

Cool Richard separated from his wife and child, moved out of 136 Park Place, rented a one-room box-car cottage on Park Court down by Venice beach in a vacant lot just west of Pacific, behind a large house that faced Brooks Avenue. Across the lot and between other houses he could see the sand, the waves, and blue water from his front door. CR continued his ethnomusicology studies at UCLA, played shakuhachi flute, kept practicing his upright piano, dealt a little heroin to pay bills, snorted or shot up once in a while, kept things under control. Richard was cool.

One day in mid-1970 while out for a rare daytime walk, I ran into Meneli from the Atlantic City gig and John King's farm prior to the Carnegie Hall concert. What a surprise! She sat beside her collie dog, Shane, on a lawn near the boardwalk. With her long blond hair, her beads and ankle-length skirt, she looked as lovely as ever.

She needed a place to stay, and more or less pushed her way into my life. I wanted no responsibility—leave me alone with my TV and goldies. But she insisted, and I gave in. We lived together for a year with that beautiful, sweet, slow-witted, inbred, pinch-brained, pedigreed collie dog. I grew to love him too.

At nineteen, Meneli was smart, assertive, and curious. Rather like myself, she couldn't cook and wouldn't clean house, but she absorbed knowledge quickly and enjoyed listening to all kinds of music, including the weird Eric Dolphy avant-garde jazz and even weirder electronic music I played. When we hung out with Tim and Judy, she thoroughly enjoyed being in their company.

When it came to making love, I had never known anyone as sensuous as Meneli. We taught each other the secrets of the ages, how to stroke every contour carefully, how to take infinite time, slowly sensitizing each slope and rise and valley, how to give and receive sensation equally, how to prolong pleasure indefinitely, how to float in dreamspaces merged with love, slow-fire passion, extended erotic intensity. Sexual intoxication often passed beyond dreams and oblivion into the no-mind serenity of meditation. Time disappeared. Ego vanished. We lost ourselves in exquisite silences.

We also lost ourselves in simple lust, and smoked pot, swallowed reds (Seconals) and Quaaludes, drank alcohol. Every way was okay, every way was good.

She got a job working with exotic animals at the Culver City Animal Hospital. When she came home, we took walks with Shane, made love, watched old movies or her favorite show, *Star Trek*, which I had never seen before. I couldn't believe it at first, but Captain Kirk and Mr. Spock were a delight to watch!

The time between the completion of *Starsailor* in 1970 and the release of *Greetings From L.A.* in late 1972 was as intense and insane for Tim as it was for me.

"They took everything away from him," Judy said. "They didn't let him record. They kept canceling recording sessions and 'postponing' them. They put him off from going on the road, wouldn't book him for gigs. He had to drive up to Hollywood once a week to pick up his 'allowance.' It just steadily got worse, more and more downhill from Friday to Friday."

While in Hollywood, Tim would occasionally score a jar of reds, driving his van, or his classic old 1940s tan and yellow Cadillac. For the most part in Laguna Beach, he stayed indoors, kept the black velvet curtains closed, drank brandy, Kahlua or Harveys Bristol Cream, watched TV, knocked himself out with Seconals. One night he wrecked the Cadillac. Didn't get hurt, but wiped out the car.

Nursing his wounds from the *Starsailor* period—vicious critics, hostile nostalgia fans, intractable business people—he searched his thoughts for ways to recover from the devastation, for ways and means to live, grow, perform, earn a living and regain some degree of economic stability and critical respect without compromising his music or his integrity.

Questions loomed, the heart ached, the days drifted on by. . . .

Dan Gordon and Tim collaborated on a screenplay called *Fully Air Conditioned Inside*, a comedy about a musician trying to make a comeback. "It's not that somber, it's very funny, but tragic the whole way," Tim told Bill Henderson. "What do they call that—black humor? Very American."

In the narrative, Tim visits Herb's office, is told he is broke, is almost given a lobotomy (tax deductible), takes the stage at the Troubadour, "knocks 'em dead" (by literally blowing the audience up), goes to jail, stands trial. Carried off by a vulture, he escapes, singing "I did it my way."

Much of the humor lies in the play's zany and often shockingly racist spoofs of American stereotypes—Native Americans, hippies, blacks, Herb Cohen–type businessmen, audiences, critics, interviewers, judges, lawyers, juries, the legal system.

Throughout the story, Dan and Tim often base their colorful characters on real-life people: Tim himself, the sexy Madame Wu, Herb Cohen, myself, and others. One-liners abound, the pace is fast, the scenes bizarre and often heart-rending. It remained unproduced, said Tim, "because nobody wants to spend a million dollars on a comedy."

Meneli decided she wanted to make love on one of the new waterbeds that were just coming into fashion. We scraped together a little money and bought one, setting it up in the living room, filling it with water, making sure Shane didn't jump on it and turn it into his personal pallet.

Coming home late one night, we saw light streaming through the glass panes of our front door. Somebody was in the living room. We approached on tiptoe and heard loud, raucous laughter from inside.

Tim and Danny were rolling around on the waterbed, both of them hilariously drunk. Shane barked as we approached. Tim and Dan sat bolt upright on the waterbed, swaying back and forth, bobbing up and down. Blood dripped from a cut in Tim's right wrist. He and Dan laughed again, "Hey, Leeeee! Meneliiiiiii! Come join us! We're rowing our way to Vahalla!"

"My God, Tim, your wrist—you're bleeding."

"Jus' a scratch, ol' buddy. Ain't nothin' like Normandy or Bastogne, thas' f'sure."

"What happened?"

"Hey, you weren't home—fist through the window—unlocked the door."

I looked. He had shattered the pane next to the knob. Broken glass littered the rug inside the door.

The cut on the inside of Tim's right wrist was not horrendous, about an inch long, not too deep. Luckily he had not slashed a vein. We wrapped his wrist and arm in a clean t-shirt, grabbed a few goldies from the fridge, piled all of us into my little Renault. On the way to the hospital emergency room we cracked a couple of beers, joking about how God saves fools, drunks, and crazy singers just to keep suffering humanity laughing.

With damp rags the next morning Meneli and I wiped dried blood off the waterbed. We swept up the broken glass, then called the landlady to replace the pane. I told her somebody had tried to rob the place, but we had chased them away.

In between gigs with Starsailor bands, Tim was thinking about writing a work based on Joseph Conrad's novel, *An Outcast of the Islands*. He scribbled ideas for lyrics in a notebook he carried, and talked with John Balkin about doing music for it. It was my understanding that Larry Beckett had also contributed some words, and that he and Tim were planning to collaborate on the project. I asked John for his recollections. . . .

"When I worked with Tim on it, I didn't know Larry was involved, and I didn't see any lyrics by Larry. I read an article written after Tim's death that *Outcast* was something he was working on with Larry near the time of his death, a different period than when I worked with him on it. The time of his death was several years later. If he was working with Larry during this earlier period, I didn't know about it.

"As far as lyrics, Tim carried a notebook with him with ideas and lyrics in it. So I assumed he was writing all the material. In '71 and '72 he and I had a few meetings and we went over thematic stuff: melodies to lyrics from his notebook, not Larry Beckett's lyrics. But I couldn't get a feel of what he wanted musically. Did he want me to take it out there and do it atonally? Or did he want it modern but not necessarily atonal? Did he want it free? We never had a meeting on that level. I couldn't get a picture of what he heard.

"So I wrote about ten or fifteen minutes of music, and Warner Bros. paid for an hour or an hour and a half of studio time. We didn't have a budget for more than four musicians, but I heard a big full sound, so I wrote the music with overdubs in mind. This time around, I just needed to get a sketch of it. So I wrote it out for four guys, an alto player, Buzz, Bunk, and a percussionist who could play odd meters without feeling awkward.

"The engineer was a pain in the ass. We had maybe 32 tracks. I told him we were going to do layers.

"'I want you to lay this down on the first four tracks. The next section, I want you to sync it in and lay it down on top of the first four.'

"He'd say, 'Well, I can't do that unless I have a score.'

"'You don't need a score, man. Just do what I'm telling you. Lay these tracks down. We'll run the tape back, then run this section on top of it.'

"So he got hostile. I had my score but didn't have a conducting score, so I threw him my score. He got shitty about it. It wasn't a good experience. Then he didn't record it right. Worst of all, he used old tape and didn't erase it all the way through—so the previous music bled through into our work. The tape was useless. I don't understand why he didn't use new, fresh tape. Warner Bros. was paying for it. So that was the end of that.

"I had a copy of it, but accidentally threw it out. There was some good music on it, but the recording quality was bad. The mix was terrible. I think they destroyed the master. I got the feeling we were just being jerked around."

After his work with Balkin in 1971–72, Tim continued thinking about *Outcast of the Islands,* and persisted in his efforts, steadily growing closer to the realization.

In the spring of 1973, a few months after the release of *Greetings From L.A.,* he told Sam Bradley, "Larry Beckett and myself have been working on a thing called *Outcast of the Islands,* by Joseph Conrad. That book is not one of his best, but the way Beckett wrote the lyrics—he did it as a character description of the eight different characters. By the time you listen to all of the lyrics, you know the story.

"It's a ballet, really—a character description of each person, done as a ballet. I've been learning how to write the music for it for the last year and a half. Because it isn't a commercial venture, I'm making money now to do it, probably as a library piece, or perhaps I'll give it to somebody like Stan Kenton to put on his mailing list. Otherwise, I can't see business people putting it out, nor do I blame them for that. They have their thing.

"*Outcast* is basically what I have my heart into. It's a beautiful piece of work on Beckett's part, and when I finally finish it, it will be beautiful musically too. It's more classical than anything, but it isn't an opera, and it isn't pretentious. It's just the story, and it covers pretty much the gamut of human emotions. It's utilizing what I've learned all these years, with the choir thing."

In April 1975, three months before his death, Tim again mentioned the project, this time to writer Michael Davis. "We wrote different songs for each of eight characters. By the end of the eight songs, you understand the whole story. It's quite an ambitious endeavor on Beckett's part. That's one of the things I'd love to work on before the decade is out. They are not things that will be done by anybody else. I've reached that place in the music where I don't fear that."

Because Tim made concrete efforts—his own notebooks, working with Balkin on music, working with Beckett—and because he continued to express interest in the project over a period of years, it is very likely that *Outcast of the Islands*—with lyrics, music, ballet dancers, orchestra, and choir—would have come to fruition. Either way, *the concept alone* reveals a great deal about Buckley's artistic evolution.

Judy Buckley told me she had Tim's lyrics to *Outcast of the Islands*, but refused access.

One Friday, Tim drove up to L.A. in his red Volkswagen van, picked up his 'allowance' from Herb's office, bought a new jar of reds, dropped by my place around 7 P.M., and asked me and Meneli to ride back down to Laguna with him. Sure, that would be fun. We packed an overnight bag. I grabbed a six-pack. Off we went.

"Lots of room at the top," he said along the way. "But you can't sit down for a second," (a line which later showed up in "Down in the Street" on *Look at the Fool*).

Somewhere south of Newport, stoned to the point of nearly falling, we stopped at a beach, shed all our clothes, staggered into the ocean, naked as babes in the night. I dove into the waves and played. Meneli lurched and staggered, protesting that she was too stoned on reds to run in the water. Tim laughed and frolicked and splashed water all over us. We had a good time.

Unfortunately, either when we hopped out of the van or climbed back into it, the reds got kicked out. We discovered the loss at Tim's house. Damn! Oh, well.

Meneli and I tumbled into the downstairs bedroom and made love until dawn. Tim's seven-year-old stepson, Taylor, watched from outside the floor-to-ceiling window. He stood naked, eyes wide, his hard little pecker rigid, quivering, eager. He knew we were aware of him. I envied him for getting to see us making love. His watching turned me on even more, Meneli, too. . . .

In the morning Tim and I drove back to the beach but couldn't find the reds. He still had a few left from the previous batch, but he was pissed. I didn't blame him. Money. Time. Inconvenience. Need. We drove back to Hollywood.

A couple of nights later, after being bombed for two days on the new reds, we all got whacked again and trouped out to a Mexican restaurant. The folk singer took a break, at which time little blond-haired Taylor jumped onstage and grabbed the mike. He started doing a Dick Cavett shtick, telling bad jokes, coming on like a comedian.

Some smart-ass in the audience booed the jokes. Taylor ignored him, tried to carry it off—"Did you hear the one about the elephant ratta-ratta-ratta. . . ." His jokes were rotten, but he had a smooth style, a fast pace, lots of chutzpah.

The heckler hollered, "How come you got blond hair when your mother's hair is black!?—Har, har, har!"

Tim strode up onstage, picked up the folk singer's 12-string guitar, sat down, started strumming. The manager and singer rushed over to stop him. I interceded, told them, "Hey, this is Tim Buckley. We played Carnegie Hall and *The Johnny Carson Show*, he's got records all over the place, he can sing his ass off, he knows what he's doing. Let him go, all right?" They grudgingly listened a few seconds, slowly smiled, said, "Okay."

Tim nodded to Taylor to sit down and play tambourine. He whomped that guitar like Leadbelly and started singing the "Train Song" from *Blue Afternoon*.

It was an extraordinary moment, one of the most beautiful I ever witnessed during those years. Tim was strumming and singing full strength, with Taylor sitting beside him wailing on the tambourine, an incredible father/son unity in the heat of battle—something Tim had never known with his father, something Jeff never knew with Tim, something I never knew with my father either.

They finished with a flourish, smiling at each other and the audience. People at the bar clapped, cheered, stood up at their tables and applauded. The owner and folk singer applauded, smiling, relieved. The heckler laughed and clapped and called for more.

Philip, one of Michael's friends from the Happy Valley days, was a lost soul, a teenager, very bright but extremely alienated, out of touch with daily life, a borderline psychotic. Although he purchased my old Epiphone guitar for $350, he had no discipline or talent and couldn't play it. He had intelligence but no direction or work skills or social skills. He just drifted, an accidental person with an accidental life. Tim liked him, felt compassion for him, took him in down in Laguna, fixed up the garage, let him live in it.

On one of those Friday treks to Hollywood, Tim and Philip got stopped by cops and searched. The cops found the reds.

"Whose are these?"

Philip said, "They're mine."

They arrested him—and Philip spent six months in jail.

When Cool Richard heard about this incident he was outraged. He felt Tim had been dishonorable in the extreme. The reds were Tim's and Tim should have taken the rap like a man. Instead, Tim proved himself a worthless coward. CR held him in utter contempt. He also felt that Philip was a wimpy sycophant who let Tim take advantage of him.

I saw things differently. To me, it was Philip's free choice, and it made perfect sense. Tim was a unique creator and a beloved friend. By the same token, Philip wanted and needed to serve Tim, and this was the ideal opportunity—what else of value could he do with his otherwise abject life? What else could he offer his hero? He felt the joy of redemption and self-esteem and pride. As well, Tim was spared the wrath of our society's imbecilic, egregiously hypocritical drug laws. Six months in jail would have killed Tim and left his family bereft of all means of support. In my view, Philip did a good thing, not only for Tim, but for himself as well.

Richard saw none of this. He didn't acknowledge Tim as an artist of worth or stature. Furthermore, just because Tim was an artist, worthy or not, he did not deserve special treatment. As for Philip, his gesture wasn't ennobling—just stupid. Richard viewed both parties and the entire incident with unalloyed scorn.

In the title track to his last album, *Look at the Fool (That Love Made Me)*, Tim spoke of feeling like "a little boy lost" when Judy wasn't there. Judy agreed.

"Very much so," she said. "I saw more of that than the other part. He was a pussy-cat who watched animal shows on television. Really. He would write erotic things, maybe after watching a documentary on sea lions. I thought that was terrific. He would really get into all the sensual things, and he would take notes. Like everybody else, he would take words and lines. I think he got a lot of his words from narrators on animal shows! Key words, you know?

"He didn't get too out of line when I was around. He was really pretty harmless. It was lucky he never got hurt. I mean, I've seen him really alienate people. I'm *amazed* he didn't get hurt in some of those things. . ."

At Bob Burns, a piano bar in Santa Monica, Judy, Tim, and Dan Gordon dropped in to hear a piano player who had been there for years. The place was crowded that night, no place to sit, so the three of them stood near the bar and waited.

Judy recalled how, "This guy, who was sitting down on a bar stool and was still taller than Tim, reaches over and taps Tim on the shoulder and says in this big voice, 'Move. Sit down. I can't see da piana player.'

"The guy was gigantic, but Tim leaned right into his face and said, 'You're a stupid muthafucker, a hangover from the Neanderthal age—and it's you who should get your ass up and be gentleman enough to give the lady your seat!'

"'You little shit, if you don't shut your mouth, I'm gonna flatten you!'

"The guy had a gun on with a shoulder strap, too. Brave Danny was pulling at me, saying, 'Come on! We gotta get out of the way! The guy's got a gun!' Dan was going to leave Tim there, can you believe it?

"Well, Tim stood his ground, told the guy to get the hell off that bar stool and let the lady sit down—and I'll be damned if the guy didn't get up and give me his seat!"

I needed to do some concentrated work on my impressionistic new approach to guitar playing, finding additional ways to merge conventional chords, discrete melodic notes, and innovative two-handed sonic effects into integrated flowing harmonic tapestries, rather like musical counterparts to Monet's water lily paintings. So I drove my rusty, aged, third-hand, pint-sized, tin-can Renault out to Lake Elsinore, rented a cabin for one month, stayed sober, and developed the spacious atonal, arhythmic concepts and techniques that had become important to me.

When I returned to Venice around ten one night, Meneli was not there, so I hopped in bed, turned out the lights, and waited for her. When she came home, she brought a huge bearded black man with her, a fierce-looking local character named Malik. They talked in the kitchen while I lay in the dark wondering what to do.

Figuring he didn't want a hassle any more than I did, I quietly cleared my throat once, twice. Meneli said to the guy, "Just a second." She came into the dark bedroom, whispered, "Lee? Is that you?"

"Yes."

"Oh, my god," she said, mortified. She sat on the bed, hugging me, "I'm so sorry, so sorry. I just met him today."

"Tell him to get out of here."

She went back to the kitchen, mutter-mutter. He left quickly. Meneli and I made love. Nothing more was said about the incident. My month away in Elsinore had been too long. I didn't blame her.

Tim called a few days later, said, "Come on. We got a gig at the Golden Bear in Huntington Beach." My now well-honed new approach to the guitar worked in each context, from older tunes, like "Blue Melody" and "Gypsy Woman," to the most recent *Starsailor* pieces.

"Wow," Tim said, after the first set. "You played every song the new way—that's great!"

Tim knocked on the door one night in Venice, staggered into the house drunk, jumped into bed with me and Meneli. We welcomed him and drank a couple of beers. Tim was making eyes at Meneli, cooing, smiling, blowing in her ear, looking at me to see if it was okay. We laughed, remembering the three of us in Atlantic City necking on the car hood before the show. Ah, yes. . . .

By this time, I had given Tim all I had—my knowledge of music and literature, my own music, creative ideas, personal appreciation, understanding, loyalty. I had even put my life on the line for him. But I didn't want to share Meneli. I didn't want to break the closeness she and I had, didn't want to include Tim, didn't want to get it on with the three of us. It just didn't feel right.

It surprised the heck out of me, but I shook my head "No." We played around a while longer, then Tim left. That little vestige of independence and autonomy eventually became a psychological foothold for me.

One night riding back home with Meneli, both of us drunk, I whimsically turned my valiant little Renault off Pacific Coast Highway, sped down the drive into a parking lot, stepped hard on the gas, loving the thrill of speed and acceleration.

We hit one of the cement parking abutments—and the car tipped over. It skidded at least fifty feet on the roof, with us upside down in it, metal screeching on concrete, showering sparks everywhere, glass breaking. The noise was horrendous. Shaken but unhurt, Meneli crawled out of a broken window on her side. I climbed out on my side. Blood gushed out of a cut on my right wrist. Lying on its back like a broken bug, gasping, wheels slowly spinning, steam spewing from its innards, my poor little Renault had been totaled. Fare thee well, dear friend.

We weren't far from Danny's house, so we staggered across beach sands to his place, woke him up, blood dripping from my hand. He drove us to the same hospital emergency room where we had taken Tim.

Back home, preparing for bed, I accidentally cut my chin shaving. Without stopping the flow, I made love with Meneli, wiping blood over her face and breasts, licking it off, dripping it into her mouth, fucking her hard, drinking my own blood from her lips and tongue, one of the most passionate nights we ever had.

The next morning, around six, Shane started howling, apparently for no reason. He just lay on the floor and howled. Within a minute, the ground rumbled violently. The whole building shook. A roar filled the air, like sustained thunder. Cups clattered on shelves. Shane howled and barked loudly. Glasses and plates rattled. Dirt sputtered out from cracks in the ceiling. Nails creaked in their sockets. The living room table jittered on the floor. Shane kept howling and barking. Meneli and I held on to each other in bed.

When the roaring and shaking stopped, I opened the front door. Early morning sun shone brightly on silent empty streets. Before long, in the distance, we heard ambulance and fire truck sirens wailing. The great San Fernando Earthquake of February 9, 1971, had struck, 6.6 magnitude, over $1 billion damage, 65 people killed.

"Why do I have blood all over me?" Meneli asked, looking down at her chest.

"Don't you remember?"

"Remember what?"

I knew things had been whirling out of control, so I withdrew again and just laid up, quietly sipping goldies all day while Meneli trotted off to work at the Culver City Animal Hospital.

A few weeks later, I woke up at 3 A.M. in physical agony—incredible pain in my lower right abdomen, the worst pain I had ever known. Pepto-Bismol didn't help. Vomiting didn't help. Meneli called the guy upstairs. He gave us a ride to the hospital.

Thorazine. Examination. More Thorazine. My liver had exploded.

Yes, we pay for our parties.

To my mortification, I had to call my parents to cover for the hospital room, the only time I ever asked them for money. I stayed several days in a ward with three other people. One afternoon when Meneli visited, we pulled the curtains around the bed and made love, much to the consternation of the humorless nurse. Tim and Judy didn't visit. Nobody visited except Meneli.

Clearly, I had to make a decision. I felt like Crazy Terry who sold hash out of his wooden leg back in New York. If I stopped drinking, I would live. If I didn't stop, I would die. Not exactly an easy decision, and, like Terry, I wasn't too quick to make it. Dying didn't look all that bad. I had been flirting with death for quite some time, hadn't I? So had Tim, had he not? Were we not alike this way? To heck with him. What about me?

Suicidal rage caused inner pain, yes, but why the rage in the first place? Exactly what was the complaint? Who or what was I so mad at? Why did things hurt so much in my heart and mind? Why did I feel so inadequate and worthless, so needing of attention? I had no answers.

Conversely, if I wanted to quit skating around the suicide rink, then why didn't I? What was stopping me? What was I getting from it? What were the payoffs? What felt so good? Intoxication? Sex, madness, transgression, expressive release of deep-seated anger, like that night I broke up the house? Getting loaded felt great. Attention from people who felt sorry for me felt great too, especially from pretty girls who wanted to help me make it through these twisted nights. How come I had to destroy myself in order to get love? Why did any sort of rejection or denial of my wishes set me off? Did it have to do with my childhood, with parents?

I suddenly flashed on the night years ago, when I had crawled on the floor over to the bookshelf in John King's apartment and looked through Karen Horney's book, *Neurosis and Human Growth*.

That was it. That was the right direction.

I asked my doctor to find me a shrink, and began the long, slow, irregular and often extremely painful journey toward sobriety. I also intermittently attended AA, as well as encounter groups at a drug rehabilitation center called Synanon. All three helped, especially the shrink. Not easy to quit drinking—I would quit for a while, off/on, off/on, like a light bulb with a short in it.

At the time I didn't realize it, but these decisions constituted a parting of the ways. Although Tim and I remained friends until his death, I had taken the first and hardest step toward sanity and sobriety right there in the hospital. Flat on my back, I embarked upon a new life that would eventually not include Tim at all.

Meneli came home one evening, sat down on the bed, held my hand, quietly said she was pregnant. A bolt of fear shot through me. No way did I want a baby. She didn't either. So we shared the cost of a legal abortion. Afterwards, she was concerned she might not be able to have children. Not to worry. One step at a time.

Shortly after that, she decided to return to New York with Shane. She had loved California, gotten to hang out with me and Tim and Judy, learned a lot about music, had a great time sexually, had worked at the hospital with panthers, bears, tigers, and other exotic animals. Now it was time to go.

We kissed good-bye and parted on good terms.

Down in Laguna, too many parties and not enough gigs made the going tough. Tim and Judy had explored the town. Alas, the rosy glow had faded. They felt lonely—their friends lived in Santa Monica, Venice, Hollywood. Money was getting short. Needed work. Boredom, stress, and general dissatisfaction—to hell with it. Sell the house, move up to Santa Monica.

When Tim talked to me about it, he called Laguna Beach "Labewka Geech" and said the whole thing was "a mistake." Judy and her former husband Darrell had been friends with film directors Francis Ford Coppola and Carroll Ballard in earlier days. Judy and Tim gave Ballard a call. He invited them to move into his apartment on Second Street while he was on the road for a few months. It was a nice two-bedroom place with a spiffy circular staircase that spiraled up to the bedroom above the living room.[1]

Tim got one of the leads in a film called *Why?*, directed by Victor Stoloff, co-starring O.J. Simpson and Linda Gillen. It was about people in group therapy trying to cope with problems and find their way out of depression. Tim played the part of a drummer whose group had broken up. He had lost friends, work, and direction, and was trying to reorganize his life—sounded a lot like Tim.

"Nobody had any idea who Tim was," Linda Gillen told writer Martin Aston, "so we weren't in awe of him." And of course O.J. showed no respect, having no knowledge of Tim's experience or point of view. "He thought Tim wasn't 'street' enough, just a phony suburbanite white kid. . . .

"Tim was fabulous," Gillen said. "He never showed a darker side. But he would get in these strange moods. Once he flew into a major rage at the person who was playing the psychologist and stomped out. Tim could be really frightening. And I remember O.J. laughing, saying, 'Come on, man, stay cool.' He was bemused that this little scarecrow figure had all this anger."

Gillen said Tim often walked several miles to work, refusing rides when she offered,

1. Years later, in 1980, Ballard's 1979 *Black Stallion* film won the Los Angeles Film Critics New Generation Award and was nominated for two Oscars, Best Supporting Actor (Mickey Rooney) and Best Film Editing. Ballard also directed *Never Cry Wolf* (1983; nominated for Best Sound Oscar) and *Fly Away Home* (1996; nominated for Best Cinematography).

and he never hustled his records or talked about his past. When Gillen asked him why he was doing "this schleppy movie," Tim replied, very quietly, "I need the money."

By this time, $420 dollars every week for six months mattered. When I asked him how he liked shooting the flick, he said, "It was a total bore. I'm glad I'm done with it." The film was never released.

With Meneli gone, I was freewheeling for a while. Sometimes straight, sometimes stoned, I did what I could to keep myself together, making steady progress. To begin with, I formed a quintet of my own, symbolically and optimistically calling it Sunrise. For fun and for free, we played a small, private, and tremendously successful concert at Synanon.

When I told Tim about it, he did not congratulate or encourage me. Instead, he brought a bottle over, asked how many people attended (50–75). Did we get reviewed? (No.) How much money did we make? (None.) Did I get a recording contract? (No.) Would the group ever amount to anything? (Maybe.) Here, have a drink, have a drink, have a drink. And I did.

He seemed to resent the fact that I had made a move on my own. He didn't like the independence I showed, and he didn't like being left out. In effect punishing me for escaping his domination, he used his questions to subtly belittle every aspect of me and my band and the concert. He got both of us loaded and "stole" the joy and happiness I felt for playing my own music with my own group and performing well. We had a great concert. Self-centeredly despising my blossoming confidence, he ripped it to shreds.

Buckley needed to be the center of attention. He had to stand in the spotlight. He had to be the star—nobody else, especially not me. He wiped out my pride and left. At first I felt baffled, then profoundly hurt, then enraged. I never said anything to him about it, but neither did I forgive him.

I returned to sobriety, but occasionally took delight in breaking my own rules. When Tim invited me over, I said to hell with it, and he and Judy and I got loaded on grass, Harvey's Bristol Cream, reds. Not once during this period did I see any heroin, or see Tim or Judy use any heroin, nor did Tim ever refer to heroin, even in a joking way.[2]

Katy, Tim's sister, remembered how happy Tim had been while he was writing and recording *Starsailor*, and how unhappy he became afterwards when he and that music had been so adamantly rejected.

"I remember his birthday on Valentine's Day in 1972, shortly before he recorded *Greetings From L.A.*," she told me in our interview. "He came over to the house, really bombed. Judy wasn't with him. He was to the point of not being able to talk. He sat in the kitchen, all hunched over.

---

2. That crack in late 1969 on *Live at the Troubadour* about "Give smack a chance," was a flippant, off-hand, spontaneous, throw-away line meant to humorously deprecate anti-Vietnam peace marchers whose anthem was "Give Peace a Chance." True, the remark was in poor taste, but that's all it was. I practically lived with Buckley during those days. He was not into heroin. Unfortunately, journalists still pick up that line and exploit it for its sensational value, as do certain critics who embrace only Tim's cynical side and do not want to grant him gentleness or compassion.

"Elaine was there. She was taking speed, because she wanted to lose weight. Her and Tim got into an argument about doing drugs. He was yelling at her for doing speed. She yelled back, 'Three years ago, Katy told me you were doing reds, and I called her a liar!'

"I was sitting there, and offered him coffee. Since he was gonna go into rock 'n' roll, I had gotten him a really bizarre sequined jacket at an antique store. It had green velvet and sequins on it. It was kind of sarcastic on my part, but it was for his new image, and I had it wrapped up.

"'Happy birthday,' I said, and gave him the box.

"He looked up at me and started to cry. 'My God, you do have a heart,' he said.

"Then he opened the box and looked at the jacket. He was really stoned, sitting in the chair—you know how hunched over he was, 'cause he never picked up his feet when he walked, just sort of shuffled. I'd watched him deteriorate over the years, getting really old. He was all hunched over.

"'Aren't you gonna put it on?' I asked.

"He got up and put it on. It looked really funny, and he started to laugh. Then he went back into his depression. And then he left.

"I think the happiest I ever saw him was when he was recording *Starsailor*. That was his highest time. After that he wasn't so happy anymore."

In early September 1972, Tim participated in a Stravinsky Marathon with Frank Zappa at the Hollywood Bowl. Zappa narrated *The Soldier's Tale*, about a soldier, a girl, a violin, and a devil that tries to separate the soldier from the other two. The *L.A. Times* said Tim was to read the part of the devil, but (according to a friend who saw the production) he read the part of the soldier, while Ernest Fleischmann played the role of the devil. Lukas Foss directed the L.A. Philharmonic Orchestra.

No matter what Buckley did, he couldn't get the respect he needed and deserved. People who loved *Happy Sad* and *Goodbye and Hello* condemned him for *Lorca* and *Starsailor*, and told him to go back to folk music, or play rock 'n' roll. When he finally did move into conceptually familiar funk-rock pop music and recorded *Greetings From L.A.*, other friends, including Larry Beckett, were "appalled" and said he had "caved in." They insisted he had sold out *Starsailor*, betrayed his innovative visions, violated his integrity.

Either way, Buckley was damned.

Larry Beckett was not alone when he said to Scott Isler, "I thought, 'They fucking got him!' He'd always said he was gonna deliver bread if they tried to take his art away. We were dedicated to total creative control and freedom and experimentation. Here they were, putting pressure on him, and instead of saying, 'Hey! I don't need you people,' he knuckles under."

I disagree. Tim had pushed *Starsailor* to its limit. As pointed out earlier, he had studied, explored, experimented, and developed every artistic shade and nuance of the concept he could conceive. He had done it, not just with one band, but with four, especially and particularly with the Balkin and Chapman groups. He worked wholeheartedly on this music and spent more time, energy, hope, love, money, and courage on it than on any other music before or after.

Knuckled under? I think not.

As for this "we" business regarding experimentation and dedication, it was

Buckley, not Beckett, who carried the flag of creative experimentation forward into battle, who struggled onward with virtually no support from businesspeople and with almost nothing but criticism from the press and turncoat condemnation from friends, including Beckett himself and Dan Gordon. It was Buckley, not Beckett, who continued with absolutely no security and no hope of financial remuneration, and who persisted in the face of titanic odds, bravely following his own blue melody to the very end.

With acknowledgment to Beckett's talent and his love for Buckley, I do not see how anybody could think Tim had failed to pursue and fulfill his vision with utmost commitment, bravery, strength, and honor. How much suffering does an artist have to endure before he is given credit for courage, artistic integrity, and valor under fire? How much dedication is required, before he gets his due respect from so-called "friends" who accuse him of "caving in" and that host of sharp-shooting killer-boy critics? Exactly how long does an artist have to "deliver bread" before he receives his fair share of well-earned accolades?

There are times when I completely understand why Tim looked the way he did on that last album cover.

Having developed *Starsailor* to the full and given it everything he had both artistically and financially, the moment finally came for a change quite naturally, and at exactly the proper time. Even as he had made exciting, surprising shifts in the past, so he could do it again. But where does one go after the fiery emotional abstractions and extraordinary intellectual flights of a dedicated Starsailor? Tim needed a fresh new direction and new energy.

Judy loved hot and funky dance music. She felt the heat and beat of it, the sexual pump and pulse, the blood-rush passion, the intoxicating fire, the primal animal urgency, the body music, the howly-yowly humor and get-down intensity of it. Buckley only had to look at her to feel turned on. And when he played "Get on Top of Me Woman," her eyes sparkled. She laughed in ways she had never laughed when confronted with the dense, sometimes cerebrally arcane complexities of *Starsailor* music.

Where to go? Make the next step a wild one: radical, no holds barred, sex-drenched, white-funk rock 'n' roll. The energizing opposite extreme from *Starsailor*—hot, danceable, fun.

Judy became the muse. *Greetings From L.A.* became the music.

Greetings hit the stands in the fall of 1972, and over time became one of Tim's best-sellers, up there with *Happy Sad* and *Goodbye and Hello*. It is still one of his most popular albums.

Captain Eddie—back in action.

GREETINGS FROM L.A.: 1972–1975

CHAPTER 15

GREETINGS FROM L.A.

ON THE ONE HAND . . .

In the *Starsailor* period, Tim suffered consequences from his choices, but did not suffer because of the choices themselves. That is, he felt fully committed to *Starsailor* music and its bold, new avant-garde directions, come what may. He made the choices he believed in—if he suffered because of those choices, so be it. In fact, there had to be times in the heat of conflict with friends, businesspeople, and audiences that he felt giddy highs in the throes of righteous martyrdom. Win or lose, there is honor in battle.

During the *Greetings* period—the last 2½ years of his life—he suffered because of the choices themselves, as well as their consequences. He lived a life of "controlled schizophrenia," inwardly divided and in conflict with himself. There seemed to be a continual underground ebb and flow between two opposing poles—two different Tim Buckleys, as it were, perhaps especially at the beginning and end of the *Greetings* phase. Whatever he loved, he hated; whatever he hated, he loved—or at least needed. The conflicts created both joy and pain. Choices were difficult.

On the one hand, for example, he loved *Greetings From L.A.* (produced by Jerry Goldstein), which formed the general directional basis for *Sefronia* (produced by Denny Randell) and *Look at the Fool* (produced by Joe Falsia, who also arranged, and played lead guitar). Tim devoted time and effort to the music, and his badass band of studio musicians sounded tight and funky.

On the other hand, he despised *Greetings*. When he first played it for me, I said, "Wow, Tim! What a great album—lots of fun, fantastically sexy, fabulous dance music!" He frowned, spat contemptuously, said, "It's a piece of shit!" That shocked me.

On the one hand, he loved growing up, getting straight, accepting responsibility for himself and his family, reuniting with Herb, earning a living, taking care of business in the so-called "real" world.

On the other, he hated the "real" world, its blindness, hypocrisy, stupidity, fear, greed and gross materialism. He held himself in contempt for the way he chose to cooperate with businesspeople and co-workers for whom he had little or no respect. He hated the fact he chose to "toe the line" when it came to music, money, and madness.

On the one hand, his white-funk "down between the sheets," "let me lick your stretch marks" rock 'n' roll raunch-music turned Judy on, and wider audiences too, and he liked that. On the other hand, he seethed with resentment that *Greetings* succeeded where *Starsailor* had failed.

When I pointed out to Judy that Tim seemed to like the music's R&B sexuality but didn't have any respect for it, she responded, "Well, he could do it as well or better than anybody, but it was really no challenge for him. It really wasn't. He could get into it, and be happy doing it, but there was so much more he had to offer that nobody wanted."

On the one hand, he put together a crackerjack touring band. With variations along the way, it consisted of Joe Falsia on guitar, Mark Tiernan on keyboards, Bernie Mysior on bass, Buddy Helm on drums. They were experienced studio musicians, first-class middle-of-the-road technicians who understood funk-rock music—and loved playing it. They performed Falsia and Tim's snappy arrangements well and improvised solos enthusiastically. They had no problems whatsoever about playing commercial music that fit business interests, radio formats, and mass tastes. They had grown up on this kind of music, and they liked it. In short, Tim had exactly the kind of band he needed.

On the other hand, it was difficult for Tim to relate to them. In talking with me, he denounced them as "lobotomized bottom-feeders, rock 'n' roll jerks weaned on radio-music, bubblegum, and baseball."

Cool Richard commented to me about how Tim laughed at them behind their backs. "To Tim, intellectual things were very important," Richard said. "He was not like Joe Falsia. Tim knew it's a big world, and that rock 'n' roll is only a small part of it. But he couldn't *act* like he thought that. He could just act a little difficult and cute and petulant. He couldn't act the way he really felt, not with *those* people around. They all kissed his ass, and he thought they were full of shit. He would tell me all the time how full of shit he thought Joe was and all those guys in that band, you know? So he had weird relations with them."

Judy said, "I saw Tim around those guys for a long time. He had nobody to hang out with. Nobody at all. Except sports, maybe, something they'd be watching on TV or something. They had a strong connection on baseball. I think it was nice that I went on the road a lot with him. I felt sorry for him, because I knew he had me with him because he didn't have anybody else to talk to.

"If he'd go on the road with them by himself, they'd be out there for a while and he would get . . . he'd get really bummed out. People would give him Quaaludes and stuff, and he'd call me on the phone late at night at weird, weird hours. And I'd end up having to . . . it was cool, I'd go to wherever he was.

"He hadn't, you see . . . ah . . . what I wanted him to acquire was . . . a little peace with himself."

I speculate that Tim condemned *Greetings* when I praised it only because the *Starsailor* intellectual in him felt embarrassed in front of me, mistakenly thinking I might be locked into *Starsailor's* values and secretly condemning *Greetings*. I think he was projecting his own values and judgments on me—and coming up short in his own eyes. There was no need to apologize to me. I thoroughly liked *Greetings*. It was a new dimension for Tim and a great change of pace.

At the same time, there may well have been a part of him that recognized the honest limitations of the music—what the heck, it was only rock 'n' roll, right?

Compared to Messiaen, Penderecki, or Miles Davis, it was simple fare. But what was wrong with that? Okay, it wasn't grand like Bach or complex like Stravinsky, but it wasn't *intended* to be. Comparisons were not only odious, they were irrelevant. I didn't make them, why should he? I saw the value of each generic kind of music for what it was in and of itself. Comparisons were worthless. But maybe Tim did not understand this.

When we talked about it, I emphasized it was important that he come to terms with himself and enjoy what he was doing. I feel sure he eventually came to accept the music's limitations, embrace its strengths, and love the power and humor and passion in it.

As for the behind-the-back condemnations of his band members, it seems to me Tim was releasing pent-up steam. He respected them as musicians. He just couldn't relate to them on levels higher than rock 'n' roll or deeper than baseball, and that frustrated him. There was nothing he could do about that, except vent a few complaints to friends.

It seems to me that his criticisms were momentary and transient, while his appreciation for Falsia, Helm, and the other musicians grew over time. Performing with them in one concert after another, he came to respect himself and his own efforts more—and was thus able to extend his self-respect to the music and the band. After the initial phase, and for almost two years during this final period of his life, he loved most of what he was doing every bit as much as he loved his previous music.

Only near the end, for the last six months or so, did he seem to have reached the end of the *Greetings* phase. At that time, he appeared to need another shift, and seemed to be searching for fresh energy and new directions both artistically and economically. Artistically, he needed to revitalize the music by reinventing himself once again. Commercially, he needed a recording contract.

CHANGES

In this new *Greetings* phase, life's kaleidoscope spun again, and a host of changes took place.

Now married, Tim legally adopted Taylor, Judy's seven-year-old son. "I hate animals, so I adopted a kid," he chuckled to writer Steve Lake.

He transformed his physical appearance. The "gentle, wandering minstrel" of *Happy Sad* and the "curly-haired mountain boy" of *Blue Afternoon* had became a short-haired, hard-edged sex-symbol who in Lake's words "looked more like Paul Newman than Bob Dylan."

Writer Chrissie Hynde said he had become "burly and aggressive—an American's American." She felt confused, and wondered where Timmy's teenage Bambi-eyed innocence had gone. "Well, when you're eighteen," Tim said, "you're sorta still right outta the choir, aren't you? And you have to consider the year [1966].

"Kids now are fourteen and strung out on reds and heroin, and pregnant maybe a couple of times. I mean, they've really been through it by sixteen. . . . So now a concert consists of thirteen-year-olds passing coffee cans of pills around and listening to Deep Purple. But I have to stay in tune with the whole thing 'cause I'm a writer and it's America."

So much for innocence.

Warner Bros. created a new marketing image—the cover of *Greetings* displayed a postcard photograph of smog-shrouded Los Angeles with the words, "Greetings from L.A." Inside the cover, shorn of hippie locks, dressed in black, Tim grimly held a gas mask on his right shoulder.

"See, in L.A. you can't get through the day without a sense of irony," Tim told Lake. "And the message the sleeve was intended to impart was that even in this horrific atmosphere there can still be a lot of musical activity going down. But of course, nobody picked up on that."

Having already explored sensitive high school love songs, social issues, the fragile emotions of young adult love, jazz improvisations, and the intellectually stimulating sonic abstractions of *Starsailor*, Tim now explored raw sex, pure, simple and, to many people, enormously attractive. Obviously, sex was not the only dimension of Tim's complex personality, but it was definitely the aspect he now emphasized.

With her Madame Wu image, Judy was an incredible muse. Tim may or may not have known the real person underneath the sexy persona, but that didn't matter at the moment. What mattered were her mesmerizing "devil eyes," her sensuous moves. The way he felt may or may not have had a lot to do with her individuality—but it definitely had a lot to do with what he needed and wanted and with how he responded to her. She had her needs. He had his. Together, they performed their roles and vied for attention. They faced each other image-to-image. She enjoyed her singer/comedian. He enjoyed his "cross-eyed flamingo" muse. Flamboyant and beautiful together, they were one of the more dashing and colorful couples of that era.

Judy said it was nice to think that she influenced his porny state of mind. "It feels that way," she told me, "and it's talked about, but it seems a little pretentious. I mean, we had running jokes about it. We also sometimes had arguments over his using something I would say or a gesture that I did in his songs, things I didn't like being told to the whole world. I mean, do you have any idea how many people have asked me do I really get on top? Or when you're sitting in the audience, and everybody is looking at you.

"One night, he knew it was really irritating, because he made me walk out across the stage with him. So everybody immediately knew where I was sitting. I never liked that. I was really pissed.

"So I sat down, and he started singing 'Get On Top of Me, Woman,' and looking right at me. I was sitting there with my hand over my chin, my middle finger extended up over the bridge of my nose. And all around me the people were looking at me and whispering and having a good time with it all.

"But it's true, he liked the feminine. And I liked being that way. He complimented a lot. It's very easy to want to be more. I enjoyed it. It was really a trip to be with somebody who didn't bother you, whatever you wore, whatever you did."

Tim also changed his musical reference points. Where once he spoke of folk singers, jazz musicians, and avant-garde composers, he now spoke of Curtis Mayfield, Marvin Gaye, Stevie Wonder, James Brown, Ray Charles, Al Green.

He changed his relationship with the business world—back with Herb, moving from Straight to Warner Bros., and then to Herb and Zappa's new label, DiscReet. He agreed to cooperate with Herb's business requirements, brought in numerous lyricists in addition to Beckett for *Greetings*, and, per Herb's instructions, included a few songs by other writers on *Sefronia* and *Fool* (not all of which were as good as Fred Neil's "Dolphins").

Tim didn't fight with business interests, but neither did he crawl. As he pointed out to writer Frankie Nemko, "You should be who you are, all the time, not just because this person or corporation is paying the money for a certain project. You shouldn't go in on your knees. And you shouldn't be overly bitchy either." Tim had discovered a healthy and viable middle ground.

In the past, he felt a certain way about performing old songs. "The toughest situation I've found is to have an audience demand a song, and then want you to play it the way they fell in love with it," he told writer Marco Barla. "You just can't grow with an old song." Hence, he refused to play old songs (the "horse shit" syndrome), or played very few, and only when he felt like it.

Now in live performances, he showcased "Buzzin' Fly," "Pleasant Street," "Blue Melody," and "Cafe" along with new material. He told Lake in 1974, "A lot of people prefer the older-type songs, and I'm happy to do them, as long as I can continue to experiment simultaneously." He now included all of himself in his sets—old, recent, brand new.

As in the past, Tim's changes left a lot of people dumbfounded, which reminded me of what modern painter Wassily Kandinsky said in 1911 about another adventurous artist of that time: "Pablo Picasso leaps boldly and is found continually by his bewildered crowd of followers standing at a point very different from that at which they saw him last. No sooner do they think that they have reached him again than he has changed once more."

COMPROMISING?

Inevitably, there were those sideline snipers who gleefully cried, "Compromise! Sell-out!"

Was it?

With *Lorca* and *Starsailor* he refused to cooperate with anybody—the "defiant rebel" stance, feeding the legend about needing and wanting nobody, ignoring everybody else's musical needs and business considerations. Artistically, he pursued a great vision. Businesswise, it was a self-defeating position—he acted as if he existed entirely independently, which he did not. Commercially speaking, it hurt him.

But was this new direction a "compromise"? Moving up the ladder of maturation, taking responsibility for his family as well as his music, he now seemed to recognize something he had only glimpsed before—the interdependent nature of art and commerce. With *Greetings* and subsequent albums, he devised an integrated way in which he could make music, play the game, earn a living, reach people, *and* keep growing. Was this a compromise to be condemned—or was it wisdom to be praised? The music was creatively new for him, and business dealings worked efficiently. Was that wrong—or was Tim Buckley simply growing up?

When Warner Bros. finally said, "Please, no more *Starsailor* music," it was okay with Tim by that time, "because I had pretty much exhausted that syndrome," he told Michael Davis. "It refreshed me to come back to writing more lyrically oriented songs. . . . And since I've done *Greetings From L.A.*, the response has been almost greater than before."

Davis was quick to ask, "So was the move to have a new band a definite attempt on your part to reach more people?"

"It wasn't a compromise, if that's what you mean. It wasn't a commercialization. In fact the new songs are *more* controversial because they're more sexual than the political ones. When I go to FM radio stations across the United States and they play something like 'Get on Top of Me, Woman,' there's a huge furor over that. AM can't sell soap with it, so they don't play it at all. . . . As for the classical things born out of the *Starsailor* period, I haven't turned my back on them. They're just more classically avant-garde. Ultimately, I would love to secure a record deal that would give me both a classical and a commercial contract."

Either way, Buckley retained his autonomy. "I don't care if you said to me, 'You're never going to record in this town again,'" he told British journalist Steve Turner. "I'd still record and I'd still create. I don't need the rock world in order to be a person or a singer or a musician or to play for people. All I have to do is walk up onstage and play. . ."

MERGER MUSIC

Musically speaking, *Tim Buckley*, the first album, was one extreme: innocence and pristine fragility. *Starsailor* was another extreme: intellectually stratospheric avant-garde. In an important sense, the three albums in the *Greetings* phase represented a major new step: musical synthesis—a unified, holistic expression of everything he knew. That doesn't mean every song was great. It means Buckley was simultaneously transcending *and including* prior viewpoints while venturing into territories that for him were new and previously unexplored.

Lake observed, "The fragile nineteen-year-old who had sung 'in the scarlet light of Valentines, our paper hearts are blind' back in 1966 had been superseded by a bellowing, super virile stud."

Musically speaking, that was true. But sexuality was only one facet of the equation. The funk-rock musical concept itself was another, even greater, dimension: It had song forms and rhythmic coherence *along with* over-the-top, free-form vocal improvisations; it had words and melodies that people could relate to, even as it had spectacular nonverbal "talking in tongues"—the "vocal gymnastics" developed during the *Starsailor* period.

In speaking with Turner, Buckley said, "My voice had always been an instrument, but I hadn't used it that way, because when you write a song you become a slave to the lyrics. So I developed vocal techniques, inspired, I suppose, by classical people—Penderecki, Boulez, Messiaen. . . . Jacques Brel tells a story specifically through his lyrics, but when I listen to [saxophonist] John Coltrane, that man tells me the story of his life just by playing what he plays. . . . I don't think you have to convey a story through words alone. In fact, words can be pretty inadequate because words which sound good in songs don't always mean what you would want them to mean. Talking in tongues is best. . . ."

Buckley told Davis that now, with the *Greetings* concept, "I can do *all* the vocal things that I do, because there's rhythm that people can relate to, and a presentation that's immediately recognizable in a lot of ways—and unique in others. That's because music itself has grown. Jazz has merged with rock with Latin. Everything has come into rock: politics, love songs, TV variety shows. . . ."

When Lake asked him about influences, Tim replied, "Ray Charles, Hank Williams, Clapton, Hendrix, Morgana King, Cleo Laine, Little Richard, Nat King Cole, Roland Kirk, Peggy Lee, Duke Ellington, strippers, classical music, avant-garde from Stravinsky on, Messaien, Penderecki, Balinese music . . ."

Viewed as a synthesis of all the elements in Buckley's life and work, these last three albums, even with their faults, represent a significant and usually overlooked step forward: Tim had stopped fighting the realities of the business world. He had found fresh, new ways to express himself emotionally. He was crafting musical concepts in which he could integrate everything he knew and celebrate everything he loved.

"We believe so strongly in what we are doing that we become reborn through the work itself," Tim said to Nemko in June 1975, shortly before his death. "We display our own purity and our own realization of the truth in whatever we do, and that is what is transmitted to the audience. When you have purity of motive, this communicates very strongly, no matter what the circumstances. . .

"It has taken me all this time of songwriting, of pop music, of jazz flowing into rock, and rock flowing into jazz, to come to this merger of all the elements. I've learned so much from Miles and his metamorphoses. And also the Latin influence, which is becoming stronger and stronger. As I go along, I absorb everything around me, and then transmute it for my own interpretations."

FEEDING THE LEGEND

Meanwhile, Buckley was having a wonderful time playing the interview game. He'd wait for a journalist such as Steve Lake to arrive, for example, and then flip through a girlie magazine.

"I found the man perched forward on the edge of an armchair in a Kensington hotel room," Lake wrote, "gazing longingly down at the suntanned, glistening, widespread thighs of a foxy young lady, splashed across a gatefold spread in one of those Paul Raymond glossy mags. 'I just adore pornography,' he moaned. 'I mean, will you just look at her?'"

It was during this period that he told some of his most colorful stories, claiming to Lake, for instance, that he worked in the Ethnomusicology Department of UCLA, and detailing how he led students in interpreting Japanese and Balinese music."

Tim had talked with Cool Richard, of course, and, as I recall, had visited one or two of Richard's classes. In the interview, he simply translated his experiences with Richard's classes into personal terms and created a colorful story around that context. Feed the legend, yes, but also bring in his honest respect for world musics and his appreciation for the way in which those particular UCLA courses were being conducted.

It was during this period that he told interviewers he had played the guitar solo on the Byrds' hit, "Turn, Turn, Turn"—he didn't; Roger McGuinn did. And that after *Starsailor* he drove a cab in L.A.—he didn't, but Danny Gordon did, and Tim copped Danny's story. (Tim and Beckett also utilized the cab driver theme in "Nighthawkin'"). He said that he disguised himself and became a private chauffeur for Sly Stone. He said he grew up in Texas and Oklahoma, and that his dad was a steel worker—all delightful fabrications, very much like his colorful father used to create. Father, Tim, Katy—a family tradition.

ORIGINS AND INTENTIONS

Steve Lake called *Greetings* an "Orgasm Suite." Noel Coppage exclaimed, "Superthroat Sings Again." Rob Steen said Tim had a voice that could "burn ice and freeze flames . . . and there's enough verbal porn to fill the Mayfair letters page. Sensitive poet my bottom."

"I want to entertain now," Buckley told the *Michigan Daily*. "I'm ready to begin again—full-out blues-type barrelhouse rock." Clearly, he was having fun and getting reactions. So how did this "avant-get-down, white-funk dance music" come to be?

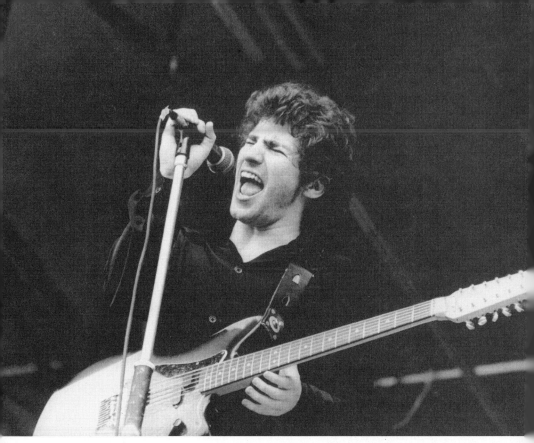

Tim "burning ice and freezing flames" at the 1974 Knebworth Festival in England.

There was no question about the R&B black influence. Buckley had been intensely involved with black culture and black music for years, "but you can't do the black lyric with any clear conscience at all," he told writer Susan Ahrens. "So if you're going to do a style of music, the only way to do it is to bring something new to it. And not necessarily a sitar—I mean a new conception, not a gimmick. Then the people who originated the music won't hate you as much."

"I don't like to repeat myself, which is great, because I can progress musically," he told writer Andy McKaie. "And the comeback has been a big thing with stars in every medium. It's part of the creative process. In fact, you're nothing unless you've come back three or four times. . . . I decided the way to come back was to be funkier than everybody else."

Tongue in cheek, he told Chrissie Hynde that his record company said he'd better make another album: "I thought, well, I have to get up to date. I saw nine black exploitation movies, read four black 'sock-it-to-me-mamma' books, and read all the rock criticisms. I took a week off, read all the *Rolling Stone* things, and finally realized that all of the sex idols in rock and roll weren't saying anything sexy. . . . So I decided to make it human and not so mysterious, and to deal with the problems as they really are. . . ."

He told Ahrens he recorded *Greetings* because "all the sex symbols, from Elvis to Jagger, had never said anything dirty or constructive about making love. You could never learn anything from *any* of those songs. So I figure, talk about stretch marks, which really lays out people in Iowa."

In addition to the three studio albums of the *Greetings* phase, recorded live performances are plentiful—including *Honey Man* (1973), live on radio station WLIR on Long Island; *Return of the Starsailor*, live at Knebworth (1974) and Detroit (1975); and *Blue Obsession—Live at the Starwood* (1975).

Reviews of the music during this period varied from blistering criticism to adulation. People who couldn't handle visceral funk-rock or raunchy humor trashed it. But people who liked it, loved it. After Tim appeared in New York at Max's Kansas City, for example, Susan Ahrens wrote, "Tim Buckley is a wet dream. He is everything your mother ever warned you about. . . . Your head starts swimming, your tongue gets thick, your stomach knots. . . . He brings you further and further, to the absolute crest of sensual experience. . . ."

For all of the whimsy and humor in Buckley's sexuality during this period, there was also an element of intensely intimate emotional honesty. The music of this final period expressed the totality of his life. "It's touching all the bases, living what you've done," he told Marco Barla. "It's experience that's communicated, onstage or in the studio. It takes guts to be that naked."

It wasn't only fun and games and boogie-boogie. Some of Tim's most beautiful, impassioned, heart-rending writings came out of these final years.

JEWELS AND DOGS

Rhythmic fun-filled sex romps during the *Greetings* period included "Move with Me," "Get on Top," "Make It Right," "Devil Eyes," and "Stone in Love." A lot of people from the *Happy Sad* and *Starsailor* days didn't like the visceral level of these songs. As well, the lyrics shocked many people and drew attention from journalists, understandably so. Until Buckley, sex in mainstream pop had been a euphemized closet item. Buckley set it front and center stage in such songs as "Get on Top," celebrating with raucous humor the delights of lusty love, squeaking bed springs, sensual delirium, and talking in tongues, urging his woman to "get on top" and get it on with abandon. In other bawdy romps, such as "Make It Right," he gets a little kinky, which set repressed right-wing prigs all a-flutter, but delighted sexually liberated listeners who had a sense of humor:

> *I'm lookin' out*
> *For a street corner girl*
> *And she's gonna beat me, whip me, spank me*
> *Aw, make it right again.*

> "Make It Right"

The rhythms of these R&B songs were intentionally libidinous, consciously designed for sexual intoxication and full-out boogie-down dancing. Judy loved the smooth pulse of it, and guitarist/arranger Joe Falsia fully appreciated the rhythmic talent and skill behind it.

One of Tim's best rhythm songs, "Nighthawkin'," moved with a sexy dance groove. Beckett's lyrics had to do with a cab driver whose fare is a drunken Vietnam veteran who pulls a knife on him. The driver responds, "I was a combat paratrooper," which hearkens directly back to Tim's dad. It also touches on a theme in Tim's life that was becoming more pronounced: his support of Vietnam veterans who were giving their lives in an unpopular war but getting no respect from Tim's peers.

Another song, "Freeway Blues," is from the point of view of a Vietnam soldier ("I joined the army just to get more fame"), and incorporates two lines from "You Can Always Tell a City by Its Graffiti" from the *Starsailor* period—*I never swallowed that cheap booze/I keep my distance from straight dudes.*

Some of his best songs during this period were not humorous, lusty dance pieces. The ballads rang with sincerity, poignancy, yearning, heartache, love, and profound passion, notably "Sweet Surrender" and "Because of You," two of Tim's personal favorites, along with "Look at the Fool," "Who Could Deny You," and "Helpless." In my opinion, these are gleaming jewels, some of the most accomplished and deeply moving songs Buckley ever wrote.

Lyrically, to the extent that they may be autobiographical (as nearly all of Tim's songs were), the ballads often reflect the searing intensity of his love for Judy. In "Because of You," for example, he gives her credit for enabling him to face life's challenges with strength and pride. He celebrates the fact that love shines through her eyes in spite of his having lied to her on more than one occasion. He passionately beseeches her to try to understand what makes him love her and want to treat her right.

They show his need for her and the resulting inner conflicts. In "Look at the Fool," he loves and hates her because of what she is doing to his health (very likely along with his own substance abuse). He loves and hates her because of the tremendous attraction and vulnerability she makes him feel. He loves and hates her because his neurotic need keeps him chained to her and he can't get away. Lost, enslaved, torn between desire and aversion, riddled with pain, he runs to the sea for comfort, but the sea "only sighs" and mocks him for being such a fool.

They show his anxiety and resentment about Judy's inability to forget her dead husband, Darrell. In "Who Could Deny You," he poignantly observes how her "first love" remains under her skin so deep that it won't let her go. He bemoans the fact that she feels alone in her misery, shutting him out, and urges her to respond to him and to his love for her. Let him revive her, he pleads. He is here and alive and young, with his whole life in front of him, so don't tease him or turn away from him. Stop clinging to the misery of lost love, torturing him with it. Come to him, lie down beside him, embrace him, let him love her alive again.

They show his anguish over the way Tim and Judy use transgressions to hurt each other. In "Sweet Surrender," he admits he cheated on her because he needed to feel the thrill of the hunt once again. But immediately he knows she will go out and do the same thing in revenge, to prove she can hurt him worse than he hurt her.

In another song, "Sally Go 'Round the Roses," which is not exactly a ballad and may not necessarily be drawn from his life with Judy, he bitterly cries about how sad it is to discover one's woman has been with another woman, and begs her not to "go down," but to come back and stroll with him the way they used to. In still another rhythmically upbeat piece with anguished lyrics, "Ain't It Peculiar," he talks about how odd it is that he and his partner laugh their way through pain, misfortune, and back-stabbing, and how peculiar it is that their love continues in spite of the "bad" and the "wrong." He calls his life a "prison," and wonders if the "long night" will ever end.

There were serious conflicts in Buckley's life during these years, clearly revealed in lyrics to these and other songs. Life was not as upbeat as some of the interviews and articles in superficial online fanzines would have us believe.

In "The Dream Belongs to Me," the title track of a posthumous CD released in 2001, Buckley puts soulful rhythmic urgency and poignant lyrics together in singing about the love he feels for his "cross-eyed flamingo," as he whimsically characterized Judy in conversation. It's a touching song, vocalized with considerable passion, portraying their joy in unity, followed by her becoming cold and then leaving—the flowering and ending of love. This song, along with the sex-romp "Falling Timber" and the Beckett-inspired comedic "Freeway Dixieland Rocketship Blues," was recorded on February 12, 1973, as part of an eight-song demo for *Sefronia*. "Dream," "Timber," and "Rocketship" were ultimately shelved, while the others were re-recorded for *Sefronia*.

Some people think that the arrangements by Falsia and other studio musicians on the last three studio albums released during Tim's lifetime are so banal that they destroy whatever grace and depth the encompassing context might otherwise have had for Buckley's singing. In my opinion, that is not entirely fair.

To test the situation, I listened carefully to these recordings, intentionally trying to imagine myself writing the arrangements, and was not able to see how they could have been done any better. It seems to me they fit the concept and the music well. Some of the funk-rock stylings are terrific, and that rhythmic dance sound is, after all, precisely what Tim was going for. We may or may not *like* the concept, but that is a personal matter and a separate issue. The point is, Tim and his fellow musicians attained the goals to which they aspired, and for the most part did it well.

If we listen to these albums with an open mind, we see that several of the songs themselves, particularly the ballads, are as musically beautiful as any Tim ever composed. The melodies are stunning in their passionate elegance. The harmonic progressions are new and fresh.

The lyrics are bed-rock honest, significantly revealing important aspects of his life and his primary relationship, not only in the pieces cited above, but also and perhaps especially in tunes such as "Ain't It Peculiar" and "Sally Go 'Round the Roses" (which, according to Falsia, had nothing to do with the old Jaynetts original). Close listening to these songs discloses key insights into Tim's state of mind during this final period.

His voice is clear and strong, aching with desire, love, pain, doubt, resentment, anger, tenderness, heartache, conflict, affirmation. In addition to vocal power, which he already had, he now included a new dimension, the intimate falsetto beauty of an Al Green, notably on "Look at the Fool."

Falsia said, "When Tim heard the playback on 'Look at the Fool,' it blew him away. He soared from the basement to the sky with absolute control, absolute smoothness. He knew then that he didn't have to scream it out or belt it out to get what he wanted. . . . Vocally, he saw himself as the real pro. He could flow into any bag he wanted to: He could be a black Smokey Robinson, he could go back to Tim Buckley 1968, he could take it anyplace."

I think these albums deserve closer attention and a more positive evaluation than they have received to date.

Of the non-original songs, Fred Neil's "Dolphins" glitters with diamond-light. Right from the early days, Tim regularly included "Dolphins" as part of his live performances, but did not record it until 1973, on *Sefronia*. With the exception of two

Starsailor tours and a brief *Greetings From L.A.* tour, I had not been a part of Tim's musical life for some time. Nevertheless, when he was ready to record "Dolphins," Tim gave me a call and included me on the session, a gesture I deeply appreciated. "Dolphins" had been part of our history together.

"Peanut Man," a Harry Nilsson (a.k.a. Nehls) tune reminiscent of "Coconut" and selected by Judy, is full of sparkling upbeat humor, delightfully entertaining. Its overdubbed three-part interweaving lines vividly display Tim's vocal range from baritone, to alto, to high tenor. It's a frivolous, lighthearted piece, which some fans resented and trashed—as if Buckley weren't allowed to have fun.

Tom Waits' "Martha" and Denny Randell's "I Know I'd Recognize Your Face" are two dogs Buckley himself would almost surely not have chosen if left on his own. However, he heard Waits rehearsing "Martha" and thought it might work on this particular album, and "Face" was included because producer Randell wrote it in a commercial format, hoping he might get a single out of it that would garner AM airplay.

"Tijuana Moon," "Mexicali Voodoo" and "Wanda Lu" brought Mexican imagery into the lyrics as well as subtle Latin rhythms. By this time, as noted, Tim had been reading Latin authors, notably Borges and Carlos Fuentes, and shortly before his death was planning a trip to Honduras.

Larry Beckett participated in a number of songs and did a good job with his lyrics—particularly on "Honey Man," a wet-dream super-stud frolic that Buckley sang until the end. Beckett also wrote "Nighthawkin'" and the beautiful "Tijuana Moon," which Tim wanted as the title tune. Herb Cohen insisted upon Tim's "Look at the Fool," a terrific song, but a painfully ironic title for what proved to be Tim's last album.

Beckett also penned "Sefronia—After Asklepiades, After Kafka" and "Sefronia—The King's Chain," once again wandering off into pseudo-intellectual literary twaddle that immediately sounded to me like a parody of Sir James Frazer's *The Golden Bough.* Nevertheless, Buckley's gentle, atmospheric music for the piece almost saves the day, and many people have greatly enjoyed both of these "Sefronia" songs, especially "The King's Chain," one of the pieces Jeff sang at his St. Ann's debut in New York.

With *Greetings, Sefronia,* and *Look at the Fool,* Herb and the others were trying to help Buckley make what they considered to be "commercial" albums. As business-music professionals, they presumed to know what "commercial" is, always a tricky proposition. In any case, Buckley faced a clear choice. If he had persisted in singing *Starsailor* music, nobody would have hired him. Having completed that phase, he now faced a new reality. If he were to have any hope of recording again and reviving his career and his life, it was incumbent upon him to bring his music into some sort of commercially viable framework, doing whatever he could to infuse it with as much grace, style, passion and creative imagination as he could. He knew the choice, he was ready for it, the time was right, and he made it. Ironically, *Sefronia* and *Look at the Fool* proved to be perhaps the least liked efforts of Tim's lifetime. Even *Lorca* got more respect.

Of all of Buckley's jewels—from the beginning to the end of his career—one might set "Sweet Surrender," "Because of You," "Who Could Deny You," "Helpless," and "Look at the Fool" in the same golden crown as "Pleasant Street," "I Never Asked to be Your Mountain," "Love from Room 109," "Anonymous Proposition," "Blue Melody," and "Cafe."

He never had a Top 40 hit. Nevertheless, these songs rank among the finest ever written by anybody of his generation.

The marketplace has always been strange when it comes to doling out roses and trophies. But that didn't trouble Buckley. "The only thing worth doing in moderation is fame, because it's such a bullshit trap. . . ." he told writer Steve Turner. "I haven't deliberately avoided fame. It's just that I'm too odd for the white middle-class. But I'm happy. I get to create. There's nobody like me, so they've got to keep me around. It's like the predicament of Roland Kirk. Nobody's going to outplay Roland, but 300,000 people aren't going to go to his concerts like they might to a Stones concert. Roland's expressing too much for people to accept."

CHAPTER 16

ON AND OFF THE WAGON

THE LAST HURRAH

In mid-May 1973, Tim gave me the old Indian Love Call, told me Joe Falsia had prior commitments, and asked if I would go out on a six-week road tour. I was in good shape—sober, seeing my psychiatrist, attending Synanon, feeling happy, healthy, and strong. I accepted the gig.

At rehearsal, Tim said, "This isn't just following along and improvising like before. It's more like the first album, you know? Parts, cues, arrangements. Write out the chords, memorize a few licks."

On June 5 we opened in Cleveland, at the Smiling Dog Saloon. Everything went well. Enthusiasm was high, the music cooked, we played a good show.

The next day my picture was published in the paper right along with Tim's. Reviewer Mark Steuve captured Buckley's performance perfectly: "Sweating, shaking and driving his voice from its highest to lowest octaves made Buckley's stage presence somewhat scary." Steuve sang my praises too: "Lee Underwood's superb performance on guitar was the surprise of the evening and left me stunned at the energy he produced from his instrument."

We were off to a good start, but before long things began deteriorating. I didn't get on well with the guys. Keyboardist Mark Tiernan was a nice fellow, but he had nothing to say. Bassist Bernie Mysior and drummer Buddy Helm were heavily into orthodox rock 'n' roll. The whole group had conventional minds, conventional tastes. I became bored with them almost immediately, and they, of course, sensed my detachment.

Tim carefully avoided favoring me. I was not special. In fact, he enthusiastically talked baseball, rock 'n' roll, and television with the guys, making it clear to me that this was a new time, a new game. These were the new relationships, with a new music that had nothing to do with the past—we had no past. Get with the program.

At first, I was confused. He gave mixed messages: On the one hand, he had said this music was shit. On the other, he was connecting 100 percent with the other guys in the band. It took me a while to understand that he was simply taking care of business. Nothing personal. But for me *that* in itself was a problem. I *wanted* it to be personal. I wanted to be favored. I wanted to be the close friend and confidant—and it wasn't happening.

Drummer Buddy Helm was a good musician, and, other than Johnny Sider and Maury Baker, the most verbally adept drummer I ever encountered. Unlike Sider and Baker, however, he seemed to take himself too seriously and was clearly accustomed to bullying opponents in debate. When he couldn't do that with me, his ego flared up, making it virtually impossible to discuss music in constructive ways.

He would criticize Tim's earlier jazz- and classically influenced concepts, for example, while elevating rock to the heights, a point of view I found offensive. All three musics are wonderful, all serve certain psychological functions, and all deserve respect and praise for what they accomplish. I could enjoy rock without condemning jazz or classical, and appreciate jazz and classical without condemning rock. Yes, I stood for conceptual excellence, but it was an excellence to which all were invited, and in no way did that mean I did not like the funky rock music we were playing.

I thought it a little silly of Buddy to elevate our funk music to sublime heights while disdainfully dumping Tim's prior jazz and avant-garde efforts into an historical dustbin, when in fact those earlier creations were still vital as art musics, eminently contemporary, and as conceptually undated then as they are now.

In truth, at this stage of Tim's journey, neither "forward" nor "backward" had any relevance to me or Tim any more. We lived in the *present*, creating whatever level of music expressed our vision. We did not feel a need to demean earlier musics or elevate this post-*Starsailor* funk-rock pop music to some sort of "leading the way" stature it simply did not warrant. With certain exceptions, notably a few of the ballads, this music was not some sort of *grand musical gesture*, nor was it intended to be. Tim had no pretensions about that. Neither did I. Most of the music we were playing was mainstream radio fare, boogie-down dance music, good ol' rock 'n' roll, a new place for Tim to go, and fun to perform. No problem for me. Evidently not so for Buddy—he had to be "ahead," whatever that meant in the world of anonymous Top 40 programming.

In my view at the time, it would have been better if Buddy had understood and appreciated Tim's earlier works, granted them their proper respect, and enjoyed the new funk music as well without trying to exaggerate its significance or demean previous phases. I could do that. Could he? I tried to explain things as clearly as I could, but my efforts failed, probably not only because of the musical principles involved, but because our values and personalities clashed.

It wasn't long before I saw Buddy as an ignorant, inflexible, mass-mind cretin programmed by corporate radio-music, incapable of learning anything new, while he saw me as an arrogant, outdated, imperious, supercilious, elitist son-of-a-bitch asshole.

I suppose both of us were at least partially right.

It wasn't all bad. One night in a motel after a gig, I spoke to Buddy of dancers and body moves and how difficult it is to move slowly and well. Naked, he got out of bed and stood silhouetted in front of the window. Back-lit by the dim light of early dawn, he performed a series of t'ai chi moves very, very slowly—a powerful, uplifting vision of grace and strength, as if he himself were an accomplished dancer. In addition to his excellent drumming onstage, he brought into our lives this moment of memorable beauty, and I thank him for it.

Generally speaking, Tim stayed in his room with Judy, never smoking, drinking, or taking any illicit substance for the duration of the tour, while I felt almost totally alienated from everybody.

Lonely, depressed, unsure of myself, I started drinking. Just a little at first, then more.

It is my understanding that Tim had been faithful to Judy on the road prior to this. However, her actual presence on this trip made it patently clear to the young ladies that Tim was not available. As a result, I received more attention than usual, which of course warmed my heart and flattered my ego. I spent time with two or three female friends from earlier years, met a few extraordinarily sensual new women, and thoroughly enjoyed the company of all.

Things went exceptionally well sexually on this tour, although in general I did not have a lot to brag about. During the full span of my years on the road with Tim, there was not exactly a plethora of women in my life. Furthermore, I proved sexually inconsistent, hardly a rock 'n' roll superstud. Sometimes young women and I had a fabulous time, thrilling, exotic, exciting, creating marvelous memories that last to this day for me, and I would hope for them too. But in more than a couple of instances I was intentionally selfish or unintentionally incompetent. Ah, well. Tim and I and the other guys in various bands never talked about this subject, so I have no idea how they fared.

For myself, whatever the outcomes proved to be over the course of those years, whether great highs or sad-eyed lows, I want to thank all of the good-hearted young women who shared their time with me, offered their companionship and comfort, and helped me make it through some of those lonely nights on the road and at home in L.A. when I lived alone. They were loving and lovely angels, saviors of my soul, each and every one.

In Atlanta we played well. But not everything went right. I was improvising free-form solos, feeling the pulse with my body, tapping my feet in time, while sailing over the top without regard to metric subdivisions. Years later, Judy told me about "somebody" who couldn't keep time in their solos—rhythm all over the place—even though they tapped perfect time with their feet. And she laughed. She didn't say so, but I suspect Tim had said that to her about me, which disappointed me to no end. I thought at least *he* had known what I was doing. Maybe not. Can't say for sure.

At the end of one of the songs, I lost my place, didn't cue the band on time. Tim said to the keyboard player, "Not much help, is he?" Mark shook his head. I was steadily losing ground.

In the dressing room, I kiddingly raised my voice and said, "I need a masochist!" A lovely girl pranced over and sat down. In the motel room she urged me to inhale a speedball combination of coke and heroin. Never before had I felt such a sublimely blissful rush. We swooned into each other's arms and made love all night long. I lasted seemingly forever each time and came again and again. I don't recall her name, but remember our passion well.

In the morning, she said she was sixteen years old, and still in high school. Boys her age bored her. Her best girlfriend couldn't understand her. This motel life was the only way to get what she wanted and needed. I told her not to overdo it with the speedballs, to contact Synanon if ever she needed help. God bless her. My Atlanta Darlin' was a sweet girl and an incredible lover. I hope she made it through the nightmares of her life.

In one of the towns, Buckley came into my room, sat down, said, "I want you to relate to the guys onstage." I asked him what he meant. As always onstage, I stood out front with him, to his right, so I could see what he was playing on guitar. "I mean, stand back there with the guys and pay attention to what they're doing—relate to them."

I figured the guys must be uptight because I stood out front with Tim. They wanted me to join them. Well, that was nice, "but I really can't get it on with them, Tim. I just don't connect with . . ."

"Do it!" he said, eyes hard, voice as cold as gun metal.

It was not the guys who wanted me back there—it was Tim! These were not the old ensemble days with Carter. This was leader and sidemen, star with backup band, an *act*. In the biz, they call it being "professional."

That night, ready for the gig, wearing my fancy white turtleneck shirt with cuff links, I waited for the elevator. When the door opened, Buddy, Mark, and Bernie stood there wearing black look-alike baseball T-shirts, big silly grins on their faces. Odd-ball out.

I tried to move closer and face them during the performance, but couldn't bring myself to do it. Instead, I stood back about halfway between Tim and the band, isolated, depressed.

That night I got drunk. Fell into a semi-stupor on the floor, ear up against the wall, eavesdropping on Tim talking with other people in the next room. Loneliness, aching bitter loneliness. Buddy suddenly walked in and almost tripped over me. Told me to get the fuck up and get my drunken ass to bed.

We were to play the Thunderbird Lodge in La Placitas, twenty miles north of Albuquerque. Tim and Judy and the band stayed at a motel in Albuquerque, while I rented a trailer up in La Placitas within walking distance of the Thunderbird so I could be by myself, away from the group, in privacy and quietude.

Opening night we played well. Happily, the stage was small enough so there was no problem with "relating" to the guys. After the gig, I walked back to the trailer with a lovely young woman who lived in a trailer across the court. We made love long and well, a beautiful memory.

A couple of afternoons later, Tim and I drank coffee in the Thunderbird while waiting for a photographer. A Vietnam veteran wearing a green camouflage jacket sat by himself at the bar nursing a beer. He was a young Hispanic, about 24, long black hair down the center of his back. His eyes looked hollow, ancient, vacant. Something vital inside had disappeared.

"Poor bastard," Tim said. "He gave his soul and now nobody gives a damn about him. World War II was my father's war. Well, Vietnam is *my* war—this guy's war too. People oughtta give us some fucking respect."

Photographer Ed Caraeff walked in, nodded at Tim. "You ready?"

"Yep."

They strode out into the afternoon heat and glaring sunshine. Tim wore a borrowed flamboyant short-sleeve green Hawaiian shirt covered with palm trees. They ambled over to an adobe ruin. Tim was in a rotten mood, but his smiles were cute. Ed snapped several pictures, including the shot that showed up on the back cover of *Sefronia*, a delightful spoof of the typical "I'm a star" pose on fifties and early sixties album jackets.

In Houston, the last stop on the tour, Tim called me to his room. He and Judy sat on the bed, comfortably propped on pillows. I sat in an armchair.

"We finish up tonight. Falsia will rejoin the band in L.A."

"I was hoping to stay on."

"You're not playing well."

"How about that review in Cleveland?"

"That's because you did it right."

"I can get it together."

"You're drinking too much."

"No problem, I'll cool it."

"The guys in the band *hate* you."

"Oh . . . well . . . oh . . . I guess, well . . . Is that it?"

"That's it."

I nodded, got up, left the room.

Onstage that night, I played as well as I ever had, including a gorgeous version of "Blue Melody," using my tapping, rubbing, sliding techniques. In the song's introduction, tears welled up in my eyes as I played. Tim looked misty-eyed, too. It was over.

Later that evening, Bernie, the bass player, pulled me aside. "Judy told me what Tim said."

"Oh?"

"Yeah, man. Hey, listen," he said, shaking my hand warmly. "I could hear you onstage, man. I think you play real good, and I don't hate you."

He was the only one to say so, but it was a comfort.

After we finished the last set, Tim stayed onstage with Buddy and did an encore that lasted 20 minutes. His short hair was thick and wavy; he wore black corduroy pants and a light gray sleeveless sweatshirt. Much of the encore featured lengthy breaks in which he sang a cappella—without playing his guitar, without support from Buddy's drums, standing in music's flames by himself, guitar draped from his neck, singing his heart out alone, in the spirit of Roland Kirk.

I stood in the audience watching him, transported beyond my personal concerns about being fired. I remembered the night he sang an a cappella encore at Carnegie Hall. On this night in Houston, he sang like never before—his voice even fuller and stronger, his emotions searing, his burning presence unfathomably intense, creativity flowing like firefalls, one new phrase after another, his words as poetic and radiant with feeling as any I had ever heard.

Standing and listening, goosebumps shivering my neck, I knew I was witnessing an extraordinary musician, an extraordinary man, a rock 'n' roll Starsailor in full flight, sailing and soaring right on out behind the sun.

The next day, I drank three beers before the airport, downed a Mai Tai at the airport, staggered off by myself to get away from Tim and the guys, got lost, couldn't remember the name of the airline, wandered around in a drunken haze trying to locate the boarding gate. Buddy finally found me and led me back, annoyed, haughty, superior.

I slouched on a bench away from the guys, hardly able to move. Tim sat on a bench opposite me, face expressionless, hands in his jacket pocket. I broke down, cried, couldn't stop myself, absolutely miserable, unable to keep from sobbing.

"God dammit, Tim, I'm so sorry—sorry about today, sorry about the guys and me, sorry 'bout everything. I tried to do a good job, man. Thought I had it together. Tried to quit drinkin', ol' buddy, tried—but jus' . . . can't . . . help it. . . . Can't . . . help . . . it."

Although our friendship lasted until the end, I never played guitar with Tim again.

But I did get straight.

RADIO INTERVIEW, JULY 1973

Tim, Judy, and Buddy Helm zipped over to the university radio station in Albuquerque, to yak-yak with the disc jockey, play a few songs off the albums, and hype the upcoming La Placitas gig at the Thunderbird Lodge.

Buckley had come a million miles from the Alan King fiasco on *The Tonight Show* all those years ago.

TB: Talk.

DJ: Sitting here with Tim Buckley and part of his backup group. Tim's going to be out in Placitas this weekend, playing Thursday through Sunday. I don't know how much it costs, but I'll bet you'll find out at. . .

TB: Three dollars.

DJ: At the door . . .

TB: Three dollars. And they'll get wine. Three dollars. Three-fifty on the weekend. You get the whole thing. Package deal . . .

DJ: Package deal!

TB: Hermetically sealed.

DJ: I hope not. It's hot in here already.

TB: Band's gonna be hot—yeah.

DJ: Your band with you now?

TB: Yeah—piano, bass, guitar, drums.

DJ: You doing pretty much stuff from *Greetings From L.A.?*

TB: No, everything.

DJ: The last time I saw you was in Baltimore, at a community college, and you played with a jazz group, three guys. It seemed like you probably met them that night, and you were making up songs.

TB: You look like a very intelligent surfer.

DJ: Uh, body surfer only. I haven't been on a board yet. My balance isn't good enough.

TB: Uh-huh. The untrained ear always says that about jazz.

DJ: No, because you *were* making up lyrics. It was fun. That is what I was going to say.

TB: Well . . .

Buddy Helm: Round two.

TB (to DJ): You have a cynical edge.

DJ: No, I'm not being cynical. I was just saying it was fun.

TB: That was a pretty good concert, actually.

DJ: It was fun, and it was like a small nightclub thing, only you had 1,500 or 2,000 people there.

TB: It can work with a lot of people in a big room. It just depends on how much humanity you have to offer. If you're a showcase group and you just put out a stock type of music, it's gonna look like that, no matter where you play it. But if you play the moment, if you play for the people, if you play what they want to hear at the moment they want to hear it, then it's going to come off with a looseness and a humanity to it. It's going to work anywhere, I don't care where it is.

DJ: So your show now, it won't be the same every night?

TB: No. Why should it be?

DJ: Most of the people who record do that. Most big acts have a 90-minute set. They take their half-hour break, then do the second half.

TB: That's because they've learned only so many songs, and they're very young, and they haven't played much. They've learned an hour-and-a-half of material, and that's it. They play it, and then they play it over again. How ya doin', glad-hand, see ya.

DJ: But you like to mess around with your audience more.

TB: Yeah. I like to play *music*, and I'm capable of playing music, so I do that, and on an extended basis.

DJ: In other words, you don't come out there and have ten songs you play. You come out and maybe you know what your first song's going to be, and then your second one might . . .

TB: When I get stuck for something, I just ask the audience what they want to hear—and they'll say, "Louie, Louie," so we'll play it.

DJ: Easy to make up lyrics for it too.

TB: I helped record that.

DJ: Really? With the Kingsmen?

TB: Yeah.

DJ: No kidding. What did you do?

TB: Bought Seconal. That's basically what they did. No, no. Manuel was the guy who stole transmissions and bought Seconal and kept the guys supplied with guitar strings and new lyrics for the songs, 'cause it was pretty loose. It varied from high school to high school. It was a territorial tune.

DJ: You started with folk songs and went through a lot of changes before you ended up with your most recent album, *Greetings From L.A.*, which is all we know you by.

TB: That's why it's hard to talk about the past, isn't it? You don't know me.

DJ: But you're playing different stuff now than before, aren't you?

TB: The sixties were a lot different. There was a lot more chance for music. You people were on better drugs or something. Your ears were more open. You had cleaner asses, I guess. I don't know what it was.

Now it's Quaaludes, sawdust, and beer: "Hi, hit me, sock it towards me, roll me in the dirt, make me human." It's depressing, stepping over bodies on the way to the stage. I'm trying to say the inner city is dying—and it's moving to places like this, your college.

Everything's kind of boring. The country's in limbo right now. We're ruining the whole political system—Watergate—and that takes time. Baseball is boring. And when boring gets popular, you know something's wrong in the taste.

DJ: All the new groups are very sensational now. They may not be very good on their albums, but in person they are flaming rockets and smoke bombs.

TB: Sure. I call them portable closet fags. They can go anywhere and do it. No, no—they're all married, and they're not really gay.

DJ: What do you think of gay rock 'n' roll?

TB: I don't think it's gay. Lou Reed's the closest.

DJ: What about David Bowie? Have you seen him?

TB: Cocktail music.

DJ: Like, "We're only in it for the money"?

TB: I know they're sincere. It just isn't saying anything for gay people. Being gay is a very valid and difficult thing to live—don't take my word for it. It's hard to come out with something that is personal, that is a whole society of people, and then program it commercially for people who buy Campbell's Soup, and say, "This is what gay is"—but then project only the queen part.

DJ: Have you seen Bowie perform?

TB: Yeah.

DJ: I haven't.

TB: It's Limey rock, you know? It's loud. Rip off the American audience.

DJ: A lot of the American audience likes loud, screaming, yelling . . .

TB: Oh, the thirteen-year-olds do. . . . Also in our country now, we're into segregation between the ages. People who are thirteen, fourteen, and fifteen don't go to things that people who are eighteen, nineteen up to twenty-five go to, and vice versa. It's not only segregation between black and white, but we have segregation now between little age groups. Over thirty, I don't know what they're doing—programming libraries somewhere.

DJ: The record companies are trying to appeal to a certain age group.

TB: Down to about *eight*. The buying public is thirteen to fourteen, and they buy the Monkees. That doesn't give you a lot of room to work with. . . . Not that I'm against thirteen-year-old people. They're fine. I just don't think they should be talked to until they're twenty-five.

DJ: Are you going to do some of the new things up in Placitas?

TB: Yeah, but nothing in the music is economic or political. What's happening is that people are in their twenties and thirties, and they're just starting to live. They're learning about one-to-one communication between man and woman and their children. They see the futility of the loose type of thing, where one guy has three women and 14 kids and a house. It doesn't work. For a period of time it does, but not for long.

DJ: Hollyweird at its best.

TB: Hey, it was communal right out here in the tepees! You know—everywhere!

But getting down to one-to-one, that's basically all I've ever talked about, and that's what I'm talking about now. It's getting to where it's harder to anchor in on it, because it's very touchy. Nobody wants to be with one person, and have that person represent them. Usually men treat women as head ornaments on Cadillacs: "Look what I got." That type of thing.

Once it gets beyond that, it starts getting into commitment. Then you're talking about more of a universal thought, more of a personal thought, and more of a frightening thought, because then you're cutting right to the bone of what life is.

Life is not war in Vietnam. It's not political. It's not economic. It's not anything like that. It's what you have to deal with every day. Basically, the news is a show. I don't think anybody really worries about it. If they did, if they really cared, then that stuff on the news wouldn't exist.

DJ: Even after this commitment, a lot of couples with children are choosing to live with other couples in communal living, sharing the responsibility. There's no such thing as an orphan.

TB: Yeah. . . . Except in L.A.

TB: That was one thing about the Beach Boys. They made the summer come alive. They sold a lot in the summer. They're good.

DJ: Their last album, *Holland*, was really fine.

TB: You know how much they spent for that? About a million dollars—for one album.

DJ: Why?

TB: Well, they bought the studio, and their sign was right—*Holland*—and they spent fourteen days on each song, and they bought homes, and Mercedes, and the wiring wasn't quite right, so they . . .

DJ: You seem quite critical of that.

TB: Oh, well, when you got it, flaunt it. Go the whole way.

DJ: It sounds like fun.

TB: Sure, what the heck. It's just that—I mean, all that money for an album, when you could be in Tahiti drinking with Brando? A song's a song. A town's a town. Why spend millions on it? Have we bored the university enough to get off the air?

DJ: Oh, I don't think so.

TB: Intellectual machos out there?

DJ: Next time we'll have the antenna on a mountain and reach the whole state. This time, we've only got the city. Anyway, everybody should go out to the Thunderbird Lodge, Thursday through Sunday night, out in Placitas.

TB: And be prepared to dance. Kick off your ski boots—it's a good floor.

DJ: Yeah, people boogie around here. People even boogie . . .

TB: What *is* "boogie"?

DJ: "Boogie"? Dance and have a good time, a general word for moving your feet, and taking whatever seems to be handy and putting it into your mouth.

TB: (Ironically) Heavens!

DJ: On that note, we'll thank Tim Buckley and Buddy and the wife of Tim Buckley and . . .

TB: Wu.

DJ: And, uh . . .

TB: Wu.

DJ: Wo?

TB: *Wu.*

DJ: And we'll go back up to Bruce, I guess.

TB: Take it away, bro's!

LONDON BEER

From the *Starsailor* days forward, Tim stayed straight while working, whether in rehearsal, in recording studios or on the road. His reasoning was simple enough: Save physical and emotional energy for the music. Handle the job professionally. No partying until after the tour.

However, on one occasion in 1974, his old nemesis—London—got to him again. Before leaving America, he had just completed *Look at the Fool*. Following an exhausting recording project like that, a letdown is inevitable. He then took a one-day promotional trip to Paris, during which he had a wonderful time talking with Jacques Brel on a radio show. Right after that, he returned to Britain and played the July 20 Knebworth Festival in Hertfordshire, just outside of London.

The placement on the bill was terrible, one of the openers; the audience was massive; it was daytime instead of night; and worst of all, it was England. At that point, after Knebworth, tired, irritable, London got to him—as it always had. He fell off the wagon.

Like his father, Tim had begun to take the abstraction of "America" quite seriously, to the point where he began attacking people who criticized America in any way, or who failed to demonstrate enough respect to satisfy him. His chauvinistic militarism was a far cry from those halcyon summer days in Venice so many years ago. Now he was talking Vietnam vets and "Nighthawkin'."

Also like his volatile Irish dad, he detested the British—their physical and emotional fastidiousness; their terror of confronting genuine emotions and expressing them freely and directly; their subtle, devious, dry, sardonic humor; their steel-willed reserve; their determination to preserve the "proper" image at all times, under all conditions.

Tim simply didn't give a damn about missing tea. Spontaneous, expressive, blunt, chauvinistic, he was as out of place in London as John Wayne at a baby shower. Dirty Harry selling women's lingerie. W.C. Fields sloshed among pedigreed aristocrats. The last thing in the world he needed was some prissy Englishman telling him to mind his manners—which, according to what he told me, is exactly what happened. . . .

Late at night, quite drunk, Tim wandered into a pub near his hotel. He sat alone at a table and ordered beer. The waiter walked across the sawdust floor with a mug, and set it on the table. Tim took a healthy swig—then spat it at the floor, spilling some on his rumpled Columbo trench coat.

"Ptah! This beer is hot!"

People at the bar turned to look at him. He was brushing dribbled beer off his coat, saying, "Jesus Christ! Hot fuckin' beer. When the hell are you Limeys gonna learn who won the *War* for you? Hot beer! Where the hell would you have been if we hadn't saved your uptight Limey asses? Gimme some goddamned ice cubes!"

The customers were amused at first, watching him hold his mug with one hand while flailing at the Columbo rain coat, trying to get the beer off. They smiled. So did the waiter.

But as Tim began lambasting their cherished World War II heroes and demanding ice cubes—which would only destroy the proud flavor of British Guinness Stout—their bland English smiles turned to contemptuous sneers.

"'Nother 'Merican can't find 'is way home."

"Won the War *for* us, indeed."

"Yer goddamned right—*for* you!" Tim continued, sounding like his "General Buckley" dad. "But in spite of losing every goddamned country you ever owned, you *still* haven't learned what a good beer tastes like! Where's my ice cubes?"

"Crude sort of chap, isn't he."

"Subtle sort, I would say."

"Soooo American."

"Ice cubes will ruin the beer."

"Give 'em to me anyway."

"Where in heaven's name are you *from*? Just who do you think . . ."

"Look, you Limey sons-a-bitches," Tim said, affecting a redneck Southern accent, "Ah am not only an ex-paratrooper Marine Air Force Commandeer head of the whole goddamned Navy—Ah am also from Texas, you better believe it, and Ah am one *hell* of a Texas-fuckin'-American. Now gimme my goddamned ice cubes!"

"We better get this fellow out of here."

"Take him, Austin."

The bartender strode out from behind the bar.

"Hold it!" Tim said, whipping his hand up—"Stop!" He sat down, sprawled his legs out, jammed his thumbs under his belt John Wayne style.

"'Fore you take one more step, bawh, I want you t'know one thing—got thet?"

"What might it be, sir?"

Tim at a press party in London, relaxing, sipping wine, socializing, promoting *Sefronia* and his upcoming album *Look at the Fool*.

"I wawnt you t'know Ah live in Texas. And in Texas, *everything* is big. It is big, it is better, it is the biggest, grandest, most powerful and *funny* place you ever heard of.

"An' you listen to me, Limey, 'cause I got *money*. I got money comin' out my socks, I got money comin' out my shirtsleeves, I got money comin' out my *ears*, you hear me?

"And that's because I got oil wells. I got oil wells rigged from one end of the sky to the other."

He stood up and slipped into his Burt Lancaster *Rainmaker* stance, palms up, light in his eyes, toothy smile, perfect teeth.

"I got oil wells in my pastures. I got oil wells in my barn. I got oil wells lining up and down my drive way. I got fourteen oil wells in my front yard, ten oil wells in back. I got four oil wells in the living room and two more in the bedroom—now *gimme my goddamned ice cubes!*"

The bartender swooped down on Timmy, bear-hugged him, smothering him in chest-hairs. Tim fought back but got tangled up in the Columbo trench coat.

The bartender hit him, and Tim found himself sliding on his ass in the sawdust toward the swinging front doors. When he got up, the bartender hit him again, knocking him out in the street. Tim heard the laughter as he picked himself up and staggered over to his hotel.

Once there, he didn't go to bed. He ran up and down the halls knocking on people's doors. He burst in on his own musicians, rousting them out of bed, tickling their women, upsetting everybody.

He then lurched back down the hall to the lobby, where he jumped up on a table and began orating to the assemblage that had trundled out in their pajamas, nightshirts, hair-rollers, and floppy slippers to see what the ruckus was about.

"I'll never know how you people think you're gonna survive in this world without an authentic Limey composer to your name. And don't talk to me about Benjamin Britten. He's as boring as your goddamn beer!

"If you had any idea how to open yourselves up, you wouldn't have to walk around all the time lookin' like you're constipated and just sucked a lemon. I mean, how can anybody eat dead *fish* for breakfast and call themselves a human being?

"You think you're better'n us because you never experience a real feeling. Now, where the hell is that? And even when you *think* you have a feeling you don't really have one—it's just another thought. If *I* can't cut through that phony façade of yours and get a reaction that has blood and love and life in it, nobody can!

"Look how your musicians come over to our country, steal our music, peddle it to you as reality—and you go for it! Where do you think the Beatles, the Stones, and Eric Clapton got it? From Benjamin Britten? Hell, no! They got it from *I got a yard-long hard-on, a bucket of balls, and enough hair on my ass to fill a mattress!*

"That's black talk, honey. That's Muhammad Ali, that's Miles Davis, that's Roland-fucking-Kirk. That's Orson Welles too, and Marlon-fucking-Brando—that's *America!*"

He teetered on the lobby table, caught himself—"And *we* won the War!"

He climbed down to the floor, straightened up his rumpled trench coat, blew a kiss and a smile to the crowd, wandered back to his room.

CHAPTER 17

YES, UP, ON

There were magnificent periods of creativity during the years between *Greetings From L.A.* and *Look at the Fool*, and equally happy periods of rest, pleasure and healthy fun. It was not all up—there were intermittent valleys of dark depression and substance abuse—but by no means was it all down.

By the time Tim reached *Sefronia* (1973/74) and moved into a house at 828 Venezia Street in Venice, he had improved considerably from earlier years. He periodically cleaned up his body, refraining from alcohol, downers, and other drugs. He embraced a state of mind that welcomed creativity. He generated lyrics, melodies and songs that spoke of the human condition with humor, compassion, insight, and tremendous heart.

At home, he took vitamins, threw basketballs into a hoop that hung from his backyard garage, began eating decent food, and spent much of his time composing and recording. To be sure, life wasn't *always* good, but when it was, it was very, very good. During these stretches, he enjoyed a middle-ground equilibrium that enabled him to feel magnanimous about himself, his marriage, his work.

Judy pointed to a photograph on her wall of Tim leaning up against a fence. "He was at a ball game between the record companies," she said to me, "unshaven, pimples—but that little fucker could really play baseball! He was a shortstop, quick, fast, a great arm. This was the DiscReet team, and they were playing Capitol, United Artists, RCA. I think they played eight games—and won seven of them. All those other guys would show up in matching uniforms, cleats, and they'd stand in parallel rows to do their calisthenics and throw the ball to each other.

"And here was Timmy's DiscReet team. They wore blue jeans. And they had blue T-shirts. That's all they bought for uniforms. They had long hair, Levis, tennis shoes.

"All the other guys on the other teams would be out doing calisthenics and throwing the ball and going, 'Yo-ho! Yaw-sah! Throw it, o' buddy! Hey!', while the DiscReet team would be laying up under a tree waiting for the game to start.

"They had teams with ten guys on them, not nine. Herb was out there in short-center field. Tim and all these musicians and executives were there. What a bunch. The catcher was a lawyer who played in his suit and street shoes! But basically, the DiscReet guys were street dudes who used to play stickball. I mean, they had their shit down. They were good. They'd hit the ball, steal bases.

"DiscReet let one of the female secretaries play, and all the guys on the other team got uptight. One of the guys walked off the field, because there was a chick playing—and beating them. They took it so seriously!

"They had their families. That was the token thing, where you take the wife and the children. And they'd get so pissed, because Timmy would be out there hollering,

'Hey, you goddamn schmucky motherfuckers, hot damn!', and he'd be spitting off to the side. Those guys got so uptight—they were gonna kill him, because their wives and kids were there!"

"One of the best times we had," Judy recalled, "was when we spent the week in New Orleans. He had been working in New York and had the week off. So I met him in New Orleans. We rented a boat with a guide, and rode back in the Bayous. We found some tombstones with my family name on them—Brejot. It's French and Indian—Creole.

"At night we stayed in the Latin Quarter. It was off-season, and we didn't go out at night. We did everything during the day. We'd get up early and go to the museums, check out the plantations, have soft-shell crab and gumbo for breakfast. It was wonderful.

"Another time was when he played in New Mexico. It was nice, because we got a bungalow way out in an old Spanish hotel with a heart-shaped pool.

"We rented a car and drove back to California, and I took him to a museum that Darrell and I had created together. That was the first time I had been back to see it. It's on the Colorado River in the Mule Mountains in Buckskin National Park, Arizona. He wanted to see it, and thought I should look at it.

"When we got there it was late. We walked all around the grounds that night. Then we rented a room and got up real early to see the sun come up in the desert. Then back to the museum. It was so strange to see the stuff. It was from so long ago in my life, another world, you know? . . .

"I've got that baseball picture of Tim in my workroom. . . . I know it's there, but I don't look at it. . . . I was going to take it down, but I can't. If I had a picture of Darrell, I'd put that up too."

It might have been Beckett who taught Tim how to play chess; I don't recall. But Tim got into it. He and Taylor played regularly, and he often went over to CR's house to play, loving the game, the competition, its subtleties and complexities, its elegance and intensity.

When he'd travel back to New York, he'd visit Washington Square and play chess with the heavies in a little chess parlor around the back of the Greenwich Hotel on the ground floor.

Whenever I saw Tim or talked with him on the phone, he'd say, "Man, you gotta get into chess—you would love it!"

I didn't learn chess until years later, but when I did—he was right!

I moved to Hollywood with Carol Zeitz, who lovingly stood by me through some of my darkest hours while I was trying to get sober. For several months, I played guitar in a soul music dance band at Jeffty's in Compton. Michael Cavanaugh played piano and got me the gig. The group was called the Mod Squad after the television black/white cop show. Michael and I were the white guys. Everybody else was black. We played cover tunes, some of the funkiest music I ever heard.

When it came time to leave Carol, I moved into my own place on Franklin Street, near Cahuenga, where I began teaching myself how to write about music and musicians. To this day I thank Carol from the heart for her love, compassion, loyalty, good humor, and invaluable help.

White shoes whimsy in Vancouver, circa 1973. Tim once rocked too far back on his stacked heels and tipped over into Buddy Helm's drum set.

In the summer of 1974, Tim visited Paris for one day. He was to do a radio interview and a press conference to promote *Sefronia* and talk about the just-recorded *Look at the Fool*.

He had a marvelous time on the radio, playing disc jockey, airing a wide variety of music from favorite albums, talking about music and musicians, and spinning his own albums as well. The great Jacques Brel called in. He loved the artists and pieces Tim selected, the things Tim talked about, and Tim's music too. Jacques's call was one of the highlights of the trip.

Next stop—interview conference at his hotel, with important press people. "But he got bored," Judy said. "He knew he was going to be in Paris only one night. So he didn't wait for the conference."

On a whim, he sneaked out of the hotel, stole a bicycle, and pedaled all over Paris. "He went to see the Seine," said Judy. "He visited Montmartre, to be around where Toulouse-Lautrec was, and the cobblestone streets. I had taken him to see my favorite movie, *Moulin Rouge,* and he had written a song about it. So when he finally got to go to Paris, that's what he wanted to see. What can I say that he didn't go to the meeting? He should have, but . . . well, Paris was there."

Just as a few people helped Tim along the way when he was in dire straits, so he helped others. Sometimes it was by remembering a musician and bringing him back into the fold. On other occasions, it was assisting a friend in trouble.

In June 1975 for example, shortly before his death, Tim and Judy and Cool Richard were excited about their upcoming trip. "We were planning a vacation," Judy said. The three of them were going to take a train through Mexico to Honduras, where they were going to stay with a friend, a painter who wanted to do drawings and paintings for some of Tim's songs. They would then put together a record with a brochure of the paintings.

However, the painter got drunk in L.A., and the cops arrested him. He did not have his papers with him, so the cops threw him in jail as an illegal alien.

To get him out of jail, Tim had to borrow money from the Musicians Union. "That was the first time in his life that Tim had ever taken out a loan," his mother said, "and I was his co-signer. He got a loan for $2,000 and used about $1,400 of it to get the friend out of jail. Originally, Tim was going to take out a loan anyway, because that was going to be the money for him and Judy to take their trip down to Honduras.

"When we went to get the loan, I asked Tim, 'Aren't you working a little too fast? I mean, who is this guy you're shelling out $1,400 for?'

"He said, 'Mother, I couldn't stand to see even a cockroach in jail, and he is a friend of mine.'"

By April of 1975, two weeks before his gig at the Starwood, Tim had opened himself up to all kinds of people and musicians, musical styles and literary influences. Journalist Michael Davis of the *L.A. Free Press* must have expected a boogie-down rock 'n' roller when he came to interview Tim, because the last album he had heard was *Greetings From L.A.,* and the Starwood was known as an urban roadhouse concert/dance hall. But after speaking with Tim, Davis said Buckley came off as a scintillating, knowledgeable, highly articulate individual, "one of the brightest people I've talked to in twelve years of interviewing."

At one point in the conversation, Tim discussed some of his views about the classical realm—a far cry from the rock 'n' roll funk he would be playing at the Starwood. . . .

"I remember when I took my band into the avant-garde, the Starsailor band, we went to New York City, and Leontyne Price came to see me. She came up and said, 'Boy, I wish they were writing things like that for us opera singers!' I said, 'Well, do what I did—get your own band.'

"That was an off-the-cuff comment, but there's truth in it. It's really hard to teach classical people how to relate to each other, in the sense of playing a lick and somebody else catching it and playing it back.

"A lot of people respect the fact that they can read and play technically terrific, and depend on the composer. But that way is becoming more and more obsolete, because the composer is dead, and he's not there to argue with the orchestra. So we've devised conductors, and we say, 'They know the real Mozart,' or, 'They know the real Penderecki,' or, 'They know the real Xenakis, Messiaen, Beethoven, or the real Stravinsky,' or that Stravinsky couldn't conduct his own orchestras because he didn't have a tremendous enough knowledge of music—but still, I get more goosebumps from his conducting than from anybody else conducting Stravinsky.

"These composers knew the power of knowing the musicians they were going to write for. Alban Berg is a classic example. He knew the orchestra inside and out, and wouldn't write until he met all of them and knew what they could do. Each instrument—its range, everything about it. Much like Duke Ellington. You have to.

"You just can't go into a rehearsal and write an outrageous thing for somebody without knowing the instrument. If you do, it's going to be out of its register, or not going to be in the character of the instrument. If you write for it, you need to know what it can do, and what effect you want.

"So the classical people are just starting to catch on—about talking into their horns, for example. At Contempo '73, Zubin Mehta said, 'Now we're going to do a new innovation. The French horn section will be talking into their horns while this piece is being played.'

"Well, Roland Kirk was doing that a long time ago!

"It's funny. It's hilarious. And I was laughing—the only one in the audience. Here's this fraud, and he's being applauded. Well, he does the Easter services real great—but he does not understand modern music.

"The only one who does is Pierre Boulez, and he's in position in New York City, thank God. He studied under Messiaen and other people who understand the extreme subtleties of contemporary music, and he's bringing it to probably the most critical public in the world—New York City—and he's making it work.

"So, finally, some new information is getting out to people, and will change music—it always does. I mean, who would have thought that Leonard Bernstein could write a Top 40 hit? But he did it, He wrote *West Side Story*'s 'Jet Song,' and Alice Cooper picked up on it. So it's a slow, painful process, but it's happening.

"It's all a matter of getting people to at least listen to it. . . . And the initiative has to be taken by the artist, not the record company, because the record company will not move from what it's making its money on.

"So here is the artist again, faced with the proposition of becoming another renegade, running on the parallel outskirts of what society loves and how he knows he can make his living.

"It takes the very best to do this experimentation—which really isn't an experiment at all. It's a voyage, a new voyage, a new exploration beyond the frontiers of what is already known. I mean, that's all there is—we've gone to the moon. We've traveled across the deserts. We've come here to California, rubbed up against each other, and been bored shitless for the last twenty years—in California, where a sucker is born every minute and can live forever.

"The explorations, the pioneers, have to be personal contacts between people."

At another point in the interview, Davis asked Tim, "So what would you do if you had your own television show?" . . .

"Well, let's see. . . . If I had an hour, it would have to be some sort of a talk show. For the last three weeks I've been reading *The Ascent of Man*, by Jacob Bronowski, who I feel is King of the Year this year. He put together a beautiful fifteen-part TV series on the evolution-of man, both science and art, which is very important.

"He didn't exclude one from the other. In fact, throughout the series, he constantly meshed art with science, with the ideals of each going side by side. Usually they're presented as separate entities. The life of Michelangelo is always presented as 'The Life of Michelangelo,' without scoping out in depth what the scientific evolutions were at the period he was doing those things in. There's one chapter in here called 'The Starry Messenger,' which shows his terrific contributions alongside his art and his morality and what he believed in. Instead of presenting Michelangelo and his times in separate little boxes, he presents them all together in relation to each other. You get a sense of the whole.

"If I had a TV show, I might show many different segments of what Bronowski did, and present him to the American public. I found out only a few weeks ago, after we played Phoenix, that Bronowski's series was shown on the Public TV stations only in New York, Boston, Chicago, Frisco, and Los Angeles. The rest of the country hasn't heard of it except by word of mouth through their colleges.

"This fifteen-part series is becoming a book in college courses. So, what I saw for free, and paid $10 or $15 for the book, somebody else is going to have to pay an entire college tuition for. This book is important. It gives you an understanding of things that's amazing. And the way it's being taught is much more logical, because it keeps you interested. It doesn't isolate things from each other. So Bronowski would be a terrific guest.

"And right after him, I would have Roland Kirk, whose talking is as interesting as his playing. He knows more about black culture in America than anybody else I've ever talked to. Not that Malcolm X or others don't know, but of the people I've met, and who is a musician and a hero of mine—Roland Kirk and Bronowski would get along terrifically. They would understand the lingo back and forth. Between music and society during that hour, it would make people realize different things and get them interested. It would make a terrific one-hour show.

"Well, that's one week! The next week, who knows?"

"Cathy Berberian and Cher?," Davis suggested.

"Cathy Berberian and Cher?! Hah! That's great! A third show, bring in Norman Mailer, tie him down, and show him clips of Ernest Hemingway. No? A low blow.

"Nevertheless, shows could be done that would be terrific. Today's variety shows are terrible. They keep authentic people off. Cher did a whole show of reggae music—without having either Bob Marley and the Wailers or Toots and the Maytals. What are these people, barbarians? I mean, why don't they think of this?

"Americans are very interested in things. They love to discover things while they're enjoying them. It's part of our nature. What makes this work? What makes that work?

"But we've been turned into sexual voyeurs. It's in the networks' interest to keep it that way too. If there's no innovation, there's no threat of losing their position. So they keep it at the same level.

"I just think there's much more that can be done with it. A lot of other people do too—and it won't happen!"

Tim was constantly coming up with new ideas. He thought of writing a novel, *Impressions of America*, and a screenplay based on Thomas Wolfe's *You Can't Go Home Again*. As noted earlier, he wanted to compose a concept album for Conrad's *An Outcast of the Islands*, using Beckett's lyrics, his own lyrics, a ballet troupe, a choir, and an orchestra.

He wanted go into the studio and record new music on one album, re-record old favorites on another, and do a series of live albums, bringing together musicians from his various groups to re-record favorite compositions from each period.

Although in late '74 and early '75 he was without a manager or a recording contract, Tim took the positive point of view. "I'm free, and it feels great," he told Davis. He indicated that he had high hopes of getting a new recording contract from either Arista or Asylum. At one point, he also had hopes of landing the lead role in *Bound for Glory*, Hal Ashby's film about Woody Guthrie.

When he spoke with writer Frankie Nemko in June 1975, just before his death, he said, off-hand, "I'm fighting for my life here." But he was so charming and confident during the interview that Frankie wrote, "Tim was excited about his career. He was so up, it was lovely."

Along the way he indicated to Nemko (and the recording industry) that he was not using drugs. Then she asked if he were under contract with anybody, to which he replied, "No, not at the moment. Things are in the wind. Right now they're getting me mixed up with Tim Hardin and his problems. I'm not the same guy." He chuckled and quipped, "Man, I can't get a flu shot without passing out."

Tim's band was cooking wherever they played, and by the late spring of 1975 they had gigs coming up in Hollywood, Detroit, and Texas.

Clearly, there were positive elements in Buckley's life. He was doing everything he could to regroup, think constructively, generate ideas, stay straight, take care of business, play the gigs, get a new contract, keep the ball rolling.

Unfortunately during these later years, Yes seemed counterbalanced by No, Up by Down, On by Off. Almost every positive step generated a backlash. Exhilarating views from the mountaintops brought vertiginous descents into darkland shadow-depths where demons lurked, snarling with glee. And sometimes Tim swooned and closed his eyes and embraced them.

CHAPTER 18

"OF TIME AND THE CITY"

For some people, there is a continual storm in the soul, a titanic battle between affirmation and negation, divine creation and demonic destruction. Mind and flesh, thought and feeling, tear each other limb from limb until Yes and No lie shredded on the ground, dying to the light.

Every effort to affirm the creative impulse while denying the destructive impulse is met with a raging force that shatters aspiring goals and dreams like cathedral windows, smashing hopes to splintered shards with a vengeance. Spirit stands by, helplessly weeping and watching while the divided heart inflicts bloody havoc upon itself.

In such divided souls, there is no light so bright that darkness cannot extinguish it, no dream so sweet that toxic rage cannot corrupt it, no pulse so strong it cannot be suffocated by that inner wrath which, if let loose, would decimate life on Earth itself. Heaven stands astonished when one of these battered children manages to rise and walk for a day or a week, much less a month, a year, or a lifetime.

If our fathers and mothers brutally bash our courage, undercut our confidence, reduce us to inner ruin, hopeless, lost, afraid, they are not to blame. They suffered such wounds from their own parents, even as their fathers and mothers before them suffered the same and passed them on. Perhaps they tried to love, but knew not how. Elders can give only what they have, and have only what they received. Nearly all remain utterly unconscious. Thus, in different forms, fashions, methods, styles, the same madness passes from generation to generation, on and on, inevitably in the name of love, help, knowledge, survival, discipline, tradition, realism.

Helpless, small, dependent, the little lost ones have no place to turn except to those who brutalize them, no one to hold except those who hurt them, no one to ask except those who betray their trust. Thenceforth, every step toward self-reliance is fiercely denied from within by fear. Every gesture toward healthy creativity is sabotaged by self-doubt. Every flicker of self-esteem is smothered by an avalanche of guilt. We dare not contradict those who teach us their own fears, anguish, anger. These are the curses and shames of elders who cannot acknowledge or accept or approve.

Later on, the weeping children know no comfort except that which numbs their pain, no joy except those intoxications that obliterate restraints and unleash fury. The divided soul transmutes retaliatory energy into self-denial, self-abnegation, self-punishment, and finally self-annihilation.

Thou shalt not murder thy sires, but thyself.

Wit, thy name is rage.

Bliss, thy name is oblivion.

Is it not an extraordinary accomplishment when one of these crippled ones manages to endure long enough to release even a single shining song to the heavens? For these spirits, damaged by those who came before, every step of the ascending path is marked by anguish and tears and blood and loss. How exorbitant the price for creative transformation. How rare the courage to grow. How wondrous each achievement, whether modest or grand. The deeper the depths the wounded ones have known, the greater the respect they deserve for whatever heights they attain.

Is it not a miracle that even one among us attains such heights?

Is it not a miracle that even one among us lives to tell the tale?

Indeed, the triumph of the human soul is a glorious adventure, most worthy of the telling.

Journalist Stanley Mieses, New York, August 19, 1973, wrote:

In the upstairs dressing room of Max's Kansas City, crowded with more boxes of equipment than people, Tim Buckley sat with his legs tightly crossed, arms wrapped around his chest, holding onto his shoulders, head tucked into his chest, like a man preparing to be shot out of a cannon, and says: "I'm bound to be more tragic than now."

He flashes a smile and quickly adds, "I'm only joking."

But a sense of predestination seems to be there, and a notion that music will chart a lonely course.

"It's in the lyrics, man," he says, arms outstretched, as if the words were right in front of him. . . . He's absolutely pale.

"Yeah, Buckley ate better and looked better," Cool Richard said to me in our interview, "but it wasn't always like that back then. I used to go over and party with them, and it was far out. Everybody got fucked up to the max, and it wasn't just on liquor. There was other stuff over there too.

"One night a girl and I went for drinks down on the pier, then stopped by Tim's. We did so much amyl nitrite that we couldn't even . . . I mean, she was just a normal person, and she was grossed out. I mean, they had the whole bottle there. Nobody could even walk, people lying around on the floor. The whole bottle had spilled on the table. I never saw so much amyl nitrite. I could hardly get home. And the downer shit was still happening, Tuinals and reds."

"I don't know why Tim wanted to get so loaded," Richard said. "It's a personal thing with everybody, you know? I mean, who can say? But I suspect one of the reasons was because he didn't always want to fuck.

"When he wanted to go to bed after partying, I think he took that extra mouthful of Seconals or Tuinals or whatever he could get, just so he could cop a plea to not fuck.

"That's what I think, and that's the impression I got from what little feedback I got from Judy—not so much anything she told me behind his back, but little things that happened between them and me when the three of us were together."

A certain incident offended Richard so much that he never forgot it and never forgave Tim for it. Based on his description of it to me . . .

Richard wasn't surprised when he heard Tim's knock at the door. It was late, around midnight, but Tim had often done this—come over to Richard's either drunk or high on downers, sometimes two or three o'clock in the morning, after the bars had closed. He would knock on the door, wake Richard up, insist Richard hang out and talk with him, have a drink, maybe snort a little. Not all that unusual, and here he was again.

So Richard didn't feel surprised, although he did feel annoyed. He wasn't making a lot of money in 1973, but his graduate studies at UCLA were going well, and his life had been on a relatively even keel lately, not a lot of heavy ups and downs, peaceful. Tonight he had been enjoying Laurie's company, feeling mellow, about to doze off, when here comes Buckley, whacked again. Oh, well . . . Richard opened the door.

"Hey, who's the chick?" Tim laughed, turning his charm on.

"Laurie, this is Tim."

"Hi," the girl smiled, pulling the covers up a bit.

"A little young for you, isn't she?"

"A friend."

"Heeey, baby, ain't nothin' wrong with a little jail bait once in a while!"

"Cool it, Buckley. What's happening?"

"Well, I got seven albums out and my name's in lights. I could die tomorrow and still be a success. 'Course I haven't had a teenybopper in my bed for a while, but the young ones are a bore anyway."

"That's enough, man. Look, it's late, and I've been feeling pretty good today. I don't want to hassle with you, so how about cooling it? Maybe it's time to go back home, yes?"

"Yeah, well, I can do that. Just thought I'd drop by and say Hi, see how things are. Everything okay for you lately? Need any money?"

"School's good, but sure, I could use fifty bucks until about the eighth. Pay you back then."

"Ha!" Buckley laughed. He reached into his pocket, pulled out a quarter, flipped it in the air. It landed on the bed. "You can have that for now. Buy yourself a new life. Come around and ask me again when you feel like it."

"Get the fuck out of here, Buckley."

"Where do you get off talking trash like that, CR? You're just a two-bit professional student who screws little girls and hides out in school his whole life because he doesn't have enough smarts or balls to earn a living in the real world. You're nothing, man, nothing at all."

"I'm gonna tell you something, Timmy, before I throw you out on your ass if you don't leave. Your success is pure bullshit. People think because you're up there singing and performing that you're some kind of big-deal lover. Well, you're not. To them, you're supposed to be more than a singer. You're supposed to be *a man*. But you don't even take care of your own wife. Now I want you to get *out* of here!"

Tim looked over at the wall, took a breath, looked back, tried to ignore Richard's remark. "Yeah, well, call me when you get ready for the loan."

"Both of them, but especially Judy, would put me up as some kind of sex figure," Richard said. "In a hundred little ways they'd put that identity on me. Not that I didn't enjoy it, because I like that stuff, but it didn't belong in their relationship. I mean, she would needle him with it, you know? She would use me to put Timmy down. In a way, I was her hammer to hit back at Timmy.

"It's like he would compensate for his normal human functions by being such a tyrannical little king around there, making everybody else feel like nothing, controlling her and making her feel like nothing too. It didn't work with me like that, so she sort of used me to get back at him."

Buckley's bandmates meant well but had little or no idea how much he put out each set, the physical energy and emotional intensity, the sheer exertion of will it took to scale those heights and plumb those depths every time he set foot onstage. While they laid back, played their parts, winked at the girls, he wasn't acting. He stood in sweat and fire, eyes closed, and burned.

When they finished their second and final set at the Brewery in East Lansing, Michigan, Tim sank into the folds of a stuffed armchair backstage, completely drained.

"This is Tim's band and the rest of us just play in it," Bernie Mysior told writer Jack Bodnar in 1973. "We don't mind just hanging back while Tim sings his music."

Emaciated, stark white, Buckley was totally exhausted after the concert. . . .

"I'm ready for one more set," keyboardist Mark Tiernan said seriously. Guitarist Ira Ingber chimed in, "Yeah, we're just getting started, man. Now's the time to play."

Buckley just hung his head down. . . .

Danny Gordon always felt great love for his Jewish homeland. As a boy he had spent time in Israel, and now, as a young man out of UCLA in the early seventies, he had returned to Israel to serve in the military.

Tim thought it was outrageous that Dan, an aspiring writer, would risk his life for political conflicts, and they had a huge fight about it in Dan's Wilshire Boulevard hotel room when Dan visited L.A. in 1974. Tim, Judy, Dan, and would-be writer David "the Baby" Thoreau were present. I was told about it later (by Judy, as I recall).

The fray started off with Tim's saying, "Why do you want to be over there risking your life when you should be writing?"

Danny responded by saying, "Israel is my home now. That is where I feel I belong. It gives my life meaning and value. It is profoundly important to me, so I'll fight for my country if I have to. It's my duty. It's my privilege. It's my honor."

That led into a heated argument about, "Why are you fighting for that country and not for this one? We've got our own wars, and America is the greatest country in the world. Israel is nothing but a province—who cares? Besides, you are an artist. You should be writing and creating art, not getting involved with politics and war. Those stupid things never change. All they do is kill people in the name of grand abstractions—flags, honor, freedom—great names masking ugly realities, and it goes on forever. You think that by facing death you're some kind of Hemingway hero? That's ridiculous. Death is nothing, and wars are bullshit. You oughtta be writing."

Dan felt insulted. He argued back. He had seen actual deaths, not just romanticized movies. How dare Tim dismiss human life so flippantly? They hassled further, and "The Baby" wound up jumping into the swimming pool from the second floor balcony with all his clothes on.

Dan wrote to me, ". . . Tim egged Thoreau into jumping off my balcony for a drunken horrible fall that almost didn't make it to the pool to show that he wasn't afraid of death, except he made that demonstration with someone else's life, and himself just pissed on doors down the hall. . . ."

Tim's ex-wife, Mary, said Tim and Dan remained friends until the end, although it was my understanding that the fight terminated their relationship.

Tim felt terrible about the squabble. He and Dan had been close buddies since childhood—and by this time, July 1974, Tim didn't have that many friends left anyway.

Buckley continued on the music path, while Dan served in the Israeli military some more and spent additional time in Israel learning the business of writing marketable television and film fare.

In a sense, it was all a pipe dream—there was no *Impressions of America* novel, no Thomas Wolfe screenplay, no completed *Outcast of the Islands*, no new recording contract from Arista or Asylum. Tim wanted those things to happen, had a few notes, lyrics, ideas. But most were hopes or projections—at best, plans. That was good. Hopes and plans were needed as goals and incentives, but they had not turned into solid realities. Maybe they would. He didn't know.

Nor was there any Woody Guthrie lead role in *Bound for Glory*—that had gone to David Carradine. Although Judy said after Tim's death that Tim had been chosen for the role and shooting was to have begun the week after Tim died, it was my understanding (through a significant phone call from Tim shortly before he left on his final tour) that the Carradine selection had already been made, and Tim knew it. (The film's producer, Harry Leventhal, later told biographer David Browne he did not recall Tim's name ever being even *mentioned* for the part. He said the Guthrie role had *always* been intended as a vehicle for Carradine.)

On every level for Tim, hope wrestled with anxiety.

Perhaps because of his painful inner divisions and conflicts during these last two years, Tim felt acutely isolated. He was being nice to key people and playing the game—with band members, with the business world, with the press, with acquaintances. But between straight periods, he was suffering serious binges, criticizing friends, feeling deeply depressed, losing ground.

It might have been difficult for him at times with Judy too. It seemed to be her nature to need attention, praise, flattery, and her nature to drift away when conversation focused on the other person's interests. One might feel profoundly lonely in her presence, craving something, anything, to numb the aching need. . . .

> *When I come home to you, honey,*
> *Oh, your little eyes never flicker,*
> *I wish I was that cool,*
> *Then your love just wouldn't matter at all.*

> "Honey Man"

Work, love, friendship—it was hard to keep hope afloat when things weren't coming through. Life was not all down for Tim, or all up either. It was sequential, like drastic swings of the pendulum.

In a DiscReet envelope postmarked September 13, 1974, Tim enclosed a typewritten letter. At the end of the letter, in a handwritten note, he asked if I might be able to get a story about him into *Down Beat* (which I was not able to do at the time). I thought the letter was his, and said so in my 1977 *Down Beat* memorial feature on him. However, as I re-read it today, I suspect it was written, not by Tim, but by his father—Tim did not type; the setting is Brooklyn and New York City; and the point of view and writing style is very much like his father's.

I do know this. Through that letter's content and tone and style, no matter who wrote it, Tim reconnected with his father, an afflicted, unfulfilled artist in his own right. The substance and atmosphere of it and the words themselves bridged them in time, brought them close again, perhaps closer than ever before. Tim sent the letter to me for a gut-level serious reason: In powerful and personal language, it conveyed much of what he himself was feeling at that particular time. Presumably through his father's impassioned words, Tim was singing his own song to me about hope and hopelessness, alienation, loss, loneliness, even as he and his father sang the same song in one voice.

I call that letter "Of Time and the City." It included these compelling paragraphs. . . .

The great vision of the city is burning in your heart in all its enchanted colors, just as it did when you were 12 years old and thought about it. You think that same glorious happiness of fortune, fame and triumph will be yours at any minute, that you are about to take your place among great men and lively women in a life more fortunate and happy than any you have ever known—that it is all here, somehow, waiting for you and only an inch away if you will touch it, only a word away if you will speak it, only a wall, a door, a stride from you, if you only knew that place where you may enter. And somehow the old wild wordless hope awakens again that you will find it— the door that you can enter . . . Then, for a moment, the old unsearchable mystery of time and the city returns to overwhelm your spirit with the horrible sensations of defeat and drowning . . .

It seems to you now that you are living in a world of creatures who have learned to live without weariness or agony of the soul, in a life which you can never touch, approach or apprehend; a strange city-race who have never lived in a dimension of time that is like your own, not measured in minutes, hours, days and years, but in dimensions of fathomless and immemorable sensation; who can be remembered at some moment in their lives only nine thousand enthusiasms back, twenty thousand nights of drunkenness ago, eight hundred parties, four million cruelties, nine thousand treacheries or infidelities, two hundred love affairs gone by—and whose lives therefore take on a fabulous and horrible age of sensation that has never known youth or remembered innocence and that induces in you the sensation of drowning in a sea of horror, a sea of blind, dateless and immemorable time. There is no door . . .

Yes, there has been beauty enough—enough to burst the heart, madden the brain, and tear the sinews of your life asunder—but what is there to say? You remember all these things, and then ten thousand others, but when you start to speak of them, you cannot. . . . For you are what you are, you know what you know, and there are no words for loneliness, black, bitter, aching loneliness, that gnaws the roots of silence in the night.

So what is there to say? There has been life enough, and power, grandeur, joy enough, and there has also been beauty enough, and God knows there has been squalor and filth and misery and madness and despair enough; murder and cruelty and hate enough, and loneliness enough to fill your bowels with the substance of gray horror, and to crust your lips with its hard and acrid taste of desolation . . .

And now the red light fades swiftly from the old red bricks of rusty houses, and there are voices in the air, and somewhere music, and we are lying there, blind atoms in our cellar-depths, gray voiceless atoms in the man-swarm desolation of the earth, and our fame is lost, our names forgotten, our powers are wasting from us like mined earth, while we lie here at evening and the river flows . . . and dark time is feeding like a vulture on our entrails, and we know that we are lost, and cannot stir . . .

It was Easter time, 1975, when I drove down to Huntington Beach to see Tim at the Golden Bear. He and Judy and Taylor were there, and, to my surprise, so were his first wife, Mary, and his eight-year-old son, Jeffrey Scott.

Tim sang incredibly well that night, covering all the bases, from early songs such as "Pleasant Street" and "Blue Melody," through all of the newer material, including another spectacular duo encore with drummer Buddy Helm and a lengthy stretch of a cappella improvisations. Jeffrey took it all in, his eyes big, his concentration intense, appreciation visible on his face.

Mary told writer Bob Niemi that she took Jeff back to the dressing room during intermission, where Jeff "flew into his father's arms. They held each other for the first time since he was a toddler . . . and the scene was the most heartrending sight I'd seen in my life.

"I left them alone and when Jeff returned to our seats he had a grin as big as his face. After the show, Tim's wife, Judy, asked if they could take Jeff home with them for a brief visit . . . They spent four days together during that Easter vacation. Jeff returned with a matchbook with his father's phone number written in it, and a new outfit.

"That was two months before Tim died . . . It was wonderful! Just think if it hadn't happened. It was glorious! It's the best thing I ever did for that boy!"

I had just bought an all-white suit with safari loops on the shoulders and a wrap-around cloth belt. Watch out, John Travolta. It was an extravagance, because I wasn't making much money freelance writing about music and musicians for the *L.A. Free Press*, *Soul*, *Players*, *Down Beat*, and other magazines. But it boosted my morale and helped me feel included in human society for a change.

When Tim appeared at the Starwood for three nights, May 9–11, 1975, I wore that new white suit and attended every night. Felt terrific. Tim wore a black shirt, brown corduroys and polished black boots each night. He looked sharp and sang well—physically strong, vocally powerful. The band was crisp, cohesive, exciting: Joe Falsia, lead guitar; John Heron, organ; Jeff Eyrich, bass; Buddy Helm, drums. The people listened, drank, danced, had a good time. To this day, the recording of that appearance, *Blue Obsession—Live at the Starwood*, is a pleasure to listen to.

Writer Richard Cromelin of the *L.A. Times* attended. He spoke of Tim's "undeniable mystique," and his "supple, roaming voice that moves from a rough, soothing baritone to a riveting, high-range scream that's close to insane." He pointed out that "when he's moving with purpose and under control, it's breathtaking."

He also observed that Tim was "a bona fide legend" looking for a recording contract, and that "no record company should be allowed to sign another country-rock act or heavy-metal group until he is back in the studio."

I sat with several of Tim's friends and acquaintances, drank ginger ale, danced to the music, felt absolutely comfortable with the white-funk concept, the combination con-cert room and roadhouse dance hall context, the band's enthusiasm, and Tim's singing.

The only thing that troubled me was when Tim hauled out a quart bottle of Jack Daniels during the last set of the final evening, slugging on it between songs, swing-ing it out over the crowd Janis Joplin style.

After introducing individual members of the band at the very end of the set, in the midst of a fast-paced cookin' showbiz finale, waving his hand toward his whole group, he passionately shouted at the crowd to give them a round of applause, "I'd like to hear a little respect for my people tonight!"

For me, if not for others, it was a shockingly poignant moment. Sure, it was a standard, upbeat finish to a great set, but I also knew Tim was expressing a deep-seated pain that had long been a problem: the lack of respect received for him and his music over the course of too many years. At the end of that final Starwood set he knew he and the band had played superbly well. He rightfully wanted the crowd to acknowledge not only himself, but also the top-flight performances of Joe and Buddy and the others. Given the harsh criticisms he had endured, first from dis-gruntled *Happy Sad* fans when he gave them *Lorca* and *Starsailor*, and then from dis-gruntled *Starsailor* fans who called him "a sell-out" when he gave them this new fun-filled, hard rockin', white-funk dance music, his proud demand to this home-terri-tory audience rang with urgent sincerity.

Because of my knowledge about the full scope of his career, it seemed to me he was addressing not only that evening's Hollywood crowd, and demanding a quality of respect long due to him, but the greater context of multiple audiences in gener-al. As well, he was poignantly articulating a profound need for understanding, appreciation, and love. Without support from the business world, he stood alone on the Starwood stage with his music. His impassioned, defiant importunity—"I'd like to hear a little respect for my people tonight!"—was the visible top of an invisible iceberg.

Then he gave one of his spine-chilling James Brown shrieks, swung the Jack Daniels bottle out over the crowd again and guzzled another shot while listeners cheered and applauded. With the funk music churning behind him, Tim gave me goosebumps when he said, "If you're bored in your kitchen, lookin' at yourself all day long, remember one damn thing, woman, Tim Buckley's back in town!"

Bobby (a.k.a. Jesse) James, the good friend to whom Tim had given both 12-string acoustic guitars, used to hang out with Tim in Hollywood and Venice. Bob was there in the early days and during the middle years, and off and on during the final years. He loved Tim and Tim's music and sang many of Tim's songs—sounding amazing-ly like Tim himself. He enjoyed hanging out with "Buck," as he affectionately called him, and found himself outraged in the years after Tim's death, when other people characterized Tim primarily in terms of drug use instead of music.

"Sure, Tim liked downers and sometimes cocaine or a few drinks, but I never *ever* saw him into heroin. Heroin was just *not* a part of the picture, and I was around him a lot. Even if he snorted once in a while—which he never did in my presence—that junkie stuff is absolute garbage. Tim was *not* a junkie, but he was definitely an incredible musician and singer and songwriter—why don't people give him credit for that? What are they, idiots?"

Even in our youth, destiny's shadow watches from the wings.

Shortly before Tim took the flight out of L.A. for what proved to be his last trip, he called me after midnight at my Franklin Street place on a rain-drenched night two or three weeks after Starwood. He was drunk—not roaring drunk, but pensive, subdued, and slurring his words.

In a way, the lapse was understandable. He had been keeping the faith and working hard and staying straight as often as he could. But for the past three years, many reviews of his concerts and recordings had been less than flattering—in some cases, scathing. And here it was, late May 1975, and after nine years, nine albums, and Carnegie Hall, he no longer had a contract or manager. Sure, freedom felt great, but not all the time. In effect, he was still paying dues. It hurt the hell out of his pride and sorely tested his confidence.

He had been bound and determined to make a comeback, and sobriety had been the intention and primary focus of his conduct. But some of those long nights were lonelier than I knew at the time, and occasionally his doubts and fears eroded his resolve.

"'S all over," he drawled without saying hello.

"Singing the 'Vodka Wallow Blues' again, y'baby? Good to hear from you."

He didn't respond. In the background behind him I heard Miles Davis's mournful trumpet playing "He Loved Him Madly" from *Get Up with It*, Miles's tribute to Duke Ellington.

"'S all over . . . won't . . . be long . . ."

I tried again. "Whatta y'mean, schmuck? I thought you were all push-ups, wheat germ, vitamin E, brussels sprouts, and distilled water these days."

"Yeah, yeah. . . . I know. . . . Thas—*rrrup!*—true . . . Doesn't matter, though. . . ." There was a lengthy pause. I could hear his slow, labored breathing. "I wan' . . . you . . . take . . . her."

"What?"

"To take her."

"What do you mean, Tim?"

"Won't be long. . . . Burned out . . . empty . . ."

"What's the matter, Tim? What do you mean it won't be long?"

"Soon . . . soon . . ." he sighed. "Ain't interested."

I waited for him to continue, but he didn't. Just slow breathing.

"Interested in what, Tim?"

"Harder and harder to . . . care." He spoke in a don't-give-a-damn whisper. "Can't get interested . . . Jus' can't . . . 'S comin' . . . I can feel it . . . soon . . . soon . . ."

He stopped talking. I listened to the sound of my own breathing through the earpiece, waiting, saying nothing. I wasn't sure if he meant he wasn't interested in Judy or the music, or both. He took a big swallow of whatever he was drinking, burped again, then came back, his voice disarmingly slow, intimate, even charming.

"Won' be long, o' buddy. . . . Then you take her."

"Who, Tim?"

He sighed sharply, irritated with me. Then nothing. Silence except for his breathing. He sounded passed out.

"Tim?" No answer. "Timmy?"

"My cross-eyed flamingo . . . Wu." He faded out again.

"Timmy? . . . Timmy?"

"Yeah."

"Look, Tim, I can't . . ."

"Yes, you can."

"What makes you think I want her?"

"Won' be long. . . ."

I didn't have the heart to talk about the deleterious effects of narcissism on all concerned, especially if each is equal to the other.

"She's beautiful and desirable, Tim, but she's your wife, not mine. I've got my own way to go. I'm creating a new life. Nor am I the one who loves her. You are, Tim. You love her.

"Yeah. . . . I . . . yeah . . . I've never loved anybody like I've loved her. . . . Won' be long . . ."

"And music."

"With all my heart."

"Then why are you talking like this? You're only twenty-eight. Doubt is natural, but it's not something to cling to, man. Doubts only create more doubt. Haven't you suffered enough?"

He took another swig.

"This phase will pass," I said. "Everything is improving. It's rough right now, but if you play your cards right, the future can only get better."

"No," he said with finality, as if he were stating a blunt fact about the rain outside. "It doesn't get better."

Again, silence except for regular breathing.

"I felt like committing suicide last New Year's Eve," he said.

"Really?"

"Yeah."

"Listen to me, Tim. There's a dark, painful thing in both of us that gets crazy sometimes, but it *can* be helped."

"Has that shrink helped you? You don't even play guitar anymore."

"Yes, I do. And, yes, he *has* helped me—and he can help you too. He can help you stop beating yourself up. He can help you live your life—not angry and suffering and full of doubts, but alive and vibrant and creative like you want to be."

"Lose the anger, lose the music."

"Not true! Your insanity wants to keep you chained to misery. You like misery and want it—and think you need it for the music, but you don't, man."

"Lose the anger, lose the music."

"Tim, if you lose the anger, you'll feel *more* open and *more* interested, *more* creative, *more* productive. Besides, you said you've already lost the music, that you can't get interested anymore."

"Thas right . . . loud . . . empty . . ."

"Then what have you got to lose? At least you could *try* therapy."

"You jus' write words, don' play."

"I play, Tim, but I also write. Besides, that's me, not you. Maybe music is something I need to do on the way to becoming a writer, and maybe they'll merge later on. For you, there's music, acting, maybe film writing, maybe other kinds of writing too. You're a first-class writer, Tim. There can be an incredible future for you."

"*Braaaap!*" he burped purposely.

"What about the Guthrie flick?"

"*Bound for Glory*?"

"Yeah."

"Bound for shit."

"What happened?"

"David . . . *brrrrrurp!* . . . Carradine. . . ."

"Doesn't matter, man. You've got enormous potential in films. Remember when I suggested you to check out Thomas Wolfe? He said you can't go home again, and . . ."

"I been readin' him . . . great book . . . great book . . ."

"And he was right, wasn't he? You can't go back. You've got to go forward. New dimensions. New levels. New music. New writing. Fresh perspectives. Forward, Tim—you taught me that a long time ago. You also taught me a guy should believe in himself. You can do it. I've got faith in you. I've got enough faith in you for both of us. Come on, Tim, grab onto it with me."

Long pause. Neither of us said anything. Wind blew rain harder against the windowpanes. Miles Davis's horn wept in the background.

Tim whispered, "I love you, Lee."

Another pause . . . *click* . . . Gone.

PART II

Timewinds

CHAPTER 19

THE TOLLING BELL

Wearing clothes he had so often performed in—his brown corduroy pants, and a black silk shirt Judy had made by hand—Tim lay in state at the Wilshire Funeral Home in Santa Monica, July 3, 1975, clutching a yellow orchid in his right hand.

Four days dead, utterly and ultimately still. Waxy complexion. Too much rouge. Slightly protruding whiskers. Scrunched down in his coffin too far. Four small chins breaking the natural lines of his neck.

I touched the back of his hand with my left index finger, lingering only a moment. . . . A quality of cold unlike any other.

"Well, ol' buddy," I said. "Here we are, the Big Gig." In a flash, I recalled some of our great performances together—Carnegie, the Philharmonic, Atlantic City, Houston . . .

I milled about inside the parlor, saying hello to Carter Collins, Maury Baker, shaking hands quietly with acquaintances, nodding appreciation to those who complimented my white suit—the same one I had worn to the Starwood, the only suit I had. I could have worn something else, something black, but didn't want to.

Jennifer and Michael attended. Bearded Bob Campbell, our true and trusted friend from the earliest days in Greenwich Village, showed up. So did Johnny Sider, our first L.A. drummer. Larry Beckett was not there. He remained in Portland with his computers and Paul Bunyan poem. Danny Gordon was not there. He remained in Israel learning how to be a cinematic businessman.

A short fellow with a thin black moustache leaned up to my ear and whispered, "The podium is ready, sir. You have five minutes."

I walked outside again, sat on the front steps alone, smoked another cigarette, tried to cry, couldn't. Doug Weston, owner of the Troubadour, sat down beside me.

"I know it's tough," he said. "I've had friends die, and now Tim's gone. But you know something?"

"What?"

"Later, after things heal up, you'll see how it all fits together."

"What does that mean, Doug?"

"Everything seems to happen because it's supposed to. It's for the best. It doesn't seem that way now, but it's true."

"Thank you, Doug."

We stood up and hugged.

Looking out over the crowd, I nodded to Judy and Taylor and Tim's mother, Elaine, and his sister, Katy, wondering for a moment where Jeff and Mary were. Didn't see them.

I cleared my throat and spoke gently, in a near-whisper. . . .

"God bless Tim for what he let us give to him, for we became enriched by loving him.

"God bless him for what he gave to us through his music, his uncanny insight, his burning strength, and the frolicking radiance of his smile. He always seemed to deftly dance behind our spoken words, and touch us deeply where we hoped and feared and cared.

"More than a friend to us who loved him, he altered the structure of many of our lives—and through the pain and happiness he generated in us, we have emerged the bigger, the fuller, the richer, and certainly the wiser for it.

"He gave in fire and fury and laughter the totality of his life's experience, which was vast far beyond his mere twenty-eight years. He had a touch of genius, and a touch of poet's madness in him. He had a beauty of spirit, a beauty of song, and a beauty of personage that re-etched the face of our lives, and of the lives of all who ever saw him, and of all who truly heard him sing.

"His passing marks the end of one era for many of us, the beginning of a new life for all of us. Let us live our new lives with the spirit of joy and courage, always aware in our moments of doubt that we were among the fortunate few directly touched by the light of his unswerving commitment, and by the heat of his sometimes awesome creative fire. . . ."

For a moment, I paused.

"I introduced Tim to several poets and their shining words, including Rilke, Lorca, and Dylan Thomas. He loved Dylan's 'Fern Hill'. . ."

I read the entire poem, emphasizing certain special lines. . .

> *Now as I was young and easy under the apple boughs . . .*
> *Time let me hail and climb*
> *Golden in the heydays of his eyes . . .*
> *In the sun born over and over,*
> *I ran my heedless ways . . .*
> *And nothing I cared, in the lamb white days, that time would take me*
> *Up to the swallow thronged loft by the shadow of my hand . . .*
> *Oh as I was young and easy in the mercy of his means,*
> *Time held me green and dying*
> *Though I sang in my chains like the sea.*

I paused, listening to the silence in the funeral room, feeling love and wonder almost palpable in the air, knowing in my heart that we would never, ever, lose Tim's presence in our lives.

"In one of his early songs, on his second album, Tim caught for all of us that same poignant spirit of youth and love and passing time when he sang. . . ."

> *Once I was a soldier*
> *And I fought on foreign sands for you*
> *Once I was a hunter*
> *And I brought home fresh meat for you*
> *Once I was a lover*
> *And I searched behind your eyes for you*

And soon there'll be another
To tell you I was just a lie

And sometimes I wonder
Just for a while
Will you ever remember me?

And though you have forgotten
All of our rubbish dreams
I find myself searching
Through the ashes of our ruins
For the days when we smiled
And the hours that ran wild
With the magic of our eyes
And the silence of our words

And sometimes I wonder
Just for a while
Will you ever remember me?

"Let us bow our heads and close our eyes, and remember some of the good times Tim shared with us. I, for one, will never forget the magic of his eyes, the silence of his words. . . . God bless each and every one of us."

What a whim, what a waste, what a mess.

Newspaper articles appeared saying Tim had died of a heart attack while climbing the stairs to his apartment. Other articles said, No, it was an overdose of cocaine that he had mistaken for heroin. Quite often newspapers cited heroin, without mentioning that alcohol was involved, which made Tim sound like a junkie. Some journalists said he was in an upbeat, positive mood and everything in his life was going swimmingly well. Others said he had a serious drug problem that had plagued him for most of his career and he was depressed and suicidal.

Fabrications, inaccuracies, distortions. Uninformed—and misinformed—writers were having a field day.

Judy initially told reporters Tim had died of a heart attack. Then she insisted the death was Richard's fault, that he had not told her Tim had snorted heroin on top of alcohol at Richard's house. Therefore, Tim had died for lack of prompt medical attention, and Judy wanted Richard busted.

Richard insisted he was innocent of any wrongdoing, that he had told her Tim had snorted heroin. Nonetheless, he was arrested on charges of second-degree murder and furnishing heroin.

Hell broke loose. Hysteria, rage, finger-pointing, chaos, fear, tears, blame.

At Richard's trial, presiding Judge Charles Woodmansee said the death seemed entirely accidental. The charges of murder and furnishing heroin were dropped when Richard pleaded guilty to involuntary manslaughter. He was sentenced to 120 days in the L.A. County jail and four years probation.

In the aftermath people kept talking about poisoned dope, an affair, a conspiracy to murder Tim. In the midst of the swirl, nothing made sense, and none of the details came out about what *actually* happened. Even after the trial, questions lingered.

Tim himself freely chose to drink alcohol and then snort heroin, so why was so much vindictive rage directed toward Richard, not only by Judy, but by numerous others? If Tim was so "upbeat," as Judy and others had said, why did he need to get loaded to the point of death? Even if things in Tim's life were *not* as "lovely" as writer Frankie Nemko characterized them, then what in particular, if anything, drove him to get as stoned as he did that day? There seemed to be an inordinate urgency to his need. Was there? If so, why?

Nothing seemed rational, nothing quite fit, things were missing.

Perhaps if I peered into these shades and shadows, I might find answers that explained the roles Tim, Judy, and Richard played in the drama. Whatever the story, upbeat or down, sordid or enlightening, it might at least reveal the context in which Tim found himself. I cared about Tim, and wanted to discover what happened, though I was unclear how to proceed.

CHAPTER 20

DARK WINDS AND
"THE SHRINKING DOLLAR"

Nearly two years went by before I finally decided to go ahead and interview several key people for a *Down Beat* article about Tim and for a possible book. The question was simple enough:

What had happened?

According to Joe Falsia, Tim's lead guitarist and arranger who also took care of road manager chores, "Tim had a few drinks on the airplane, but no way was he drunk. The gig at the Electric Ballroom in Dallas Saturday night had been fantastic. He was great, we were great, the people loved us. In the motels after the gigs on the trip he had been reading Thomas Wolfe's novel, *You Can't Go Home Again.*

"But when we got on the plane Sunday morning, everything was different. I could tell something was bothering him, because he wasn't himself that day. The whole day Sunday was different. It was all . . . a strange day. Right off when we checked out of the hotel, he said, 'You gotta keep me on the road longer.' On the plane, he wasn't reading Thomas Wolfe. He was reading *The Story of O*, laughing and showing us kinky passages and saying, 'Here, you gotta read this!' . . . That whole day was weird. . . . I think there was a major upset in his life. Something must have happened that I don't know about."

Jeff Eyrich, Tim's bass player, gave Tim a ride from the airport. "There didn't seem to be anything different about Tim's mood that day," he said, seemingly contradicting Joe. "Tim seemed real upbeat, you know? Everything was cool. He got a little drunk on the plane, two or three drinks, but that was normal after a tour. Everybody was having a good time."

Jeff said they and two of Jeff's women friends stopped in a bar, had "one drink," then dropped Tim off at Richard's house without any other stops.

According to Richard . . .

. . . He and his new friend Jackie were at the beach near Richard's house, enjoying a drink and the afternoon warmth. Nearby on the boardwalk, old Ted Hawkins, a well-known gray-haired black musician, strummed a guitar and sang.

Suddenly Richard sat up on his beach towel, squinting in the sunlight. A yellow Volkswagen had pulled up to his house. "Shit," he said, "somebody's trying to rip me off." He jumped up and ran toward the house, scotch in hand. Getting closer, he saw Buckley getting out of Jeff Eyrich's car. Tim waved. Richard waved back, relieved.

"What's happening?" Richard asked. "What are you doing here?"

"Can you take me home?"

Richard thought the request a little strange. Eyrich said goodbye and drove off.

"How come you didn't go home with Eyrich?"

"Just wanted to kill a little time with you. Give me lift home later?"

"Yeah. Like a drink?"

"Sure, man."

Richard helped Tim with his luggage. Opening the front door, he said, "I'll get us a drink, and we can go down to the beach and hear this old guy sing and play guitar. He's good."

"That's cool."

They set Tim's gear down inside.

"Can I have a little toot?" Tim asked.

"Okay. But we'll do that later. Let me fix a drink first."

Richard poured scotches for himself and Tim and Jackie. While Tim went to the john, Richard took Mexican heroin from his hidden stash and patted some out on top of a 4" x 3" rectangular piece of translucent plastic that contained a one-dollar bill inside, folded into pleats, like an accordion. Words inscribed on the plastic read, "The Shrinking Dollar." Richard set the plastic rectangle and heroin on his desk. Tim came out of the john.

Richard picked up two of the three glasses of scotch.

"There's a glass for you. Grab it, and let's go down to the beach."

"Maybe I could have a little toot?"

"My friend Jackie's waiting for us down at the beach. Let's go hear the old guy play. We'll come back and do some then."

Tim didn't respond with his usual cheer. He wasn't joking with Richard, and seemed sullen.

"Okay," Tim said, not smiling.

Richard described what happened next . . .

When we came back, Tim started getting real ugly with Jackie. First he said a couple of things insulting about women in general, then he started wrestling with her on the bed.

I said, "Look, man, the dope's over there. You can either snort it or not snort it, but I want to take you home. I want to be alone with Jackie. We haven't slept. We haven't eaten. And now's the time to give you a ride home."

Tim rolled up a dollar bill and snorted heroin off the "Shrinking Dollar" plastic rectangle. Within five minutes he started staggering.

He didn't fix it, didn't shoot it, and he had only about a dime, about—oh, if you put a cigarette ash out there, not very much, very little, so I couldn't see why he would start staggering so soon, unless he was just fucking around.

You remember how he'd take a bunch of reds and then he'd lay back and pretend to be almost asleep while other people would be talking, and then he'd come out and say something real clever? How he was there the whole time, just playing possum?

So I assumed he was fucking around like that, 'cause I've carried him home a lot of times over the years, and laid him down, just like that. He liked the attention, you know? Liked being waited on, even if it's carrying him around. So we took him home and put him to bed to sleep it off. . . .

According to Judy . . .

. . . Tim had a lot of positive energy at that time. He was straight and healthy. He was up for Hal Ashby's Woody Guthrie movie, *Bound for Glory*. A couple of record companies were talking to him about new contracts. His band was good.

That final weekend, Tim went to Texas to play some concerts. He had been worried about Richard, and every time he called home he told me to check on Richard to see how Richard was doing. He partied in the airplane on the way home Sunday, and stopped to check on Richard. Tim just didn't know how drunk he was.

I don't know why he did the heroin. Was it to test Richard? I really don't know. It didn't have anything to do with me. I had been behaving myself, and so had Tim, for quite a while. We weren't having any problems. We really weren't. . . .

Richard brought Tim back here Sunday and told me Tim was drunk but okay. He said it was just liquor—and you could really smell it. He also said Tim had taken some downers. Well, how many times had Timmy taken downers and drank all the time? So I put him to bed for a nap. Michelle [Judy's sister] and Maury Baker came over and picked up Taylor and took him to the movies. I went in and lay down next to Timmy and started to read.

After a while, I noticed he was cold and sweaty, and his face was gray-white, like paste. I got scared. He was still alive, and I was hitting him on the chest trying to get him to wake up, but he wouldn't even open his eyes. I screamed for the paramedic who lives next door and called Richard. "What did he have? What did he have? Get over here quick!"

Richard came and the paramedics came, and I had to make the decision for them to do shock treatments. They said that was the only thing they could do to keep him alive. But it totally destroyed his mind. If the treatments had worked, he would have been a complete vegetable. That's what the medics told me. I really had strange feelings. It was awful. He would have been conscious and alive, but he would have had to be waited on, and he couldn't have done anything for himself.

The apartment building at 2811 Third St. in Santa Monica, where Tim faded to black.

Richard was there, and at first he was denying that Tim had used anything at all. And then he said he might have had some downers. . . .

When Richard arrived he found Judy crying hysterically, her face lined with mascara and creases. As Richard recounted . . .

"We can say anything at all that will help Tim," he told Judy. "But there is no reason to tell them I was the one who gave him the dope. As far as his system is concerned, it doesn't matter who gave it to him. Stay in the living room with Jackie while I take a look."

As Richard described the scene in his writings, he rushed into the bedroom. Tim lay on the maroon satin quilt as if asleep, but he looked terrible. His face was pasty-white. He had turned blue around the mouth. Richard bent over and held Tim's nose, opened his mouth and gave him mouth-to-mouth resuscitation. Nothing. He couldn't be sure whether Tim was alive or dead. He ran into the bathroom, looking for a mirror.

When Judy saw Richard leave the room she bolted away from Jackie, jumped on the bed, straddled Tim and began beating him on his chest with her fists, screaming his name into his face, "Ti-i-mmm-e-e-y-y, Ti-i-mmm-e-e-ey! He's dead! Oh, God, he's really dead! *Ti-mmm-e-e-y!*"

Exhausted, she began sobbing, beating him with both fists at the same time, throwing the whole weight of her upper body against his, slowly, over and over again.

Richard grabbed Judy by her shoulders, pulled her off the bed, hustled her into the living room, roughly sat her down in a chair between the marble table and the ferns.

"Shut up, Wu!" he screamed at her, shaking her. "Just shut up. This is Richard! Everything is going to be okay. Timmy will be all right. He can't die from that little bit of shit. He's just passed out, and the fire department will be here any minute. Sit here. Stay out of the way."

He turned to Jackie, "Make sure she stays here, no matter what you have to do."

A neighbor paramedic heard the screaming and rushed over from next door. He and Richard pumped Tim's chest hard—up, down, up, down. . . .

Rescue squad paramedics burst into the bedroom, shoved Richard aside, quickly set up their equipment. Police arrived, looked in through the doorway. Richard, Judy, and Jackie stood near the bed, watching, waiting.

"Is he alive?" the paramedic asked.

"Can't tell," Richard said.

"What happened to him?"

"He took some dope somewhere."

"What kind?"

"He usually takes reds, barbiturates, but he could have had heroin,"

Richard responded ambiguously. "He sometimes takes downers, but I think he could have had heroin."

Judy didn't say anything. Richard repeated himself two more times, "He could have taken heroin. It might be heroin."

Everybody in the room watched and waited . . . Nobody spoke.

The paramedics administered an electric shock—*wham!* Another—*wham!*

No brain waves.

"Get him to the hospital."

On Sunday, June 29, 1975, at 9:42 p.m, Tim died at the hospital from "acute intoxication resulting from ingestion of alcohol and inhalation of heroin to the point of overdose, age twenty-eight."

Los Angeles County Medical Examiner Dr. Joseph H. Choi testified at Richard's preliminary examination in Santa Monica Court on September 18, 1975. According to Choi, there were no needle marks and no evidence of sustained heroin usage— Tim was not a junkie. The amount of heroin in itself was probably enough to kill Tim, alcohol aside. Heroin converts to morphine in the system; the blood morphine level was 0.02 milligrams, and the bile morphine level was 3.31 milligrams. These levels indicated that there was a total 1.5 milligrams of morphine in the body at the time of death. Because of the burn-off factor—some four hours between the inhalation and the death—the actual amount of pure heroin Tim snorted had to have been *more* than 1.5 milligrams in order for 1.5 to remain.

"This is the minimum," Dr. Choi told defense lawyer James Epstein. "More than this amount went into the body."

After it was established that Tim was not an addict, and that more than 1.5 milligrams of pure heroin had been inhaled, defense lawyer Epstein asked, "Are you saying that in your opinion a great majority of non-addicts [with 1.5 milligrams] in the blood die?" Choi replied, "Yes."

In other words, having snorted 1.5 milligrams or more, it was almost certain that Buckley had snorted enough to kill himself, even without the alcohol. With the alcohol—0.13 percent, well over the 0.08 percent that legally constitutes drunkenness in California—the combination proved devastating. It caused acute intoxication, which caused respiratory failure, which killed Tim.

There was no indication by Dr. Choi that the heroin was in any way contaminated, tainted, toxic, or "bad stuff," an important point, because some people had accused Richard of giving Tim tainted heroin.

Dr. Choi went on to state that, "[Tim] was in good physical condition. There was nothing wrong with his organs. . . . His body was healthy. Nothing was wrong with his heart and no heart attack was involved."

Lying there on the living room floor, fading fast, Tim knew he was sailing toward the far shore.

Richard bent down close. "Timmy? Are you all right?"

In a small, nearly inaudible voice that only Richard heard, Tim whispered, "Bye-bye, baby."

"I am sure I am the only one who heard it," Richard told me. "He definitely articulated it in a real little voice, a real little voice. As far as I know, that was the last thing he ever said. He said it right to me, like it was natural."

I know the depth of Tim's love for Judy. Those whispered words were not for Richard, but for her. She missed them.

When the *Down Beat* feature came out in June 1977, Judy missed again. If she had read it, she would have learned about Tim's heart-wrenching farewell to her. Later, when other writers picked up on those words that had been whispered "in a real little voice, a real little voice," she missed still again. Sneering at the writers and laughing at the "bye-bye, baby" utterance, she said to me on three occasions, "How could they possibly know his last words? They weren't even there." Three times I had to tell her, "They got it from the *Down Beat* feature, and I got it directly from Richard. Why don't you read the article?"

Poor Timmy. Alive, dying, or dead, was he ever seen? Was he ever heard? Was he ever truly known? What a shame.

CHAPTER 21

GIVING UP THE GHOST

In my *Down Beat* feature I bypassed the questions surrounding Tim's death, and instead celebrated his very real attributes: his talent, his intelligence, his amazing evolutionary ascension, his impressive accomplishments as a singer, songwriter, and recording artist. I remembered him as the gifted musician he was, and felt proud of having done so.

However, I continued to examine the issues over the course of several years, interviewing all the parties involved and delving into the complexities. My conclusions? There was no "conspiracy," and nobody forced Tim to snort the heroin. His action was his own responsibility, nobody else's. He had on dozens of occasions ingested heroin or downers on top of alcohol and then passed out, so on the fateful day there was no reason for Richard or Judy to think he had overdosed to the point of death. It seems to me that Richard got painted black and paid a mean price for Tim's action. In my opinion, he should never have been brought to trial, much less convicted and sentenced to four months in jail. He got a raw deal.

I moved in with Sonia Crespi almost immediately after Tim's funeral, and continued evolving toward sanity, sobriety, and equilibrium, developing myself as a music journalist, initially in soul and jazz.

In February 1977 I had finished writing the *Down Beat* story. Exhausted from the effort, I felt mentally and emotionally spent, wired but not tired. Worse, I needed a drink. It was after midnight. Sonia was asleep. Maybe take a nite-ride.

I wheeled out of the driveway, radio blaring rock 'n' roll, headed inland from Santa Monica to Hollywood. Neon lights, erotic red, soothing green, alluring blue. Coors, Bud, Miller. Rainbow Bar, Dew Drop Inn, Saints and Sinners. Gorgeous girls, lips full-red, long hair, t-shirts, belly buttons, breasts eager to be squeezed, hot pants, naked legs, willing, ready. Pretty boys with cut-off jeans, tumescent cocks, thumbs out hitch-hiking. Wailing music, bar lights spinning, Hollywood wired, electrified, poised in the night for the kill.

I drove up the Boulevard, letting my eyes drink in sights and sounds that used to titillate me. But none of it felt right that night. I punched the radio off. "Get out of this stupid phantasy," I told myself. "Go home."

I turned around, drove down Olympic Boulevard, over to Broadway, bypassed my Harvard Street apartment where I had been living with Sonia for two years, kept on driving to Venice, our old stomping grounds, passing Big Pink, where Jennifer and I had lived, where Tim and the rest of us partied so long ago. . . . Distant, almost inaudible laughter and faraway music echoed in my ears.

I drove slowly down to the beach and parked near the old Pacific Ocean Park site, got out, stood for a moment on the empty boardwalk. It had been almost two years since Tim's death, and several years since they had destroyed POP. Only rubbish remained—huge piling posts knocked over, shattered concrete blocks, jagged boards, nails, rubble, glass, rust, decay.

Gone, forever gone. Listening to the wind, I heard Janis singing inside the Cheetah dance hall, heard Tim and me and Carter playing there and saw hundreds of innocent hippie boys and long-haired rosy-cheeked girls dancing happily to the music in the flower of their youth. I heard POP's roller coaster clacking its wheels, voices squealing in delight. Breathing deeply, I smelled cotton candy, popcorn, soda pop, fish sticks, hot dogs. I saw the carousel, Ferris wheel, bumper cars, darts and balloons, people pitching pennies, little kids with mommas, dads . . . laughter . . . music. . . .

There in the night, I stood in solitude on the boardwalk. Ocean waves tumbled quietly down by the shoreline. Whispering winds skittered across the sands. Darkness glowed in shadows and moonlight. . . .

A rumpled newspaper blew out across the beach. A new volleyball net at the boardwalk's edge fluttered in the breeze. How could they put up a net, instead of a shrine to Tim?

Time whooshed back to '68 and '69. Lovely blond-haired Manda appeared, walking along the shoreline, barefoot in moonlight, her long white cotton dress wafting in the wind. In afternoons remembered in this night's moonlight, Tim and Michael and I threw footballs over there, running in sand beside the pier. Jennifer and Jainie, Michael, Larry, Manda, and Tim and I spread red and yellow and blue towels down by the shoreline and lay side by side. These shimmering moonlit waves were the very same waves we rode in glittering summer sunlight.

Where was the shrine? How could they not erect a great pile of stones with a bronze plaque in Tim's honor? How could they not stop time itself?

Slowly stepping off the boardwalk, gradually leaving the street lamps' circles of dim yellow light, walking toward the ocean, I could see the waves, creamy white, quietly tumbling in moonlight. Eternal music, these waves. They sang to Odysseus. They sang to Tim. They sang to me.

A gentle breeze caressed cheeks and arms. I felt slightly uncomfortable, but didn't mind. I had walked here many times in a T-shirt. No cooler tonight than other nights.

Another breeze rustled my hair. A brooding chill rose up slowly from deep inside my gut, spreading in concentric circles. I shivered, kept walking. The chill intensified. I clutched my sides. Teeth started chattering.

What's wrong?

Now teeth clattered hard.

Better turn back.

I wrapped my arms around my torso and headed for the car. The chill worsened. I walked faster. Teeth banged together, out of control. I ran. My whole body shook uncontrollably. Terrified, I hurled myself into the front seat.

Stop, stop, I told myself. I sat up, clutched the wheel. My scalp crawled. Bones shook. Body quaked. I clenched my teeth as hard as I could to stop their clattering.

Am I dying? A heart attack? What's happening?

Suddenly, without my willing it, a howl ascended from the bottom of my soul up and out into air—"*Ahhhhhh!*" I screamed as loud as I could. Screamed again, again, again—"*Eeeeyeowwwahhhhhh!*"

And I cried. Tears I could not shed for Tim two years ago ran down my cheeks in rivers. Shivering, teeth rattling, clutching the steering wheel, I let it out, crying without resistance, crying all my heartache, all my love and loss, crying and crying until the tears stopped flowing.

Slowly, the shivering subsided. I sat in the car, muscles limp, mind exhausted, emotions drained.

It was as if *Timmy had come out of me.* The moment the terror and shivering stopped, I understood what people meant by "giving up the ghost."

Not mine. Tim's.

"I don't belong in Venice anymore," I said aloud, wiping tears off my face. "Tim's gone. That whole life is gone." I turned the key, started the motor, revved the engine. "So am I."

I drove home to Santa Monica without drinking, and made slow, sweet love with Sonia.

CHAPTER 22

TIMEWINDS

Was it all a dream?

Sometimes it seems like it.

The whirl and swirl of years gone by, flashing images . . . Tim's bright smile, flicker-quick moments onstage, winter highways, a beautiful girl, a whisper, a nod, a kiss, concert halls, laughter, misty breath on New York streets, music's pounding pulse, California's sunlight beachglare, ocean waves, exquisite passion, lost love spiraling down into the maw. . . . In one of my poems—

> Time's an abyss
> I fill with roses
> Sprung from blood,
> Cast into the void
> With memory's aching smile

If we set each album picture in a row, it's easy to see a passage from innocence, to whimsical youth, to introspection, into a kind of hard, cynical bitterness. In fact, John Balkin suggested Tim's story was an American tragedy, a disastrous conclusion to an ennobling problem that many artists face in every era.

The artist needs a sense of self, a strong ego, a feeling of identity. He or she needs to be able to create in freedom, drawing energy from autonomous inner resources and from appreciative audiences too. If the artist's need for self-expression exceeds commercial parameters, the symbiotic pact between art and business dissolves, and a struggle ensues. Balkin called it "the battle with the sentinel toll collectors at the gateways to fame and fortune. Elsinore revisited."

Sometimes the artist wins. Picasso did. Miles did. Sometimes the artist crashes and burns. Maybe that's what happened to Tim.

But I think the truth is greater than those final album covers. I don't think his life was a tragedy. Whatever its sadness at the end, I think it was a certain kind of triumph.

The final chapter in Tim's life happened to be laced with difficulties, but almost everybody experiences difficulties—and they conquer them. Could he have reinvented himself? Maybe. Maybe not. He died before that question was resolved. I like to think he would have survived the slump, come back strong, and flourished again. Even as he mastered each kind of music he developed, so he would master the comeback. He had already come back after *Starsailor*. Like a Miles Davis or a Muhammad Ali, he would come back again. All he needed was a new direction, which he was seeking even as the flame flickered and died.

Tim did not live safely. That was his glory. He lived honestly. Even his lies were honest. They weren't always factual, but they had truth in them. They sparkled with humor and insight. Like metaphors, they illustrated something of value every time. At the very least they inspired laughter, and in many ways laughter and its pleasures was one of Tim's greatest legacies.

The whole of his life was bright with vitality, creativity, generosity, humor. He didn't live to snatch things from life. In fact, he died more than $100,000 in debt, owning only his Rickenbacker guitar and a Fender Twin Reverb amp. For all of his undeniable selfishness and self-centeredness, he gave us everything he had. His songs were not artificially concocted decorations. They were gems mined from the essence of his life experience. He was a human being, yes, but he served music, and in so doing he transcended character flaws. He disappeared into music, and music became his glory.

Ultimately, his life was so intense, so real and artistically true, that it soared far beyond mere personal considerations. In this sense, there was no Tim Buckley. For him, only the music existed, and only the music remains. He knew the music was more important than he was, and so he journeyed through idiosyncratic individuality into the universality of the human heart. That is what we celebrate to this day—not only Tim the individual, but the music flowing through him and the many ways in which he devoted his life in selfless service to it.

Like every artist of stature, he gave us insight. Our span is but a fleeting moment. Death is arbitrary and absolutely democratic. Young or old, the *quantity* of time doesn't matter. Life—and death—are now. Only quality matters. Let us live our brief flash of consciousness in a state of love, rapture, heartache, joy. Let us live with passion, courage, enthusiasm. He did. He was constantly questioning the givens, pushing boundaries back, soaring beyond limitations. That took courage. He led the way. We can learn from him.

It is as if he were saying, Let us not fear love, although we know we can lose it. Let us dare to love even fear, for life's exhilaration pulses and throbs on the brink of the abyss. Let us not hide within the secure folds of the known, but sail into the unknown. As a universal positive, life is where the challenge is—where the past ends and the creative Now begins. Let us transform the shining mystery of our lives into art.

He did. So can we.

Perhaps above all, Tim showed us how to explore ourselves and the world around us in terms of the beautiful. Whether that beauty be uplifting or depressing, violent or tender, corrupt or innocent, we can embrace it. Life sings its blue melody through each of us. Flatland gray is a safe place, but it's as dead as last week's weather report. Let us celebrate evolutionary exploration. Let us forever be Starsailors, winging into eternal light. With all our pain and glory, let us lead lives not of quiet desperation, but of strength, creativity, purpose. Even when we're down, let the song raise us up.

As for Tim's death, the "sentinel toll collectors" did not get him. He tripped up on his own.

Part of his divided self was on the rise again, back up from despair, from substance abuse, from depression as a way of life. Nevertheless, even as he ascended, making plans, putting ideas in motion, creating opportunities, the discipline sometimes proved difficult. He found a workable compromise—straight for rehearsals, gigs, tours, as confirmed by Falsia, Helm, Balkin, and myself. Afterwards, oblivion. But that final time, he partied too hard on his clean system. He visited Richard's house a little too drunk, snorted heroin—strong stuff, it was—and the combination proved catastrophic. Bye-bye Starsailor.

From a certain perspective, an accident, a horrible mistake.

From a different perspective, a stupid, heartbreaking waste.

From another perspective, the "sentinel toll collectors" *did* get him. He just could-n't take it anymore. Time to give up the struggle. Enough, *no mas*, fuck it. Gone.

I often wondered why I was spared the same demise Tim Buckley suffered. Looking back from today's vantage point, I suspect it was because certain work still remained to be done by me in service to music and musicians in general and to Tim in particular, not the least being the writing of this book.

It is true, he was not a perfect person. He made mistakes, even as we all do, often shredding other people's ego without mercy, especially if they combined ignorance and stupidity with arrogance. The path he trod is strewn with people who curse him as an intolerably self-centered smart-ass. He was not always a nice guy, not by any means.

Nevertheless, through his music and wit and precocious wisdom, through the sheer magnitude of his talent, charm, warmth, generosity, and sparkling humor, he left this mad world a far better place than he found it. He gave us music, laughter, beauty, and love in abundance. None of us will be the same. In pain and joy, our lives are richer, deeper, and better for having been touched by his flame.

Although Tim is gone, he sings in the timewinds to this very day. We hear his golden voice, and hold his pain and joy in our hearts forever. Where the smiles are, where sorrow is, where hope abides, we see Tim onstage, eyes closed, dreamweaving melodies that will forever accompany us into the shifting tides and timelines of our lives.

There were seawaves then, my friend,
Moonlight glittering among
Spikey shadowed palm leaves
Spread like veils 'cross
Luminescent Venice summer beaches,
Sea-salt in balmy night air,
Midnight ocean waters
Brushing close,
Whispering our youth to us,
Gentle kisses lapping sand-swaths,
Cream-foam licking shoreline edges—

Time passed inside an hourglass,
Stared up at stars,
And laughed.

Now, again—
After more than 30 years,

Finally recognized, appreciated, celebrated,
Given your proper respect—
You speak to me from far across these waters,
Your voice alluring, entrancing, seductive,
Your gentle windsong
Whisper-intimate,
Brimming with tears,
With yearning's aching arc,
Compassion's understanding,
Jingling silver in moonlight,
Bitterly sweet in
Empathy, hope, heartbreak,
Happy/sad again,
And here you are,
Calling from afar—
And I hear you.

How the music
In our life and love
Made all the difference.
We were exactly
What we needed
At the time.
Few have known
A melody like ours,
And, yes,
I hear you calling.

Soon enough,
I softly cry,
Soon enough
I will join you, yes,
When the hourglass tilts,
And laughs again.

CODA

JEFF BUCKLEY

When I answered the knock and opened the door in late 1989, Jeff Buckley stood leaning against the porch wall, jacket draped over one shoulder, hand in pocket, knee slightly bent, intentionally striking precisely the same pose as Tim had on the first album cover. He looked almost exactly like Tim too, astonishingly so—a full head of hair, high cheekbones, full lips, bushy eyebrows, dark brown eyes, the same charming smile.

He said he was soon leaving L.A. for New York, and was talking to Tim's friends about his father before his departure. He had already spoken with Dan Gordon, Judy, Daniella. Could he talk with me too? We sat in the living room.

"You ask, I'll answer," I said.

He leaned forward, his voice a hiss: "How did he die?"

"Ha!—You go right for the jugular, don't you!"

We started with the death, moved into the albums, traveled through the various creative stages. For two hours, I painted the most honest portrait of Tim that I could—his love of music, his dedication to it, his honesty, wit, intelligence, creative evolution.

When I mentioned that Tim loved him, Jeff spat out, "He did not!"

"Have you listened to the song, 'Dream Letter'?"

"Yes. Other than that, what did he say?"

"Well, 'Dream Letter' says a lot. To me personally, he expressed his love for you, and the guilt he felt at not being able to take you into his life. He told me he fully intended to talk with you when you got older. He hoped to make things up. His departure before your birth had nothing to do with you. He said he didn't know Mary was pregnant when he left. That's no small thing, man. When he split for New York, he did not know Mary was pregnant. Even if he did, he did *not* leave *you*—he left your mother. Besides, given the choice—her and you, or fulfilling his calling as a musician—would you have had him give up music and keep working at the Taco Bell? Is that what *you* would have done in the same circumstance?"

Jeff returned two days later. This time, he had slashed half his hair off, leaving one side bald, the other side with a Mohawk on top, long hair on the sides. It was as if he had intentionally decimated his beauty and was defiantly and belligerently presenting himself as an ugly stupid two-bit sleazy grunge-rock street-rat. I ignored his appearance, and we talked another two hours.

Except for that "He did not!" in our first visit, Jeff did not indicate the profound and deep-seated antipathy he felt toward Tim. In this way, he was dishonest. From my side, I regret the fact that we talked only of Tim, not of Jeff. Looking back, I can see how Jeff gave subtle indications of his rage. But at the time, I missed them. I had no idea Jeff felt so hostile toward Tim, no idea of the extent of his inwardly searing love/hate conflicts. I thought he would welcome hearing the truth about his father. Otherwise, why did he contact me? If I had asked questions, opened Jeff up, become aware of his anger, I might have framed some of my answers differently, perhaps helping him come to terms with his own animosity and with Tim.

From Tim he got his voice, his looks, his intelligence, his exceptional musical talent. Mary obviously contributed talent too, for she was also a musician. But the distinctive and characteristic cast of Jeff's handsome features, the particular tone and range of his voice, the oblique slant of his sparkling intellect, and the idiosyncratic Buckley viewpoint—its brilliant insight and verbally poetic expressiveness—seemed to descend from his warrior grandfather, down through Tim, directly to him. Physically, intellectually and musically, Jeff was a Buckley to the core. If you looked, you saw it. If you listened, you heard it. The resemblance was uncanny, unequivocal, indubitable.

In New York, Jeff sang and played guitar in the East Village, landed a recording contract with Columbia, recorded a four-song Extended Play CD, *Live at Sin-è*, followed by a full-length CD, *Grace*, and became a hit around the world.

Instead of embracing and celebrating his heritage, however, and giving credit where it was due, Jeff fiercely turned his back on Tim. "Genetics be damned," he told writer Robert Hilburn. "I have completely different musical choices."

Even as he denied the biological influence, so he denied the artistic influence. He said in print numerous times that he had not listened to Tim's music, and yet at the St. Ann's Church commemoration of Tim in Brooklyn, April 26, 1991, he sang four of Tim's songs—"I Never Asked to Be Your Mountain," "Sefronia—The King's Chain," "Phantasmagoria in Two," and "Once I Was."

He added some of his own extraordinary lyrics to "I Never Asked to Be Your Mountain," lyrics which eerily foreshadowed his own death—

> *My love is the flower that lies among the graves,*
> *My love is the thousand souls that each saves,*
> *And all the insane madmen tell me I am not a smoky haze.*
> *Lay me not in lands of men to spread my ash along the way,*
> *I want to feel the tide pull through me, like a woman drunk in sin,*
> *I want to feel the fish swim through me. Let the water take my skin*
> *Wrapped around the pebble that you choose to warm your hand*
> *Just as I dream every day, as I pray you'll understand.*

In his own recordings, it was patently apparent to me that he had listened carefully to Tim's every album, had wisely chosen Tim as his foremost mentor, had learned dozens of vocal inflections, phrasings, and "gymnastic" techniques from Tim, and had masterfully incorporated his knowledge and experience of Tim's music into his own unique, powerful, and exceptionally heart-touching creations.

[According to biographer David Browne, Jeff indicated that he was especially moved by *Lorca* and *Starsailor*, writing in his journals, "Check out the electric piano on 'Lorca.' Hah!! The vocal—haa! . . . That work Tim did was it. That was *it*. In my memory of my father, when I die, you can all remember my admiration of that period. They hit it. They certainly hit something that no one can touch.... *Starsailor* wasn't a failure. It was an untouchable beauty. . . ."]

More than any other artist before Jeff or since, Jeff was directly influenced by Tim and his music, perhaps particularly *Starsailor*—and there was absolutely nothing wrong in that. He was the only singer I have ever heard who was vocally or temperamentally even *capable* of being influenced to that degree. Like his father, he blended knowledge, influences, and vocal talent with brilliant originality, and out of that synthesis created extraordinary music of his own—unique, impassioned, enchanting, potent, communicative. He was a beautiful musician and a beautiful young man.

Much to my dismay, however, he criticized Tim's singing in numerous interviews, denigrated his albums, ridiculed him as a man and artist, and malevolently identified him exclusively with drug use instead of music.

He told writer Matt Diehl he had spoken with me and other friends of Tim's: "I talked with all the cast of characters, and then I was done with it. It revealed a lot of ugliness that I can't talk about." Well, it also revealed a lot of beauty, love, passion, creativity, joy, and humor. Clearly, Jeff was not ready to hear that. [In his journal, according to Browne, Jeff contemptuously minimized my offerings, as he did Dan Gordon's; characterized the whole of my contribution as "the mantra"; and said he wasn't interested in being a "disciple" to his own father.] Obviously, poor Jeff could not handle the potent realities he was being given. Instead of incorporating them into his thinking and expanding and deepening his own view of Tim, he rejected them outright. Evidently, everything Gordon and I said to him was wasted.

In public, Jeff wasn't just putting down his father, which was sad enough. He was also putting down my best friend, which was upsetting and offensive to me personally.

If he had given credit to Tim's music, it could and would have been called an influence. He would have been carrying on a family tradition. He would have psychologically brought Tim and himself together harmoniously within his own heart and mind. But unlike Natalie Cole, Hank Williams Jr., or other sons and daughters of stars who have made it through this dark and difficult passage, Jeff had not resolved his crippling conflicts. Because he could not give proper credit to Tim, he exacerbated the melancholic, self-destructive wars within his own psyche. The question was not of origins and influences. Of *course* he was influenced genetically and musically. The question was of acknowledgment and respect and self-acceptance. The battle was not with Tim. It was with himself.

Certainly Jeff's pain was understandable. Deep psychological wounds seemed to pass from one generation to the next. Tim's father suffered—I don't know exactly why, but indications suggest a serious father problem. Tim suffered because his tormented father was physically present as a critical adversary but absent as a loving mentor. Jeff suffered from the horrific void his father's almost total absence left. All three—lost souls living and brooding in a gothic hell.

In several interviews, Jeff indicated how angry he was at not being invited to Tim's funeral. He had not been able to say goodbye, and he and his mother had been snubbed. His anger was justified, but he made it sound as if it were Tim's fault, not Judy's. How could he be angry at Tim for not being invited to the funeral? Obviously irrational, although consistent with his pain.

When writer Mark Kemp asked me about Jeff, I observed how Jeff's rage was preventing him from fulfilling his gifts. Like Tim before him, he writhed in discord, yearning for his father, denying his father, trying to please *and* defeat the very man he loved and needed most. Unfortunately, Kemp included in his *Option* magazine article virtually *none* of the compassion and understanding I felt for Jeff and indicated to Kemp. That made Jeff and me both look bad.

There are other factors involved as well. Jeff knew he had a great voice, but he also knew he did not have the strength or range that Tim had. He found it immensely difficult to write songs. At the beginning, it was almost impossible to face a microphone. At the end, it still seemed enormously difficult to write and record. Competition with his father had stifled his creative output from the beginning. Even when Columbia gave him three years and almost unlimited moral and financial support, Jeff found it virtually impossible to squeeze out a coherent tune (as Browne documented throughout his book). At the end, Jeff was more obsessed with his father than ever, and still couldn't produce under pressure, although he was making herculean efforts to do so, and, according to one Columbia executive, he seemed to have made a significant conceptual breakthrough (as was later demonstrated on Jeff's self-recorded four-track demo tape tagged on to the posthumous release of *Sketches for My Sweetheart, the Drunk*).

Jeff fought with his record company because he could not formulate a coherent artistic direction and commit himself to it without psychologically sabotaging himself. He fought because he had no musical vision and could not transcend his pain-riddled fears of creative and popular success. Sometimes Tim fought with record companies, too, but not because he could not write or meet deadlines or keep appointments or handle recording sessions confidently and professionally. He fought because he was an innovator and dedicated musical visionary who courageously struggled to realize and fulfill that vision, even when nobody wanted to buy it.

Fears of success tormented both young men, as did self-destructive behavior. This is often noted when it comes to Tim, but rarely pointed out when it comes to Jeff. Tim did it primarily through substance abuse, while Jeff did it primarily through creative inhibition and an inability to commit himself to a musical vision or to follow through on agreements.

Tim did not let his behavior get in the way of creativity, while Jeff couldn't manage a second full-length album. By the time Jeff died, he had completed one Extended Play CD and one full-length CD. He and the record company had been dissatisfied with a third effort (*Sketches*), and scratched it. Jeff was preparing to record a new CD when he died at age thirty. It is not from cynicism, but from the heart of compassion, that I wonder if his death was not an unconscious escape from impending rehearsals and recording sessions, and an enormous release and relief from a deep-seated sense of inadequacy and its resultant fears. By way of contrast, Tim died at age twenty-eight having completed and released nine albums. It is not quite fair to characterize Tim as "self-destructive" and Jeff as merely "loveably loopy" [in Browne's words]. Jeff's problems were every bit as profound and debilitating as Tim's, albeit manifested in somewhat different ways.

Although Jeff was not as prolific as Tim, he was enormously successful. Tens of thousands of people around the world loved him and his music, and critics rightfully celebrated him as a master vocalist. Along the way, he won the French award, Grand Prix du Disque (past recipients include Leonard Cohen, Bruce Springsteen,

Edith Piaf). *Mojo* magazine named *Grace* the best album of 1994. *Rolling Stone* gave him the 1994 Best New Male Singer award. He did well, and his father and father before him undoubtedly would have felt proud of him.

One of his close friends, Penny Arcade, told me Jeff had been seeing a therapist for four years before his death and making progress. I do not know if that is true, and I have not seen it indicated by other writers. But perhaps he *had* been seeing a therapist. I hope so. It is not easy to recognize the need for change, but if he did, his wisdom and courage are to be commended.

With or without the help of a therapist, near the end he commented on how his anger was not so much with his father as it was with the intrusive press, how he had come to understand more clearly what Tim had to do as an eighteen-year-old young man, and that Tim would have tried to make things up to him had he lived. These and other remarks in print indicated that he was coping with his conflicts. In the years to come, almost surely he would have been able to liberate his talent and flower into an even greater presence on the international music scene. He was a beautiful poet and musician, an extraordinary young man full of promise. I personally have been moved to the depths and heights of my being by his music, and miss him with almost the same burning intensity that I miss Tim.

[Except where specifically indicated, the observations and comments in this chapter were written well before the publication of David Browne's *Dream Brother.*]

Jeff was fond of wearing eight-inch high-top, lace-up, thick-soled Doc Martens work shoes that looked like the black combat paratrooper boots his father and grandfather wore. On May 29, 1997, the night of his death in Memphis, just before the first rehearsal for the new recording, Jeff whimsically went swimming in the Mississippi River wearing all of his clothes, including a pair of black combat boots. Swirling waters dragged him under. Authorities did not find him until he floated to the surface six days later. The coroner said no drugs or alcohol were involved.

Father, son, grandson—all three Buckleys struggled, and shared everything they were capable of. In spite of the fact that self-destruction plagued each of them, all three left extensions of themselves that reverberate down to this very day. Their greatest conflicts and barriers were psychological. Their greatest positive energy was creativity. Their greatest strength was the will to keep on trying in the face of overpowering odds. Like Dylan Thomas, they "sang in their chains like the sea," gave us all they could, and made our world a stronger, more beautiful and compassionate place than it was before their arrival.

The Buckley story is ultimately a tremendously uplifting story, glorious in its artistic beauty, radiant in its tragic sadness. Father, son, and grandson—the Buckleys graced our earth, and we are the better for it. Bless them, every one.

We disappear in rain, but forever remain in light.

Bye-bye, baby. You made it all worthwhile.

DISCOGRAPHY

I—STUDIO ALBUMS

1) *Tim Buckley* (LP, mono)—Elektra Records. Released: October 1966.
2) *Tim Buckley* (LP, stereo)—Elektra Records. Released: October 1966.
3) *Goodbye and Hello* (LP, mono)—Elektra Records. Released: September 7, 1967.
4) *Goodbye and Hello* (LP, stereo)—Elektra Records. Released: September 7, 1967.
5) *Happy Sad*—Elektra Records. Released: March 7, 1969.
6) *Blue Afternoon*—Straight Records. Released: January 1970.
7) *Lorca*—Elektra Records. Released: February 1970.
8) *Starsailor*—Straight Records. Released: November 1970.
9) *Greetings From L.A.*—Straight Records. Released: October 1972.
10) *Sefronia*—Warner/DiscReet. Released: May 1973.
11) *Look at the Fool*—Warner/DiscReet. Released: November 1974.

II—POSTHUMOUS RELEASES

1) *The Late Great Tim Buckley*—WEA. Released: 1978.
2) *The Best of Tim Buckley*—Rhino. Released: 1983.
3) *Dream Letter: Live in London 1968*—Demon. Released: 1990.
4) *The Peel Sessions: Tim Buckley (1968)*—Strange Fruit/Dutch East India Records. Released: 1990.
5) *The Peel Sessions* (LP)—Strange Fruit. Released: 1991.
6) *Morning Glory*—Band of of Joy Music. Released: 1994 (1968 *Peel Sessions*, plus "Dolphins" and "Honey Man," from 1974 *Old Grey Whistle Test* show.)
7) *Once I Was*—Strange Fruit. Released: 2000 (1968 *Peel Sessions* and 1974 *Old Grey Whistle Test* sessions, plus "I Don't Need It to Rain," recorded in Copenhagen, October 12, 1968).
8) *Live at the Troubadour 1969*—Bizarre/Straight Records. Released: 1994.
9) *Honeyman*—Manifesto Records. Released: 1995 (recorded live, 1973, on radio station WLIR, Long Island).
10) *Works in Progress*—Rhino. Released: September 1999.
11) *The Copenhagen Tapes*—generic import. Released: 2000.
12) *Morning Glory: The Tim Buckley Anthology*—Elektra/Rhino. Released: 2001.
13) *The Dream Belongs to Me*—Manifesto. Released: 2001 (rare and unreleased recordings, 1968–73).

III—SINGLES

"Wings"/"Grief In My Soul" (7") Elektra (US) (1966)
"Aren't You The Girl"/"Strange Street Affair Under Blue" (7") Elektra (UK) (January 1967)
"Once Upon A Time"/"Lady Give Me Your Heart" (7") Elektra (US) (1967)

"Morning Glory"/"Once I Was" (7") Elektra (US) (1967)
"Morning Glory"/"Knight Errant" (7") Elektra (UK) (November 1967)
"Once I Was"/"Phantasmagoria In Two" (7") Elektra (UK) (January 1968)
"Wings"/"I Can't See You" (7") Elektra (UK) (March 1968)
"Pleasant Street"/"Carnival Song" (7") Elektra (US) (October 1968)
"Happy Time"/"So Lonely" (7") Straight (UK) (February 1970)
"Morning Glory"/"Once I Was" (7") Elektra (UK) (September 1976)

IV—UNOFFICIAL RELEASES

Happy Mad—(*Top Gear*/Denmark '68)—no label. UK, 1983.
Blue Obsession—*Live at the Starwood 1975*—no label. UK, 1983. (*Blue Obsession* was/is also available as a unauthorized CD.)
Return of the Starsailor—(live at Knebworth, 1974, and Detroit, 1975).
Live at the Santa Monica Civic Auditorium—December 13, 1969.
Starsailor Band, circa 1970.

V—CDS

Most of the above albums (except *The Best of Tim Buckley*, *Starsailor*, and *Blue Afternoon*) are currently available on CD in the UK or USA. *Live at the Troubadour* and *Honeyman* are available only in CD format.

VI—TELEVISION

PBS Boboquivari #107 (seventh program of a nine-part pop-rock concert series), aired September 15, 1971, 8:30 P.M.

Note: We have made every effort to acquire accurate information for our Discography. However, due to the inconsistency of various sources, there may be inaccuracies in the month and day dates.

SOURCES

Ahrens, Susan. "Tim Buckley: His Songs Are Sexier the Second Time Around." *Good Times* (December 4–17, 1974).

———. "Tim Buckley: Max's Kansas City." *Good Times* (December 19–25, 1973).

Andy (last name not given—possibly McKay). *Zig Zag* #48, Vol. 5.

Arkow, Phil. "Tim Buckley: White Soul." *The Daily Pennsylvanian* (October 25, 1967).

Aston, Martin. "The Million-Dollar Bootleg." *Mojo* (1994/95).

author uncredited. "Greetings From L.A.—Tim Buckley." *Watford Observer* (March 4, 1975).

author uncredited. "Scene U.S.A." *Melody Maker* (October 20, 1973).

Aysha (Dianne Quinn). Telephone notes, February 2000 and letter to author, June 14, 2000, used by permission.

Balkin, John. Taped interviews with the author, March 1977 and June 12, 1997.

Bangs, Lester. "Starsailor—Tim Buckley." *Creem* (December 1970).

Barla, Marco. "Tim Buckley: Naked Guts." *Circular* (September 24, 1973).

Beckett, Larry. Letters to the author, May 4, 1977 and June 28, 1977, used by permission.

Bell, Max. "Tim Buckley: Greetings From L.A." *New Musical Express* (January 3, 1975).

Billany, Fred. "Tim Sings." *Lancashire Evening Telegraph* (April 20, 1968).

Bodnar, Jack, "Buckley's Singing Stands Alone." *Michigan State News*, East Lansing (October 12, 1973).

Bodoin, Suzanne. Tim Buckley Archives. http://timbuckley.net.

Boudreau, Gerry. "Tim Buckley: Friday." *URI Beacon* (February 18, 1970).

Bourne, Michael. "Tim Buckley: *Lorca* & *Starsailor*." *Down Beat* (March 4, 1971).

Bradley, Sam. All Bradley quotes are from Bradley's unpublished taped interview with Tim Buckley, 1973, used by permission.

Brolly, Jack. www.geocities.com/jzero2149/TimBuckleyandFriendsindex.html, Interviews online with Lee Underwood, Larry Beckett, Mary Guibert, Jerry Yester, others.

———. Room 109 Pleasant St., Phase III (with links). http://jzero2149.tripod.com/room109pleasantstreetphase3/id3.html.

———. Tim Buckley and Friends . . . The Room 109 Interviews. http://timbuckleyandfriends.com.

———. Tim Buckley, Room 109 Pleasant Street . . . Sights and Sounds. http://timbuckleyroom109.homestead.com/Homepage

———. Room 109, Pleasant Street . . . The Tim Buckley Discussion Forum. http://forums.delphiforums.com/purestcandle/start

Brown, James. "Ex-Zombie Blunstone No Longer Whispering." *Los Angeles Times* (April 26, 1973).

Brown, Stephen. "Tim Buckley's Blue Afternoon." *Georgia Straight* (May 6-13, 1970).

Browne, David. *Dream Brother: The Lives and Music of Jeff and Tim Buckley.* Harper Entertainment, 2001. (Except where specifically indicated in the text, all of *Blue Melody* was written prior to *Dream Brother*'s release in 2001.)

Buckley, Elaine. Taped interview with the author, June 11, 1977.

Buckley, Kathleen "Katy." Taped interview with the author, June 17, 1977; notes of subsequent conversations.

Buckley-Llewellyn, Judy. Taped interview with the author, April 14, 1977; notes of subsequent conversations; recollections.

Buckley, Tim. "Even If You Can't Play Him On The Guitar." *The New York Times* (November 22, 1970).

Buckley, Timothy Charles Jr. "The Father Song" letter, read aloud by Katy Buckley and taped by the author September 18, 1978, used by permission.

———. "Of Time and the City," mailed to the author by Tim Buckley, September 13, 1974.

Burke, Casey. "Tim Buckley, We Love You." *Georgia Straight* (January 13, 1971).

Burr, Debbie. "Blue Afternoon, Tim Buckley." Publication uncited.

Cage, C.T. "Blue Afternoon." *The Image* Vol. 1, No. 16 (December 26, 1969).

Campbell, Bob. Taped interview with the author, June 1977.

Campbell, Scott. "Free's big liberation." *The Arizona Republic* (August 30, 1970).

Charlesworth, Chris. "Los Angeles Report." *Melody Maker* (October 20, 1973).

Copeland (first name, publication and date not on copy). Circa 1971/72.

Coppage, N. "Tim Buckley: *Lorca.*" *Stereo Review* (September 1970).

———. "Superthroat Sings Again." *Stereo Review* (December, 1972).

CR, see Richard, Cool.

Cuscuna, Michael. "Buckley's Yodeling Baffles Audience." *Rolling Stone* (April 2, 1970).

Davis, Michael. All Davis quotes are from Michael's taped interview with Tim Buckley, April 1975, used by permission. Davis published parts of this interview in the *Los Angeles Free Press* (May 9–15, 1975) and in *Goldmine* (May 10, 1985).

Diehl, Matt. "The Son Also Rises." Interview with Jeff Buckley, *Rolling Stone* (October 20, 1994).

Drake, Nadine Beth. "Tim Buckley: Poet of Dreams." 1968, publication uncited on copy. Without giving credit, Drake apparently drew her material from "Tim Buckley: A 1943 Individualist," by Bob Garcia, *Open City,* 1967. I used Drake's words instead of Garcia's, because Drake did some rephrasing that made Buckley's comments more cogent.

Dula, Louie. Personal letter to the author, April 29, 1989, used by permission.

Eberle, Paul. "Tim Buckley Raps." *Jazz & Pop* (March 1969).

Edmonds, Ben. "Dreamy, Driven and Dangerous." *Mojo* (June 2000).

Elwood, Philip. "Stupendous Show by Tim Buckley." *S.F. Examiner* (March 2, 1973).

Erlich, Nancy. "Tim Buckley Racks Up Fans With an Impressive Range." *The New York Post* (November 15, 1969).

Eyrich, Jeff. Taped interview with the author, June 21, 1977.

Falsia, Joe. Taped interview with the author, April 12, 1977; notes of conversations; recollections.

Ferguson, Jayne. "Single Artist Displays Versatile Singing Style." *Richardson Daily News* (July 20, 1969).

Garcia, Bob. "Tim Buckley's Acid Test." *Open City* (October 18–24, 1967).

———. "Tim Buckley: a 1943 Individualist." *Open City* (1967).

Gearhart, Tom. "Buckley Croons Love Tune for Marlene Dietrich." *The Blade,* Toledo, Ohio (April 4, 1970).

Georgia Straight, The (May 6–13, 1970).

Goff, John. "Bitter End West." *Hollywood Reporter* (December 22, 1970).

Gordon, Dan. Letter to the author, October, 1975, used by permission.

Guibert, Mary. Online interview with Bob Niemi, hosted by Jack Brolly, May, 1999.

Heckman, Don. "Buckley at His Best." *The New York Times* (January 25, 1970).

Henderson, Bill. "Tim Buckley Talk-In." *Sounds* (August 3, 1974).

Hentoff, Nat. "Tim Buckley: *Goodbye and Hello*." *Stereo Review* (1968).

Hilburn, Robert. "Tim Buckley Headlines Troubadour's Twin Bill." *Los Angeles Times* (early September 1969).

———. "Jeff Buckley." *Los Angeles Times* (February 19, 1995).

Hohman, Marv. "Bitin' the Green Shiboda with Tom Waits." *Down Beat* (June 17, 1976).

———. "Buckley's Mysticism and Sexuality." *Chicago Express* (October 18, 1972).

Holzman, Jac, with Daws, Gavan. *Follow the Music.* First Media Books, 1998.

Horst, Brian Vander. "Who's Singing." *Westside News* (October 5, 1967).

Hoster, Jay. "Tim Buckley: 'An incredibly thin wire—Dylan thin.'" *The Haverford News* (April 14, 1967).

Hynde, Chrissie. "How a Hippie Hero Became a Sultry Sex Object." *New Musical Express* (June 8, 1974).

Isler, Scott. "*Goodbye and Hello*: The Tim Buckley Story." *Musician* (July 1991).

Jahn, Mike. "Pop: Tim Buckley." publication not stated on copy.

———. "Poet-Singer Draws Throng With Band at Philharmonic." *The New York Times* (March 17, 1969).

Jopling, Norman. "In Britain—Buckley and Guthrie." (1968).

Kamper, Bob. "*Blue Afternoon* Is Bittersweet." Publication not on copy, (February 24, 1970).

Kandinsky, Wassily. *Concerning the Spiritual in Art.* Trans. by M.T.H. Sadler. Dover Publications, N.Y., 1977.

Karmon, Mal. "Inside Track to Success." *St. Louis Post-Dispatch* (date unlisted).

Kelly, Geoff. "Tim Buckley Opens Youth Musical Series on KCET." *Upbeat* (October 3, 1970).

Kemp, Mark. Sidebar to "God Bless the Child." *Option* No. 63 (July–August 1995).

Lake, Steve. "Tim Buckley: *Starsailor*." *Melody Maker* (May 25, 1974).

Lawless, John. Interview with Tim Buckley. *Luton Post* (London publication) (April 1968).

Loggie, Robin. "Van Morrison, Linda Ronstadt, Tim Buckley." *Billboard* (November 28, 1970).

Mangelsdorff, Rich. "*Starsailor*." *Kaleidoscope* (January 8–15, 1971).

Mackie, Rob. "The Peach Melba Man." *London* (May 25, 1974).

McKaie (first name not on copy; probably Andy), *Rock* (September 20–25, 1972).

Micklo, Anne Marie. "Tim Buckley Interview." *Changes* p. 29, Vol. I, No. 7 (1969). One of Buckley's very best interviews, given shortly after *Lorca* and *Blue Afternoon* had been recorded, just as he was moving into *Starsailor*.

Mieses, Stanley. "Singer Tim Buckley Sends His 'Greetings From L.A.'" *Leisure* (August 19, 1973).

Nemko, Frankie. From Frankie Nemko's unpublished taped interview with Tim Buckley, June 1975 (Tim's last interview), used by permission.

Niemi, Robert. Interview with Mary Guibert, on internet chat session hosted by Jack Brolly, May 10, 1999. A few selected details about Amsterdam are from Niemi's *Wayfarin' Stranger* (unpublished), used by permission. The body of family history and Amsterdam information was provided for LU not by Niemi, but by Tim's mother, Elaine.

Richard, Cool. Taped interview with the author, April 19, 1977; various writings of CR's given by CR to the author for use; and notes and recollections of conversations thereafter.

Riny's Tim Buckley web site. http://www.timbuckley.com.

Rockwell, John. "Tim Buckley Displays Talent with Diversity." *The New York Times* (April 9, 1973).

Roxon, Lillian. "Albert Hotel." photocopied article, publication not indicated.

Scourtis, Ted. "Insight Into Tim Buckley." *New England Scene* (March, 1968).

Senoff, Pete. "Tim Buckley: *Starsailor*." *Jazz & Pop* (March 1971).

Shadoian, Jack. "Tim Buckley: *Starsailor*." *Fusion* (March 19, 1971).

Shelton, Robert. "Blue-Rock Bag Sung by Buckley." *The New York Times* (November 14, 1967).

Sherman, Michael. "Buckley Sings Folk, Progressive Jazz." *Los Angeles Times* (April 1, 1970).

Smith, Bob. "Quintet Generates Warmth." *The Sun* (January 13, 1971).

Steen, Rob. "Tim Buckley: Honeyman." *Mojo* (date not on copy).

Terence, Malcolm. "Hard-driving or mellow, Buckley wails happy time." *Los Angeles Free Press* (December 1, 1967).

Thomas, Dylan. From "Fern Hill," *The Collected Poems of Dylan Thomas (1934–1952)*. New Directions, 1971. Reprinted by permission.

Thomas, Michael. "In Person, Tim Buckley." *Cheetah* (December 1967).

Turner, Steve. "Tim Buckley: Talking in Tongues." A 1972 interview published in *Mojo* magazine (July 1995).

Tusher, William. "The Troubadour." *Hollywood Reporter* (April 2, 1970).

Underwood, Lee. "Tim Buckley: Chronicle of a Starsailor." *Down Beat* (June 16, 1977).

———. Liner notes for *Dream Letter: Live in London, 1968* (see Discography).

———. Liner notes for *Works in Progress* (see Discography).

———. "T.B. 1" poem from *Three Ascensions: The Warrior, The Lover, The Mystic*. 2000. (Originally in *5 Brief Tim Buckley Moments*; individual poems published from unpublished book.)

———. "Time's an abyss." Excerpt from "Memory's Smile," from *Poems From the Blue Book, Vol. II*, (also included in *I Have Heard the Sirens Sing*; individual poems published from unpublished book).

Von Tersch, Gary. "Tim Buckley: *Lorca*." *Fusion* (October 2, 1970).

Ward, Alex. "Buckley: Down to It." *Washington Post* (September 27, 1972).

Warner Bros. Bio. (1972).

Wilber, Ken. "Integral Art & Literary Theory 2." *The Eye of Spirit* (Shambhala, 1997), pp. 133–134.

Williams, Michael. "Go Live Your Own Life." *The New York Times* (April 6, 1969).

Wilson, Howard. Letter to the author, July 10, 1977, used by permission.

Wilson, Tony. "Don't Call Me a Poet." April 13, 1968, publication not cited on copy.

PHOTO CREDITS

ABOUT THE AUTHOR

The years with Tim were among the most exciting of my life.
Exploring beauty, joy, and dark-side demons, I found the gateway
to consciousness, wholeness, and creative vitality. My motto today:
Transform obstacles into steppingstones, and keep-keep-keepin' on!

Musician, writer, poet, and photographer Lee Underwood has been witing about
about music and musicians and his own experiences for some thirty years.
Underwood lived in Los Angeles for twenty-five years and in Santa Fe, New Mexico,
for seven. With his mate Sonia Crespi, he moved to Oakhurst, California, near
Yosemite National Park, in 1997.

During the sixties and early seventies, Underwood played lead guitar with singer/
songwriter Tim Buckley on seven of the nine albums during Buckley's lifetime, and

on several Buckley CDs issued posthumously, including *Dream Letter: Live in London 1968* and *Works In Progress.* He toured America and Europe with Buckley for seven years, and remained one of his best friends until his death in 1975.

While living in Los Angeles, Underwood wrote extensively about music and musicians, publishing regularly for nineteen years. His articles, interviews, and reviews appeared in dozens of periodicals, including *Down Beat* (West Coast Editor, 1975-1981), *L.A. Times, L.A. Weekly,* Billboard, *Rolling Stone, Pulse, Jazz Forum, Players, Soul, L.A. Free Press, Coda, Body/Mind/Spirit, New Realities, Players, Yoga Journal, New Age Journal,* and many others. In Santa Fe, Underwood mounted seven exhibitions of his own photography.

He co-authored flutist Paul Horn's autobiography, *Inside Paul Horn* (HarperCollins; 1990), and in 1991 received the Crystal Award for Music Journalism at the NAM (New Age Music) Convention in Hollywood.

As a poet, he co-hosted a radio show in Fresno for two years with Preston Chase, *Between the Lines: Poetry to Take You Home.* He has given numerous readings in San Francisco, Yosemite, Sacramento, Mariposa, Oakhurst, Fresno and elsewhere. He has published poems in *Light of Consciousness, ZamBomba, In the Grove,* and *The Central California Poetry Journal.* Whenever possible at his readings, he plays original piano music.

INDEX